T0326481

# Globalization and Challenges to Building Peace

Anthem Studies in Development and Globalization

Nolan, Peter *Capitalism and Freedom* (2007)

Nolan, Peter *Integrating China* (2007)

Boyce, James K., Narain, Sunita and Stanton, Elizabeth A. (eds.) *Reclaiming Nature* (2007)

Fullbrook, Edward *Real World Economics* (2007)

Ringmar, Erik *Why Europe Was First* (2006)

Rangaswamy, Vedavalli *Energy for Development* (2006)

Buira, Ariel (ed.) *Reforming the Governance of the IMF and the World Bank* (2005)

Ringmar, Erik *Surviving Capitalism* (2005)

Ritzen, Jozef *A Chance for the World Bank* (2004)

Fullbrook, Edward (ed.) *A Guide to What's Wrong with Economics* (2004)

Chang, Ha-Joon *Kicking Away the Ladder* (2003)

Chang, Ha-Joon (ed.) *Rethinking Development Economics* (2003)

# Globalization and Challenges to Building Peace

Edited by
ASHOK SWAIN, RAMSES AMER AND JOAKIM ÖJENDAL

ANTHEM PRESS
LONDON · NEW YORK · DELHI

Anthem Press
An imprint of Wimbledon Publishing Company
*www.anthempress.com*

This edition first published in UK and USA 2008
by ANTHEM PRESS
75-76 Blackfriars Road, London SE1 8HA, UK
or PO Box 9779, London SW19 7ZG, UK
and
244 Madison Ave. #116, New York, NY 10016, USA

*British Library Cataloguing in Publication Data*
A catalogue record for this book is available from the British Library.

*Library of Congress Cataloging in Publication Data*
Library of Congress Cataloging-in-Publication Data

Globalization and challenges to building peace /
edited by Ashok Swain, Ramses Amer, and Joakim Öjendal.
p. cm. — (Anthem development studies and globalization)
Revisions of papers presented at the Annual Conference of the Swedish Network of
Peace, Conflict, and Development Research held in 2006 in Uppsala, Sweden.
Includes bibliographical references.
ISBN 978-1-84331-287-1 (hardback)
1. Peace-building—Congresses. 2. Globalization—Political aspects—Congresses.
I. Swain, Ashok. II. Amer, Ramses. III. Öjendal, Joakim. IV. Swedish Network of Peace,
Conflict, and Development Research. Conference (2006 : Uppsala, Sweden)

JZ5538.G584 2007
303.6'6—dc22
2007026891

ISBN-10: 1 84331 287 5 (Hbk)
ISBN-13: 978 1 84331 287 1 (Hbk)

1 3 5 7 9 10 8 6 4 2

Printed in India

# CONTENTS

# ACKNOWLEDGEMENTS

The inspiration for this edited volume began in the Fall of 2006 at the Annual Conference of the Swedish Network of Peace, Conflict and Development Research, sponsored by the Swedish International Development Cooperation Agency (Sida) through its Department for Research Collaboration (SAREC).

The conference held in Uppsala, Sweden was attended by eighty people over the course of three days. Fifty-one researchers presented their papers on globalization and its influence on peace, conflict and development in the South. We would like to sincerely thank those conference participants whose papers are not included in this volume, but who contributed immensely to the success of the conference and to our thinking about this important topic.

In this volume thirteen revised papers from the conference have been included together with an introductory chapter. Contributors have followed a tight schedule in revising their contributions and in responding to various queries and comments.

Tej P. S. Sood of Anthem Press guided us through the review and editing processes and oversaw the publication of this volume.

We would also like to thank Jonathan Hall and Andreas Jarblad of the Department of Peace and Conflict Research, Uppsala University for their editorial support.

Ashok Swain, Ramses Amer,
and Joakim Öjendal
Editors
April 2007

# LIST OF CONTRIBUTORS

**Ashok Swain** is a Professor at the Department of Peace and Conflict Research, Uppsala University, Sweden and Coordinator of the Swedish Network of Peace, Conflict and Development Research.

**Ramses Amer** is Associate Professor and Senior Lecturer at the Department of Political Science, Umeå University, Sweden.

**Joakim Öjendal** is a Professor at the Department of Peace and Development Research at Gothenburg University, Sweden.

**Oliver P Richmond** is Professor of International Relations and Director of the Centre for Peace and Conflict Studies at the University of St Andrews, UK.

**Richard Sannerholm** is a doctoral candidate in law at the University of Örebro, Sweden.

**Anna Jarstad** is Assistant Professor and Coordinator for the Conflict & Democracy Programme at the Department of Peace and Conflict Research, Uppsala University, Sweden.

**Ralph Sundberg** is Research Assistant at the Department of Peace and Conflict Research, Uppsala University, Sweden.

**Patrik Johansson** is a doctoral candidate at the Department of Political Science, Umeå University, Sweden.

**Jonathan Hall** is a doctoral candidate at the Department of Peace and Conflict Research, Uppsala University, Sweden.

**Katarina Månsson** is a doctoral candidate at the Irish Centre for Human Rights, National University of Ireland, Galway, Ireland.

**Annika Björkdahl** is Lecturer and Researcher at the Department of Political Science, Lund University, Sweden.

**Cyril I Obi** is Programme Coordinator for the Programme Post-Conflict Transition, the State and Civil Society in Africa at the Nordic Africa Institute, Uppsala, Sweden.

**Linnea Bergholm** is a researcher at the Department of International Politics, University of Wales, Aberystwyth, UK.

**Michael Schulz** is Senior Lecturer in Peace and Development Research, Head of the Regional Studies Section and Director of the Centre for Middle East Studies, School of Global Studies, Göteborg University, Sweden.

**Fiona J Y Rotberg** is Research Fellow and the Environmental Security Project Director at the Central Asia-Caucasus Institute & Silk Road Studies Programme, Johns Hopkins University and Uppsala University, Sweden.

**Niklas Swanström** is Programme Director of the Central Asia-Caucasus Institute & Silk Road Studies Programme, Johns Hopkins University and Uppsala University, Sweden.

# Chapter One

# BUILDING PEACE
# IN THE ERA OF THREE WAVES

## Ashok Swain, Ramses Amer
## and Joakim Öjendal

## Introduction

During the last few decades, the nature of peace and development in the international system has shifted considerably so has the measures applied in support of those values. Whereas 'war' has structurally shifted from being interstate concern to becoming intrastate in nature, 'development' has moved from one of typically defining national development strategies to one of tapping into a neo-liberal global order in the most efficient way possible. As such, the values and processes of, and measures to support, peace and development have, to a large extent, conflated. Moreover, internal war is typically founded in a particular political economy further feeding – or even being the origin of – conflicts; adaptation to the neo-liberal globalization has, on the other hand, turned 'development' into a conflict prone process, marginalizing large number of people. Globalization which – for good and bad – is driving the processes described above will not fade within the foreseeable future, but rather it is likely that the trend will increase in the decades to come. While undeniably, this shift in 'order' has brought some positive values, globally the problems may be even more severe, including the creation of social and internal conflicts, ethnic strife, political instability (often related to democratization), pauperization, forced migration and rampant natural resource extraction with severe livelihood losses for millions, just to mention a few of the far too prevalent problems.

One of the major policy responses from the international community has been the invention of a battery of 'repairing', 'reconstructing' and 'reconciliatory' policy approaches. Perhaps the most comprehensive of these attempts has been branded 'peacebuilding' that dates back to the tenure of General Secretary

Boutros-Boutros Ghali. Its origin in the UN system was an early attempt to respond to the first cycle post-cold war conflicts and its ambition was to adapt to a post-cold war world. At bottom, it contains an ambition to deal with the problems described above comprehensively including both peace and development aspects. However, hitherto few successes have been recorded in these efforts. The international responses have been largely separated into conflict resolution as carried out from the UN offices, or traditional development activities carried out by different actors and agencies, missing the obvious connection between these two values. Self-critically, it could also be observed that research has to a large extent followed that path too.

This volume aims to present a broad inventory of the study of the contemporary peace, conflict and development research in light of the above-mentioned *problematic*. The chapters, in various degrees, take as their point of departure the ongoing globalization and reflect upon the viability of various peacebuilding efforts. Below follows a brief review of the themes we have chosen in order to illuminate the issue at hand. Neither the themes, nor the coverage of them, are comprehensive, but rather a dip into a wide sea of possible themes and approaches whose full treatment goes beyond the scope of this volume.

## Globalization and Conflicts

The world has gone through a major transformation in the last two decades. The end of the cold war in Europe has directly led to massive increase in the private capital flow and indirectly to an information and telecommunication revolution. In this new interdependent and interconnected world, the international trade and investment has overtaken the importance of national economies. Globalization has created new opportunities as well as many risks and challenges. The World Commission on the Social Dimension of Globalization in its report in February 2004 praises globalization for promoting open societies, open economies and better exchange of goods and ideas. At the same time, the Commission finds the current working of global economy 'ethically unacceptable and politically unsustainable'.

Globalization is generating new wealth and encouraging technological innovations, but at the same, it has failed to support and promote sustainable human development (Swain, 2006). So far, it has had largely negative impact on the poor and underprivileged sections of the society. In 1990s, the global growth in gross domestic product has been sluggish compare to previous decades. The debt burden of developing countries has multiplied, which impedes their development. The gap between the ratio of per capita income in the developed and the developing countries has widened further, from 50 to 1 in the 1960s to more than 120 to 1 in 2006.

**Table 1.** ODA* as a Percentage of GNI* for DAC* Donors 2003

| | |
|---|---|
| United States | 0.15 |
| Italy | 0.17 |
| Austria | 0.20 |
| Japan | 0.20 |
| Greece | 0.21 |
| Portugal | 0.22 |
| New Zealand | 0.23 |
| Spain | 0.23 |
| Canada | 0.24 |
| Australia | 0.25 |
| Germany | 0.28 |
| United Kingdom | 0.34 |
| Finland | 0.35 |
| Ireland | 0.39 |
| Switzerland | 0.39 |
| France | 0.41 |
| Belgium | 0.60 |
| Sweden | 0.79 |
| Netherlands | 0.80 |
| Luxembourg | 0.81 |
| Denmark | 0.84 |
| Norway | 0.92 |

Source: UNDP Human Development Report, 2005.
*Note: ODA = Official Development Assistance; GNI = Gross National Income;
DAC = The Development Assistance Committee of the OECD.

The number of poor and unemployed people is at its highest level ever. There is no doubt that the globalization's benefit has failed to reach the majority of the poor.

While the key to the sustainable growth lies in the countries' own efforts to pursue sound policies and strengthen institutions, these efforts need to be complemented with financial and technological support from the international community. Unfortunately, the foreign aid is decreasing overall. In the last decade, the Official Development Assistance (ODA) of the OECD (Organization for Economic Cooperation and Development) countries has gone down from 0.35 per cent to 0.22 per cent of the gross national income and far below the 0.7 per cent target the developed countries had promised to meet. In 2003, only five donor countries reached or exceeded the UN target. According to the World Bank estimate, due to this failed promise, developing countries are loosing USD 100 billion every year. The donor community has been increasingly alleging that development assistance intended for crucial social and economic sectors are being used directly or indirectly to fund unproductive military and other expenditures.

Globalization, so far, has not been able to foster sustainable human development; it instead has generated anguish and deprivation, resulting in growing civil unrests and, in some cases, in armed conflicts in the developing world. However, peace and conflict research has till now somehow overlooked the influence of increasing globalization on the formation and management of the emerging conflicts. The study of globalization also tends to overlook a proven fact that the conflicts in the South have been invariably influenced by the global powers and their strategic politics.

Thus, the causes of major violent conflicts need to be monitored and assessed, particularly in developing countries. What concrete measures exist and are likely to be effective in addressing the causes of conflict in an increasingly interdependent world? The problem areas need to be identified as significant in a particular developing country, in a region or on a given continent or generally in the developing world. Research in the field of peace and conflict is concerned with possible major violent conflicts that arise within states, while it takes into account their global and regional sources and effects. Put differently, globalization has reached such depths that it cuts deep into national affairs, causing structural changes loaded with potential conflicts. Such conflicts may be civil wars, revolutions, intercommunal violence, genocides or general state breakdowns, including possible consequences such as massive humanitarian crises. Since violent conflicts in the developing regions may follow a series of stages at which international intervention may occur, conflict prevention turns into a contemporary concern. Also our ability to identify these stages and to intervene in an appropriate manner becomes increasingly prioritized.

## Democratization and Conflicts

Coinciding with this third wave of globalization (the first wave was colonialism while the second was the imperialism), there is another wave of democratization (Huntington, 1991). Parallel to the collapse of Communism in Eastern part of Europe, a process of democratic reform ran its course in Latin America, Africa and Asia (O'Donnell and Schmitter, 1986; Simensen, 1999). The notion that democracy is the ideal form of government has almost become axiomatic. There is a strong belief that a community of democratic nations is the best way to maintain domestic and international peace. In fact, in contemporary Western academic discourse on Afghanistan and Iraq, mere imposition of democracy was prescribed as the most important step towards peace, as it previously was in Mozambique and Cambodia (Öjendal and Lilja, 2006). However, in the later two cases there was an international consensus and a broad domestic acceptance of the peacekeeping efforts of the international community.

This has not been the case in Iraq and international lawyers have criticized the military intervention of 2003. Internal opposition to the intervening forces is also in evidence in Iraq and Afghanistan. The notions of 'pro-democratic' and 'pro-self determination' military interventions have been and still are seriously challenged with the scholarly debate.

Theoretical works on democratic transition and democratization have also emphasized the conflict resolution capacity of democracy. The idea that democracy, as such, rather than any other form of government, is the best way to resolve interstate conflicts has been stressed. Several theorists have also extended the democratic peace thesis to argue that a 'democratic peace' is evident within intrastate conflicts as well (Mathew and Myers, 1997; Rummel, 1985). It should be noted that the 'democratic peace' notion was first put forward in the context of interstate relations. In the context of domestic developments it has been reasoned that democracy reduces the likelihood of discrimination, especially of ethno-political minorities, and thus the likelihood of political repression (Gurr, 1993). However, as Errol A Henderson (2002) points out, 'the democratic peace proposition' has not been explicitly tested with reference to third world post-colonial states, where most civil wars take place. It has also, significantly, been pointed out by Mansfield and Snyder (2005) that in periods of democratization – which may be prolonged for decades – the risks of political instability, social turmoil and severe conflicts are enhanced, putting a spin on the democratic peace theory.

It is also true that democracies are more prone to host violent secessionist movements. According to the Uppsala Conflict Data Project, Russia, Turkey, India, Indonesia, Sri Lanka, Senegal, Philippines are among the democracies that faced separatist violence. There is no doubt that democracies face more separatist violence than non-democracies. Even several 'mature' democracies either are facing a number of violent separatist challenges at present or have faced them in the recent past.

Democracy, which introduces competitive elections, is commonly offered as a solution to political problems. While this is a reasonable, overall and long-term argument, it carries, nevertheless, problematic aspects. In contexts of post-conflict resolution, the introduction of competitive politics often resembles the conflict it was supposed to solve and often in a situation where institutions to absorb tensions and instability around this is lacking. Hence it may contradict its purposes. Moreover, as Przeworski (1999) points out elections may not represent the will of all population groups. There are several democracies that refuse to follow international human rights standards, subjecting minorities to arbitrary power by a predatory majority (O'Brien, 1983; Roeder, 2005; Swain, 2005). In a democracy, the majority has the ability to abuse its electoral power against the minority or to elect a government that imposes laws and mores of one religion (Clemens, 2002). This does not mandate an abandonment of democracy, but it suggests that efforts at democratization should be guided by the realization that it is a conflict-driven process which may exacerbate inequalities and encourage affected groups to pursue insurgency (Henderson, 2002).

## Migration and Conflicts

The world, at present, is not only experiencing third wave of globalization and democratization, but also the third wave of large-scale human migration. In that first wave up to 1914, nearly ten percent of the population of the world moved from one country to another – and in many cases from one continent to another. The second wave of human migration came up after the World War II, caused by massive destruction and redrawing of state boundaries, particularly in Europe.

Migration is a highly multifaceted term, which includes all types of voluntary as well as forced movements of a population. A series of demographic, economic, socio-cultural and psychological issues influences the nature, pattern and direction of voluntary human migration, while forced migrations are the results of civil war, political and ethnic persecution, famine and environmental disasters (Swain, 1996). The present wave is a combination of both voluntary and forced migration of large number of population.

In the last decade, the number of internal conflicts increased and that displaced a large number of people. Though, there is a drop in the number of civil wars in recent years, the population migration has not decreased. It is one of the safest of predictions that the population migration will increase in the decades ahead. There is no holding back to this tsunami. The United States alone detains more than 1.5 million people along the Rio Grande border to Mexico every year.

Every year, world population is increasing by 78 million, roughly the equivalent of another Germany. Some describe world demographic trends as 'revolutionary', because though the human species emerged perhaps 150,000 years ago, most of its growth has been in the last forty years. More than 90 per cent of population growth is taking place in the developing countries. Recently, research has found pressure of population growth to have a significant impact on the likelihood of state becoming involved in interstate military conflicts. Whether the population growth directly affects the decision making of the state to go to war or not, but it undoubtedly generates scarcity of resources in a technologically underdeveloped country. In spite of the tall claims by the agricultural scientists, it is true that 700 million people on this earth do not get the 2,200 calories per day generally accepted as the nutritional bottom line, and 40,000 die every day of hunger and hunger-related diseases. The availability of fresh water has also fallen short of meeting its increased demand. One billion people in the world lack access to clean water and nearly two billion do not have adequate sanitation facilities. The loss of living space and source of livelihood due to civil war and/or environmental change could force the affected people to migrate. Ethnic conflicts and food scarcity have already forced a large number of people to move across international borders. This phenomenon has been one of the growing concerns to the international community. This mass movement of population creates security concerns for a nation state.

It is true that the refugee statistics showed a downward trend from 2001 to 2005. International community claimed that this drop in refugee population was due to the peacebuilding efforts in the conflict zones and voluntary repatriation. However, the refugee statistics of these years fail to tell the whole story. In reality, the total population of concern to United Nations High Commissioner for Refugees (UNHCR) increased from 19.5 million persons at the beginning of 2005 to 20.8 million by the end of the year. This 6 per cent increase is due to increasing numbers of internally displaced people and stateless persons. In 2005, in Iraq alone, 1.2 million people have been internally displaced. Moreover, the declining security situation in Iraq, Afghanistan and Sudan has again contributed to increased number of refuges in 2006.

The anti-regime activities of the migrants on foreign soil or the attempt of the host state to repatriate them back to their own country might deteriorate the relationship between sending and receiving states and even can incite armed struggle. Migrants may pose a structural threat to a developing host country by increasing pressures on its already scarce resources. Competition with the

*Table 2*. **Refugee Population, 2005**

| UNHCR Bureau | Start 2005 | End 2005 | Annual change |
|---|---|---|---|
| Central Africa and Great Lakes | 1,267,700 | 1,193,700 | −5.8 % |
| East and Horn of Africa | 770,400 | 772,000 | 0.2 % |
| Southern Africa | 243,100 | 228,600 | −6.0 % |
| West Africa | 465,100 | 377,200 | −18.9 % |
| Total Africa (excluding North Africa) | 2,746,300 | 2,571,500 | −6.4 % |
| Central Asia, South West Asia, North Africa and Middle East | 3,062,100 | 2,467,300 | −19.4 % |
| Americas | 581,300 | 564,300 | −2.9 % |
| Asia and Pacific | 836,900 | 825,600 | −1.4 % |
| Europe | 2,316,900 | 1,965,800 | −15.2 % |
| Total | 9,543,500 | 8,394,500 | −12.0 % |

Source: UNHCR, 2005 Global Refugee Trends, 9 June 2006.

host population over scarce resources may cause conflict with migrants and lead to political problems for the government of the receiving country. At the same time, the migrant communities are also playing significant role in the economic development of the host and home countries. Many countries draw a significant portion of their revenue from remittances. Even in some cases, the diasporas are contributing to peace negotiations in their homeland conflicts.

## International Community and Peacebuilding

Peacebuilding has emerged as a significant concept in the last decade and a half. The reason for its success (as a policy idea) is, we claim, threefold. First, as few other approaches, it takes both the development and the conflict approach into consideration, daring to make a connection and try to work on the nature of the interrelation between these (or at least that's the idea). This was a break with previous attempts, such as for instance the much older UN idea of 'peacekeeping', and the more recent 'peacemaking'. In line with the UN charter, but not with previous practices, the problematic of peace, conflicts and development were integrated. Second, since 1992, the UN machinery has consistently pursued the idea, 'marketed' the concept, produced high-level reports, and (to a minor extent) implemented projects based on its ideas. As such, the UN offices have become the 'guarantee' for its validity. Third, peacebuilding is clearly an idea whose time has come: 44 per cent of the 'solved' conflicts in the last few decades have resorted to renewed violence within a decade; a fact crying for attention to a more comprehensive view on conflict resolution as well as on 'development' (Junne and Verkoren, 2005). In the post-cold war world, it is not alliances with great powers alone that determine the pattern of major conflict, as argued above, the emerging global political economy and how it positions countries in the South in relation to it, is likely be a key factor for which, where, when and how conflicts break out and eventually become resolved. Hence, 'globalization' as an underlying factor provoking social, economic and political change, requires 'peacebuilding' as a policy response.

So what is 'peacebuilding'? It stems from the immediate post-cold war period. The process UN searched for at the time was to contain 'disarming', 'restoration of order', 'repatriation of refugees', 'retraining of security personnel', 'monitoring of elections', 'increased human rights monitoring', 'reformation of government institutions' and 'promotion of formal and informal ways of political participation' (UN 1992). A decade later, the irony of this approach may be that while this list of 'goods' has in many places largely been achieved, societal stability and reconstruction have not; neither has the risk of returning to a situation marked by violent conflict, social instability and endemic underdevelopment. The most obvious explanation to this might be that the UN was at the time thinking in terms of interventions and projects with a limited extension in time and addressing the most urgent problems, while little regard was extended to the specific societies and their particular historical, cultural and violence based legacies. This has been the dominant approach to recovery during a 'decade of reconciliation' (cf. Chandler, 2000; Roberts, 2001; cf. Orjuela, 2003).

The international community realized the inadequateness of the approach and put up a high-level panel led by Algeria's former Minister of Foreign Affairs, Lakhdar Brahimi, producing the highly influential 'Brahimi Report' (UN 2000), which, to date, is the most concerted effort in raising the significance and discussing the capability of 'peacebuilding'. Kofi Annan, the then Secretary General of the UN, characterized its 'analysis [as] frank, yet fair'. The report immediately set the tone when stating, 'the United Nations has repeatedly failed to meet the challenge' of its key mandate, to 'save succeeding generations form the scourge of war'. And although it takes a keen interest in 'conflict prevention', the effort, again, falls short of thoroughly integrating a development perspective in its analysis and recommendations. Instead it remains within the limiting terminology of 'missions', 'contingencies' and 'peacekeeping' and remains preoccupied with internal UN organization/ administration. Hence, from our perspective failing to update and reinvigorate peacebuilding to the contemporary needs. This is at large echoed by the many practitioners' cries for more efficient and comprehensive approach to the problem at hand.

In spite of the 'conceptual success', and the need for it, peacebuilding remains a contested, or even empty, concept with limited progress in reality. Below we will find a range of views on how it has been perceived, worked with and how it actually corresponds to the problems of peace, conflict and development 'out there'. The chapters in this volume address these new issues, which challenge the peace projects undertaken in the different parts of the world, particularly in Asia, Africa, Balkans and the Middle East.

Oliver P Richmond, in Chapter 2 examines the development of the liberal peace, identifying its internal components, and the often-ignored tensions between them. The construction of the liberal peace, and its associated discourses and practices in post-conflict environments around the world is far from coherent. It is subject to significant intellectual and practical shortcomings, not least related to its focus on political, social, and economic reforms as mainly long-term institutional processes resting on the reform of governance. It thereby neglects interim issues such as the character, agency and needs of civil society actors, especially related to the ending of war economies, and their replacement with frameworks, which respond to individual social and economic needs, as well as political needs. The resultant peace is therefore often very flimsy and 'virtual' at best, rather than emancipatory.

In Chapter 3, Ramses Amer examines the ongoing legal debate surrounding pre-emptive self-defence. The study examines the legal debate surrounding the regulation of the use of force in the provisions of the Charter of the United Nations, and explores the possible interconnection between pre-emptive self-defence and anticipatory self-defence. The political ramification of the possibility of weakening of the regulation of the use of force, as expressed in the Charter of the United Nations, is discussed. Given the fact that the United States has been one of the most vocal countries in articulating the doctrine of pre-emption and pre-emptive self-defence, the policies of the US are examined in the study. The analysis displays that pre-emptive self-defence is, in essence, synonymous with anticipatory self-defence. The policies pursued by the United States, as expressed in National Security Strategies of 2002 and 2006, are geared more towards preventive use of force then the use of force in self-defence. The later poses a challenge to regulations of the use of force in interstate relations as established in the provisions of the Charter of the United Nations.

In Chapter 4, Richard Sannerholm argues that the international community has taken the position that to recover the post-conflict societies need a healthy dose of the rule of law. Behind this diagnosis is a conception of the rule of law as the main instrument for law and order, increased human rights protection, justice and peace. The impact of rule of law programmes has not reached the high ambitions. While rule of law reformers blame lack of funding, coordination and political will, it is argued in this chapter that the main problem lies in a misconception that rule of law is synonymous with criminal justice and human rights. The rule of law template currently promoted ignores other pressing post-conflict issues such as: corruption, discrimination by administrative agencies, and inconsistencies in the civil and administrative legal framework. These legal and administrative barriers impede a return to stability and normality. Consequently this chapter argues for a substantial shift in policy towards the rule of law in order to make the approach more needs based and systemic in scope, and to include issues outside the criminal justice system.

The Chapter 5 by Anna Jarstad and Ralf Sundberg focuses on the implementation of power-sharing pacts in peace agreements. Much scholarly work has been devoted to how the design of peace agreements can pave the way for peace. In this regard, power sharing is seen as a viable solution to end civil war. Agreement on the sharing of power is a concession by warring parties that can be seen as a sign of credible commitment. Such concessions often entail compromises on how political, territorial and military power is to be shared or divided in a future form of governance. However, the implementation of such power-sharing pacts has only to a limited extent been the focus of quantitative analysis. This chapter presents new data, namely the IMPACT dataset, which explores all peace agreements signed between 1989 and 2004 and analyses the implementation of provisions for political, military and territorial power-sharing pacts. The chapter addresses a number of claims based on literature on durable peace and peace agreements. Conventional wisdom holds that the failure to implement peace agreements is an important explanation of the recurrence of war. However, the IMPACT dataset demonstrates that a majority of power-sharing pacts in peace agreements are indeed implemented. In addition, the authors find that the relative share of pacts in peace agreements has increased over the years. How long implementation takes varies across the different types of pacts. It is also shown that political pacts are less associated with peace than military and territorial pacts.

In Chapter 6, Patrik Johansson argues that the refugee repatriation is often seen as a necessary condition for peace in peacebuilding literature. This claim is usually presented as an assumption rather than as a hypothesis that merits testing. The author argues that depending on the circumstances, repatriation may contribute to peace, it may be irrelevant to peace, or it may be unfavourable to peace. The essay addresses the question of how to test the claim about refugee repatriation as a condition for peace, the main focus being on how to operationalize repatriation as a condition. Previous research on the relation between refugee repatriation and peace is discussed and categorized, and some methodological considerations related to testing necessity are presented. In the main part of the chapter, four ways of approaching the operationalization of repatriation are discussed, based on the international refugee law, the organized repatriation processes, the major protracted refugee situations and the relative number of returnees, respectively.

While there are pros and cons of all four approaches, the conclusion is that the one based on the relative number of returnees is the most reasonable.

Jonathan Hall and Ashok Swain's Chapter 7 discusses an emerging debate over the influence of diasporas on civil wars in their homelands. Many prominent scholars claim that diasporas are especially prone to political extremism and the use of violence to resolve political disputes. In their view, residing in the homeland and experiencing the atrociousness of war sobers previously idealistic goals of gaining territorial sovereignty or state power and tempers rather than exacerbates tensions among groups. Those who migrate during civil conflicts however avoid the moderating costs of war. While abroad, diasporas are empowered by economic upliftment, and by the freedom to pursue extremist agendas unobstructed by homeland government oversight. Other scholars have challenged these views, offering evidence that diasporas are actively involved in peacebuilding and conflict resolution in their homelands. In this chapter, the authors provide an examination of the arguments offered in support of these opposing claims. In the process, the debate is situated within the broader context of globalization and the challenges and opportunities it presents for building peace. By way of conclusion, the authors present some of their own reflections on the arguments for viewing diasporas as extremists and/or moderates, and point out some possible directions for future research that would help to bring forward the debate over diasporas and their roles in conflict and peace in the homeland.

Katarina Månsson in Chapter 8 argues that while assessing the potential of peace operations to protect and promote human rights, it is important to take into factor the ability of civilian and military peace actors to engage in constructive interpersonal and intergroup communication on human rights. The author argues that for the UN missions to operate as successful 'norm entrepreneurs' vis-à-vis the local society, a common understanding of human rights must first be imbued in the inter-agency relations between different mission components.

The author argues that for the UN missions to operate as successful 'norm entrepreneurs' vis-à-vis the local society, a common understanding of human rights must first be imbued in the inter-agency relations between different mission components. Human rights officers, police and military are key actors in this regard. By analysing interview material gathered in Kosovo (UNMIK/KFOR) and the Democratic Republic of the Congo (MONUC) through Jürgen Habermas' Theory of Communicative Action, it is suggested that fruitful cooperation on human rights in peacekeeping is contingent on three main preconditions: mutual empathy and knowledge; the existence of a common 'lifeworld'; and equality of actors and equal access to the discourse. Data collected in the field furthermore underscore the role that institutional structures play in enhancing the forging of a common understanding on human rights based on these three premises. In this vein, the chapter explores some pioneering initiatives underway in MONUC with respect to cooperation between the military and the human rights officers. By engaging in joint reporting on human rights and by designating military observers as human rights focal points, MONUC represents an interesting case study on how communicative action on human rights between the human rights actors and the military may forge. Drawing on these and other findings, the chapter concludes with several recommendations for future peace operations.

In Chapter 9, Annika Björkdahl states that the United Nations Interim Administration Mission in Kosovo (UNMIK) is a bold experiment of post-conflict reconstruction and an unparalleled opportunity to promote norms pertaining to liberal democracy. Yet, the obvious gap between what the UN preaches and what it practices challenges the conventional assumption that norm advocates respect and comply with the international norms they champion and attempt to diffuse to norm-takers. Furthermore, the democratic deficit and the authoritarian style of governance of UNMIK has undermined its norm advocacy, efforts to build sustainable democratic institutions and practices in Kosovo, as well as created tension in the relationship between UNMIK and the Kosovars, and it has potentially also contributed to distort the Kosovars' vision of democracy. This failure to respect and comply with the norms of liberal-democracy has eroded the authority of UNMIK as a norm advocate, weakened the norms and closed a channel for norm promotion.

In Chapter 10, Cyril I Obi critically examines the dominant perspectives to the causes of civil wars in Africa. It makes the case against the wholesale acceptance of monocausal explanations that the root causes of violent conflict lies solely in the pathology of predatory states/corrupt elites, retribution from the 'resource curse' or the opportunities that the 'production of violence' provides men (and women) with guns to loot. By drawing upon post-cold war civil wars in West Africa, it shows why more attention needs to be paid to historically constructed socio-economic contradictions and inequities that alienate large sections of the populace, and how the processes of globalization, and the activities of transnational actors lie at the 'complex' roots of conflict. Thus, wars in West Africa have multiple causes that include internal and external factors. It is therefore necessary to go beyond the dominant perspectives of the causes of war, in order to transcend the tendency towards broad generalizations that are partly informed by the penchant of the international community for 'short-cut' explanations, which also drive, ineffective 'quick-fix' solutions. Such transcendence would enhance explanation of war that is more likely to influence socially equitable and sustainable peace in the region.

Chapter 11 by Linnea Bergholm marks the pronounced change in emphasis between the Organization of African Unity (OAU) and the African Union (AU) when it comes to its peacekeeping and peacebuilding framework. The AU has set out to steer away from the OAU's non-interventionist agenda and to take a non-indifferent stance instead in situations of massive ethnic cleansing or genocide in the continent. The AU has to date had two opportunities to deliver on these commitments; in its peacekeeping missions in Burundi and Darfur. The author argues that these two cases are pivotal in terms of reflecting how human beings are more centrally placed in the African peace and security agenda today. These two cases present a mixed record and the AU remains severely hampered in terms of logistics, finances and forces. But a case can be made that the AU has, in a limited but very important sense, promoted human security and carried out important civilian protection functions. The relative stabilization of conflict, the protection of lives and of the humanitarian operations in zones of Darfur offer precedents and the lessons learned are likely to contribute to a capacity-building process that is well worth studying. To look at the positive developments should in no way be interpreted as an attempt to belittle the challenges still remaining, the opportunities lost in Burundi or the large areas of Darfur that remain entirely unprotected even today.

Chapter 12 of Michael Schulz is concerned with the unresolved issue about where to locate the Palestinian–Hamas movement in relation to democracy and democratic peace. The chapter evaluates whether Hamas is evolving into a more democratic organization, or it is retreating to its theocratic foun dations instead. The study focuses particularly on the period after Hamas effectively took control of the Palestinian Authority (PA) following its democratic election victory in January 2006. Many expect Hamas to pursue an Islamic *Sharia* rule, similar to that of the Iranian regime, while stifling the more secular and democratic elements within the PA. The study demonstrates that Hamas is a movement that has gradually accepted the political realties of the Oslo process, and is increasingly more flexible in relation to Israel and to democratic pubic demands. This readiness to engage in new realities has encouraged a more pragmatic strategy within Hamas. Palestinian public pressure, in concert with international coercion, can be seen to have been responsible for dramatic shifts in certain strategic positions of the Hamas organization, most significantly concerning relations with Israel. The author indicates that Arab Islamist parties, such as Hamas, have the potential to evolve into a Demo-Islamic position, similar to those of European Christian Democratic parties and the Islamic Justice and Development party in Turkey.

Fiona J Y Rotberg in Chapter 13 analyses the way scarcity of renewable natural resources, such as forests and cropland, and water leads to intrastate conflicts. The linkages between resource scarcity and the state's capacity to provide for its people are also explored. The chapter poses the question: Do resource scarcity issues lead to security concerns and violent conflict? Nepal serves as a case study to test the hypothesis that natural resource scarcity issues do contribute to intrastate conflict. The chapter argues that natural resource scarcity and unequal access to natural resources can be linked to a decline in state capacity and thus to civil strive and internal conflict.

Chapter 14 of Niklas Swanström deals with security challenges posed by opium (heroin) and other illegal narcotics in the Northeast Asian region. China in particular has been a main actor, partially as a producer but more importantly as consumer and as an important transit country. The present drug threat to China emanates from multiple sources ranging from states in its periphery, regional criminal networks as well as domestic actors, such as local triads, which accounts for the bulk of the production and sale of narcotics. As China is gradually opening up the drug problem is becoming increasingly serious and is threatening China's progress, especially in the field of health, economy and public security. This development is driven by the rapid economic development and the creation of a strong consumer base in China for narcotics. As seen in Central Asia, Afghanistan and some South East Asian states, economies seriously affected by the narcotics trade usually have a worsened health situation with a rapid rise in HIV/Aids, Hepatitis C and other drug-related diseases. There have also been cases of 'narcotization' of states leading to political instability. They are usually associated with decreased competitiveness of the national economies as drug related industries offer steady incomes in states with high unemployment and fewer opportunities for a secure income at the legitimate market.

One of the most problematic effects in such states has been weakening of the state apparatus by the criminal networks that deals with drugs; such networks thrive in weak states where they exercise control over the political elite or simply become a part of the elite. The chapter makes an assessment of what the current effects are for China and how long-term implications can be prevented.

# Chapter Two

# THE PROBLEM OF PEACE: UNDERSTANDING THE 'LIBERAL PEACE'[1]

## Oliver P Richmond

*To remember Hiroshima is to commit oneself to peace.* Pope John Paul II, 1981
*Pax Invictis*[2]
*Virtue runs amok.* Attributed to G K Chesterton

## Introduction

What is peace? This essay examines the genealogy of the 'problem of peace'. This is not as commonly thought caused by the contestation of power by sovereign actors (Carter, 1936, p. xi) but rather by the absence of debate on the conceptualisation of peace, and the consequence of assuming it is a negative epistemology that can never fully be achieved (Rasmussen, 2003, p. 174). Instead, it is generally assumed that the 'liberal peace' is acceptable to all. This is essentially what Mandelbaum and others have called the combination of peace, democracy and free markets (Mandelbaum, 2002, p. 6; Duffield, 2001, p. 11; Paris, 2004). These assumptions are also prevalent in most policy documents associated with peace and security issues (United Nations, 2004; International Development Research Centre 2001). The liberal peace is assumed to be unproblematic in its internal structure, and in its acceptance in post-conflict zones, though its methodological application may be far from smooth (Paris, 2004, p. 18–20). Yet, the liberal peace's main components – democratisation, the rule of law, human rights, free and globalized markets, and neo-liberal development – are increasingly being critiqued from several different perspectives. These critiques have focused upon the incompatibility of certain stages of democratization and economic reform, the ownership of development projects and 'thick and thin' versions of the neo-liberal agenda, the possible incompatibility of post-conflict justice with the stabilization of society and human rights, the problem of crime and corruption in economic and political reform and the establishment of the rule of law. These terrains are relatively well explored (Snyder, 2000, p. 43; Annan, 2002, p. 136; Chopra and Hohe, 2004, p. 292; Rieff, 2002, p. 10; Paris, 2002, p. 638). What has received rather less attention is the scope and conceptualization of the liberal peace itself.

Understanding the different conceptualizations of peace, and the different graduations of the liberal peace, offers an important contribution towards unravelling the dilemmas of making a sustainable peace for others as claimed by the liberal peacebuilding consensus. This would provide a better awareness of what the objectives of multiple interventions engendered in the contemporary peacebuilding consensus (Richmond, 2004) might construct, and what different decisions, actions and thinking imply about the achievement of these objectives. This indicates a weak consensus between the UN, major states and donors, agencies and NGOs that liberal peace should incorporate a market democracy, the rule of law and development, and that all international intervention, both humanitarian and security oriented should be contingent upon this. This consensus masks a deeper dissensus in terms of the application of resources, the use of force to establish the basis for such a reform, and the efficacy of different actors involved in the many roles this requires (Richmond, 2004). To know peace provides a clearer understanding of what must be done, and what must be avoided, if it is to be achieved. First, we must know peace.

This essay briefly outlines the main theoretical underpinnings of the assumed conceptualization of peace in most academic and policy documentation and literatures (Bleiker, 2000, Introduction), which contribute to the conceptualization of the 'liberal peace'. It then focuses on the liberal peace, its implications and internal tensions. It argues that the liberal peace is subject to four main graduations. These reflect its theoretical antecedents, and carry important implications, for humanitarian intervention (both military and non-military), peace operations and peacebuilding for the sustainability of the peace to be constructed, and for the exit strategies of internationals and other interveners. What is more, this opens up a research agenda in IR associated with the conceptualization and critique of the contemporary form of peace. It also points to fundamental weaknesses in the relationship between the liberal peace and the economic prosperity of individuals, which are not generally dealt with directly or as a matter of urgency in liberal peacebuilding.

## Understanding Contemporary Thinking About Peace

There are four main strands of thought within the liberal peace framework, influenced by the key antecedents of, and debates in, international theory.

These four strands are the 'victor's peace', the 'institutional peace', the 'constitutional peace' and the 'civil peace'. The victor's peace has evolved from the age-old realist argument that a peace that rests on a military victory, and upon the hegemony or domination of a victor peace is more likely to survive. In its extreme form this can be seen as a Carthaginian peace, and the only way of containing both Hobbesian anarchy and the profligacy of human nature. The institutional peace rests upon idealist, liberal-internationalist and liberal-institutionalist attempts to anchor states within a normative and legal context in which states multilaterally agree how to behave and how to enforce or determine their behaviour, which also informs the thinking of the English School. It can be traced from the Treaty of Westphalia, through to the founding of the UN and beyond. The constitutional peace rests upon the liberal Kantian argument that peace rests upon democracy, free trade, and a set of cosmopolitan values that stem from the notion that individuals are ends in themselves, rather than means to an end (Doyle, 1983, pp. 205–35). This became a common refrain spanning the many European Peace projects of the medieval period after (see for example William Penn, 1993 [1693], pp. 5–22), through to Versailles in 1919, and on into the post-cold war period. All of these three strands have been influential across the scope of the first and second 'Great Debates' of IR.

The final strand identifiable is that of the civil peace. This is something of an anomaly in thinking about peace because it requires individual agency, rather than state, multilateral or international agency. The civil peace is derived from the phenomena of direct action, of citizen advocacy and mobilization, from the attainment or defence of basic human rights and values, spanning the ending of the slave trade to the inclusion of civil society in IR today (Haliday, 2001, p. 35). It is derived from liberal thinking on individualism and rights, and has been taken up by more recent constructivist, critical and post-structural thinking on the problem of hegemony and domination, self-other relations, identity, particularism and pluralism, as well as the need for human security and justice beyond the states-system.

These aspects of the liberal peace are both contradictory and complimentary, and each brings with it a certain intellectual and empirical baggage. The victor's peace framework has been subject to the *hamartia* of territorial and strategic overextension, greed, and an inability to control unruly subjects despite its impositionary qualities. The civil peace discourse is often drowned out by the overwhelming weight of official discourses, even though it is moti-vated by claims for enhanced human security and social justice, which blames the state for war or liberal states for self-interest. The institutional peace discourse is subject to many discordant voices and issues, and the enormity of its systemic project, which requires the consent of a broad range of actors.

Its development and implementation has drawn the UN system, International Financial Institutions (IFIs), and agencies into the quagmire of multilateral governance in an international milieu where states jealously protect their a priori sovereignty. It has struggled to create consensus or to communicate with those involved at the civil level, or to receive and respond to feedback on its overall systemic project. The constitutional peace is a challenge to those who do not want to share power in domestic constitutional situations, and who do not want the certainty of domestic legal structures that might outlaw their activities. It struggles to overcome the simple binaries it depends upon the territorial inside/outside, and the identity of friend or enemy.

Some important questions arise from these different components of the liberal peace and the problems they raise. How does one emancipate without dominating, without ignoring difference, without knowing the mind of the other? How do these different discourses interweave, play themselves out, and communicate with each other, without competing, dominating or negating each other. How can those who 'know' peace talk to those who do not? So arises the question of the nature of peace, and how it is to be achieved. The fact that peace is so rarely openly conceptualized and explicitly defined in much international discourse other than in negative terms is, in the light of the above, the problem of peace (Richmond, 2005).

The liberal peace is a discourse, framework and structure, with a specific ontology and methodology. Its projected reform of governance entails a communicative strategy on which depends its viability and legitimacy with its recipients, both at a social and a state level. It cannot be achieved without significant resources. The allocation of those resources, the power to do so, and their control, is often the new site of power and in post-conflict societies, despite or because of the emancipatory claims of the liberal peace. The liberal peace and its usage in the relevant, mainly Western literatures and policy discourses (the dominant forms of 'print capitalism' (Anderson, 1983) in the context of peace) requires a clear ontological, epistemological and normative agenda. This opens up the conceptualizations and imaginings of peace as a serious research agenda, moving away from the ever present assumption that peace is an ideal form. The emergence of the liberal peace reflects Augustinian thinking on the 'tranquillity of order' (Augustine, 1991, pp. XIX, 1, 13), the contradictions of Hobbesian thinking on containing the state of nature (Slomp, 1996) and the project outlined by Quincy Wright that peace is represented by a community in which law and order prevail, both internally and externally (Wright, 1964, p. 174). War is made in the 'minds of men' and therefore 'in the minds of men the defences of peace must be constructed' (Wright, 1964, p. 257). This is telling of the liberal peace project: it merely constructs a defence against the worst excesses of the state of nature, or anarchy and hegemony implicit in its victor's peace component (Duffield, 2001, p. 11).

This indicates that liberal peace is a hybrid form which rests mainly on the age-old victor's peace – the Enlightenment and often Christian based work on constitutional peace – and twentieth century secular attempts (but also tinged with non-secular, mainly western claims) to create an institutional peace, and civil society building, are of course important but are often overshadowed by the assumption that basic security can exist a priori to an institutional, constitutional and civil peace. Yet, the liberal peace also claims to be a Platonic ideal form and a Kantian moral imperative, it is also a discourse or a master signifier that may sometimes silence any thought or discussion of other alternatives. It is presented as an ideal form, though there are divisions about whether this ideal form is practical or unobtainable. The subjectivity of the debate on the liberal peace is generally disguised by the objectification and universalization of peace in theoretical and policy usage.

What is clear from this debate is the privileging of the Western experience of peacemaking, which of course has been on an enormous scale since the Treaty of Westphalia, but in particular during the twentieth century. The basic characteristics of both thought and practice on peace are rooted in the Enlightenment, and the notions of rationality and sovereignty, underpinned by various forms of liberalism and progressivism found therein. All four strands of thinking about peace effectively nominate omniscient third parties, which are then placed in a position to transfer external notions of peace into conflict societies and environments. The liberal peace depends upon intervention, and a balance of consent, conditionality and coercion (Ceadel, 1987, p. 4–5). The following diagrams outline the liberal peace framework developed above.

These notions have lengthy antecedents and the victor's peace has remained a key aspect of the liberal peace, even possibly including the emancipatory discourses, which still seem to depend on others being able to know, and install peace for those caught up in conflict. But, the victor's peace increasingly became diluted and disguised by the long-line of peace projects in the post Enlightenment period, which were mainly European in origin and eurocentric in nature, the emergence of a private discourse on peace with the growth of NGOs and civil society actors, and then in the twentieth century the formalization of an institutional discourse on peace. This later discourse, again underpinned by the victor's peace, formed the basis for the hybrid form that was to become the liberal peace, in which multiple actors at multiple levels of analysis in rigid conditional relationships with each began its universal construction according to a mixture of conservative, liberal, regulative and distributive tendencies (Clark, 2001, pp. 216–41). This construction requires a specific ontology of peace, a methodology, mechanisms and tools deployed

**Figure 1.** A genealogy of the liberal peace.

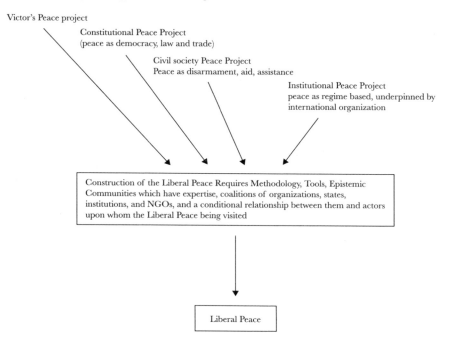

by epistemic communities which have the necessary expertise, by coalitions of organizations, states, institutions, involved in a conditional relationship between them and locations where the liberal peace is being constructed.

The liberal peace is created through the methodologies associated with a 'peacebuilding consensus', where like-minded liberal states coexist in a Western-oriented international society and states are characterized by democracy, human rights, free markets, development, a vibrant civil society and multilateralism. This represents a superficial consensus of states, donors, IOs, ROs, and non-governmental organizations (NGOs) as to the objectives entailed in the different components of the liberal peace. At the same time, there is also disagreement on the methodologies to be applied for its creation, and also which aspect of the liberal peace should be prioritized. Yet, being part of this framework of liberal peace provides certain rights. Knowing peace empowers an epistemic community, legitimately able to transfer the liberal peace into conflict zones. This represents a continuum from war to absence of war to peace.

Despite the assured nature of the liberal peace from this perspective the peacebuilding consensus is heavily contested both in discourse and in practice.

Indeed, it has been argued that institutional and local capacity is actually being destroyed by intervention in conflict environments (Fukuyama, 2004, p. 53). This is partly because those working from the top-down to construct the liberal peace tend to focus more on the state and its institutions. This is often resisted by those working on bottom-up versions of peacebuilding. Their conditional relationship with recipients, donors, international organizations and international financial institutions, means that many non-state actors have developed the capacity for the most intimate forms of intervention in states and in civil society in order to develop a civil peace and to contribute the broader liberal peace project. This important capacity is, of course, of great benefit to the predominantly state-centric liberal peace project, in which such actors are deployed as norm entrepreneurs promoting the validity of its components (Keck and Sikkind, 1998, p. xi).

This means that victor's peace continues to hold legitimacy, though it is heavily disguised. It underpins the constitutional and institutional peace. These versions of peace combine governance, law, civil society, democracy and trade, enshrined in domestic constitutional documentation, and in international treaties at the heart of the new peace, along with the emergence of a civil society and NGO discourse of peace (the 'civil peace'). What is rarely discussed in this context is which of these strands of the peace are the most evident in any particular post-conflict environment. This mainly depends on where the observer is located, but it is undeniable that the form of peace perceived is dominated by its main sponsors, which in the context of the liberal peace, is without question the key states, funders, and executors of its components through the many agents of the peacebuilding consensus. Of course, these dynamics are also subject to change, so it is likely that different aspects of the liberal peace may receive more attention at different periods in the post-conflict peacebuilding process. Yet, the outcome normally reflects the work of the earliest political theorists in the Western tradition, and their focus upon the form of government required to create a durable peace.

The reform of governance is directed by an alliance of actors, who become custodians of the liberal peace. Their control of this process rests upon a combination of inducement, consent and cooperation, occasionally verging upon the coercive, or even the outright use of force. There is essentially a conditional relationship between different states and other actors involved in projecting the liberal peace, the agents they use to construct the peace, and the recipients of the liberal peace. There is little questioning of the validity of the liberal peace, or the way in which its various components fit together with some notable exceptions (Chopra and Hohe, 2004; Paris, 2004; Lund, 2003). Thus, it is assumed that democratization, development and economic reform are complementary, along with human rights reform and legal processes.

There is also little questioning of the motivation of the projectors and agents of the liberal peace, other than among its recipients, who, whether official or non-official actors, tend to be suspicious of outsiders' objectives. Most of the critical focus therefore tends to be on the methods used to construct the liberal peace most effectively, efficiently, and as quickly as possible.

As a result, the different strands of thinking about peace, derived from debates in political theory and philosophy, the constitutional peace plans of the medieval peace, the empowerment of civil society, and the institutional peace plans of the imperial and post-imperial periods have converged on a contemporary notion of what I term *peace-as-governance*. This is the most common form of peace applied through a methodological peacebuilding consensus in conflict zones where international actors become involved, in which a reordering occurs in the distribution of power, prestige, rules and rights. Peace-as-governance in state building terms focuses on the institutions of state as the basis for the construction of the liberal peace. For NGOs and agencies, it focuses on the governance of society. In terms of bottom-up peacebuilding different actors contribute to the liberal peace model by installing forms of peace-as-governance associated with the regulation, control, and protection of individuals and civil society. The balance of power, hegemony, institutionalism and constitutionalism, and civil society converge in this version of peace in an era of governmentality, which is super-territorial, and multi-layered (Foucault, 1991, p. 103). It incorporates official and private actors from the local to the global, institutionalized in the alphabet soup of agencies, organizations, and institutions. But, in its top-down guise it is also a form of the victor's peace, relying on dominant states, in the context of the states-system. The next section examines the different graduations of the liberal peace.

## Conservative, Orthodox and Emancipatory Graduations within the Liberal Peace Framework

The liberal peace project can be broken down into several different graduations. There is first the conservative model of the liberal peace, mainly associated with top-down approaches to peacebuilding and development, tending towards the coercive and often seen as an alien expression of hegemony and domination, sometimes through the use of force, or through conditionality and dependency creation. This equates to a hegemonic and often unilateral, state-led peace, which diplomats are fond of describing as the 'art of the possible'.[3] Such charges are often levelled at the World Bank or the UN, but more often at recent US unilateral state-building efforts. This represents a fear of moving peacebuilding into a terrain where coercion and even force may used to apply it, and where it becomes an expression of external interest rather than external concern and responsibility. The militarization of peace in this context, especially as has been seen in Somalia, the Balkans, Afghanistan and Iraq represents a hyper-conservative model, heavily informed by the victor's peace in the preliminary stages of intervention.

The next discourse is provided within an orthodox model of the liberal peace in which actors are wary and sensitive about local ownership and culture, but still also determined to transfer their methodologies, objectives, and norms into the new governance framework. This framework is dominated by consensual negotiation. This equates to a balanced and multilateral, and still state-centric peace. This is generally projected by international organizations and institutions as well as international NGOs. It represents a bottom-up approach, peacebuilding peace via grassroots and civil society oriented activities, as well as a top-down approach, through which peacebuilding is led by states, donors, officials, IOs and IFIs. It focuses upon and contests needs-based and rights-based activities (Chandler, 2002). However, top-down peacebuilding activity tends to dominate particularly through the conditional models and practices of donors, organizations and institutions, as does the interests of major states and donors. This model is exemplified by the UN family's practices of peacebuilding and governance reform, which started at the end of the cold war and culminated in UN sovereignty for a time over East Timor. Both the conservative and orthodox models assume technical superiority over recipient subjects, as well as the normative universality of the liberal peace. These two models generally assume neo-liberal strategies are sufficient to deal with the problems of war economies and their replacement.

A third discourse is provided by a more critical form of the liberal peace, the *emancipatory* model, which is concerned with a much closer relationship of custodianship and consent with local ownership, and tends to be very critical of the coerciveness, conditionality and dependency that the conservative and orthodox models operate through. This is mainly found within the bottom-up approach, and tends to veer towards needs-based activity and a stronger concern for social welfare and justice. This critical approach to the liberal peace still envisages its universalism, but accentuates its discursive and negotiated requirements. These different actors, mainly local and international NGOs in association with major agencies and some state donors, and associated types of the liberal peace, tend to become more or less prominent in different phases of the conflict and the peacebuilding process. This peace equates to the civil peace, and generally is not state-led, but shaped by private actors and social movements.

These main aspects of the liberal peace model often tend to be combined in the peacebuilding consensus and are expressed to different degrees in any one peacebuilding intervention, depending upon priorities associated with dominant state interests, donor interests and the capacity of peacebuilding actors.

**Figure 2.** Graduations of the liberal peace model.

| | Hyper-Conservative | Conservative | Orthodox | Emancipatory |
|---|---|---|---|---|
| **Geography:** | limited area of strategic allies | Limited area of norm sharing allies | Still geographically bounded but aims at universal coverage. | Aims at universal coverage |
| **Threat:** | Reguar and irregular war and capacity for war; obstacles to necessary resources; terrorism. | Regular and irregual war and capacity for war; obstacles to trade and resouces; terrorism. | War; structural violence; identity conflict; under–development; terrorism; obstacles to trade; barriers to noms and regimes. | War, structural violence; identity conflice; under–development; obstacles to trade; terrorism; free communication and represetation; social justice. |
| **Sustainability of Peace:** | Negligible | limited | high | complete? |
| **Exit of Internationals:** | Unlikely | possible in long term? | Likely in medium to long term | likely in medium to long term |

| | Hyper-Conservative | Conservative | Orthodox | Emancipatory |
|---|---|---|---|---|
| **Method** | Use of Force | Force and Diplomacy military intervention leading to ceasefire, mediation or negotiation. | Top-down peacebuilding; bottom–up peacebuilding | Top-down and bottom–up Peacebuilding |

**Actors**

State officials and regular/irregular military forces

**Nature of Peace**

Victor's Peace defined Solely by military superiority.

**Ontology of Peace**

Peace is not possible, very limited, or is territorially bounded; peace is utopian

**Actors**

State officials and regular/irregular military forces

**Nature of Peace**

Victor's Peace, constitutional peace settlement/international peace treaty (but not an institutional peace). Quasi military measures such as peace keeping deployed for long periods.

**Ontology of Peace**

Peace is a product of force and elite diplomacy; universal form of peace should be aspired to but is unreachable

**Actors**

State officials and regular/irregular military forces; IO, RO, IFI, which control Agencies and NGOs.

**Nature of Peace**

Constitutional and institutional Peace; elements of victor's peace through hegemony rather than use of force. As with conservative model, but long–term measures for sustainability also included: institutional, constitutional, and civil governance measures for political, economic, development, and social issues imported through conditional relationship between agents of peacebuilding and recipients; settlement more importantthan justice.

**Ontology of Peace**

Peace rests mainly on constitutional and institutional measures; it is universal and can be achieved through epistemic transference of technical knowledge and frameworks.

**Actors**

Combinations of state officials and regular/irregular military forces; IO, RO, IFI, Agency, and NGO personnel but led by local actors.

**Nature of Peace**

Civil Peace; focus on social movements, social actors, and issues, social welfare and justice as a pathway to peace. Wary of external forms of domination being imported through external intervention.

**Ontology of Peace**

Peace rests on social justice and open and free communication between social actors, as well as state/official actors; recognition of difference and otherness.

Local actor's responses may also have some impact, as has been seen in the case of the 'Timorisation' campaign in East Timor (Smith, 2003, p. 63), or in Kosovo (Rupnik, 2005). The nominal unity of the peacebuilding consensus often breaks down exactly because of the internal competition, interests and capacity of its different components. Clearly, conservative, orthodox and emancipatory versions of the liberal peace may actually contradict and undermine each other, leading to disruption in the broader peacebuilding process.

During an emergency period the hyper-conservative or conservative version of the liberal peace may find their raison d'etre at the top-down level and operate partly as a way of fulfilling the norms of the liberal international community, but also to preserve and reinforce the sanctity of the liberal peace model within the states-system. In a post-conflict reconstruction phase official actors may begin to shift to the orthodox version of the liberal peace, which focuses on the development of institutional relationships, institutions and constitutions that preserve or redefine the state but also provide for the interests and requirements of the general population. Agencies and NGOs often operate in both phases upon the basis of the more critical emancipatory version of the liberal peace, mainly because they are much more dependent upon local and donor consent. Those actors, mainly agencies and NGOs, working within the critical model tend to be wary of the conservative approaches and their associated actors, while those working in the latter tend to be disdainful of consensual requirements and local ownership while 'results' are more pressing than sustainability in an emergency, or immediate post-conflict phase. Clearly, however, once sustainability becomes key in a post emergency phase, and internationals begin to think about their exit strategies, even top-down actors begin to move towards more critical emancipatory models of the liberal peace. This latter discourse appears to be the most legitimate of all of these models, despite its breadth, and lack of parsimony. All of these strands of the liberal peace are often presented as emancipatory in policy discourse.

This raises some important policy implications in terms of the different versions of the liberal peace outlined above. It is clear that there seems to be shifts between these different approaches, depending upon the conditions and thinking prevalent within the international community and within conflict zones. One could draw a broad teleological evolutionary line in which the victor's peace gave way to a constitutional peace, to which was then added an institutional and civil peace in European and Western thinking and policy-making. This has, of course, occurred in the broader context of a belief in the superiority, infallibility and universality of the liberal peace. Depending on the strength of this position, the project of the liberal peace may move from the conservative coercive models, to the more consensual orthodox model, or even to the emancipatory model, or a specific combination of all of the above.

**Figure 3.** Current examples of the liberal peace.

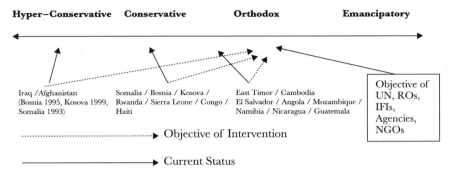

It is vital to identify the graduations of the liberal peace that are being constructed through different types of intellectual and policy analysis, and by different actors, in order to evaluate the effectiveness and sustainability of peacebuilding approaches. This is represented by a configuration of the main four discourses of peaces, and the four graduations of the liberal peace outlined above. This should lead to a better understanding of (i) the type of peace being created, (ii) impediments to peace, and (iii) the sustainability of this peace. This analysis and comparison opens the way for a greater intellectual and policy understanding of the agendas inherent in the different aspects of the liberal peace project. The figures above illustrate the axis along which the nature of the liberal peace can be located, and from which the implications for sustainability of the peace, its costs, and likely areas of resistance, can be drawn in a number of cases. It indicates the general tendency of peacebuilding interventions, though it should be acknowledged that interventions often show some crossover between these graduations.

What the above seems to illustrate is that entry into a conflict zone is often predicted on a conservative version of the liberal peace, with the aspiration of moving towards the orthodox position. A significant number of examples can be provided for this movement, as Figure 3 illustrates, but a significant number also remain mired within the conservative graduation of the liberal peace. No cases can be located within the emancipatory graduation, and indeed, as much of the literature attests, the lack of social justice, and socio-economic well-being and development seems to mar all international involvements in the post-cold war era (Paris, 2004; Bellamy and Williams, 2004; Chandler, 2002; Chopra, and Hohe, 2004; Cousens and Kumar, 2001; Caplan, 2002). Clearly, the above diagrams illustrate the tendency for internationals to enter a conflict environment somewhere within the conservative graduation, and then aspire (both the internationals and local recipients included) to move along the axis to the orthodox peace, which is both sustainable and allows the internationals to withdraw. However, experience seems to show that where force is used in a hyper-conservative initial approach, moving along the axis towards the orthodox category tends not to occur. The best illustration of this appears to be Bosnia and Kosovo, where the political entity (state or not) is weak, and socially and economically unsustainable despite the length of time the internationals have been involved.[4] Where entry is based upon a peace agreement with broad consensus, it often occurs within the conservative graduation but moves rapidly towards the orthodox, as many of the cases in Figure 3 indicate.

This raises the question of what the requirements are for the construction of a specific graduation of the liberal peace, which may then shift from the conservative to the orthodox. Clearly, the liberal peace discourse focuses on constitutional democracy, human rights, neo-liberal development, as well as a civil peace, these providing the general framework through which the liberal peace can be achieved. In practice, however, the processes have created very weak states, and institutions, and civil society is marred by unemployment, lack of development, forms of nationalism, and the often tortuous slowness of the shift from the pre-intervention situation to even the most limited and conservative form of the liberal peace. In these conditions, a lack of confidence in the new polity, and in the economy are often key problems, as well as suspicion of the intentions of internationals, and of local actors. For instance, throughout the Balkans, there is suspicion of the intentions of internationals, of local politicians, as well as a lack of confidence in constitutions, the viability of the states being formed, and acute problems relating both to unemployment and ethnic chauvinism. This is despite the lengthy presence of the many internationals.

All of these versions of the liberal peace identify geographical zones that are to be made safe from war, terrorism and political violence, under-development, human rights abuses and other forms of structural violence. The liberal peace ranges from the virtual and highly interventionary to the more consensual versions which are also concerned with social justice. All of these strands of the liberal peace have graduated approaches to consent and conditionality, but they all share an assumption of universality, which legitimates intervention, and of the superiority of the epistemic peacebuilding community over its recipients. The conservative approaches tend to be more conditional, though this can also be seen in the more critical liberal peace approaches in relations between grass roots actors and donors. In the conservative discourse, however, conditionality is imposed from the top-down by the external actors involved. In the more critical approaches, conditionality is subject to negotiation, thus acquiring a bottom-up aspect and being coloured more by social justice concerns. This conditionality is also two-way. Internationals are now learning that where they set conditionalities so local actors also expect conditionalities to be observed. Furthermore, local actors are becoming adept at manipulating conditionalities in their favour. If a sustainable peace is to be constructed there can be no exit until both locals and internationals have agreed that such a version of peace has actually been achieved. What is more, the emphasis of different aspects of the liberal peace – the victor's peace, constitutional, institutional, and civil – depends on which actors take the lead in intervention or coordination. The UN family tends to focus simultaneously on all aspects, despite the fact that they may not be complementary, but the institutional peace provides its raison d'etre (though this is constrained by the imperative to foster and preserve state sovereignty as part of its charter). The US tends to focus on the victor's peace as well as the constitutional peace, though it must be noted that on all terms apart from per capita, the US is the biggest contributor to all of the different aspects of the construction of the liberal peace. NGOs and agencies tend to focus on the civil peace, as do major donors such as Britain, Japan, Canada, and Norway, which also emphasise the institutional peace and associated forms of multi-lateralism. The OSCE and EU have probably the most explicit view of their end goals, which are constituted in terms of the orthodox category above, but moving along the axis towards the emancipatory version (Fearn, 2004).

All of these different approaches within the liberal peace framework often claim to be emancipatory, though there are no empirical examples which incorporate social welfare institutions which would act at least in the interim for a replacement for war economies and grey markets. They all find their raison d'etre in the identification and response to specific threats identified against the liberal peace project. Furthermore, they exist side by side, and in tension which each other. The conservative notions of liberal peace and the critical notions act, both in theoretical, conceptual, and policy terms, as brakes upon each other and upon the worst excesses of hegemony, domination, and relativism. This raises the question of what is emancipation, who carries it out as its agents, who understands and transfers it, and who receives, and why, and what impact this has upon the recipients identity? Again these open questions underline the subjective ontology of peace.

Most contemporary peacebuilding cases can be placed somewhere between the conservative and orthodox liberal peace components in terms of their pre-ponderant approaches. Cambodia, Angola, and East Timor generally fit into the orthodox frameworks. Somalia, Bosnia, and Kosovo, and more recently, Afghanistan and Iraq, would fit somewhere between the hyper-conservative and conservative frameworks (of course, this depends upon which phase of the peacekeeping/peacebuilding intervention was under review), perhaps slowly moving toward the orthodox model. These general positions can be broken down further by examining the different actors involved. The orthodox and emancipatory models would be more significant if one focuses on agencies and NGOs and their peace projects. It must be acknowledged, however, that the preponderant framework relates to the reconstruction of the state, meaning that the conservative and orthodox discourse are the most commonly expressed through these peace operations. This then raises serious questions about the sustainability of the peace that is being created, and the limits of the liberal peace. There is a general tendency to respond to the seriousness of conflict or war by moving the intervention along the liberal peace axis toward the hyper-conservative framework, and then as peacebuilding consolidates, to push the focus back along the axis toward the orthodox framework.

Given the significance of the experience of internationals and local actors in the specific context of East Timor, it should not be surprising that the East Timorese President argued that the experience of East Timor indicated that peace was a basic human right and this involved not just responses to international and civil violence, but to socio-economic deprivation, a lack of development, and required an engagement with the experience of recipient communities on the part of internationals (Gusmao, 2004). In the UN triptych of *Agendas*, democratization and development are also seen to be a right and in the recent report on the *Responsibility to Protect* the broader international community is called upon to protect communities and individuals where their host states are unable to (Chandler, 2004). This is a far more interventionist agenda for peace than ever before: the liberal peace works only by creating a basis for liberal states and organizations to intervene to correct abnormalities in others' political, social and economic practices. Thus, creating the liberal peace is about disciplining those deemed to be responsible for such abnormal practices through conditionality and effective transnational governance regimes controlled by liberal states, organizations, NGOs, donors and IFIs. Liberal peacebuilding has created the conservative or orthodox rather than emancipatory model, as can be seen in the context of Afghanistan and Iraq. If liberal peace is a right, then clearly this raises the question of which form of liberal peace? It is clear that while the conservative versions may have some legitimacy in an illiberal transitional phase, the orthodox graduation would probably provide a minimum long-term aspiration.

## Theoretical Implications

The evolution of thinking about peace seems to show that it is an ontologically unstable concept (indicative of ontological insecurity) (Giddens, 1991, p. 35–69). But the history of engagement with the construction of peace indicates that it has been generally thought of as an ontologically stable concept. Much of the discourse of the liberal peace is derived from the development of a governance approach, which since 1945 has focused on the reform and regulation of both domestic government and global governance, in a regulative and restrictive fashion (Clark, 2001, p. 216–41). Thus, the liberal peace project has endeavoured to produce a peace that is stable and consensual, but within a cosmopolitan framework of governance which is both a representation of the individual, the state and the global. This complex position on peace needs to be clearly elucidated before we can begin to decide whether it has the potential to become ontologically stable and a positive epistemology. As Walker argues the construction of binaries has been one of the key approaches for mainstream theories of IR (Walker, 1992). This has meant that a common pattern has emerged which depends upon the identification of threats and of an 'other' (Wilmer, 2002, p. 95). This is what Rasmussen has called a 'negative epistemology' of peace (Rasmussen, 2003). This is played out in a discourse of moral superiority versus inferiority. The peacebuilding consensus and peace-as-governance have been constructed as ways around the incessant problem of seeing peace as a negative epistemology revolving around short-term 'threat assessments'. Peace has long been a policy goal (Cooper, 2003, p. 111), but the conservative and orthodox graduations of the liberal peace appear to be a form of 'imperial sovereignty' (Hardt and Negri, 2000, pp. 183–204).

Such approaches are indicative of a critical and post-modern construction of a counter debate to the general mainstream essentialization of negative epistemological assumptions about peace – often to be found in protective securitization discourses within the traditional liberal, realist and structuralist traditions. Drawing on the work of critical theorists and post-structuralists (Linklater, 1998; Jabri, 1996; Bleiker, 2000; Pugh, 2004; Cambell, 1992; Walker, 1993; Der Derien, 2001; Cox, 1981), who themselves draw upon Foucault, Gramsci, Habermas and others, an emancipatory project in IR vis-à-vis peace has emerged. This challenge to the mainstream has been constructed in terms of the creation of a positive epistemology of peace, and one which attempts to avoid 'orientalism' and totalism, while still aspiring to the plausibility, if not possibility of universalism. Part of the problem with this critical approach is its complexity, but this is also where its sophistication lies. The recognition of the sheer complexity both of conflict, and of the peace projects of internationals is necessary because there is evidence that the liberal peace is in practice often little more than a 'virtual peace'.

The liberal peace is generally understood to be geographically limited, often to be achieved in or for the future, legitimates the use of force for its ends, and is understood in opposition to threats. Both the acts of defining and constructing peace are therefore hegemonic acts dependent upon international institutionalisation, governance and regimes, and the dominant threat discourses present in the international system. Many assertions about peace are actually forms of orientalism in that they depend upon actors who know peace, then creating it for those that do not, either through their acts or more basically through the peace discourses that are employed to describe conflict and war as located in opposition to agents of peace.

Peace, in Howard's words, is a visualization of a social order in which war is controlled and ultimately abolished, specifically in the context of Western Enlightenment and post-Enlightenment thinking (Howard, 2000, p. 8–9). It is of little surprise that the political and social institutions of both war and peace always coexist. War and peace are both social and political inventions (Mead, 1990, p. 415–21); but war is generally seen as abnormal and peace needs to be juxtaposed with a non-peace situation in order to have any meaning. As the sociologist William Graham Sumner has argued, a universal understanding of peace may be a fallacy:

> It is a fallacy to suppose that, by widening the peace group more and more, it can at last embrace all mankind. What happens is that, as it grows bigger, differences, discords, antagonisms, and war begin inside of it on account of the divergence of Interests. (Sumner, 1911)

In other words, as peace spreads it collapses. Peace is contested. Peace becomes war. War becomes peace.

## Virtual Peace, Virtuous Peace

Rather than starting with the problems caused by conflict, war, underdevelopment, and so forth, a research agenda is needed which starts with the type of peace envisaged in a particular situation and at a particular level of analysis, by particular actors whether they are intervening or are local actors. This require extensive and ongoing consultation and research in order to develop these ideas so that they are ready to be negotiated, accepted, rejected and constructed when and where becomes necessary. When internationals engage in conflict zones, one of the first questions they might ask of disputants at the many different levels of the polity might be what type of peace could be envisaged? Working towards such an explicit end goal would be of great benefit both to internationals and recipients of intervention. This would have to occur in the explicit context of responses to the root causes of the conflict, meaning that peacebuilding occurs at two starting points. Rather than merely beginning from the identification of the root causes of the conflict, it would concurrently build peace from the perspective of the specific notion of peace deemed to be appropriate for the specific environment. This appropriateness would be negotiated from the perspective of the internationals, custodians, and other interventionary actors, and most importantly, local actors. Where one set of actors could not agree, the other would compensate, upon the explicit understanding that this would be merely an interim (and possibly illiberal) measure.

Clearly, the use of strategies and theories for understanding conflict, war and terrorism that do not move beyond the strategic analyses of state interest runs the risk of remaining 'virtual'. As represented in Figure 3, the tendency appears to be for interventions to enter a conflict environment somewhere within the conservative category, and to aspire to move towards the orthodox framework where the liberal peace becomes self-sustaining, more concrete, and the internationals can withdraw. Yet, the reality – apparent from the Balkans to East Timor – is that intervention focuses upon the creation of the hard shell of the state and rather less so on establishing a working society, complete with a viable economy which has an immediately beneficial effect on the labour force or provides a welfare system. This results in a virtual peace – one which looks like the virtuous orthodox liberal peace from the outside, but looks and feels like its more conservative version from the inside – especially from the perspective of those who are experiencing it.[5]

Indeed, the possibility is that the 'virtuous' distinction between peace and war, which creates a situation of virtual peace, is explicitly advantageous for western liberal states and their interventionary policies in that this allows the superficial distinction based upon domestic and international public law to obscure the fact that in reality, on the ground in many parts of the world, peace and war are synonymous in actuality. Indeed, war to create the liberal peace – the victory of 'democratic theory' – underlines exactly this. But, is the democratic peace in post-conflict societies much more than a virtual construction by outsiders for the consumption of their own audiences? Of course, much has been achieved in conflict zones by the agents of the peacebuilding consensus, but these achievements are mainly measured by their own frameworks and standards. It is also clear that the internationals' representation of their achievements is often skewed in favour of what donors and the main actors in the international community want. The peace being constructed in the various contemporary conflict zones around the world looks very different from the perspectives of local communities, polities, economies and officials. This is clear in the discourses about peace that is in evidence, and is emphasized by the fact that these discourses are so rarely acknowledged. In a rather orientalist manner, Western political thought and policy has reproduced a science and methodology of peace based upon political, social, economic, cultural, and legal frameworks, by which conflict in the world is judged and dealt with. Indeed, this is an expression of hegemony – a tempered victor's peace in which its agents and its recipients clamour to be heard and to influence the outcome. The post-Gramscian notion of plural 'hegemonies' (Hoare and Geoffrey Nowell-Smith, 1973, pp. 56–9) encapsulates the liberal peace as a form of both multiple hegemonies and a single dominant discourse promoted by powerful states. Peace can be problem-solving or emancipatory, but in either case it is always laden with agendas related to actors' interests and objectives. In this sense, a virtual peace may be of a problem-solving character despite its 'virtuous' claims to be emancipatory. Such claims have to be made on behalf of someone or something and the voices of the marginalized are often swamped by such hegemonic voices. This is particularly problematic in the areas of marketization and development, which are driven by neoliberalism and therefore leave labour markets and civil society more generally at the mercy of elite corruption, grey markets, and of course, poverty.

Because the liberal peace is virtual and highly interventionary, it engenders a whole range of debates about hegemony, the moral equivalence of interveners and the recipients of intervention, the motivations of interveners and recipients in their relationship, neutrality, impartiality and conditionality. Yet, most work dealing with peace both directly or indirectly fails to present a working definition of the peace that is being imagined, nor engage with any of the epistemological, methodological, or ontological issues it raises. Top-down approaches to the creation of peace have been based upon a mix of idealism associated with humanitarianism and implemented through political, social and economic interventions, and the militarist strategies associated with the realist project. This has increasingly taken the form of military occupation. Again, this represents a hybrid of the civil, constitutional, institutional and victor's strands of thinking about peace. It is in this context that it becomes clear that the liberal peace may well be a virtual peace, certainly in its more conservative forms, despite the fact that it is based upon deep-rooted intervention in governance. This is, essentially, a form of rehabilitation of imperial duty and a liberal imperative. The top-down construction of the liberal peace dominates the epistemic community engaged in the construction of the institutions the liberal peace, which treads a narrow path between dependency, conditionality and sustainability. Peace-as-governance is often presented as a transitional phase but a final outcome may remote. The liberal peace legitimates the use of force and external long-term governance, but peace without external governance may not be achieved.

Peace has thus been transformed from a possibly unobtainable utopia coloured by the ideology and norms of the perceiver to an objectified graduation of the liberal peace – an actually existing and obtainable peace propagated through an epistemic peacebuilding community, involving political, social, economic, and even cultural intervention through external governance. Examining a research agenda on the nature of peace rather than merely the nature of conflict and intermediate responses, provides a much clearer vision of the specific project of peace implied and engaged with by specific intellectual and policy approaches to international order, war and conflict. It underlines the possibilities of this project – in this case of the liberal peace – and its key problems. The graduations of the liberal peace are implicit in the construction of peace in the contemporary era but dangers in this project have become apparent, not least the relationship and indeterminacy of forms of peace and war. For peace to be acceptably transformed, it first needs to be understood, negotiated and mediated, in fora designed for multiple voices and free communication. This process is still little more than embryonic endorsing recent and critical claims about a regulative and distributive, but highly conditional understanding of, contemporary liberal peace as hegemonic (Clark, 2001, p. 248). This peace project needs to respond to the suspicion that '[L]iberalism destroys democracy' (Strong, 1996, p. xxiii) and that different forms and components of the liberal peace may effectively be incoherent. Ironically, the liberal peace treads a fine line between a coercive peace based upon 'wars to determine once and for all what is good for all, wars with no outcome except an end to politics and the liberation of difference'. (Schmitt, 1996, p. 69) and a peace based upon consensual, universal governance. In looking at the transformation of war economies, it also needs to make a much stronger provision for social welfare and justice in order to enhance the contract between citizen and state, to undermine grey economies, and to replace them with more immediate opportunities than neo-liberal strategies tend to provide. We still need to know how one gains consent for liberal peacebuilding, how it is legitimated, how actors learn in this context, how human rights, humanitarian assistance and aid, democratisation, zdevelopment, free market reform and globalization actually fit together, how they overlap, and where they may impede each other. If we claim we now 'know' what peace is, then these oversights are inexcusable.

# Chapter Three

# PRE-EMPTIVE SELF-DEFENCE NEW LEGAL PRINCIPLE OR POLITICAL ACTION?*

## Ramses Amer

## Purpose and Structure

The purpose of this study is to examine the ongoing legal debate surrounding pre-emptive self-defence. The study examines the legal debate surrounding the regulation of the use of force in the provisions of the Charter of the United Nations. The possible interconnection between pre-emptive self-defence and anticipatory self-defence is explored. The political ramification of the possibility of a weakening of the regulation of the use of force as expressed in the Charter of the United Nations is discussed.

The study is structured into two main sections. The first relates to the Charter of the United Nations and the Articles relating to the use of force and the scholarly debate relating to the key Articles is outlined and assessed. The second is an overview and analysis of the renewed attention and interest in issues relating to the use of force in self-defence in interstate relations, in particular the notion of pre-emptive self-defence and related developments in the post-cold war era particularly after 11 September 2001.

## The Charter of the United Nations and the Use of Force by States

### The provisions of the Charter of the United Nations[1]

There are three clauses in the Charter of the United Nations that regulate the use of force by the individual member states, namely Article 2(3), Article 2(4)

---

* The Author wishes to acknowledge the assistance of Mr David Valijani.

and Article 51. Furthermore, in Article 39 the regulations pertaining to the use of force by the United Nations are outlined. Article 2(3) states that all members of the United Nations shall settle disputes by peaceful means. In the context of this study the focus will be on Article 2(4) on Article 51. Article 2(4) reads as follows:

> All Members shall refrain in their international relations from the threat or use of force against the territorial integrity or political independence of any state, or any other manner inconsistent with the purposes of the United Nations.

Article 51 reads as follows:

> Nothing in the present Charter shall impair the inherent right of individual or collective self-defence if an armed attack occurs against a Member of the United Nations, until the Security Council has taken measures necessary to maintain international peace and security. Measures taken by Members in the exercise of this right of self-defence shall be immediately reported to the Security Council and shall not in any way affect the authority and responsibility of the Security Council under the present Charter to take at any time such action as it deems necessary in order to maintain or restore international peace and security.

### Assessing the Scholarly Debate on the Interpretation of Article 2(4) of the Charter [2]

The debate among international lawyers pertaining to the provisions of Article 2(4) of the Charter relating to the use of force by states in interstate relations displays considerable controversy as to how these provisions should be interpreted. This controversy can partly be ascribed to the wording of Article 2(4). The wording of Article 2(4) and for that matter the whole Charter was based on considerations and decisions among the original member states of the United Nations. It is the result of a series of compromises reached by these states after having reconciled each other's views and, consequently, the text is in some instances 'ambiguous' and 'unclear'.[3]

In the case of Article 2(4) the term 'force' has caused the scholars some trouble. The wording of Article 2(4) does not give a clear answer as to which actions of a state that should be defined as 'force'.

- A restrictive interpretation is that 'force' refers to the threat or to the use of 'armed force' against the territorial integrity or political independence of a state.

- An extensive interpretation is that 'force' refers to any threat of 'action' or to any 'action' initiated against the territorial integrity or political independence of a state.

The restrictive interpretation prohibits the threat or the use of 'armed force' but does not, in principle, prohibit an economic embargo directed at another state. Scholars adhering to such a restrictive interpretation usually point to the fact that other forms of intervention in the internal affairs of a state than by 'armed force' are addressed by the provisions of Article 2(7) and the principle of non-intervention. The extensive interpretation implies that the threat or the use of 'force' in whatever form in interstate relations is prohibited, i.e. 'any' kind of interference which is not acceptable to the government of the target state.

Another point of disagreement is how the wording 'against the territorial integrity or political independence of any State', in Article 2(4), should be interpreted.

- A restrictive interpretation is that only the threat or the use of force that directly affects the territorial integrity or the political independence of a state is encompassed by the prohibition.
- An extensive interpretation is that not only the threat or the use of force affecting the territorial integrity or the political independence of a state but also any action against the political authority of a state is encompassed by the prohibition.

The interpretation of the wording 'against the territorial integrity or political independence of any State', in Article 2(4), has a bearing on what kind of interstate behaviour that would fall under the phenomenon known as 'use of force'. Nevertheless, despite the divergent interpretations of Article 2(4) there is a consensus that this Article provides a general prohibition of the threat or the use of 'force' in interstate relations.

The scholarly interpretations of the provisions of Article 2(4) have their weaknesses from the point of view of restricting the use of 'force' in interstate relations.[4]

- A restrictive interpretation of the term 'force' would not prohibit economic and political activities that could undermine the political stability in a state or create hardship for its population. Furthermore, it would not prohibit foreign interference in a state as long as such interference does not involve direct engagement of troops in the affected state.
- A restrictive interpretation of the wording 'against the territorial integrity or political independence of any State' would imply that many kinds of

foreign interventions short of armed attacks would not be prohibited, notwithstanding their effects on the political structure of the affected state.

### Interpreting Article 51 of the Charter

#### The Scholarly Debate on the Interpretation of Article 51

The debate among international lawyers pertaining to the provisions of Article 51 of the Charter of the United Nations displays considerable controversy as to how these provisions should be interpreted. This controversy can partly be ascribed to the wording of Article 51. As in the case of Article 2(4) it must be stated that the wording of the whole Charter was based on considerations and decisions among the original member states of the United Nations. It is the result of a series of compromises reached by these states.[5]

If the wording of Article 51 is looked at from the purely literal point of view, a state or a group of states can use force in self-defence only 'if an armed attack occurs against a Member of the United Nations'. Thus, contrary to the wording in the case of Article 2(4), the provisions of Article 51 can be literally interpreted. Nevertheless, the interpretation of the right of self-defence has been subject to controversy in the scholarly debate and, as in the case of Article 2(4), a restrictive and an extensive line of interpretation can be identified.

Scholars in the restrictive camp include Brownlie (1962, 2001), Mrazek (1989), and Kelsen (1948). Scholars in the extensive camp include Asrat (1991), Bowett (1955–6), Sapiro (2005) and Waldock (1952).

To start with the first group, Brownlie has argued that the permission to use force in self-defence, as expressed in Article 51, is exceptional in the context of the Charter of the United Nations and that it is exclusive of any customary right of self-defence (Brownlie, 1962, p. 240). Brownlie is unequivocal in defending his interpretation, as can be seen in the following:

> It can only be concluded that the view that Article 51 does not permit anticipatory action is correct and that the arguments to the contrary are either unconvincing or based on inconclusive pieces of evidence. (Brownlie, 1962, p. 245)

Brownlie gives an interpretation of what exactly can be regarded as 'armed attack' in accordance with the provisions of Article 51. He argues that 'armed attack' refers to 'a trespass, a direct invasion, and not to activities described by some jurists as "indirect aggression"' (Brownlie, 1962, p. 260). However, Brownlie says that if there is control by the 'aggressor State' and actual use of force by its agents, then there is an 'armed attack' (Brownlie, 1962, p. 260).

To summarize, Brownlie's line of argumentation is that a state has the right to resort to force in self-defence only if it has been subject to an armed attack. Furthermore, such an armed attack must be directed against the territory or territorial waters of a state (Brownlie, 1962, pp. 266–7). Brownlie also says that anticipatory self-defence is unlawful. Finally, he claims that forcible intervention to protect the lives and/or property of its own nationals, living in another state, is also unlawful.

In a more recent study Brownlie revisits his book on *International law and the Use of Force by States* published in 1963 and in reference to Article 51 he states:

> The author's general position on the use of force is sometimes caricatured as the 'restrictive view', chiefly because the book is unfavourable to anticipatory self-defence. In this respect the author remains unrepentant. (Brownlie, 2001, p. 26)

This confirms the continuity in Brownlie's interpretation of Article 51 and his opposition to anticipatory self-defence. His reference to the 'restrictive view' should be noted.

Kelsen has argued that the provisions in Article 51 restrict the rights of member states to use force in self-defence to the case of an 'armed attack' actually being made by one state against another (Kelsen, 1948, p. 791). Kelsen also says that the intention of the Charter is that the use of force in the exercise of self-defence under Article 51 should be:

> [...] a provisional and temporary measure, permitted only "until" the Security Council takes the necessary measures to restore peace, especially until collective security comes into action, and not as a substitute for it. (Kelsen, 1948, p. 795)

Mazrek has carried out a comprehensive analysis of the various interpretations of Article 51 including scholars from both the restrictive and extensive schools. from both the restrictive and the extensive schools.

In his conclusion his clearly states his interpretation of the provisions of Article 51 as can be seen in the following:

> The right of individual and collective self-defence is defined in Article 51, which limits it to cases of armed attack. Contemporary international law does not authorize anticipatory or preventive self-defence. A right of self-defence based on customary law outside Article 51 does not exist. (Mrazek, 1989, p. 108)

Among the scholars representing the 'extensive' group Bowett has argued that the effect of Article 51 is to recognize the rights that existed before the Charter of the United Nations was written and not to create new rights. One of the cardinal pre-existing rights referred to by Bowett is the 'anticipatory' right of self-defence (Bowett, 1955–6, p. 131, 148). He argues that 'the right of self-defence is not limited to cases of an "armed attack"' (Bowett, 1955–6, p. 144).

Waldock has made some interpretations of the reference in Article 51 pertaining to the inherent right to self-defence 'if an armed attack occurs' and to its connection to the customary rights of states. Waldock argues that it would be a misinterpretation of the intention of Article 51 to assume that it prohibits the use of force in self-defence in resistance to an illegal use of force not constituting an 'armed attack' (Waldock, 1952, pp. 496–7). Waldock also argues that, if the reaction of the United Nations is 'obstructed, delayed, or inadequate' when a state faces an imminent threat of an armed attack, that state can use force in self-defence (Waldock, 1952, p. 498). Finally, Waldock is of the opinion that the general principle of 'self-protection' has not been touched upon by the Charter of the United Nations. According to Waldock, this implies, among other things, that a state has the right to use force against another state in order to protect its nationals living in that state (Waldock, 1952, pp. 502–3).

Asrat is also preoccupied with the term 'armed attack', and he argues that if an 'armed attack' was the sole ground on which a state could act in self-defence, other violations of Article 2(4) would be left unattended by the unilateral protection of self-defence. Such a state of affairs would undermine the prohibition expressed in Article 2(4). Following from this line of argumentation Asrat states that

> It would not appear consistent with the maintenance of international peace and security to construe Art. 51 so restrictively. [...] The Article should rather be seen as recognizing the inherent right of self-defence *per se* and not as setting a limit to the ground of its exercise. (Asrat, 1991, p. 222)

Asrat also moves into the realm of 'anticipatory' self-defence by arguing that

> Since it has been submitted that the prohibition of force in Art. 2(4) subsumes and engenders the exception of self-defence whose content is not restricted by Art. 51, the target state could exercise its right of self-defence against the illegal threat of force. (Asrat, 1991, pp. 222–3)

Thus, Asrat makes the interpretation that the Charter of the United Nations does not prohibit anticipatory self-defence.

Sapiro recognizes that there are different views on whether or not the 'pre-emption doctrine' is till valid after the adoption of the Charter of the United Nations given the fact that Article 51 'requires' and armed attack in order for a state to invoke self-defence. However, she goes on to argue that

> The better line of reasoning argues that the requirement of an "armed attack" is broad enough to accommodate the prospect of an imminent attack, when there is a high level of certainty and the other criteria – necessity and proportionality – are met. (Sapiro, 2005, p. 366)

This displays that Sapiro adheres to an extensive interpretation of the right to invoke self-defence in the event of an imminent attack.

The scholarly debate on the interpretation of the provisions of Article 51 of the Charter displays that the basic differences between the restrictive interpretation and the extensive interpretation can be summarized as follows:

- Scholars making a restrictive interpretation of the provisions of Article 51 argue that the use of force is only allowed when an 'armed attack occurs' against a member state of the United Nations and under no other circumstances.
- Scholars making an extensive interpretation do not regard Article 51 as comprehensive in assessing the right of self-defence. They argue that the customary right of self-defence is still valid under the Charter of the United Nations. From this follows that 'anticipatory' self-defence is not necessarily a violation of the provisions of the Charter.

## Assessing the Scholarly Debate on the Interpretation of the Article 51

The scholarly interpretations of the provisions of Article 51 have their weaknesses from the point of view of restricting the use of 'force' in interstate relations.[6]

An extensive interpretation of the right of self-defence could have serious implications. First, it would not prohibit the pre-emptive use of force against a state under the guise of self-defence in a situation in which no real threat of force could be proved. Second, it would not prohibit the use of force against another state under the guise of rescuing its own nationals, residing in that state, without sufficient indications that the well-being of these nationals was really threatened. Third, and more fundamentally, an extensive interpretation of self-defence could contribute to opening the way for the condoning of the use of force claimed to have been carried out in self-defence but in fact aiming at changing the political structure of another state. It is true that the representatives of the school of extensive interpretation put strong emphasis on the aspect of proportionality and on the action to be temporary when force is used in self-defence but this does not sufficiently address the possible implications as outlined above.

## Anticipatory, Pre-Emptive and Preventive Self-Defence – An Analysis

The scholarly debate relating to the right to use force in self-defence in accordance with the provisions of the Charter of the United Nations, i.e. Article 51, is as old as the Charter itself. The debate has been closely associated with the debate and interpretations of Article 2(4) of the Charter that relates to the use of force and the prohibition of the threat and the use of force against the territorial integrity and/or political independence of a state. Since Article 51 is but one of two exceptions to this ban of the use of force – the other being the right of the Security Council to make decision involving the use of force in accordance with Article 42 of the Charter – it is of fundamental importance to assess the developments of both legal and political debate relating to the right to use force in self-defence.

The traditional division in the legal debate has pitted a school centred around a restrictive interpretation of the Article 51 arguing that the use of force in self-defence is only permitted when an armed attack occurs and under no other circumstances, as against a school centred around an extensive interpretation of the right to use force in self-defence which does not rule out anticipatory self-defence.

In the post-cold war era and in particular since 11 September 2001 there has been renewed attention to the question of self-defence with, not only the emergence of the notion of pre-emptive self-defence, but also broader attempts at legitimizing the use of force in self-defence prior to an armed attack in view of the perceived challenge of the threat of terrorist attacks. The United States of America (USA) has been most vocal in pursuing a pre-emptive or pre-emption policy not always explicitly linked to self-defence but nevertheless relevant in this context. A key development in the policy of the USA was the publishing of the National Security Strategy (NSS) on 17 September 2002.

The NSS has provoked scholarly debate. Franck notes that the NSS extended 'far beyond' the notion of anticipatory self-defence and even exceeded of the notion of 'preventive measures' to outline a new claim to the 'lawful use of force pre-emptively' (Franck, 2004, p. 425). He continues his analysis of the NSS by stating under the doctrine that it formulates: '[...] an attack need not be imminent, it need not even be threatened, it need merely be *expected*, sometime' (Franck, 2004, p. 425). He then moves on to argue that

'What the United Sates wants to pre-empt is the right of another state to *aspire* to threaten us' (Franck, 2004, p. 426).

On the Iraq case in 2003 she argues that 'The US decision to invade Iraq was "preventive" in nature, relying upon a concept of questionable legal pedigree and a high degree of subjectivity' (Sapiro, 2005, p. 367).

On the issue the case of Iraq in 2003 the NSS from 2006 does include it within the context principles of self-defence and 'pre-emption' and links the intervention to the issue of weapons of mass destruction. The NSS states that 'It was Saddam's reckless behavior that demanded the world's attention, and that it was his refusal to remove that ambiguity that he created that forced the United States and its allies to act' (NSS 2006, p. 24).

The arguments for a the legitimization of pre-emptive use of force when faced with an imminent threat of attack has been expressed from within the United Nations, in particular in the 'Report of the Secretary-General's High-level Panel on Threats, Challenges and Change' in 2004. In the Executive Summary of the Report it is stated that

> The UN Charter provides a clear framework for the use of force. States have an inherent right to self-defence, enshrined in Article 51. Long-established customary international law makes it clear that States can take military action as long as the threatened attack is imminent, no other means would deflect it, and the action is proportionate. (Executive Summary, 2004, p. 4)

Thus, the Executive Summary explicitly stated that pre-emptive use of force in self-defence is permissible in the face of an imminent threat of an attack. In other words, the High-level panel unequivocally adheres to an extensive interpretation of the Article 51. Interestingly, neither 'anticipatory' nor 'pre-emptive' is used in the text. More alarmingly no reference is made to the fact that the use of force in self-defence is an exception to the prohibition of the threat or the use of force as stated in Article 2(4) on the Charter.

As it appears, pre-emptive self-defence does not, in essence, differ from anticipatory self-defence since both are intended to fend-off an imminent attack. In fact Sapiro seems to treat them as synonymous as indicated by the following: 'Anticipatory – or pre-emptive self-defense traces its historical origins back to the famous Caroline Case' (Sapiro, 2005, p. 366). It seems to more a choice of vocabulary and possibly also a result of a shift away from what used to be threats of attacks from other states to threat of attacks from non-state actors. The later has led to a discussion on the impact of attacks from non-state actors, i.e. terrorist attacks, on the right to use force in self-defence. This debate is not necessarily linked to the debate on pre-emption since it relates to responses to attacks that are carried out. It relates more to the question if armed attacks by non-state actors fall within the scope of the provisions of Article 51 of the Charter.

In a recent study Mahmoudi has investigated the relationship between self-defence and international terrorism and the conclusion he reaches is that

> The applicability of the right of self-defence against international terrorism, which gained vast support after the unprecedented attacks of 11 September 2001 in the US, cannot be seriously challenged today. (Mahmoudi, 2006b, p. 179)

> He does acknowledge that this has yet to be recognised by an 'authoritative international judiciary instance', but he argues that state practice 'seems to indicate that an expansion of the right of self-defence has probably taken place'. (Mahmoudi, 2006b, p. 179)

If we accept that the right to use self-defence when attacked by a non-state actor falls within the scope of Article 51, then the problem does not relate to the right of self-defence of the presumed target of the attack but rather to the question how self-defence can be carried out against a non-state actor operating from outside the target state itself. In other words, if a self-defence strike is aimed at a country that did not carry out the attack then the strike would violate Article 2(4) of the Charter. The dilemma is, thus, not if non-state actors attacking a country generate the right to use force in self-defence but rather that any such action against another country would violate the prohibition of the use of force in the Charter.

The problems with non-state actor is also if they operate within one country or if they operate from another country when carrying out an attack, e.g. 11 September 2001 in the USA was carried out by people residing in the USA using civilian air planes to crash into targets in New York and Washington DC.

One of the rationales for the adherents of a restrictive interpretation of the right to use force in self-defence in accordance with Article 51 is that the only exception to the prohibition of the use of force in Article 2(4) should be in the event of an armed attack. Any attempt to permit the use of force in self-defence in response to a threat would open the door to abuse by countries. The controversy surrounding both the arguments used by states to argue anticipatory self-defence, e.g. Israel in 1981 against Iraq gives credence to the restrictive interpretation. The 1981 claim was rejected by many countries and by the Security Council (Schachter, 1984, p. 1635). Even claims of self-defence to armed attacks have generated controversy due to a perceived lack of sustainable evidence for such armed attacks as exemplified the case of the so-called Tonkin Gulf incident of 1964 when the US instigated an attack against its own warships in the Gulf of Tonkin and then claimed to have been attacked by North Vietnam. This claim persisted up to the release of classified documents that displayed the fallacy in the claim made by the USA (The Gulf of Tonkin). Self-defence claims were also made in two cases of foreign military intervention in the 1980s. First, the intervention in Grenada initiated in October 1983 and carried out by the USA and several Caribbean states members of the Organization of East Caribbean States (OECS), and second, the intervention in Panama initiated in December 1989 and carried out by the USA. The self-defence argument in the case of Grenada has been rejected on the basis that it was not in accordance with the OECS Treaty and because the self-defence claim was not substantiated (Audéoud, 1983, pp. 221–2; Beck, 1993, pp. 803–4; Doswald-Beck, 1984, pp. 366–8). In the case of Panama, legal scholars analysing the claim by the USA did not find any evidence to substantiate the self-defence claim of the USA (Nanda, 1990, pp. 496–7; Quigley, 1990, pp. 281–8; Rumage, 1993, p. 16).[7]

In more recent time the case of Iraq, 2003 is of relevance. The prelude to the intervention against Iraq centred around attempts by the USA and the United Kingdom (UK) to gain support in the Security Council for a resolution authorizing the use of force against Iraq on the grounds that Iraq was in 'material breach' of its obligations under earlier Security Council resolutions, in particular S/RES/687 (1991) and S/RES/1441 (2002). These efforts continued up the day preceding the initiation of the military intervention, i.e. up to 19 March 2003. In letters to the Security Council dated 20 March 2003 both the UK and the USA argued along the similar lines. The letter from the UK stated that Iraq's behaviour had resulted in 'material breach of the conditions for the ceasefire at the end of hostilities in 1991 laid down by the Council in its resolution 687 (1991)'. The letter from the USA (S/2003/351) stated that the 'actions being taken are authorized under existing Council resolutions, including its resolutions 678 (1990) and 687 (1991)'. The lines of argumentations pursued by the two intervening states were that the authorisation to use force in response to Iraq's intervention in Kuwait in 1990 provided a legal foundation for the use of force against Iraq in March 2003.

In terms of self-defence, the letter from the UK did not contain any such references or claims whereas the letter from the USA contained a self-defence claim as stated in the following:

The actions that coalition forces are undertaking are appropriate response. They are necessary steps to defend the United States and the international community from the threat posed by Iraq and to restore international peace and security in the area. Further delay would simply allow Iraq to continue its unlawful and threatening conduct. (S/2003/351)

Thus, the USA was pursuing a self-defence argument.[8] However, the USA did not claim to have been subject to an armed attack carried out by Iraq. In fact reference is made to the 'threat' posed by Iraq. Thus, USA's claim was not sufficient to invoke the right to use force in self-defence according to a restrictive interpretation. This is in accordance with the interpretation of the provisions of Article 51 pertaining to the right of self-defence, i.e. that self-defence can only been claimed when a state is the subject of an armed attack.

Interestingly enough, it is questionable if the argument by the USA would even fall within the realm of a pre-emptive self-defence interpretation of Article 51. The letter to the Security Council does not stress an imminent threat and it is – to say the least – vague since it is not a threat to a specific country but to the 'international community' at large, furthermore, it is not referred to as imminent. It would seem that the line of explanation pursued by the USA would rather fall within the notion of prevention and preventive armed attack rather than as a pre-emptive self-defence measure. This is in line with Sapiro's argumentation about the 'preventive' nature of the action of the USA (Sapiro, 2005, p. 367).

The fact that the UK did not include any self-defence argumentation in its letter to the Security Council considerably weakens the self-defence argumentation made by the USA. After all, either it is a self-defence action or it is not and the two major intervening parties cannot diverge on such a fundamental dimension and issue as self-defence.

Since it is already difficult at times to assess if an armed attack has taken place when a state claims to have launched military action in self-defence then it will be even harder to assess if an attack is imminent when a pre-emptive self-defence action is launched. As in the context of anticipatory self-defence claims there is a risk of abuse of the pre-emptive self-defence argument. However, the basic fallacy of both anticipatory and pre-emptive self-defence is that it implies that a country uses armed force against another country and thus the action is a breach and violation of the prohibition of the use and threat of use of force as enshrined in Article 2(4) of the Charter. The following chain of events can illustrate this:

- If an armed attack takes place then the target state of the attack can invoke the right of self-defence in accordance with Article 51 of the Charter and an armed response would be in accordance with the provisions of Article 51 as long as it is proportionate.
- If a state claims that an armed attack is imminent and launches an armed attack with the claim that it is an act of self-defence (anticipatory/pre-emptive) in accordance with the provision of Article 51 then the armed attack will constitute a breach of the prohibition of the threat and use of force as expressed in Article 2(4) of the Charter.

- If attention is turned to the attacks on the USA on 11 September 2001 their impact can be most obviously be seen in two Security Council Resolutions (S/RES/1368 (2001), S/RES/1373 (2001)) reaffirming the inherent right of individual and collective self-defence in accordance with the Charter of the United Nations following the attacks. This taken together with the fact that no attempt was made in the Security Council to censure the bombing campaign launched by the USA and the UK against Afghanistan on 7 October 2001, but rather it was openly or tacitly supported by some states and tolerated by other states, a pattern of reactions that has been interpreted as not only condoning but supporting the campaign and by doing so accepting that the attack on Afghanistan was a legitimate act of self-defence. This line of interpretation of events is supported by a number of scholars among them are Bring (2006, pp. 77–88), Franck (2004, p. 433) and Mahmoudi (2006a, p. 137–41; 2006b, p. 170–6). However, things are not as simple as this line of interpretation argues. First, the bombing campaign in Afghanistan neither was explicitly authorized in any Security Council resolution nor did the USA seek such an authorization.

Second, the fact that the Security Council has in subsequent resolutions legitimized the outcome of the intervention does not imply that the intervention as such has been condoned or legitimized.[9]

Third, to argue that the bombing and intervention in Afghanistan was an act of self-defence in response to the attacks on the USA on 11 September 2001 is problematic for two reasons, first the Taliban Movement which controlled the major part of Afghanistan did not carry out the attacks against the USA, thus there was no case for self-defence argument against it, and second, if the bombing was in self-defence it ought to have been carried out in response to the attacks on 11 September and not several weeks after they occurred. Seen from a restrictive interpretation the Afghan campaign does not qualify as self-defence, no matter which of the two dimensions is assessed.

As seen from the extensive interpretation of self-defence it is also difficult to find support for a self-defence argument. The only way to construe a case for pre-emptive self-defence would be to argue that there was an imminent threat of a new attack on the USA and that the threat came from the Taliban Movement in Afghanistan. If harbouring Al-Qaida is seen as legitimizing a pre-emptive strike, then the case of Afghanistan could fit into the extensive interpretation of self-defence if Al-Qaida attacks on the USA were imminent at the time of the bombing campaign against Afghanistan. However, the criteria of proportionality would also have to be taken into consideration and it is highly doubtful that the massive bombing campaign can be considered proportionate to such a threat.

The case of Afghanistan exemplifies just how complicated it is to assess self-defence claims in the post-11 September 2001 international system. The nature of the events of 11 September also complicates self-defence argumentations. People legally residing in the United States hijacked the planes used in the attacks and thus they hardly qualify as external attacks. Furthermore, none of the hijackers were citizens of Afghanistan, in fact several were citizens of Saudi Arabia. Thus, the Afghan connection was limited to the presence of the Al-Qaida leadership in that country. These factors raise several questions. Can the 11 September 2001 motivate any self-defence claims against external actors and if so which ones? The first part of the question can be answered in the negative by stating that the matter ought to have been an internal USA issue since people residing in the country carried out the actions with no military materials from external actors. If the answer is yes, since they were citizens of foreign countries and/or linked to a foreign actor, then the question is who could the USA target with a self-defence action? The country in which the hijackers were citizens, e.g. Saudi Arabia, the organization to which they were linked, i.e. Al-Qaida, and/or Afghanistan, where the Al-Qaida leadership was based? Any of these three dimensions do create problems from an international law perspective, as all would involve attacks against a country that had not carried out the attacks of 11 September 2001.

The case of Afghanistan also highlights the criteria of proportionality in the armed response given the large-scale bombing campaign that eventually undermined the Talibans, compelling the organization to withdraw into the countryside and to abandon power. The use of force on such a large-scale cannot be assessed as a proportionate use of force in self-defence. In fact the same can be said for the intervention in Iraq in 2003 in relation to the self-defence claims by the USA. More recently, the question of proportionality was once again discussed in relation to Israel's attacks on Lebanon. In fact, the Israeli claim to have acted in self-defence in response to a cross-border attack by Hezbollah, is not without dispute. Early reporting indicated that the Israeli soldiers were taken prisoners on 12 July 2006 on the Lebanese side of the border and that the killings of other Israeli soldiers also took place on the same day inside Lebanon (Franck, 2006). In addition, repeated Israeli violation of Lebanon's territorial integrity through the activities of Israeli air force and navy preceding the events in July 2006 clearly indicate that the situation was very complex. Reverting back to the question of proportionality in the way in which Israel carried out its claimed self-defence, it is difficult to argue that it was proportionate. The fact that Israel encountered stiff resistance and that Hezbollah managed to continue strike missiles into Israel do not make the Israeli mode of military operation more proportionate. Targeting of civilian infrastructure on a nationwide scale, the attempt to forcefully remove the civilian population from the South Lebanon, and the attacks on factories with non-military production, all indicate that the military campaign was not proportionate. The massive use of cluster bombs by Israel in the run-up to the international brokered cease-fire appears to have had no military strategic importance but rather to have been aimed at affecting the returning refugees after the cease-fire came into effect. The later is another evidence of the non-proportionate use of force by Israel.

## Concluding Remarks

In conclusion it can be argued that pre-emptive self-defence is in line with an extensive interpretation of the right to use force in self-defence in accordance with Article 51 of the Charter. In essence, anticipatory and pre-emptive self-defence have the same implication, namely a state can claim self-defence when facing the threat of an imminent attack.

As seen from a restrictive interpretation of the right to use force in self-defence both anticipatory and pre-emptive self-defence are not permitted. Thus, from a legal interpretation perspective pre-emptive self-defence is not a new legal principle but is in line with anticipatory self-defence.

The main impact of the events of 11 September 2001 has been that self-defence is debated and claimed in response to attacks and the threat of attacks from non-state actors often referred to as 'terrorist' groups and organizations. As exemplified actions credited or claimed by such groups and the military responses direct against other countries in response to such attacks do generate a number of controversial questions relating to the compliance of such self-defence claims and relating to how the armed response is carried out in particular relating to the question of proportionality. Given the issues that self-defence claims and actions taken in response to so-called 'terrorist attacks' raise, the debate relating to self-defence will persist in years to come. The issues and claims of pre-emptive self-defence will continue to be highly controversial and hotly debated.

The political dimension of pre-emption is linked to how the term has been used in the context of the original NSS from 2002 and the new NSS from 2006 of the USA. In the two NSS' pre-emption is used as synonymous with prevention as has been noted by some scholars. In the NSS of 2002, it displayed that the USA considers that there is an established legal basis for its policy of 'pre-emption'. The NSS also notes that legal scholars and international jurists 'often conditioned the legitimacy of pre-emption on the existence of an imminent threat' (NSS 2002, p. 15). Interestingly, the NSS argues that the US 'must adapt the concept of imminent threat to the capabilities and objectives of today's adversaries' (NSS 2002, p. 5). This line of argumentation finally leads to the core formulation of the US policy of 'pre-emption' namely that: 'The United States has long maintained the option of pre-emptive actions to counter a sufficient threat to our national security' (NSS 2002, p. 15). In the NSS of 2006 the USA reiterates the right to act 'pre-emptively in exercising our inherent right to self-defense' (NSS 2006, p. 18).

Although it is more a question of the direction chosen by the USA then an attempt of shifting the boundaries of international law and the use of force, it still does impact on the legal debate and by so doing it is the extensive interpretation of the right to use force in self-defence that stand to loose the most. The reason why this is the case is that the way in which the USA uses the term pre-emption will be perceived as being an extension of the extensive interpretation of the right to use of force in self-defence. However, this should not be interpreted as implying that the terminology by the USA in the context of the two NSS has altered the international regulations pertaining to the right to use force in self-defence.

# Chapter Four

# BEYOND CRIMINAL JUSTICE: PROMOTING THE RULE OF LAW IN POST-CONFLICT SOCIETIES

## Richard Sannerholm

### Rule of Law in Post-Conflict State-Building

The rule of law has been hailed as a panacea for developing and transition countries. Despite the fact that it has now been almost a decade since Carothers (1998, p. 95) wrote '[...] one cannot go through a foreign policy debate without someone proposing the rule of law as the solution to the world's troubles' there are no signs of a rule of law fatigue.

On the contrary, as some commentators recently stated, rule of law 'is like apple pie and ice cream', it is a concept that no one can dislike (Stromseth *et al.* 2006, p. 58). Typically within development cooperation, donors push for rule of law based on two rationales – rule of law is an essential prerequisite for market economy and it enhances protection of human rights (Messick, 1999; Carothers, 2001).

In relation to post-conflict settings, a third rationale can be added, namely rule of law in the achievement and maintenance of peace and security. This is a rather late contribution to the field of rule of law promotion. Stripped to all essentials the argument goes something like this: human rights violations and high levels of insecurity cause conflict and crisis, and if the rule of law is an essential condition for making human rights a justifiable claim, not merely rights on paper, then it is the key strategy for post-conflict recovery.

Despite a concerted effort to promote rule of law in the aftermath of conflict, few projects and programmes can be said to have had a successful impact on post-conflict peace processes. This chapter will argue that the poor track-record of rule of law promotion has little to do with the rule of law as such, but more to do with how the concept is acknowledged and operationalized by donor agencies.

Several projects and programmes launched under big fanfare in Liberia, Sierra Leone, Afghanistan and other post-conflict scenes focus predominately on criminal justice and civil and political rights, while failing to support rule of law in other areas desperate for attention; for example administrative agencies (dealing with licenses and permits), land registration systems, the state financial system (and in particular public procurement and handling of natural resources) and non-state justice systems. These areas are vital for a post-war recovery and return to normality, but they rarely attract the attention of rule of law reformers because they are seen as vaguely, if at all, connected to rule of law.

It is argued here that they are. The rule of law is a systemic concept that expands the full breadth and the full width of state institutions and is a concept for how to best organize a state and a state's relationship to its citizens. To secure the principle of legality in relation to public procurement can be just as vital a reform strategy for state-building as fair criminal law trials. It is not argued here that the international community should pick and choose between projects and programmes, but to treat rule of law as a holistic concept. Inevitably, however, a certain selection is necessary due to constrained resources. The international community cannot be expected to support a too broad reform menu. But in the selection, sequencing and prioritizing of reforms this chapter calls for reflection before venturing into rule of law promotion, and to match the needs of post-conflict societies with adequate responses.

In order to set the stage for this article's central argument, section two will discuss the rule of law template in post-conflict state-building. This will be followed by a discussion on what's gone wrong, highlighting the dominance of models as a result of a misconception of the rule of law. The need to go beyond the narrow rule of law focus is then discussed in section four against the backdrop of some recent developments in state-building practice. Section five will summarize and provide some concluding remarks.

## The Rule of Law Template

The post-conflict reconstruction scene is characterized by a multitude of donor agencies. A precise constellation is difficult to present because it varies from mission to mission, but a crude list of the 'usual suspects' can nevertheless be presented. Besides the ten or more UN departments and agencies involved, from the Department of Peacekeeping Operations to the High Commissioner for Human Rights and the United Nations Development Programme, bilateral support is given through state's development agencies, regional organizations such as the EU, international non-governmental organizations and foundations, and international financial institutions. Despite this diversity most of the reforms initiated and implemented in the legal sector follow a similar model and form and focus, more or less, on the same areas of the legal system.

The current effort at promoting the rule of law is frequently referred to by critics as a 'template', 'menu' or 'orthodoxy' (Carothers, 1998; Upham, 2006; Golub, 2006). These terms are used to characterize the rationales for why rule of law is promoted and the principal methods used. Although presented slightly differently by different commentators, most tend to agree on the rule of law template rationales as being assumptions of its necessity for economic development, human rights protection and to the achievement and maintenance of peace and security.

Carothers (1998, pp. 99–100) divides the key features of how the rule of law template operates into three broad categories: law reform, strengthening of law-related institutions and efforts to increase government's compliance with law. The rule of law model focuses primarily on state institutions because of the influence that legal professionals have in the formulation of strategies and programmes. This results in a tendency to define problems in the legal system in narrow terms, most often including courts, prosecutors, lawyers, contracts, law reform and other processes where lawyers play a dominant role. The role played by the civil society, the perceived end users of the system, is thereby marginalized and they are often consulted towards the end of the reform process (Golub 2006, p. 108).

In concrete terms, the rule of law template translates into projects and programmes that focus on constructing and repairing court houses, supplying technical equipment, drafting of new laws or wholesale 'importation' of foreign model codes, training programmes for lawyers, judges and prosecutors on the new laws or in gender-sensitivity, supporting human rights commissions, bar associations, and police and prosecutorial offices.

The United Nations Secretary General (UNSG) has attempted to establish a comprehensive rule of law definition to guide the work of the UN's various agencies, programmes and departments. Rule of law, following this definition, '[…] refers to a principle of governance in which all persons, institutions and entities, public and private, including the State itself, are accountable to laws that are publicly promulgated, equally enforced and independently adjudicated and which are consistent with international human rights norms and standards. It requires as well, measures to ensure adherence to the principles of supremacy of law, equality before the law, accountability to the law, fairness in the application of the law, separation of powers, participation in decision-making, legal certainty, avoidance of arbitrariness and procedural and legal transparency' (UNSG 2004a, Para 6).

This definition integrates formal (procedural) aspects of rule of law with material (substantive values) and by and large manages to summarize the commonly shared view that international donor agencies have of the rule of law (see Conference on Security and Cooperation in Europe 1990, I (2)). The growing body of UN conventions, resolutions and declarations support a substantial interpretation of the rule of law, and so does the corpus of instruments developed by regional bodies.[1] From the perspective of modern international legal sources, rule of law is equated with democracy and human rights.

With its value-laden connotation and focus on institutions, the rule of law template has become equated with criminal justice reform on the post-conflict scene (see Making Standards Work 2005). Thus when it comes to law reform, international agencies have sought to review and strengthen the criminal laws and criminal procedure laws and the legal framework for the judiciary. Reformers often anchor law reform on foreign models, promoting what they know based on their epistemological backgrounds, which results in a substantial amount of 'cut-and-paste'. Many of the new commercial laws in Iraq, for example, bear close resemblance to US commercial laws (Kassinger and Williams).

International norms and principles are also frequently used as blueprints or yardsticks for measuring the standard of the laws in place. There is a strong push for post-conflict states to ratify and accede to international human rights and criminal law conventions early on in the post-conflict phase. Liberia is an evocative case in point where the UN assisted the transitional government to become a part to a host of international conventions (UNSG 2004b). International human rights law, in addition to United Nations norms and standards, are perceived to be a solid basis for guidance and for offering '[…] orientation and inspiration, as well as an appropriate framework for establishing and re-establishing and strengthening criminal justice systems' (Making Standards Work 2005, Para 43). In the same vein the UNSG has argued that international norms and standards bring a legitimacy that cannot be said to attach to the export of national law (UNSG 2004a, Para 5).

Thus, law reform under the rule of law template constitutes a rather unique interaction among the post-conflict society's own legal framework, model codes from leading donor countries, and international norms and standards (Ehrenreich–Brooks, 2003).

As regards strengthening the institutions of the legal system, international agencies tend to take a similarly narrow focus as in law reform activities. The issue of institutional building has in the past (and still to a large extent) been treated as a technical or practical problem and activities have focused on rebuilding court houses, supplying legal materials and equipment to courts and training programmes for the judiciary, lawyers and prosecutors on the newly revised laws, or in gender sensitivity and international human rights. But the problem lies elsewhere. Enhancing the capacity, accountability and accessibility of justice delivering institutions requires a change in behaviour, and technical assistance and continuing legal training have had a limited impact in this regard.

When it comes to international agencies efforts at enhancing governments' compliance with the law in post-conflict societies it is predominately a matter of securing accountability mechanisms in relation to law enforcement agencies and among the judiciary. Supporting other accountability mechanisms such as parliamentary oversight bodies, anti-corruption commissions, financial audit institutions and civil society's capability to access and use these oversight institutions is a rarely pursued strategy in post-conflict state-building.

## What's Gone Wrong?

It is a commonly shared perception today, among scholars and practitioners alike, that the rule of law template has a poor track record in post-conflict reconstruction (e.g. Stromseth *et al.* 2006; Studdard and Hurwitz, 2005). It is in a way as Ehrenreich–Brooks (2003, p. 2280) described it, 'a string of expensive disappointments'. The same could be said about rule of law promotion in development cooperation, although it is generally viewed to have been more successful (see Garth, 2003; Hammergren, 2003; Channell, 2006).

Disappointing results of rule of law reforms are reported from nearly all post-conflict reconstruction scenes. In Kosovo serious problems in the legal and administrative systems persist despite a concerted effort of the international community. The UN, EU and OSCE assumed executive authority over the territory in 1999 under the form of an international administration. In a series of OSCE reports on the criminal and civil justice system, a lack of enforcement, misconduct by the judiciary and violations of fair trial standards are frequently cited (OSCE 2004; 2006).

Similarly in East Timor, where the UN assumed executive authority the same year as in Kosovo, the judicial and administrative system is still in a state of disrepair (UNSG 2006c). Sobering results are also reported from Sierra Leone, Liberia Burundi and Afghanistan.

When it comes to answering the question of what's gone wrong, the field is filled with a raft of suggestions. The 'remedies side' is overflowing with lessons learned and proposals for best practices. Several lessons learned tend to focus on the technical side of rule of law promotion. Thus, it boils down to lack of leadership, vague mandates, absent political will and weak funding as key elements in need of improvements (e.g. Carlson, 2006). Donor inconsistency as a result of a lack of coordination is another factor often cited as the reasons behind the poor track record. This is not a flaw in rule of law aid specifically but a structural problem relating to all forms of international development assistance. Nevertheless, inconsistency and lack of coordination has been a particularly salient feature in rule of law promotion.

Reports from the field frequently stress the need to improve donor policy to make rule of law reform a more concerted effort, but the problem has thus far proven difficult to solve.

Moreover, it is not just that policies are inconsistent among donor agencies; there is also inconsistency within agencies. The United Nations Mission in Kosovo (UNMIK) is one good example. Being the de facto administrator since 1999, UNMIK decided that all higher education should be three years instead of four in line with the Bologna process, making the University of Prishtina the first university in Europe to adopt the Bologna criteria (UNMIK Reg 2003/14). At the same time the reformed three year legal education is not accepted by the Kosovo Bar Association as sufficient in order to practice law, and it causes undue delays and additional costs for students while it also deprives the justice sector of new legal professionals.

Implicit in this technical critique of rule of law promotion is an assumption that given the right amount of financial, human and material resources, rule of law would more easily 'take root'. It is not, and we know this by now, that easy. Rule of law is not a binary code that is either on or off. As Carothers (2006, p. 20) has aptly put it, law is not just the sum of the courts, legal codes, and legal professionals but 'also a normative system residing in the minds of the citizens of a country'. While technical issues of operationalizing the rule of law need to be improved, they are secondary to questions of what rule of law is, or is not, and for what reasons the concept is promoted.

### A Misconception of the Rule of Law

Problems with coordination and technical issues aside, it is argued here that the main factor behind the poor track record of rule of law reform is that it is based on a flawed understanding of what the concept actually means (Carothers, 2006, p. 15; Goodpaster, 2003). This should come as no surprise since the discourse in legal theory frequently point to the rule of law as a contested concept (see Rosenfeld, 2001; Fallon, 1997; Fletcher, 1996; Shklar, 1987). Generally in legal theory the rule of law is presented as a concept with two basic purposes: to protect against arbitrary power and to guide human conduct (Raz, 1979; Summers, 1999). This is the core 'message' of the rule of law. As such, the rule of law is a principle of governance that encompasses all forms of exercise of power whether it is in criminal justice, administrative matters, or constitutional issues.

While opinions tend to differ on the actual content of rule of law, many agree on a similar set of background principles which laws and legal institutions need to respect, including the principle of supremacy of law, equality before the law, legal certainty and separation of powers (Tamanaha, 2004). This is a modest and scaled-down interpretation in comparison to how international agencies present it where, typically, human rights, democracy and substantial notions of justice are included as key characteristics.

There are indications that international agencies are beginning to acknowledge that failing to grapple the complexity of rule of law reform constitutes a major part of the meagre list of success stories (Stromseth *et al.* 2006, p. 9). From the field of rule of law in development cooperation (and lessons learned from the law and development doctrine) a synopsis of what's gone wrong focuses on the difficulties of external support in domestic legal transformation, in particular the issue of so-called 'transplanting' of law (e.g. Legrand, 2001; Berkowitz *et al.* 2003; Markovits, 2004); that rule of law is a complex concept difficult to define and even more difficult to externally support (Orth, 1999); the need to recognize the political and cultural aspects of rule of law (Faundez, 2001); and that patience and a modest adjustment on the expectations of what rule of law programmes can do is needed (Peerenboom, 2005).

These experiences parallel those in the field of rule of law promotion in post-conflict state-building. The UNSG (2004a, Para 15) notes that international assistance has too often been based on foreign experts using foreign models for foreign devised solutions, 'but we have learned that effective and sustainable approaches begin with a thorough analysis of national needs and capacities, mobilizing to the extent possible expertise resident in the country'.

Rule of law promoters have not succeeded in defining or justifying the goals of legal transformation or to ask the basic question of what role law plays in society. Ehrenreich–Brooks (2003, p. 2285) charge the present rule of law promotion for failing to acknowledge that it involves norm creation and that we need to study the intersection of international law, domestic law and comparative law in order to grasp the intricate workings of promoting legal change in post-conflict societies. But, it could also be added that rule of law reformers have failed to embrace the systemic character of the rule of law in the sense that they have failed to see the concept as an intersection between criminal, civil, administrative and constitutional law, and that the concept has a bearing in all situations involving state-individual interaction.

### *Exporting Good Law is Sometimes of the Mark*

Implicit in the rule of law template is a notion of the rule of law as the rule of *good* law. Regardless the fact that this interpretation has scant support in legal theory, it is a flawed approach to post-conflict state-building for another reason, namely that it ignores crucial issues of legal and administrative reform.

Or put differently. Since rule of law is equated with human rights and substantial notions of justice, reforms are implemented in areas where the most flagrant and egregious violation of rule of law takes place – the criminal justice system. This means that securing rule-based governance in other areas of state-individual interaction is left in the dark. Moreover, it is more attractive for reformers to draft a new criminal law code than to address administrative discretion in public procurement process. The fact that rule of law promotion has become a big business means that donor agencies are motivated by contradicting rationales; the desire to do good and the possibility of attracting funds.

The argument here is not that equal weight automatically should be given to problems in the civil/administrative sphere as in the criminal justice arena. The principles of legality and legal certainty quite naturally carries significantly more weight in criminal justice than in civil law.

At the same time, many post-conflict societies display a dysfunctional civil and administrative legal framework (often existing prior to the conflict), which reinforces discriminatory practices, violates human rights and effectively hinders the return to normality. This undermines the rule of law even though criminal justice might have attained excellence in high standards and efficiency.

Another argument against equating rule of law with rule of good law is that it risks 'blunting' the concept. This is a frequently voiced criticism from legal scholars (e.g. Raz 1979, p. 211). Krygier (2006) suggests that we must not start with the specific attributes of the rule of law, forms of rules and institutions, because this can result in goal displacement where we mistake means for ends. Reformers should start by asking, what the point of the rule of law is and what the problem is to which it is the supposed solution; and then should approach the concept teleologically.

Thus, instead of struggling with the issue of what institutions to 'export' or establish in a recipient country, international agencies should start with the idea of how to best prevent arbitrary rule and ensure that laws have a capacity of guiding human conduct, and then ask how this can be done in line with the cultural, social and legal tradition of a particular context. This is made difficult by the tendency to promote a material rule of law as the rule of good law, because it requires a definition of the term 'good'. If the discussion on the rule of law is instead limited to a formal conception it avoids being bogged down in endless discussions on the superiority of different political theories.

Those who advocate for a formal rule of law in relation to development assistance and post-conflict reconstruction does so for the primary reason that since the formal rule of law says nothing about the content, and does not try to expound a specific political morality, it is more or less politically neutral. While this may seem as an 'empty' project, promoting rule of law in order to make governments comply with the law, and ensuring that the law is capable of guiding human conduct, stands on its own merits in war-torn societies where discretion, political corruption and discrimination are seen as contributing factors to conflict and crisis. Making governments act according to the laws is less of a legal–technical exercise as it is a matter of changing behaviour and attitudes. Moreover, emphasis on rule governance also implies compliance with the post-conflict states' obligations under international law, including international human rights, and thus works indirectly towards increasing people's access to the international legal system.

Summers (1999, pp. 1710–11) gives three principal reasons for why rule of law should continue to be defined according to a formal conceptualization. The first relates to the fact that formal rule of law principles will, most likely, command general support. If material considerations are brought into rule of law, controversies are more plausible to occur, because different views exist over substantive issues.

Secondly, and this is perhaps a more useful argument, keeping rule of law formal enables the criticism of a violation of rule of law to be sharper and more focused. If material norms are included, criticism risk stranding on different interpretations of what type rule of law for material goods is supposed to realize.

Thirdly and lastly, separation between formal and material makes it more plain and open to see when a court departs from the formal rule of law grounds because substantive policy or justice are seen as overriding it, or vice versa, when a court reject calls for a departure from a substantive value due to formal grounds. Or as Fallon (1997, p. 54) put it, by making a too close link between rule of law and 'good' law, broader disputes over substantive justice can deprive the concept of an 'independent analytical bite'.

### A Needs-Based Rule of Law Template

The exclusion of rule of law reform areas outside the criminal justice system, and the focus on 'good' laws has made non-state justice systems and non-state justice actors a forgotten reform imperative. This is remarkable considering that these systems and actors often stand for a majority of justice delivery. Research by Chirayath, Sage and Woolcock indicates that non-state justice systems are the providers of justice for as much as 80 to 90 per cent of the population in many parts of Africa (Chirayath *et al.* 2005).

This exclusion is linked to the scarcity of empirical assessments of legal and administrative systems in developing and post-conflict societies. International agencies often fail to ask the most fundamental questions before engaging in post-conflict rule of law reform, namely who provides 'justice' and for whom?

The United Nations High Commissioner for Human Rights have developed a set of post-conflict rule of law tools intended to function as guidelines for reformers including guidelines for monitoring and mapping legal systems (Office of the United Nations High Commissioner for Human Rights (OHCHR), 2006). Valuable as they are for a more evidence-based approach, they have one serious flaw, namely that they take a narrow reading of the rule of law. Despite the fact that the 'tools' talk of rule of law in a generic sense, the specific activities in, for example, mapping and monitoring, fails to include civil law, administrative law and non-state justice systems.

Evaluations of rule of law programmes have, to this point, been ad hoc, fragmented and overly technical. In spite of its popularity, the field of rule of law promotion is remarkably free from empirical studies (Hammergren, 2003, p. 301). As Krygier (2001, p. 301) writes, 'looking at the mixed success of attempts to implant the rule of law in unfamiliar soil, for example, it might be clear that we have not always done well, but it will not always be clear why'.

Since aid providers define the rule of law from an institutional perspective, with a strong slate towards international human rights and reformers' own backgrounds, little room is left to local approaches. This is evident in constitutional drafting when there is a substantial external involvement. The prospect of helping the post-conflict society to craft an ideal constitution sometimes overshadows the need for inclusion and transparency in the process (Carothers, 1999, p. 161).

A similar position exists in relation to any other reform activity, criminal law, judicial reform, human rights training, etc. The desire to 'do good' and to share or inform values makes the process of how to 'get there' secondary. The important question of local participation in legal transformation runs the risk of being reduced to referendums in order to approve an already drafted constitution, or invitations to promotional conferences of already established legal codes.

This speedy 'cut-and-paste' situation is typical for how legal reform is promoted in development and post-conflict state-building and it is remarkably empty of ethical discussions concerning the role and responsibility of international agencies. As Channell (2006, p. 141) puts it, 'it is hard to imagine any rule of law aid specialist pursuing law reform in his or her own country in this fashion'. All the same, it remains the standard approach to less developed countries.

The challenge for reformers is not only to provide assistance to a broad set of rule of law structures, but to promote a cultural challenge so that the legal and administrative systems receives cultural and political commitment. What legal culture consists of, however, remains as contested as the concept of the rule of law (see Cotterrell, 1997).

While some see it as meaning mainly shared values and understandings among the legal community, others tend to take a view of legal culture as a more broad-based societal phenomenon (Freidman, 1997). Nevertheless, the merit of including legal culture in rule of law promotion is that it informs and reminds of the fact that legal change does not take place in isolation (Nelken, 2001). Legal culture in a broad sense shows that law comes in packages of sorts and that different elements influence legal change, including legal norms, form and structure of legal and administrative institutions, social behaviour in using law or not using law, as well as legal consciousness and awareness regarding law. (Blankenburg, 1997).

Furthermore, making people feel they have a stake in the legal and administrative systems is important, not merely as end users but as active participants in the reform process. Several hard-learned lessons from the field point to the crucial importance of listening to local perceptions on law and to closely study the role of law in society in the client state.

In Kosovo the Special Representative of Secretary General (SRSG) issued in the first United Nations Mission in Kosovo Regulation that the applicable law would be the law in force prior to the international presence. This created indignation among Kosovar judges. They preferred the pre-1989 law in force prior to the Milosevic regime (see Strohmeyer, 2001).

Similar events took place in Somalia where the SRSG declared that the applicable criminal law would be the law in force prior to the breakdown of hostilities. The community of northern Somalia protested and proposed instead the pre-1969 criminal code (Ganzglass, 1997). In both cases, a certain type of legal regime was seen as a symbol of repression and although the rejected law was technically more 'advanced' it failed to meet other more deeply rooted criteria for acceptance.

Rwanda provides yet another disheartening example of how international agencies turn a blind eye to local legal culture. Following the post-genocide intervention, the international community focused on prosecuting perpetrators of the genocide, resulting in a number of training programmes for the few remaining judges and other legal professionals. Many of the international experts within the training programmes, however, came from common law backgrounds with little or no understanding of the Rwanda's legal tradition, a mix of French and Belgian civil law, which effectively impeded the reform process (Mburu, 2001, p. 29).

Attempting to enhance a rule of law culture inevitable involves an examination of the existing legal culture. This is difficult for outside actors to do. It requires an understanding of the social and political goals rule of law is to further in the client state, as well as a clear understanding of the difficulties of the present system. In large part, supporting a rule of law culture necessitates the move towards seeing individuals as active actors in society, not merely as passive receivers of reforms, and towards an enhanced understanding of how rule of law can be employed as a means to create an enabling legal environment.

Providing incentives for rule of law as a cultural change also requires that methods involving non-legal assistance are used to strengthen civil society groups (grassroots movements, indigenous groups, business interests, human rights activist, etc.). In Liberia, Sierra Leone and Burundi, for example, the UN has supported societal educational initiatives to inform on changes in the legal framework. Laudable as these initiatives are, however, they still position civil society groups as passive receivers of rule of law promotion to be enlightened, informed and aware of the law. Since reforms directed towards building civil society support are slow and resource demanding, donors tend instead to focus on building political will and support for reforms within the political elite and groups with vested interests in reforms, i.e. judges, lawyers and prosecutors (Bergling, 2006, p. 65). Thus, enhancing participation and ownership over rule of law issues tend to, by default, take a top-down institutional focus.

## Beyond the Rule of Law Template

Today's heavy emphasis on judges, lawyers, and courts, Golub (2006, p. 106) writes, '[…] is analogous to what the public health field would look like if it mainly focused on urban hospitals and the doctors staffing them, and largely ignored nurses, other health workers, maternal and public education […]'. Indeed, rule of law reform in post-conflict societies have channelled resources into erecting the formal institutions of the legal system, with a concerted effort towards the criminal justice system, and failed to acknowledge the importance for a systemic scope of reforms. This creates a dualism in legal and administrative systems where progress in one end is outmatched by failure in another. Recent reports from the field testify to the inability of the current template to effectively address the main factors undermining post-conflict recovery and the rule of law. Going beyond the rule of law template is a necessary shift in policy. But this requires, first of all, a re-evaluation of the relationship between law and security.

### *The Role of Law in Relation to Security*

In large part the present rule of law template in post-conflict state-building can be described as founded on a conception of security that translates into law and order and an absence of violations of physical integrity rights.

While these issues are clearly associated with security there is more to the concept (Human Security Centre 2005). In a series of reports from the World

Bank called *Voices of the Poor: Crying Out for Change* based on extensive worldwide interviews, eight factors of insecurity were listed: insecurities of work and livelihood; natural and human made disasters; crime and violence; persecution by the police and lack of justice; civil conflict and war macro policy shocks and stresses; social vulnerability; and health, illness and death (Narayan *et al.* 2000, p. 155). The voices of the poor provide a more nuanced picture of the insecurities poor people face. Several recent studies point to a cumulative approach towards insecurity and highlights the fact that ineffective, rigid or obsolete legal and administrative systems actually constitutes an effective barrier for people's access to a number of common goods (i.e. engaging in economic activity, legal protection in business transactions, titles to housing and property, employment) (World Bank 2006; High Level Commission on Legal Empowerment of the Poor, 2006).

Seeing insecurity in this broad perspective has also been singled out as a root cause to conflict. The Truth and Reconciliation Commission for Sierra Leone concluded that a number of factors are at play in a crisis situation, and that it was years of bad governance, endemic corruption and the denial of basic human rights that created the conditions that made conflict inevitable. Furthermore the Commission noted that if these causes are not adequately addressed they remain as potential cause of conflict. (Sierra Leone Truth and Reconciliation Commission 2004, p. 37).

That these issues had indeed been left unaddressed by the international community was later confirmed by the UN High Commissioner for Human Rights. In a report from 2005 it was noted that progress in the area of human rights in Sierra Leone had been lopsided in favour of civil and political rights and that Sierra Leone was unlikely to meet the Millennium Development Goals in any of the areas of economic, social and cultural rights (OHCHR 2005, p. 33).

The basic argument here is that these 'other' issues of insecurity, which exists outside the realm of a law and order perspective, are crucial to effectively address potential causes of conflict. What's more, addressing these issues is all about rule of law promotion because remedying the impediments and stumbling-blocks to post-conflict recovery, which insecurity of livelihood, work, social vulnerability and corruption represents, requires the use of legal and administrative reform strategies.

## *A Rule of Law Deficit in Civil and Administrative Legal Frameworks is a Threat to Security*

Sierra Leone provides here yet another poignant example. The first report of the UNSG on the establishment of the United Nations Integrated Office in Sierra Leone concluded that while economic development will gain traction as peace becomes further consolidated, the elimination of administrative barriers is an important prerequisite and that the economic climate suffered from a 'largely outdated, inconsistent and ineffective laws affecting business activities' (UNSG 2006a, Para 47). The report recommended that further technical and financial assistance was needed in order to reach a more focused regime of legal, administrative regulatory measures, and to intensify the fight against corruption.

The most remarkable aspect of the UNSG's report on Sierra Leone is not that the need for legal reforms in relation to economic reconstruction and governance are gaining traction as a post-conflict strategy, or that it addresses the challenge of legal informality. Instead, the remarkable aspect is that this is done six years after the first UN mission was established in Sierra Leone.

Developments in Burundi have followed that of Sierra Leone. The president of Burundi requested in April 2006 that the UN peacekeeping mission in the country should be transformed into an integrated support office, focusing more on reconstruction and development priorities.

On the basis of this request, the UNSG proposed that the integrated office should strengthen the capacity of national intuitions to address the root causes of conflict and to focus, in particular, on reforms in administrative and economic governance, increase transparency and accountability of the public administration, combat corruption and review the issue of land and property rights (UNSG 2006b, Para 59).

Similarly, a World Bank report on reconstruction in East Timor singled out the deficiencies in the civil and administrative legal frameworks as constituting one of the major challenges facing the country after the closure of the UN administration. Inconsistency, gaps in the legislative framework and 'roadblocks' in the justice sector constrained further development. Moreover, private sector development was impeded because businesses could not rely on the existing property rights regime or the efficient and impartial enforcement of contracts. Taken together, these legal and administrative barriers if sustained were considered a threat to conflict and as a source of social unrest (Cliffe and Rohland, 2002, p. 20).

Establishing rule of law by enhancing the capacity of the judiciary, police and correctional centres only responds to one portion of the menu of 'legal' problems post-crisis states display. Several important rule of law deficits are found within the executive, administrative agencies, and incoherent administrative and civil law frameworks. Developing, least developed and post-crisis states are often plagued by a sector by sector administration of society, with inconsistency and lack of coordination between state agencies and a multitude of government organs with the competence to take binding decisions (Bergling, 2006, p. 83).

A World Bank assessment report on administrative structures in Afghanistan clearly illustrates the inconstancy and confusion often inherent in a post-conflict bureaucracy (Hakimi *et al.* 2004). The predominant problem is singled out as an absence of formality. There are no job descriptions and little clarity on the function of various units and departments. Changes in the legal and administrative framework governing their operation have only been partially operationalized while contradictions in the administrative law remain. As a result, administrative practice has been developed differently by various sectors, and implementation of changes has been ad hoc and pending the inclination of individual ministers (Hakim *et al.* 2004, p. 10). The report notes that governance in Afghanistan rests upon two elements of power, de jure and de facto, with a predominance of the latter outside Kabul.

Another poignant example is provided by a recent UN report on the status of Liberia's rubber plantations, a crucial source of revenue for the war-torn economy (UNMIL, 2006). Here, the issue of unclear legislation on bidding and procurement is brought forward as a source of illegal business practices. Moreover, issues concerning worker's rights as well as the obligations of international companies involved in tapping rubber remain uncertain. In this case the laws regulating rubber plantation (and the same goes for other natural resources) suffers from a deficit in clarity and enforcement. At the same time, the executive power, the central government and regional authorities, are suspected of corrupt practices in relation to the granting of concessions to companies (UNMIL, 2006, p. 22). In short, there is a rule of law deficit, resulting in the violation of worker's rights, squandering of financial revenues and environmental degradation.

Despite the importance of addressing these issues it has rarely been more than a distant blip on the international community's rule of law radar because remedying these sorts of rule of law deficits does not involve the typical institutions of the justice sector.

### *Going Beyond Criminal Justice Requires New International Strategies*

International assistance to Liberia illustrates an interesting example of an emerging paradigmatic move from the present rule of law template. Indeed, recent developments in Liberia could mark the trend of a new form of international administration.

For nearly three years the international community has invested in rule of law reforms in Liberia. It is argued that after international assistance to legal and judicial reform activities in Kosovo and East Timor, Liberia is the place where the rule of law template has received the strongest attention.

Nevertheless – notwithstanding the creation of a special rule of law component within United Nations Mission in Liberia (UNMIL) comprising a Legal and Judicial System Support Division, Corrections Unit, Civil Affairs Section, Civil Police Mission, Human Rights Protection Service and a Gender Office – the most basic and essential component of rule of law, ensuring a law abiding state, has failed to take root.

One explanation is simply that it has never really been the primary focus of the international assistance to Liberia. Rule of law reforms in Liberia have been focused on high-profile areas that attract international attention but not, generally, on how the transitional government administration in Liberia should be organized, or how the relationship between the state and citizens in a wider sense should best be regulated, outside the realm of securing protection in criminal justice.

Two audits carried out by the Economic Community of West African States (ECOWAS) and the European Commission in 2004 and 2005 came to the conclusion that 'theft and fraud within the transitional government were so great that they were sabotaging any possibility for durable peacebuilding' (Dwan and Bailey, 2006, p. 10). The audits met with fierce resistance; several members of the Transitional National Government of Liberia attempted to obstruct the investigations, and the Liberian Institute for Certified Accountants filed a writ of prohibition to the Supreme Court, in order to restrain public officials of cooperating with ECOWAS and the European Commission. The Supreme Court, however, refused the writ after civil society groups filed an *amicus brief* on behalf of the investigation (Dwan and Bailey, 2006, p. 5). Previous pressure from the donor community had resulted in the formation of a Task Force on Corruption and a Cash Management Committee but none of these measures were sufficient in tackling the rule of law deficit within the transitional Liberian government. (Security Council Res. 2003; 2004; 2005).

As a response, a congregation of donors[2] proposed a Governance and Economic Management Assistance Programme (GEMAP). This agreement, concluded in September 2005, represents an intrusive and radical form of international control and supervision and includes six components: financial management and accountability; improving budgeting and expenditure management; improving practices and granting of concessions; establishing effective processes to control corruption; supporting key institutions; and capacity building.

A striking feature of GEMAP is that several components call for the deployment of international experts with binding co-signature authority in state-owned enterprises and revenue generating agencies. No major transactions can take place without being examined by both a Liberian manager and an international counterpart. For example, under the financial management and accountability component, an international expert will have co-signing authority over matters relating to banking and for ensuring that internal controls and audits are carried out according to established rules (GEMAP 2005, p. 3).

The Liberian justice system has been severely damaged by the long civil war. One fundamental implication from Charles Taylor's rule is rampant corruption in the judiciary and frequent executive interference. The possibility of accountability, judicial review and means of redress against has traditionally been severely limited. GEMAP proposes in this regard the establishment of an effective and independent Anti-Corruption Commission to assist in the investigation of fraud and corruption and other economic crimes (GEMAP 2005, p. 4).

The Commission, consisting of both Liberian and international experts, will have full prosecutorial powers. In addition, an independent prosecutor will be installed to work on corruption charges, and international technical assistance will be provided to enhance the investigative capacity of the prosecutorial office (GEMAP 2005, p. 13)

The Commission is mandated to investigate cases brought before it by any person or group, including donor organizations who suspect that their funds and assistance programmes have not been properly used by the government.

International legal experts will support and advice the Liberian judiciary in the dispensation of justice, particularly in cases of corruption in a form of 'co-location programme' where international judges sit with national judges (GEMAP 2005, p. 3).

This falls short of the original proposal by ECOWAS to let international judges dispense justice, but nevertheless represents an intrusive initiative. It can also be discussed what level of de facto discretion and independence the Liberian judges will have in relation to international experts 'advising' on the adjudication of high-profile cases.

Besides the Anti-Corruption Commission another interesting development is the establishment of a Contract and Concession Review Committee with a mandate to review contracts entered in the past (Economic Governance Steering Committee 2006). A new procurement A new procurement law has also been passed and came into effect in early January 2006. Procurement practices and the lack of an adequate and respected legal framework for granting concessions have been an infected issue and reform initiatives taken in this area is a necessary strategy in order to ensure that public assets are not used for private political gains.

Although it is too early to draw any conclusions on the impact of the GEMAP, a first year review noted an increase in revenue collection and a strengthened fiscal discipline. Several of the reforms required under the agreement are also underway. A challenge for the agreement is to link it closely to rule of law reform activities implemented by other donors in theatre, most notably by UNMIL, so as to bridge the gap between conflict and development strategies.

## Concluding Remarks

This chapter has argued that the present effort of the international community to promote rule of law in post-conflict societies rests on a flawed definition of what rule of law is. From the perspective of the international community, rule of law means human rights, criminal justice, and law and order. The result is a promotion of rule of law in relation to only a small part of the legal and administrative system, while ignoring issues of corruption, inconsistent legal framework for the economy and for administrative agencies, land and property rights and economic governance.

To go beyond the narrow rule of law template requires a substantial shift in policy. Among other things, this chapter argues for a more modest interpretation of rule of law based on a rather minimalist set of principles: supremacy of law, legal certainty and equality before the law and separation of powers. International agencies should exercise caution and not overload the concept by equating it with international human rights and democracy, thereby making the reform of laws and legal institutions synonymous with reform of 'good' laws and 'good' legal institutions.

Rule of law promoters must increase the use of baseline studies, needs assessments and evaluations. The absence of an empirical tradition among rule of law reformers is a frequently voiced criticism, but even when needs assessments are carried out they are often inadequate in the sense that they map the justice sector, ask questions based on how legal systems are structured in the West, and tend to focus excessively on formal institutions.

These sorts of assessments do not reflect the actual state of the legal and other forms of normative systems in many developing countries, but reflect the epistemological background of the international agency instead. Non-state justice systems constitute a large portion of dispute resolution in developing countries. Leaving them out of the rule of law equation will render any reform initiative inherently flawed.

Although a gloomy picture has been presented, there are indications that international agencies are beginning to re-evaluate their rule of law support. Liberia is one example. Though concerns can indeed be raised regarding the intrusive mandate of the GEMAP, it nevertheless represents some light in the end of the tunnel in the sense that rule of law deficiencies with the potential to disrupt the fragile peace are now being addressed. Developments in Burundi and Sierra Leone seem to be following suit, perhaps marking the beginning of a paradigmatic shift in the policy of rule of law promotion in post-conflict societies.

# Chapter Five

# PEACE BY PACT: DATA ON THE IMPLEMENTATION OF PEACE AGREEMENTS[1]

## Anna Jarstad and Ralph Sundberg

### Introduction

Is the implementation of a peace agreement a severe obstacle for peace? Conventional wisdom holds that the failure to implement peace agreements is an important explanation of the recurrence of war. Much scholarly work has been devoted to how the design of peace agreements can pave the way for peace. In this regard, power sharing is seen as a viable solution to end civil war. Agreement on the sharing of power is a concession by warring parties that can be seen as a sign of credible commitment. Such concessions often entail compromises on how political, territorial and military power is to be shared or divided in a future form of governance. However, the implementation of such power-sharing pacts has only to a limited extent been the focus of quantitative analysis. This chapter presents new data, namely the IMPACT dataset, to fill up this empirical deficit within the literature on post-civil conflict settlements. The IMPACT dataset contains data on internal armed conflict settlement provisions in 83 peace agreements struck in the period of 1989–2004. It includes data on the most important components of a peace agreement, with regard to the contested incompatibilities, namely political, military and territorial pacts.[2] Furthermore, it includes unique data on to what degree such pacts were implemented following the signing of a peace agreement.

The chapter is structured in the following way. We begin by discussing literature on durable peace and peace agreements, and formulate four expectations based on this research. Firstly, power-sharing pacts are expected to be more common in recent peace agreements, than in the beginning of the analysed period. Secondly, it is expected that implementation of power-sharing pacts is rare. Thirdly, we discuss why we expect a variation in terms of the length of the implementation phase across the three different types of pacts that we study; political pacts are expected to be implemented relatively swiftly, compared to military and territorial pacts. Fourthly, we expect implementation to be important for peace to hold. We then move on to define and operationalize the key concepts in the dataset: peace agreements, pacts and implementation. In our subsequent analysis we investigate the four expectations. In short, we find that the relative share of pacts in peace agreements indeed has increased over the years. Surprisingly, a majority of pacts are implemented. How long implementation of the pacts takes varied in line with our expectations. Finally, political pacts are less associated with peace than military and territorial pacts.

## Implementation of Pacts as a Sign of Credible Commitment

There is a growing literature on different types of power-sharing pacts, such as political, territorial and military pacts.[3] Power-sharing pacts effectively divide or share power between one or more actors to allow for a levelled balance of power in the spheres that the parties deem to be of relevance. Previous research has shown that such guarantees of post-conflict power are the best way to get warring parties to sign on to peace settlements, and that this can have positive effects on durable peace in the post-settlement environment (Walter, 1999; Walter, 2002; Hartzell and Hoddie, 2003; Hoddie and Hartzell, 2005). More specifically, pacts can serve to mitigate the problems of credible commitments and security dilemmas. The credible commitment problem stems from a lack of trust between the parties to a settlement concerning the other's future behaviour. In other words, there is a belief that the other party will renege on the agreement when it suits them. This commitment problem can be mitigated through the use of costly signals, i.e. signals of intent that are costly to one of the parties. Seeing one's foe perform actions that are costly to them might induce oneself to perform similar activities, and thus build trust.[4] Sharing power in the most important spheres of influence can be such a costly signal, by virtue of the concessionary nature of giving up power. However, such costly signals are problematic in conflict and post-conflict environments, due to high levels of insecurity and risk (Walter, 2002, pp. 24–6).

Power-sharing pacts entail a guarantee of power in a future system of governance, thereby also serving to resolve, or at least 'freeze', the security dilemma that often exists between the former warring parties. The security dilemma refers to the spiral of violence where the experienced uncertainty and threat of an opponent drives states or groups to acquire more and more power and capabilities to protect itself, in turn forcing the other to act in the same way, perpetuating insecurity (Posen, 1993). The use of power-sharing pacts in peace settlements provides a possible way out of this dilemma by promising sharing or division of power to provide for a levelled power balance, which may be guaranteed by external actors (Hartzell, 1999, pp. 6–7). Such a power balance can portray one's opponent as being less threatening than before, breaking the spiral to allow for the building of trust.

Thus, in order for a peace settlement to lead to its ultimate goal – peace – the parties' commitment to stick to the deal is central. However, for peace to hold, it is conceivable that the promises of power sharing need to be implemented. As Walter (2002) suggests, pacts that guarantee warring parties a share of power can be seen as a sign of credible commitment, given that both parties will attempt to implement the provisions of the deal. However, mere efforts to implement an agreement are not as strong a sign as full implementation of the provisions.

Furthermore, it has been suggested that the short-term implementation of peace agreements should be separated from the long-term tasks of peace building (Stedman 2001, pp. 739–40). There are few statistical studies that address the relationship between implementation of peace agreements and durable peace. In such previous research, the implementation of a peace agreement is often seen as successful if war did not recur within five years of the signing of the agreement (Hartzell, 1999; Walter, 2002; Hoddie and Hartzell, 2005).[5] Such interpretations of implementation success could be misleading, as there is a possibility that provisions are implemented but that peace still does not hold. For example, the successful implementation of the 50–50 power-sharing government in Guinea-Bissau in 1999 failed to stop the military junta from effectively ousting their Guinea-Bissauan government partners later that year. Likewise the opposite occurs: peace endures despite failure to implement the promised pacts. A case in point is the Mexican government's failure to implement constitutional changes agreed with the Zapatista rebels in 1996. In this case, failure to implement the agreement did not lead to a resumption of fighting. To include these types of outcomes in our investigation of the relationship between implementation of peace agreements and peace, we adhere to the suggestion of theoretically distinguishing between 'implementation success' and 'peace'.

Rothchild and Roeder have suggested that political power sharing is an invention of the late 1990s and the first years of this century (Rothchild and Roeder, 2005, p. 5). We find it important to address this claim since many of their volume's concerns regarding power sharing are based on the notion that it is an expanding phenomenon. We would thus expect the IMPACT data to display a marked increase in the use of political pacts as a conflict-solving mechanism in the later part of the post-cold war period, compared to the early years of the analysed period.

A second claim regarding peace agreement implementation concerns the possibilities of implementing settlements at all. For example, Stedman argues that '[i]t is a wonder that any peace agreement in civil war is successfully implemented' (Stedman et al. 2002, p. 663), implying that the implementation of peace agreements is indeed a challenging task. Crocker and Hampson agree with this pessimistic view of negotiated settlements of civil conflict, stipulating that '[a] major reason is that implementing peace agreements is no less formidable a task than negotiating them' (Crocker and Hampson, 1996, p. 55). We thus expect that a significant number of pacts in the IMPACT data are not implemented.

## Implementation by Pact Type

In the realm of the political science, power sharing is often viewed as a viable solution to a dispute between belligerents concerning government power (Spears, 2002, p. 123). Walter uses the term 'political pact' to refer to an agreement under which the warring parties are each guaranteed seats in a post-conflict executive or legislative branch of government, sharing power and influence on a vertical continuum (Walter, 2002). Walter suggests that political pacts can mitigate the problem of credible commitments and contribute to solving the security dilemma through the promise they hold for future influence.

In the sphere of political pacts, Spears contends that such pacts are 'difficult to arrive at [and], difficult to put into practice' (Spears, 2002, p. 123). Likewise, Rothchild while analysing power-sharing pacts in Africa, states that implementation of such pacts is likely to be hampered by unreliable information, lack of credible commitment and inappropriate external protection (Rothchild, 2005, pp. 256–9), and be very complicated and challenging indeed. From such statements it seems reasonable to theoretically induce a claim that the implementation of political pacts should take time, and that more political pacts will fail in the implementation stage than will be successfully implemented.

If the literature on settlements presents a bleak picture for the implementation of political pacts, the outlook for territorial pacts is even worse. While political power sharing is commonly used for regulating conflicts regarding government power, territorial pacts may be a preferred solution in peace agreements to territorial conflicts. The conflict-mitigating characteristics of territorial pact are different from that of the political pact, because territory is more concretely divisible than government power. Still, a territorial pact aims to regulate conflict through the sharing of power along geographical lines. A guarantee of autonomous control over a specific piece of territory leaves the rebels with a political base, and an additional sense of security (Walter, 2002, p. 31). Through making use of such guarantees in a peace settlement, the government can signal commitment to the deal by costly concessions (Walter, 2002, p. 24).

While discussing territorial pacts, Lake and Rothchild claim that '[...] there are few successful cases of actual implementation of territorial decentralization after civil wars to substantiate the high hopes of contemporary proponents' (Lake and Rothchild, 2005, p. 110). In fact, their list of all civil war settlements during 1945–92 does not include a single conflict that has ended with an implemented territorial decentralization. They even contend that territorial decentralization is extremely unlikely to take place, because of the centrifugal forces of power consolidation that inevitably occur as peace stabilizes itself. In the same book, Keller and Smith claim that being extremely costly in a situation where a state lacks resources due to the civil conflict that brought on the settlement, the implementation of decentralization schemes often fails to materialize (Keller and Smith, 2005, p. 234). From these statements we can induce that the implementation of a territorial pact is likely to be a temporally lengthy process, due to the high logistical and economic costs of implementation, and because territorial restructuring is dependent on the passing of new laws or constitutional amendments. Thus, we would expect comparatively few pacts to be implemented than are partially or not implemented at all, and that implementation of territorial pacts should take longer time span than implementation of political pacts.

A third type of pact, which is seen as power sharing by Walter, is military pacts. Such pacts can play a vital role to provide credible commitments and mitigate the security dilemma in post-settlement environments, which warrant their inclusion in the same category of determinants as the other pacts. For example, Rothchild argues that 'a primary focus on security issues during the transition to a self-enforcing peace is essential' (Rothchild, 2002, p. 117). Just as a stake in the political power is essential as the 'price for peace' (Walter, 1999, p. 137), a stake in the military power in the post-conflict setting allows rebels to have some sustained leverage against those in power, hindering the government's military power from becoming dominant (Walter, 2002, pp. 30–1). Such a guarantee provides the rebels with a minimum sense of security, and the leverage to force compliance with other parts of the settlement.

The implementation of military pacts has been examined by Hartzell and Hoddie (2003), in a study in which they conduct a survey of 16 military pacts between 1980 and 1996. The authors find that 8 out of the 16 pacts (50 per cent) are successfully implemented, 5 are partially implemented (31 per cent) and 4 are not implemented (25 per cent). Hoddie and Hartzell, however, include in their power-sharing variable, cases in which there is no integration into the national armed forces but joint collaboration between opposing forces: something that most likely is easier to achieve and does not expose the former warring parties to the same hazards of vulnerability, logistics and economic costs as does integration. Such cases of mere collaboration are not included in the IMPACT dataset. It is therefore highly probable that IMPACT data will present a more pessimistic picture than Hoddie and Hartzell's study. On military pacts in general the picture is once again bleak in the literature, with many scholars outlining the many hazards of demobilization, disarmament and integration (e.g. Spear, 2002; Walter, 2002; Knight and Özerdem, 2004). In addition, efforts to implement military provisions are economically very costly and should take a long time to implement due to the number of individuals that need to be demobilized or integrated. It also threatens the 'last line of defence' for combatants – their military forces – which makes former warring parties sensitive to such moves (Walter, 1999, p. 129). We would thus expect implementation ratios to reveal that a majority of military pacts see only partial or no implementation and that implementation should be a temporally lengthy process, compared to the implementation of political pacts.

Finally, we will address our own assertion that implementation success should have a positive association to the concept of durable peace i.e. maintaining peace between signatories for at least five years. Walter (2002) and Hoddie and Hartzell (2005) have shown that the inclusion of power-sharing pacts in peace agreements significantly increases the prospects for such a period of peace. It is relevant to address whether or not implementation can provide the same positive association. Thus, our final expectation is that when a settlement provision is fully implemented there will be a positive association with peace within that five-year period.

## Defining and Operationalizing Armed Conflicts and Peace Agreements

For the purpose of analysing the implementation of political, territorial and military pacts struck following civil conflict, we focus our attention on peace agreements signed between warring parties in intrastate armed conflicts in the period 1989–2004. In studying intrastate conflicts in this post-cold war period, we make use of the UCDP definition of internal armed conflict. In such conflicts there must have been at least 25 battle-related deaths in the same year, with the conflict concerning a contested incompatibility between at least two actors, with one side being the state (UCDP 2006). UCDP data contains a total of 114 internal armed conflicts in the selected time frame, of which 33 were active in 2004 (Harbom *et al.* 2006). Using UCDP data provides us with a larger sample of armed conflicts and peace agreements than, for example, Correlates of War (COW) data. UCDP data contains more recent conflicts and also includes minor armed conflicts.[6] The definition of a peace agreement is also based on UCDP criteria: a 'peace agreement should address the problem of the incompatibility, either by settling all or part of it, or by clearly outlining a process for how the warring parties plan to regulate the incompatibility' (UCDP 2006). We have chosen not to include cases that can be classified as peace-process agreements (agreements simply outlining a process towards reconciling the parties, or creating a timetable for such a process), and accords whose implementation depends upon the signing of a final, comprehensive peace agreement. This has been done in order to create a list of agreements in which the process of implementation can be coded in a valid way that allows for comparison across agreements and conflicts. Finally, for an agreement to be included in the IMPACT dataset, it must have been signed by the government and at least one of the rebel groups in the conflict.[7] These definitions yield a list of 83 peace agreements in total for the period 1989–2004, found in 40 separate conflicts, and 38 separate countries around the globe.

## Defining and Operationalizing Pacts

In defining what constitutes a 'pact' in a peace agreement we build mainly upon Walter's 2002 book *Committing to Peace*, in which the author identifies political, military and territorial pacts. Hoddie and Hartzell (2003; 2005) identify similar mechanisms, labelling them political, military and territorial power sharing.[8] We apply Walter's narrower definitions which aptly capture the essence of the power-sharing logic and our own definitions lean more on her work, rather than on Hoddie and Hartzell's broader categories. Applying Walter's more narrow definitions, more aptly captures the essence of the power-sharing logic and our own definitions lean more on her work, rather than employing Hoddie and Hartzell's broad categories. The keyword in our definition of 'pacts' is guaranteed control that includes guaranteed representation in central government, guaranteed influence in a new national army and/or guaranteed control of a specified territory. These guarantees are what make pacts so appealing to the warring parties: both are included in the key spheres of power and thus both have stakes in the proper implementation of the agreement. A political pact is defined as a provision in a peace settlement that offers the combatants guaranteed positions in a new government or assembly (transitional or permanent). A military pact is defined as a provision in a peace settlement that offers the combatants guaranteed integration into the national armed forces and/or command structures,[9] or a provision that allows the rebels to maintain their own separate armed forces. A territorial pact is defined as a provision in a settlement that guarantees the rebels some form of local self-government,[10] or a provision that allows rebels to continue to administer an area under their de facto control. In the IMPACT dataset the pact variables have been adapted from the TOPAD v1.1 dataset (Nilsson *et al.* 2006). Employing these coding criteria, yields a total of 100 pacts in the 83 peace agreements.

## Defining and Operationalizing Implementation

Peace agreements vary a great deal with regard to which tasks are regulated and how far-reaching and detailed the provisions for implementation are. This means that some agreements merely reflect a status quo situation and thus do not require any actions to be implemented. Other agreements set up a detailed timeline and even include a new constitution. Therefore, defining implementation is no easy task. In *Ending Civil Wars*, Downs and Stedman argue that the study of implementation of peace settlements is modest at best, mainly because the post-conflict environment to be studied is not conducive to systematic evaluation. In their chapter on settlement implementation, Downs and Stedman claim that operationalizing the success or failure of implementation should be contingent on whether violence ends, and on whether the war is terminated on a self-enforcing basis (Downs and Stedman, 2002, pp. 50–1). Their main focus is on implementation strategies though, and this type of operationalization is not transferable to the study of the relationship between implementation of pacts and peace. Walter also measures implementation success in a similar manner and includes absence of war in the definition (Walter, 2002, pp. 53–4). For this reason Walter's definition is not suitable for our study.

The present chapter uses a definition of implementation that examines whether the core provisions of the settlement were executed or not. It does not observe if they led to stable peace. A possible problem with such an approach is that a working definition of this type is not suitable for analysing a *whole* peace agreement, since it is not analytically possible to evaluate implementation through studying the exact extent to which every paragraph of a settlement is adhered to or not adhered to, especially when many provisions are open to negotiations, arbitration or interpretation.

But such a definition is suitable for assessing implementation of the above mentioned pacts. Also, it separates what we wish to study – peace as a dependent variable – from what might affect it – implementation of settlement provisions as a possible independent variable – instead of claiming deterministically that successful implementation is the same as peace. Angola's 1991 Bicesse Accords are a case in point. The agreement regulated the conflict over government power by allowing UNITA to become a political party and take part in elections. Elections were held (i.e. the provisions of the agreement were implemented), but UNITA returned to war anyway. Thus, fulfilment of a provision, or pact, does not necessarily lead to peace if the provision in itself is flawed.

In the IMPACT dataset, implementation success and failure is determined by to what degree the guarantees and guaranteed quotas in a stipulated pact are fulfilled. We have chosen to categorize implementation of pacts as being 'full' (successful), 'partial' (implementation began but was not completed) and 'none' (no implementation). These definitions effectively separate the peace and the peace deal, and open up the possibility of analysis of implementation and its relationship with peace.

We have chosen a five-year time period for the analysis of pact implementation. There is a risk in using a strict time frame while classifying implementation, as failed implementation may be revived or partial implementation may be completed just beyond the stipulated period of five years. Despite such drawback, the length of this time period should allow for valid measurements of the attempts of the warring parties to implement political, military and territorial pacts. The five-year time frame is a standard measurement for peace settlement analysis, employed by Walter (1999; 2002), and also by Hoddie and Hartzell (2003) in their article on the implementation of military power sharing. As Hoddie and Hartzell (2003) points out, use of a shorter time period would probably miss out on committed efforts to implement a pact. These time frames start from the date of signing.

A pact has been coded in the IMPACT dataset as being fully implemented if the guarantees provided by a pact are accommodated within the specified time frame. For a political pact this means that the stipulated number of seats in the government and/or assembly must be claimed and taken up by the rebels, the new government and/or assembly must be inaugurated, and the government and/or assembly must begin carrying out normal government functions (such as holding meetings, issuing executive decisions etc.) within a time frame of five years. For a military pact, the stipulated quota or guarantee of integration into the armed forces and/or command structures must be fulfilled within a time frame of five years. Alternatively the rebels must be allowed to maintain their own forces for the entire time frame. For a territorial pact, the definition entails that a pact is coded as being fully implemented if the laws/bills/constitutional amendments needed for decentralization are passed and executed by the government within the time frame, or if the rebels were allowed to retain control of their captured territory during the entire time frame (if it is a territorial pact of this kind). Partial implementation is coded for pacts whose implementation begun but can not be completed before the end of the specified time frame. This can occur in cases where constitutional amendments are discussed, but never passed, where integration of forces is ended before the quota has been satisfied, or where a transitional government is appointed but never inaugurated. No implementation is coded in those cases where there have been no discernable moves to fulfil the pact.

In coding implementation of settlement provisions we have made use of wide variety of sources, such as Keesing's Record of World Events, Factiva searches in Reuters, AFP, All Africa, BBC Monitoring and IRIN news wires, Amnesty International's country reports, State Department country reports, selected academic and policy-oriented case studies, MAR qualitative data, the Accord series on peace processes, UCDP conflict summaries and more. Each pact has been subjected to in-depth study from these various sources.

## Pact Proliferation in Peace Agreements

The IMPACT dataset contains data on internal armed conflict settlement provisions in 83 peace agreements signed in the 114 conflicts that took place between 1989 and 2004. These 83 peace agreements were signed in 40 conflicts in 38 different countries around the globe, meaning that only 35 per cent of conflicts have been subjected to a peace agreement. Out of the 83 identified peace agreements 56 (68 per cent) have been reached in conflicts concerning government power, implying that peace agreements are more common in conflicts over government than in conflicts over territory.

Region-specific data shows that the vast majority of peace agreements (64 per cent) are signed in African conflicts, while other regions display figures below 15 per cent. Analysing the geographical dispersion of agreements further, Africa has the highest agreement-to-conflict signing ratio, with nearly half (46 per cent) of all African conflicts experiencing the signing of an agreement. The Middle East displayed the bleakest outlook for settlement signing, and only 11 per cent of the conflicts saw a peace agreement in this region. The other regions cluster between roughly 25 per cent and 35 per cent. The data clearly shows that the majority of signed peace agreements can be found in Africa, where we also find the majority of post-cold war conflicts. One might have expected Europe to show a comparatively higher propensity towards signed agreements when taking into account regional and superpower interest in this region, but the low figures might be explained by many of the European conflicts being short-lived military-coup-style conflicts.[11]

Out of the 83 identified peace agreements 70 contain one or more pacts, while 13 agreements lack any type of pact. A total number of 100 pacts are identified in the list of 83 agreements, and out of these 36 are political pacts, 31 are military pacts and 33 are territorial pacts. Broken down across the spectrum of conflict type and type of conflict-resolution mechanism, the data shows that out of 56 government conflict settlements 55 per cent contain political pacts, and out of 27 territorial conflict settlements 89 per cent contain territorial pacts. Military pacts are more common in conflicts concerning government power: 45 per cent of agreements contain such a pact while the same figure for territorial conflict settlements is 22 per cent.

A small number of peace agreements also contain all types of pacts, or regulate the incompatibility through making use of both territorial and political pacts. A case in point is the Bosnian Dayton Accords, which contains provisions for both territorial autonomy and guaranteed ethnic quotas in the government and assembly, and allow the Srpska Republic to maintain its own fighting force.

The governments are often reluctant to give up territorial control. As Reiter argues, the states do not willingly cede territory due to the costly signals this entails (Reiter, 2003, p. 30). However, the data demonstrate that 89 per cent of territorial conflicts contain territorial pacts. The types of solutions incorporated into the definition of a territorial pact are wide-ranging, including both different forms of autonomy, and possible secession.[12] The many possible solutions make for a wide inclusion of 'less costly' concessions that governments may make use of. However, only 32 per cent of signed peace agreements concern territorial conflicts, pointing instead towards the conclusion that states rarely accept territorial decentralization, and not the other way around.

The comparatively less number of military pacts in territorial conflicts can be explained by the driving factors in such conflicts. It has been suggested that while government conflicts are about conquering of power at the centre, territorial conflicts are commonly about removing pieces of power from the centre and bringing them down to a regional or local level (Fearon, 2004, p. 288). Rebels in territorial conflicts may not be as concerned with being integrated into the national military structures, but instead prefer influence in the sectors of internal coercive power that exist on lower levels of government, such as the police. Empirical data suggests that integration into, or the yielding of, policing powers is relatively common in territorial conflicts, lending support to this argument.[13] This arrangement to some degree replaces the need for an integration of rebel forces into the national army.

Rothchild and Roeder (2005, p. 5) claim that political pacts have become more common in contemporary international mediation. According to our data, 55 per cent of government settlements contain such pacts, suggesting that they are fairly common. We can further address this claim directly by looking at the proliferation of political pacts in peace agreements throughout the post-cold war period, divided into shorter time periods that allow for comparison between the early post-cold war period (1989–92) and the later period of this era (2001–4).

**Figure 1.** Trends of pacts in peace agreements.

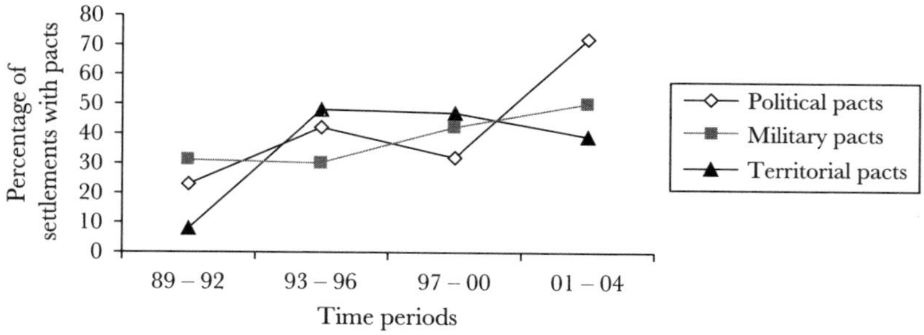

Notes: Cases are from 1989–2004, N = 83. 13 settlements 1989–92, 33 settlements 1993–6, 19 settlements 1997–2000, 18 settlements 2001–4.

The IMPACT data firmly supports Rothchild and Roeder's claim about political power-sharing pact proliferation, from being employed in only circa 20 per cent of settlements at the end of the cold war, political power sharing at the dawn of the new century can be found in as many as over 70 per cent of all peace agreements. The use of military pacts shows a more varied trend, but has slowly risen from the early 1990s to being included in almost 50 per cent of settlements in the early years of the twenty-first century. Territorial pacts were rare in the years following the cold war, but show a relatively stable trend from the mid-1990s and onwards. Pacts in general appear to have been rare in 1989–92, but there has been an increase in proliferation in the decade that followed – a trend that appears to be constant.

## Implementation of Pacts

To address the other claims that were identified in the section on theory we turn to the implementation of settlement provisions. The IMPACT dataset identified a total of 100 pacts within the 70 peace agreements that contained one or more pacts. However, to analyse implementation ratios for these pacts we need to exclude from the analysis all those pacts that were not given the full five-year time frame for implementation, i.e. the analysis excludes all agreements signed after the year 2000. This yields a total of 71 pacts found in 65 peace agreements, of which 23 are political pacts, 22 are military pacts and 26 are territorial pacts. By employing our coding criteria for implementation on the identified pacts we categorize implementation as being 'full', 'partial' and 'none'. The data is summarized in the graph below. Out of the 23 political pacts, 17 are fully implemented, one is partially implemented

**Figure 2.** Implementation of pact.

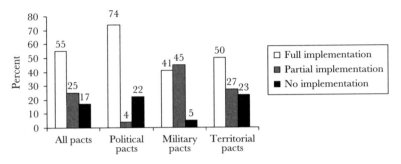

Notes: Cases are from 1989–2000, N = 71. The percentages for categories 'All pacts' and 'Military pacts' do not add-up to 100 per cent due to missing data.

and five are not implemented at all. Corresponding figures for military pacts are 9, 10 and 1. For territorial pacts the figures are 13, 7 and 6.

Analysing the data through the lens of the theoretical claims on implementation yields interesting results, and there appears to be no strong support for the notion that comparatively few peace-agreement provisions are implemented than are partially or not implemented. Overall the data does not support the statement of Stedman *et al.* on peace agreement implementation. Instead, more than half of the identified pacts are implemented. A significantly large portion of provisions are fully implemented than provisions that are either partially or not implemented at all. Still, that only 55 per cent of peace agreement provisions are implemented means that almost half of all peace agreements are not fully implemented within five years of the signing of the agreement.

The data on pact implementation, in general, might not be completely clear-cut, but for political pacts the data is more telling. The data does not support the harsh claims of some scholars that political pacts are hard to implement, in that the vast majority of political pacts are in fact implemented (74 per cent), most likely because they – in contrast to military and territorial pacts – have low economic costs, are not reliant on large-scale logistical operations or warrant the drafting of new constitution to allow for decentralization of authority. This high figure of successful implementation presents us with some optimism regarding conflict resolution: if many political pacts (power-sharing agreements) can be implemented then the incompatibilities between the warring parties can be solved through such arrangements. This, of course, hinges upon whether the political pacts *do solve* the incompatibility, and not just displace it, as claimed by Spears

(2002, pp. 129–30). At the least, political pacts are not as difficult to implement as has been previously contended.

Analysing the data on territorial pacts also yields interesting results in relation to previous research. The data presents a radically different picture compared to Lake and Rothchild's data and their theoretical expectations for the post-cold war period. Contrary to their claim that hopes for decentralization should be low, the IMPACT data shows that 50 per cent of all territorial pacts are fully implemented, 27 per cent are partially implemented and only 23 per cent are not implemented at all.[14] This data clearly shows that the pessimistic view found in the literature is not applicable to the post-cold war period. One explanation for the high implementation ratios for territorial pacts might be, in relation to the argument on such implementation being very costly, that out of 13 fully implemented pacts, ten (77 per cent) are found in Europe and in the Israeli-Palestinian conflicts – conflict zones that are wealthier than the other regions under study, and also attract more international interest. It is, therefore, possible that the resources that these settlements attract from their environments skew the ratio of implementation. That 27 per cent of territorial pacts are only partially implemented lends some support to the notion that such pacts take a long time to implement.

Turning to military pacts and the reference point for implementation given by Hoddie and Hartzell, the analysis shows that the numbers do not overlap completely. The IMPACT data, as a whole, presents a bleaker picture, with only 41 per cent of pacts being fully implemented, 45 per cent being partially implemented and 5 per cent being not implemented at all. That Hoddie and Hartzell include collaboration between opposing forces in their pact-variable, might explain this discrepancy. The data barely supports the claim that comparatively more pacts see failed implementation than successful processes. The data, however, lends support to the notion that the implementation of military pacts is a protracted process, since such a large number of pacts are only partially implemented within the five-year time frame. This also supports the argument that such processes are economically costly, and that giving up one's armed forces is a highly sensitive move that hampers implementation.

To address the claims on the protracted nature of the process of territorial and military pact implementation we turn to an analysis of the length of implementation processes for these types of pacts. The first column in the table below gives the total number of pacts by type. The second column focuses on pacts that were reached no later than 2000, in order to allow for a five-year period for implementation. Pacts where one party is simply allowed to continue to administer a territory or retain its armed forces – 'status quo' pacts – are also excluded from the analysis to avoid another possible bias in the data. We then employ the data on the time in months from the signing of

**Table 1. Average Length of Implementation Processes of Fully Implemented Pacts**

|  | Number of pacts (89–05) | Analysed pacts (89–00) | Implemented pacts | Average (in months) |
|---|---|---|---|---|
| Political pacts | 36 | 23 | 17 | 7.1 |
| Military pacts | 31 | 22 | 9 | 16.1 |
| Territorial pacts | 33 | 26 | 13 | 16.7 |
| Total | 100 | 71 | 39 | 13.3 |

Notes: 'Average' denotes the average time in months from the signing of the settlement until full implementation of a provision was reached.

the agreement until the completion of implementation. The data is summarized in the Table 1 above.

As expected from analysing implementation success and failure, especially taking into account the arguments of the hazards each type of pact faces, political pacts have the shortest implementation duration with 7.1 months on average, followed by military pacts with a 16.1 month average, and territorial pacts with an average implementation duration of 16.7 months. There is however a wide dispersion of cases across the temporal space: especially so for territorial pacts, which show large variations in the time it takes to implement this type of pact.

This data confirms the expectation that political pacts are easier to implement, and are implemented more swiftly, than military and territorial pacts. One reason for the difference regarding implementation time of different types of pacts could be the economic and logistical costs associated with military and territorial pacts. The data also shows that when pacts are fully implemented they are commonly implemented within one and a half years, implying that international implementation missions do not necessarily have to be long-term commitments. However, also after a peace deal is implemented, international monitoring may be pivotal for durable peace.

Next we present a simple cross-tabulation to address the question of implementation as a mechanism for peace. By employing the commonly used five-year time frame for durable peace we attempt to create a preliminary sketch of how implementation relates to this concept. We make use of UCDP data on dyad activity to code whether or not a signatory dyad returned to warfare within five years after the signing of the agreement. We present data for all three types of pacts, divided into categories of successful and failed implementation, with the latter category including partial and no implementation.

*Table 2*. **Durable Peace and War Recurrence in Successful or Failed Implementation (Peace or War Recurrence Within Five Years after Signing)**

| Type of pact | Successful implementation (full) | | | Failed implementation (partial or none) | | |
|---|---|---|---|---|---|---|
| | Durable peace | War recurrence | Cases | Durable peace | War recurrence | Cases |
| Political pact | 9 | 8 | 17 | 2 | 4 | 6 |
| | (53%) | (47%) | (100%) | (33%) | (66%) | (100%) |
| Territorial pact | 12 | 1 | 13 | 10 | 3 | 13 |
| | (92%) | (8%) | (100%) | (77%) | (23%) | (100%) |
| Military pact | 9 | 0 | 9 | 5 | 6 | 11 |
| | (100%) | (0%) | (100%) | (45%) | (55%) | (100%) |
| Total number | 30 | 9 | 39 | 17 | 13 | 30 |

Notes:  Cases from 1989–2000, N = 69. Missing data for two military pacts are excluded from the analysis.

The data fits our initial expectation that implementation, in general, does matter for peace during the first five years. However, the data does not provide us with the expected results for all types of pacts, especially so regarding political power sharing. In cases where a political pact was fully implemented within five years, nearly half of all conflicts saw the recurrence of warfare within this time period. One interpretation of this result is that the implementation of political pacts does not necessarily resolve the root cause of the conflict. However, the record for failed implementation processes is even worse, with two thirds of such failed processes seeing a recurrence of war within five years of the signing of the agreement. A preliminary conclusion, which would have to be validated through more advanced statistical methods, is that the implementation of a political pact in general does not serve to mitigate or end violent conflict.

The data on territorial pact implementation shows that in those cases where there was successful implementation of a territorial pact a full 92 per cent saw peace last within the time frame. Only in one case of full implementation did war recur. More surprising is the observation that in the cases of failed implementation (partial or none) the majority of conflicts did not recur despite such failure. Territorial pacts still seem to be associated with peace as the figures for full implementation in the cases where peace prevailed are significantly higher than in the cases where it did not. The data for military pacts is clear – not a single instance of full implementation saw a recurrence of war within the five-year time period. In cases of failed implementation processes, war recurred in the majority of cases.Overall, the cross-tabulation supports the notion of a positive association between successful implementation and durable peace for territorial and military pacts, but not for political power-sharing pacts.

## Conclusions

This chapter has presented new data on the implementation of peace-agreement provisions related to political, military and territorial power sharing. We have addressed four theoretical claims made in the literature on peace and peace settlements. Firstly, in line with previous research, we have demonstrated that the inclusion of political pacts in peace settlements has increased in the later years of the 1990s and the early years of the new century.

Our second conclusion challenges the previous notion that peace agreements are seldom implemented. On the contrary, the analysis of IMPACT data shows that more than half of all pacts were implemented. An overwhelming majority of political pacts (17 out of 23) were implemented following the peace settlement. A clear majority of territorial pacts were also implemented, while less than half of the military pacts were fully implemented within the five-year time frame. Thirdly, as expected military and territorial pacts took longer to implement than political ones. Of those political pacts that were fully implemented, most were executed within a year.

Fourthly, our cross-tabulation on the association between implementation and peace showed that even though political pacts are implemented they only yield five-year peace in about 50 per cent of all conflicts. Hence, political pacts are no 'sure-fix' solution. The cross-tabulation showed that the implementation of military and territorial pacts have a positive association with peace. This is especially true for military pacts where a fully implemented pact saw no recurrence of conflict. This finding points to the importance of demobilization and reintegration to avoid a recurrence of conflict.

Our results suggest that it is possible for formerly warring parties to change the political, territorial and military power balance by a peace agreement. However, it is yet too early to evaluate the long-term consequences for durable peace. Considering that power-sharing pacts have become increasingly more common, this warrants more research into such long-term effects on democratization and peacebuilding.

# Chapter Six

# REFUGEE REPATRIATION AS A NECESSARY CONDITION FOR PEACE

## Patrik Johansson

*The conventional wisdom of most refugee experts holds that there is a necessary connection between forging and implementing a peace agreement and ensuring the successful return of refugees. Peace depends on refugee repatriation, and every peace agreement must provide for it, or so it is widely believed.*[1]

*Howard Adelman*

## Introduction

There are around 12 million refugees around the world today. The total population of concern to the United Nations High Commissioner for Refugees (UNHCR), including asylum seekers, internally displaced persons (IDPs) and stateless persons, is nearly 20 million, many of whom are displaced as a result of armed conflict (US Committee for Refugees 2006; UNHCR 2006). There are three types of durable solutions to refugee situations: return/repatriation, local integration and resettlement in a third country. Repatriation has over the past twenty years become the distinctively most important solution, preferred by the UNHCR as well as most host states. Having long been the ideal solution only in theory, in the mid-1980s repatriation started to be endorsed as the ideal solution also in practice, and today the other two solutions – local integration and resettlement – are applicable to less than 1 per cent of the world's refugees (Chimni, 2003, p. 195; 2004).

In an Agenda for Peace, under the heading 'Post-conflict peace-building', Boutros-Ghali (1992, Para 55) included refugee repatriation among factors that will help to consolidate peace after war. In 1997, then High Commissioner Ogata (1997, p. vii) wrote that 'peace-building requires just solutions for refugees and displaced persons. In UNHCR's experience, such solutions are indispensable for lasting peace and true stability'. Kumar (1997, p. 15, 41) argues that the 'return and resettlement of the refugees and IDPs are necessary for social peace and economic growth', and describes the repatriation and resettlement of refugees and IDPs as 'an essential prerequisite to political stability in many war-torn societies'. UN Secretary General Annan (United Nations 2005), in an address to the UNHCR Executive Committee argued that '[t]he return of refugees and internally displaced persons is a major part of any post-conflict scenario. And it is far more than just a logistical operation. Indeed, it is often a critical factor in sustaining a peace process and in revitalizing economic activity'.

These are just a few examples. The tendency is that in the academic literature on conflict resolution and peacebuilding, as well as in many policy statements, the blessings of post-conflict refugee repatriation come across as an article of faith. The claim about refugee repatriation as a condition for peace is presented as an assumption rather than as a hypothesis to be tested. In Adelman's words, it is part of conventional wisdom. Sometimes, however, conventional wisdom needs to be questioned.

In this essay I consider some aspects of how to question the conventional wisdom about refugee repatriation and peace. In the next section I provide a necessarily brief overview of research on the relation between refugee repatriation and peace, and specify which angle I find most interesting. I then discuss some methodological concerns related to the practice of formulating claims about refugee repatriation and peace in conditional rather than correlational terminology. In the concluding section I consider four alternative ways to approach the operationalization of refugee repatriation as a condition for peace, and argue that one based on the relative number of returnees is the most promising one.

I want to point out at the outset that refugee repatriation as a condition for peace is not necessarily the same as sustainable resolutions to refugee situations. A refugee situation may be resolved through other means than repatriation, and the claim that refugee repatriation is a (perhaps necessary) condition for peace is probably not intended to require that a sustainable solution is found for every single refugee. Further, the discussion in this essay is limited to the role of refugee repatriation as a condition for peace. There are of course many other reasons to argue for (or against) repatriation. Further, the focus of this essay is the operationalization of refugee repatriation as a condition; I do not discuss the operationalization of peace as an outcome.

It should also be noted that there are many important differences between displaced persons recognized as refugees and displaced persons not so recognized. However, I believe that arguments about the relation between refugee repatriation and peace are usually intended to apply equally to all displaced persons, with or without refugee status, whether internationally or internally displaced. For reasons of convenience I therefore refrain from enumerating several categories of displaced persons every time I need to mention them, and instead use the terms refugee and refugee repatriation throughout this essay.

## The Relation between Repatriation and Peace

When post-conflict refugee repatriation is discussed in a peacebuilding context, the approach is often one of rebuilding societies, reversing ethnic cleansing, and the right to return. Repatriation is perceived as the humanitarian solution that puts the interests of displaced persons first. Perhaps this sympathetic notion is partly responsible for the scant attention paid, in the peacebuilding literature, to question the need for repatriation. The perspective is strikingly different when (post-conflict) refugee repatriation is discussed in an international legal context. The legal focus is more often on the securitization of migration, human rights protection in asylum procedures, and non-refoulement. In terms of humanitarian considerations, the increased focus on repatriation as a solution to refugee situations is seen as highly problematic (Bell, 2000; Costello, 2005; Crépeau and Nakache, 2006; Noll, 1999; Thielemann, 2004).

Adelman (2002, pp. 274–5) has described four positions on the relationship between refugee repatriation and the implementation of peace agreements. First, he identifies two soft positions: the Soft I position views any resolution of a refugee situation as a sign that peace is in place, and the Soft II position specifically sees repatriation as a sign.

Viewing repatriation as a sign that peace is in place should not be confused with treating repatriation as an indicator of peace. An example of Adelman's Soft II position is Wallensteen's (2002, p. 160) argument that '[...] the return of refugees is important, as this signifies, more than many other actions, that the extreme conditions that gave rise to their flight have been remedied to some extent'. This is different from Ali & Matthews's (2004, p. 405–6) use of repatriation as an indicator of peace – as an empirical criterion by which peace is measured:

Even in Mozambique, South Africa, and Zimbabwe, where the international community can fairly claim some responsibility for a successful transition from war to peace, measured by such criteria as effective economic recovery, free and fair elections, the repatriation of refugees, the decommissioning of former combatants and their integration into society, external intervention has also had a negative impact.

If repatriation is used as an indicator of peace, it cannot be meaningfully analysed as a condition for peace, because by definition there can be no case of peace without repatriation.

Adelman also presents two hard positions: the Hard I position considers peace and refugee repatriation as necessary conditions for one another, and the Hard II position claims mutual causation between peace and refugee repatriation. Two phenomena can certainly be mutually reinforcing, but as demonstrated in the next section claiming that two phenomena are necessary conditions for one another has certain noteworthy implications.

Having analysed several case studies, Adelman concludes that none of the four positions is supported by empirical facts (2002, p. 276). His argument is not that there is never any type of relation between refugee repatriation and peace, but rather that no one relation is valid across all cases. Depending on the circumstances, repatriation may contribute to peace, it may be irrelevant to peace, or it may be unfavourable to peace.

The claim at the centre of this essay, namely that refugee repatriation is necessary for peace, is a unidirectional version of the Hard I position. This may well be the most commonly held position, and is the one referred to by Adelman in the epigraph. Another alternative position would be that any solution to a refugee situation (i.e. not necessarily repatriation) is a necessary condition for peace, the idea being that peace cannot be achieved so long as a significant refugee situation prevails (cf. the major protracted refugee situations-approach in the final section of this essay). An example could be Lischer (2005).

Previous research on the relation between refugee repatriation and peace can be categorized on other grounds as well, into at least four categories. The first category deals with the relation between refugee repatriation and peace in general terms, uses cases for the purpose of illustration, and pays limited attention to theoretical explanations of the relation. Much of the peacebuilding literature ends up in this category, along with Adelman (2002), Cousens (2001) and Chimni (2003) who in various ways questions the generalizability of the claim of necessity.

The second category is very empirical. It studies peace processes, peacebuilding etc. on a case by case basis, and includes repatriation among other conditions. Studies in this category usually do not attempt to draw general conclusions about that relation between refugee repatriation and peace, but rather to analyse the nature of that relation in the particular case. Several of the case studies in Stedman, Rothchild and Cousens (2002) are examples of this category.

The third category contains systematic analyses of several cases, and tries to find theoretical explanations of why repatriation is good/necessary (or bad) for peace. Representatives of this category are Kaufmann (1996; 1998), who argues against refugee repatriation, and Sambanis (2000), who argues against Kaufmann. This is the type of research most relevant to a problematization of the claim that refugee repatriation is necessary for peace. Unfortunately, while both Kaufmann and Sambanis draw conclusions about the relation between refugee repatriation and peace, neither of them uses data on repatriation. Instead, in different ways, they both use territorial/political partition (or rather the absence of partition) as a proxy for repatriation.

The fourth category concerns the achievement of durable solutions to refugee situations, and how this is affected by the context of armed conflict. For example, Bhatia (2003) and Naqvi (2004) both warn against using repatriation as a tool to achieve peace. Studies in this category do not accept refugee repatriation as a condition for peace, but instead argues that peace is a condition for repatriation.

## Methodological Considerations

As noted in the introduction, the claim that refugee repatriation is necessary for peace is usually presented as an assumption rather than as a hypothesis to be tested. It is usually expressed in conditional rather than correlational terminology. Consequently, if it is to be treated as a hypothesis to be tested, that hypothesis needs to be a hypothesis about conditions rather than a hypothesis about correlations. The hypothesis, 'Refugee repatriation is a necessary condition for peace', makes a very different claim compared to the hypothesis, 'The more refugee repatriation, the better (or more likely) the peace' (see Goertz and Starr, 2003a, p. 17). This has significant implications for how the hypothesis can be tested. Most importantly, instead of using independent and dependent variables that can take on any number of different values, we need to use conditions and outcomes that are either present or absent.

In the basic test of necessity, both the condition and the outcome are dichotomous – they are present or absent, conventionally coded as 1 and 0, respectively. Testing for necessity requires, first of all, identification of all 'instances of the outcome', meaning cases where the outcome is present and second, determination of the presence of the condition in all these cases. If so, then we can speak of a necessary condition. Expressed in set theoretic terms, a condition is said to be necessary for an outcome if the outcome is a subset of the condition.

However, if there are cases where the outcome is present, but the condition is absent, then the outcome is not a subset of the condition, and the condition is not necessary for the outcome. According to Seawright, a claim about necessary causation

> [...] is not a claim about the frequency of the cause, the frequency of the outcome, or even the frequency of the outcome given the cause. It is only a claim that the outcome does not occur without the cause. (Seawright, 2002a, p. 183)

In the context of refugee repatriation and peace it is perhaps more reasonable to talk about conditions than causes, but Seawright's comment remains equally valid.

The abovementioned procedure – identifying all cases where the outcome is present – is described in variable-oriented research as 'selecting on the dependent variable', and is strongly criticized. For a test of necessity it is much more legitimate (see Dion, 2003; Ragin, 2003), not least because it can be argued that cases where the outcome is absent are irrelevant to a test of necessity. To continue Seawright's argument above, a claim about necessity is strictly a claim about cases where the outcome is present, but it is not a claim about cases where the outcome is absent; therefore, cases where the outcome is absent have no bearing on the validity of the claim.

The argument is aptly illustrated by the hypothesis that 'twins always resemble each other' presented by Hempel (1945). What the hypothesis states is that in order for two persons to be twins, these two persons must resemble each other; resembling each other is the necessary condition and being twins is the positive outcome. As Hempel explains (1945, p. 10), in an analysis of the hypothesis 'twins always resemble each other':

> […] any two persons who are twins and resemble each other would confirm the hypothesis; twins who do not resemble each other would disconfirm it; and any two persons not twins – no matter whether they resemble each other or not – would constitute irrelevant evidence.

Friends, married couples, cousins, colleagues, neighbours – cases where the positive outcome (being twins) is absent – can neither confirm nor disconfirm the hypothesis that twins always resemble each other. In set theoretic terms, the example means that the set 'twins' constitute a subset of the set 'persons who resemble each other'. Because people may look alike without being twins, the set 'persons who resemble each other' would contain not only twins, but a lot of other people as well, irrelevant as they may be to the hypothesis at hand. What is important is that the set 'twins' is a subset of the set 'persons who resemble each other'.

The subset principle can be used to analyse sufficient and necessary conditions. A condition is said to be sufficient for an outcome if the condition

*Table 1.* **Condition is Necessary but Not Sufficient**

|  | Condition absent | Condition present |
|---|---|---|
| Outcome present | no cases here | cases here |
| Outcome absent | not directly relevant | not directly relevant |

is a subset of the outcome (see Ragin, 2000, Chapters 8–9; 2003). It should be emphasized that demonstration of one set as a subset of another set is not enough to determine the existence of a necessary or a sufficient condition, or the cause involved. The analysis must be built on a theoretical rationale about the necessary or sufficient relation. (This is true also for analyses of correlations). This can be illustrated with the help of the twins hypothesis. The two hypotheses: 'Resembling each other is a necessary condition for being twins' and 'Being twins is a sufficient condition for resembling each other' are supported by the set 'twins' constituting a subset of the set 'Persons who resemble each other', yet one of them may make more theoretical sense.

On the basis of the subset principle it can be argued that if two phenomena are necessary conditions for one another, then they are also sufficient conditions for one another. This is why Adelman's Hard I position described above is problematic. It is possible to argue that peace is necessary for repatriation, meaning that the set 'cases of repatriation' constitutes a subset of the set 'cases of peace' (i.e. cases where the outcome is present).

It is equally possible to argue that repatriation is necessary for peace, meaning that the set 'cases of peace' constitutes a subset of the set 'cases of repatriation'. However, if these two hypotheses are true at the same time, as the Hard I position claims, then the set 'cases of repatriation' constitutes a subset of the set 'cases of peace' while simultaneously the set 'cases of peace' constitutes a subset of the set 'cases of repatriation'. This is not a contradiction in terms, but rather an overly complicated way of expressing the set-relation that the two sets 'cases of peace' and 'cases of repatriation' completely overlap, implying all cases of peace are cases of repatriation and vice versa. From this follows logically that in order for two phenomena to be necessary conditions for one another they must also be sufficient conditions for one another. The way to address this problem is, as stated above, to present a good theoretical argument in favour of one phenomenon being a necessary and sufficient condition for the other phenomenon.

The important point in the present context is the requirement that we distinguish between cases where the outcome and the condition, respectively, are either present or absent. The condition as well as the outcome must be (or be made) dichotomous if an analysis of necessity is to be possible.

Claims about necessary conditions are usually considered to be very strong. Strictly speaking, a single contradicting case is enough to disconfirm the claim. There are ways to loosen the demand on necessity, and still analyse causation and conditionality in set-theoretic terms. One way of doing this is through Qualitative Comparative Analysis (QCA), a method which allows for multiple conjunctural causation and INUS conditions (cf. Table 2). Multiple means that there are different causal paths to the same outcome; conjunctural means that different conditions need not have any independent effect, but may still be very important in combination with other conditions. An INUS condition is an Insufficient but Necessary part of an Unnecessary but Sufficient condition (INUS). In the example of multiple conjunctural causation in Table 2, all four conditions (C, D, E and F) are INUS conditions.

The details of QCA will not be discussed here (A good introduction to QCA is provided by Ragin, 2000, Chapter 5.). The important point here is that QCA uses Boolean algebra to calculate how the combined presence and absence of various conditions are related to the outcome. In other words, QCA, like the basic test of necessity, uses dichotomous conditions and outcomes.

Many social science concepts, however, do not easily lend themselves to being divided into dichotomies. For example, determining whether two persons belong to the set 'twins' or not may be rather straightforward, but the distinction between a democracy and a non-democracy is less clear-cut. While some states are definitely democracies, and some are definitely not, many states comprise some democratic features while lacking others, and it is difficult to determine whether they belong to the set 'democracies' or not. This problem can be addressed with the use of fuzzy sets. Fuzzy set social science combines the qualitative distinctions between categories of social phenomena with the quantitative variations within these qualitatively distinct categories.

Crisp sets require each state to be either a full member of the set 'emocracies' or a full non-member of that set (which can also be expressed as being a full member of the set 'non-democracies'). With the use of fuzzy sets, a state can be a partial member of the set 'democracies', and at the same time a partial member of the set 'non-democracies'. Unambiguously democratic states receive a membership score of 1.0 in the set 'democracies', and states that are unambiguously non-democratic receive a membership score of 0.0 in that set. The membership degree of 0.5 is called the cut-off point, and represents the most ambiguous cases. A fuzzy set has at least these three degrees of membership, 0.0, 0.5 and 1.0, but more can be added in between. A five-value fuzzy set has the membership degrees 0.0, 0.25, 0.5, 0.75 and 1.0; a seven-value set has the membership degrees 0.0, 0.17, 0.33, 0.5, 0.67, 0.83 and 1.0. A fuzzy set can also be continuous.

*Table 2.* **Different Types of Causal Relations (Plus (+) Means Logical OR; Multiplication (*) Means Logical AND)**

| monocausal | $X \rightarrow Y$ |
|---|---|
| multiple | $A+B \rightarrow Y$ |
| conjunctural | $P*Q \rightarrow Y$ |
| multiple conjunctural | $C*D + E*F \rightarrow Y$ |

However, a fuzzy set is not a mere standardization of a continuous variable. Constructing a fuzzy set means providing theoretical justifications – 'qualitative anchors' – for the various membership degrees, most importantly full membership, full non-membership, and the cross-over point. The hypothesis that 'refugee repatriation is a necessary condition for peace' can be analysed with a basic test of necessity, with QCA or with fuzzy sets. Whichever method is chosen, there is a need to operationalize refugee repatriation as a condition. In the next section I discuss four ways to approach that operationalization.

For more on necessary conditions, QCA and fuzzy sets, see Braumoeller and Goertz (2002), Clark (2002), Goertz and Starr (2003b), Ragin (1987; 2000; 2004), Seawright (2002a; 2002b) and Smithson and Verkuilen (2006).

## Four Approaches to Operationalizing Repatriation as a Condition

The most important conclusions of the previous sections are first that depending on the circumstances, repatriation may contribute to peace, it may be irrelevant to peace, or it may be unfavourable to peace, and second that in order to conduct a systematic study of refugee repatriation as a condition for peace (in conjunction with other conditions), repatriation needs to be operationalized as a condition, i.e. coded as either present or absent in each empirical case. (The use of fuzzy sets, too, requires qualitative anchors for at least three degrees of membership, and should not be confused with a continuous variable.) The focus of this final section is the empirical basis for such an operationalization – what indicator(s) to use in that operationalization.

As soon as the first refugee is repatriated, repatriation has taken place to some extent, but this is obviously not what is intended when it is claimed that refugee repatriation is necessary for peace. It is also safe to assume that the idea is not that peace will not be achieved unless every single refugee returns. Yet, to treat the claim that refugee repatriation is necessary for peace as a hypothesis to be tested, we need to determine when the condition 'repatriation' is present, and when it is not.

In light of the incidence of the claim that refugee repatriation is a condition for peace, surprisingly little attention has been paid to how to determine when that condition is present. In the following I consider four ways of approaching the operationalization of refugee repatriation as a condition. The first one is based on international refugee law, the second deals with organized repatriation processes, the third one takes the concept of major protracted refugee situations as its starting point, and the fourth one involves the relative number of returnees.

## Alternative 1: International Refugee Law

The primary instrument of international refugee law is the 1951 Convention Relating to the Status of Refugees (the Convention). A central element of the Convention is the definition, in Article 1. A (2), of a refugee as a person who

> [...] owing to well-founded fear of being persecuted for reasons of race, religion, nationality, membership of a particular social group or political opinion, is outside the country of his nationality and is unable or, owing to such fear, is unwilling to avail himself of the protection of that country[.]

Article 1.C – often referred to as the cessation clause – lists the circumstances under which the Convention shall cease to apply to a person. This shall be the case, inter alia, if he has voluntarily re-availed himself of the protection of the country of his nationality (Article 1.C (1)), or if he has acquired a new nationality and is protected by the country of that new nationality (Article 1.C (3)). Most important in the present context is Article 1.C (5), which states that the Convention shall cease to apply to a person if

> [h]e can no longer, because the circumstances in connexion with which he has been recognised as a refugee have ceased to exist, continue to refuse to avail himself of the protection of the country of his nationality[.]

Until 2001, the cessation clause has twice been invoked by the UNHCR with reference to the settlement of civil conflict: in 1973 concerning Sudan, and in 1996 concerning Mozambique and Malawi. It has also been invoked seven times on the basis of 'independence', and twelve times on the basis of 'regime change/democratization' (Bonoan, 2001, p. 22). With reference to the Convention, it was determined that it was no longer reasonable for persons that once fled from these countries to continue to refuse to avail themselves of the protection of the country of their nationality.

There are two main problems with using the cessation clause as a basis for operationalizing repatriation as a condition. The first problem is that the cessation of refugee status is compatible with all three durable solutions to refugee situations (repatriation, local integration, or resettlement), not only repatriation. Displaced persons may for various reasons lose their refugee status without having found any solution, and that would not satisfy the condition 'repatriation' in the claim that refugee repatriation is necessary for peace.

The second problem is that the cessation clause is invoked because of changed circumstances in the country of origin (settlement of civil conflict, independence, or regime change/democratization), not because refugees have repatriated. In the cases of Sudan 1973 and Mozambique and Malawi 1996 substantial repatriation had taken place before the cessation clause was invoked by the UNHCR. It is possible that this repatriation was necessary for the fundamental and durable changes in circumstances referred to by the UNHCR as the reason for its decision to invoke the cessation clause. However, in both cases, the cessation clause was invoked because peace was in place, not because refugees had repatriated. (Invoking the cessation clause may even be seen as a message to refugees that there is no longer any need to remain in flight, that it is time to start repatriating.) In other words, the cessation clause was invoked because the outcome was present, not because the condition was present.

For IDPs, there is no legal framework corresponding to the Refugee Convention. On the international level, the Guiding Principles on Internal Displacement (United Nations 1998) is a comprehensive framework, but it lacks legal authority. On national level, a handful of countries do have legislation that treats IDPs as a special category, but in general, IDP – as opposed to refugee – is not a legal status, but an empirical description (Beau 2003; Kälin, 2003). Just like the cessation of refugee status is compatible with resettlement, local integration and repatriation, the end of internal displacement does not require repatriation (cf. US Committee for Refugees regarding Guatemalan IDPs below).

## Alternative 2: Organized Repatriation Processes

Another possibility is to argue that the condition 'repatriation' is present when an organized repatriation process has been successfully concluded. In many instances, the UNHCR organizes repatriation processes as part of or in parallel with the implementation of peace agreements. Commonly used examples, where successful repatriation processes have been important for peace, are Cambodia, Guatemala and Mozambique. While case studies of repatriation during peace processes usually do not use the language of (necessary) conditions, it is reasonable to argue that these three cases are examples of the condition 'repatriation' being present, because the organized repatriation processes were largely successful.

In Cambodia, 'the repatriation in safety and dignity of Cambodian refugees and displaced persons' was 'an integral part of the comprehensive political settlement' of the conflict (Article 20 of the Paris Agreement). Repatriation was explicitly related to the ability of refugees and displaced persons to participate in elections, as provided for in the peace agreement (Annex 4, Article 6). During 1992 and 1993, more than 360,000 Cambodian refugees repatriated from Thailand on UNHCR convoys, more than 95 per cent of them in time to vote in the May 1993 election (US Committee for Refugees 1994, p. 78). The process was tainted by Thailand's forcible return of the few hundred Cambodians who did not repatriate voluntarily (US Committee for Refugees 1994, p. 78), and it has been criticized for failing to reintegrate the refugees properly (see Eastmond and Öjendal, 1999). However, if a successful repatriation process is an indicator of the condition 'repatriation' being present, it is reasonable to consider Cambodia in 1993 as a case of repatriation.

In Guatemala, the active participation of refugees in planning and implementing repatriation has contributed to the assessment of it as a success.[2] After a 1992 agreement between the Guatemalan government and representatives of the Guatemalan refugee community in Mexico, organized repatriation began several years before the conflict was finally brought to an end in 1996. It is interesting to note that the US Committee for Refugees in its yearbook for 1998 argued that those Guatemalans that remained in Mexico should no longer be considered refugees, despite the fact that both the Mexican government and the UNHCR still considered them as such. The US Committee also decided not to include remaining internally displaced Guatemalans in its listing of internally displaced populations, despite the Guatemalan government's view of them as internally displaced. In both cases, the US Committee argued that nothing prevented repatriation, and that those who had not repatriated by the end of 1998 should be considered to have voluntarily decided to resettle elsewhere, and should therefore no longer be considered displaced (US Committee for Refugees 1999, pp. 266–7).

The Mozambican repatriation process is one of the most massive repatriation processes to date. Between the signing of the peace agreement in 1992 and the end of 1995, almost 1,500,000 refugees and around 3,000,000 IDPs returned home, in a process that was clearly considered successful. As noted above, in 1996 the UNHCR invoked the cessation clause for refugees from Mozambique. It was also concluded that IDPs who wanted to return had done so by the end of 1996 and the rest decided to resettle elsewhere. Therefore, virtually no Mozambicans were officially displaced at the end of 1996 (US Committee for Refugees 1997, p. 82).

As opposed to the cessation clause discussed above, using organized repatriation processes to determine when the condition 'repatriation' is present, is directly related to repatriation, and is, therefore, clearly relevant in the present context. The problem with this approach is its dependence on a determination of what constitutes a successful repatriation process. That determination is done on a case-by-case basis and is related not only to the number of persons who actually repatriate and how well they re-integrate, but also to ambitions of the process. If the aim of a particular organized repatriation process is to end a certain refugee situation by repatriating all

200,000 refugees, then a repatriation of 180,000 can probably be called a success, and the condition 'repatriation' can be considered present. If, however, the aim is to repatriate 25,000 out of a refugee population of 200,000, then success in that regard does not necessarily mean that repatriation – as a condition for peace – should be deemed present. The example illustrates that it is difficult to ignore numbers in an operationalization of refugee repatriation as a condition for peace. An operationalization based only on the success of particular repatriation processes is, therefore, problematic.

## Alternative 3: Major Protracted Refugee Situations

In 2004, the UNHCR introduced the admittedly 'crude measure of refugee populations of 25,000 persons or more who have been in exile for five or more years in developing countries' as a way to identify what was termed as 'major protracted refugee situations'. The number 25,000 is the basis for the designation 'major', and the reference to five years makes a situation 'protracted'. This measure resulted in a list of 37 protracted refugee situations, with a total of 6,200,000 refugees. Palestinian refugees assisted by UNRWA were not included (Loescher and Milner, 2005; UNHCR Executive Committee 2004).

The number 25,000 has attracted attention and criticism, and in *The State of the World's Refugees 2006*, the UNHCR points out that this number should not lead to other smaller groups being excluded from attention. An often cited example of such a group is the Rohingya in Bangladesh. In the early 1990s, they numbered around 250,000, but in recent years most Rohingya refugees have returned to Myanmar. However, around 20,000 Rohingya remain in Bangladesh (US Committee for Refugees 1996, p. 79).

It is possible to use the concept of major protracted refugee situations as a starting point for operationalizing repatriation as a condition for peace. This approach means that the condition 'repatriation' would be present once the number of refugees is fewer than 25,000. If 20,000 remain, as in the case of the Rohingya in Bangladesh, they would still constitute a protracted refugee situation, but no longer a major one. Even if it is likely that those who remain displaced the longest are the ones for whom solutions are the most difficult to find, one could argue that once the number goes below 25,000 the situation is no longer significant enough to prevent peace. Consequently, the condition 'repatriation' may be considered present.

There are some disadvantages to using an absolute number of remaining refugees (whether 25,000 or any other number). First, just like the international law version discussed above, a major protracted refugee situation can be resolved through the use of any of the three durable solutions, not just repatriation. Second, even if a particular situation is resolved primarily through repatriation, it is counterintuitive to argue that the repatriation of 10,000 out of displaced population of 30,000 refugees (leaving 20,000) satisfies the condition 'repatriation', while the repatriation of 750,000 out of 800,000 (leaving 50,000) does not. The number of refugees, who do repatriate is reasonably as important as the number who do not.

The cases of Cambodia, Guatemala and Mozambique illustrate the problem. With around 15,000 remaining refugees, the case of Cambodia would clearly be considered successful. With 26,000 refugees remaining in Mexico, Guatemala would be a borderline case. However, in the case of Mozambique, 106,000 persons lost refugee status when the cessation clause was invoked. Despite being one of the most massive repatriation processes ever, often (though not always) considered very successful, 106,000 remaining refugees show that on the basis of the major protracted refugee situations-approach the condition 'repatriation' was definitely not present.

## Alternative 4: The Relative Number of Returnees

A fourth way to determine when the condition 'repatriation' is present is on the basis of the repatriation that has actually taken place (whether organized or spontaneous). The absolute number of displaced persons who have repatriated could be relevant, but I believe that the share of displaced persons that have repatriated is more important. If 30,000 out of a displaced population of 40,000 (75 per cent) have repatriated, this is more to the point than if 50,000 out of 200,000 (25 per cent) have repatriated. Similarly, to use the example above, if 750,000 out of a displaced population of 800,000 (94 per cent) have repatriated, this is more to the point than if 10,000 out of 30,000 (33 per cent) have repatriated.

It is reasonable to argue that a 75 per cent repatriation rate is a better indicator of the condition 'repatriation' than a 25 per cent repatriation rate. It is not obvious what rate to require for the condition 'repatriation' to be present. There is no theoretical basis in previous research for determining what repatriation rate is most useful for separating cases of repatriation from cases of non-repatriation. Another look at Cambodia, Guatemala and Mozambique gives an indication of what rates can be expected in cases that are considered successful (data from various years of the World Refugee Survey).

For Cambodia, the peak year of displacement was 1991 with 392,700 refugees. By 1993, when the official repatriation process was completed, 377,500 refugees had repatriated – a repatriation rate of 96 per cent. For Guatemala, the peak year of displacement was 1989 with 58,700 refugees. By 1997, when the US Committee for Refugees argued that there was no longer any reason to consider anyone displaced, and that all those who had not yet repatriated should be considered to have chosen to resettle elsewhere, 31,628 refugees had repatriated – a repatriation rate of 54 per cent. For Mozambique, the peak year of displacement was 1992 with 1,725,000 refugees. By 1996, when the cessation clause was invoked by the UNHCR, 1,396,000 refugees had repatriated – a repatriation rate of 81 per cent.

A conservative suggestion would be to use Mozambique's repatriation rate of around 80 per cent to guide the determination of whether the condition 'repatriation' is present in other cases. This would mean that the condition was present in the Cambodian case, but absent in the Guatemalan case. It is also possible to be more generous, and use Guatemala's repatriation rate of around 50 per cent when judging other cases. This would mean that the condition was present in the Cambodian case, but absent in the Guatemalan case. It is also possible to be more generous, and use Guatemala's repatriation rate of around 50 per cent when judging other cases.

This approach also has its weaknesses. Most importantly, there is no theoretical basis for selecting the repatriation rate used to determine whether the condition 'repatriation' is present or absent.

## Conclusion: Refugee Repatriation as a Condition for Peace

The various approaches discussed above build on different logics as to why refugee repatriation would constitute a condition for peace. According to the *refugee law-approach* and the *major protracted refugee situations-approach*, refugee repatriation is a condition for peace because the continued presence of large-scale displacement is seen as an impediment to peace. Two underlying principles may be at work: the refugees themselves may constitute a direct security threat if they have, or try to acquire, the capacity to force their way back (as in the case of Rwanda), or, when the position of the refugees is very weak, it may still be impossible for those who represent the refugees to accept a peace agreement that leaves the refugee situation unresolved (the Palestinian situation comes to mind). According to this logic, what is required to make peace possible is to end large-scale displacement, and as pointed out above, this goal can be achieved through any of the three durable solutions to refugee situations – return/repatriation, local integration and resettlement.

The repatriation processes-approach and the relative number of returnees-approach, on the other hand, build on the logic that establishment of peace after armed conflict is dependent on the return of displaced persons. Here as well, two underlying principles may be at work: the returning refugees' contribution to rebuilding society can be said to be indispensable, or their presence as such is important because of its impact on the social structure of the society – particularly in cases of ethnic cleansing that needs to be reversed (both principles commonly expressed regarding Kosovo and Bosnia-Herzegovina). According to this logic, local integration and resettlement are inadequate solutions to the refugee situation. Repatriation is the only effectual one.

The refugee law-approach and the major protracted refugee situations-approach are both too loosely related to repatriation to provide a useful basis for an operationalization of refugee repatriation as a condition for peace. The repatriation processes-approach is clearly related to repatriation, but it is also vulnerable to different levels of ambition of repatriation processes. All three are insensitive to the relative size of refugee situations. The relative number of returnees-approach is both directly related to repatriation and sensitive to the relative size of refugee situations, and is, therefore, probably the most promising alternative. The problem with the relative number of returnees-approach identified above (the lack of a theoretical basis for selecting the repatriation rate used to determine whether the condition 'repatriation' is present or absent) can be significantly reduced with the use of fuzzy sets, including the 'dialogue between theory and data' that is an important component of fuzzy set social science (Ragin, 2000, pp. 35–42). The other three approaches can be included in the analysis without being part of the condition 'repatriation'. So can other potentially relevant factors, such as ethnic diffusion (related to the reversal of ethnic cleansing) and political partition (the proxy measure used by Kaufmann and by Sambanis).

Chapter Seven

# CATAPULTING CONFLICTS OR PROPELLING PEACE: DIASPORAS AND CIVIL WARS

## Jonathan Hall and Ashok Swain

### Introduction

In research on armed conflict, a debate is emerging over the influence of diasporas on civil wars in their homelands. Many prominent scholars claim that diasporas are especially prone to political extremism and the use of violence to resolve political disputes. In their view, remaining in the homeland and experiencing the atrociousness of war sobers previously idealistic goals of gaining territorial sovereignty or state power and tempers rather than exacerbates tensions between groups. Those who migrate during civil conflicts however avoid the moderating costs of war. While abroad, diasporas are empowered by economic upliftment, and by the freedom to pursue extremist agendas unobstructed by homeland government oversight. Other scholars have challenged these views, offering evidence that diasporas are actively involved in peacebuilding and conflict resolution in their homelands. In this chapter we provide an examination of the arguments offered in support of these opposing claims. In the process, the debate is situated within the broader context of globalization and the challenges and opportunities it presents for building peace. By way of conclusion, we present some of our own reflections on the arguments for viewing diasporas as extremists and/or moderates, and point out some possible directions for future research that would help to bring forward the debate over diasporas and their roles in conflict and peace in the homeland.

### Civil War and the Challenge of Building Peace

Armed conflict peaked in the early 1990s as the cold war came to an end in Europe and new states were formed in the aftermath of the collapse of the

Soviet Union and Yugoslavia. Since that time the world has experienced a precipitous decline in the number and severity of international and civil wars (Gleditch *et al.* 2002; Lacina *et al.* 2006; Mack, 2005; Marshall and Gurr, 2005; Mueller, 2004). Today's armed conflict levels are the lowest; they have been since the decades immediately following the Second World War. The humanitarian effects of civil war, including the number of civilians killed and forced migration, reflect similar trends (Melander *et al.* 2006). However encouraging these global patterns may be, as reports of daily violence in places such as Iraq, Afghanistan, Sudan and Somalia poignantly illustrate, human suffering induced by conflict is far from disappearing. Although international wars are now limited, civil wars continue on every continent of the planet. Each year thousands lose their lives in battle or are victims of one-sided violence, and many thousands more are forcibly displaced from their homes. In 2005 alone the world witnessed 31 armed conflicts fought in 22 locations around the world (see Table 1).

*Table 1.* **States Experiencing Civil War in 2005**

| Location | No. conflicts | New refugees | Total refugees |
|---|---|---|---|
| Afghanistan | 1 | 12,310 | 1,908,052 |
| Algeria | 1 | 820 | 12,006 |
| Azerbaijan | 1 | 2,136 | 23,365 |
| Burundi | 1 | 30,179 | 438,663 |
| Chad | 1 | 889 | 48,400 |
| Colombia | 1 | 12,358 | 60,415 |
| Ethiopia | 2 | 9,842 | 65,293 |
| India | 5 | 896 | 16,275 |
| Indonesia | 1 | 8,653 | 34,384 |
| Iran | 1 | 11,938 | 98,722 |
| Iraq | 1 | 21,299 | 262,142 |
| Israel | 1 | 608 | 350,305 |
| Myanmar | 3 | 30,372 | 164,864 |
| Nepal | 1 | 558 | 2,065 |
| Philippines | 2 | 85 | 465 |
| Russia | 1 | 18,633 | 102,965 |
| Sri Lanka | 1 | 3,666 | 108,059 |
| Sudan | 1 | 87,799 | 693,267 |
| Thailand | 1 | 224 | 424 |
| Turkey | 2 | 4,573 | 170,131 |
| Uganda | 1 | 2,670 | 34,170 |
| United States | 1 | 5 | 683 |
| 22 Locations | 31 Conflicts | 260,513 | 4,595,115 |

Sources: Harbom and Wallensteen (2006); UN (2006).[1]

The effects of these armed conflicts continue to be devastating to the collective well-being of nations. As witnessed recently in the aerial assault of Lebanon by Israeli warplanes in the summer of 2006, poor countries are further submerged by the disruption of the formal economy, the destruction of physical infrastructure and renewed tensions between social groups. While many states struggle to cope with the ongoing effects of wars, others are struggling to consolidate recent gains. Peace agreements have taken place in one third of the 121 conflicts active since 1989 (Harbom *et al.* 2006, p. 622). After the cessation of violence, societies cope with precarious situations of insecurity, as identities and intergroup tensions forged in the caldron of violence persist in the face of attempts to reinvigorate the economy, rebuild infrastructure and fashion a new national ethos.

The process of rebuilding the economy is challenged by the dynamics of war-induced environmental disasters made worse by deregulation and increased resource extraction during and after conflict, when exit of the population from the formal economy to the informal and illicit economies combined with a breakdown of state legal structures and traditional means of regulation lead to a tragedy of the commons (Conca, 2006). Even international aid and humanitarian assistance do not escape complications, sometimes compounding environmental problems by increasing the capacity of local actors to extract resources before sustainable practices have been implemented. Aid, relief and financial investments themselves may increase the risk of conflict through uneven distribution, altering the power relations between actors, providing legitimacy to illegal groups, and leading to security dilemmas and a lack of credible and sustainable commitment. In Bosnia-Herzegovina for example, even a decade after the termination of violence reconciling political differences between ethnic groups continues to be a daunting task. Among both local political elites and their constituencies, opposition remains strong to international nation-building efforts and attempts at constructing an inclusive national identity (Kostic, 2007).

The international community has taken a more active role in supporting democratic transition and consolidation since the end of the cold war (Pevehouse, 2002; Ottoway and Carothers, 2000). However, research on the promotion of democracy has not been very optimistic about its efficacy in ethnically divided societies (Bunce, 2005). In the aftermath of severe violent conflict, divisions along ethnic dimensions often prove highly durable and resistant to be influenced by external actors. Without reconciliation, prospects for democratic consolidation and development are extremely limited by a lack of cooperation among ethno-political groups and the possibility of a return to ethnic war. A pressing question for the international community is how to prevent, manage and successfully resolve civil wars, fought within multi-ethnic states, the effects of which are felt locally, regionally and globally.

## Globalization, Diasporas and Homeland Conflicts

Internal armed conflicts and their effects do not occur in isolation, but are spread across borders. Globalization further facilitates this diffusion process through the increasing movement of people, capital, information, goods and services around the world without reference to national borders. Through ethnic ties, refugee movements, cross-border sanctuaries, and the spread of international terrorism, violence spans the boundaries of states, incorporating new actors or creating new conflicts. War economies are linked through migrant networks to the global economy. Global communications deliver around the world the sense of insecurity experienced at the local level during civil wars. And the costs of war are shared internationally through their effects on economic relations, the accommodation and repatriation of refugees and asylum seekers, and the demand for international development aid, peacemaking and peacebuilding which require taking risks and the investment of substantial monetary, diplomatic and military resources.

A central element of globalization is the circulation of migrants. The world is currently experiencing a mass wave of international migration. Although recent figures suggest that refugee flows may have stabilized (UN 2006), global migration is increasing exponentially. According to UN estimates, the global stock of immigrants rose more than 30 per cent in the twenty-year period between 1960 and 1980, from 75.9 million to 99.8 million (UN 2004). However in the twenty years between 1980 and 2000, there was over 75 per cent increase in the number of immigrants worldwide, as the total stock reached 174.9 million. It is impossible to estimate the number of people who migrate voluntarily to escape the costs of war. However in terms of forced migration across borders, refugees in the world totaled nearly 8.4 million at the end of 2005, over half of which are displaced from states in which there are active civil wars (see Table 1).

Conflicts directly and indirectly force people to migrate. Other push and pull factors such as environmental degradation, natural disaster, poverty at home and economic opportunity abroad also account for global trends in migration. This leads to the dispersion of a 'nation' that was formerly concentrated in one place. These communities constitute a 'diaspora' when an orientation towards the homeland and boundaries between the dispersed community and the host community are maintained over time (Brubaker, 2005). Diasporas are becoming an active and potentially crucial link between migrant receiving countries and conflicts in war-torn countries of origin. In this way they offer both challenges and opportunities. On the one hand, members of diaspora communities have been found to finance war efforts and to promote extremist ideologies and uncompromising political views in the homeland (cf. Anderson, 1992; Collier, 2000; Duffield, 2001; Kaldor, 2001). On the other hand, a nascent body of research has begun to identify their peacebuilding potential (cf. Mohamoud, 2005; Newland and Patrick, 2004; Zunzer, 2004). Diasporas have campaigned abroad for conflict resolution in their homelands and supported ongoing peace processes. They provide a major source of investment and tourism to war-ravaged economies, and supply aid and relief via family-to-family remittances to their homelands in times of crisis. They are able to use their influence with warring parties in the homeland to reach a negotiated settlement (Cochrane, 2007). And in the aftermath of war, they provide trained human resources to the homeland in support of democratic consolidation and post-conflict reconstruction (Fagen and Bump, 2006).

In sum, scholarship has highlighted the potential for diasporas to promote both conflict and peace. The emergence of these opposing perspectives in research on civil war reveals a controversy with two main components. The first is theoretical and has to do with understanding the effects of either remaining in the homeland and experiencing the costs of war, or avoiding those costs by virtue of being in the diaspora. The second element of the controversy involves evaluating the catalogues of available evidence that supports the respective claims. Below we present the opposing theoretical perspectives and review the available evidence on both sides of the controversy over diasporas and their roles in conflict and peace in their homelands.

## The Controversy: Diasporas and Civil Wars in Their Homelands

### Diasporas as Extremists

Regarding the negative influence of diasporas on civil wars in their homelands, two debates among scholars that had the greatest impact are 'greed vs grievance' (Berdal and Keen, 1997; Berdal and Malone, 2000; Collier, 1998, 2000; Collier and Hoeffler, 2004; Grossman, 1999; Keen, 1998) and 'old wars vs new wars' (Anderson, 1992; Duffield, 2001; Gray, 1997; Holsti, 1996; Kaldor, 2001; Kaldor and Vashee, 1998; Shaw, 1999; Snow, 1996). Within both debates, no one disputes the concept that diasporas are violence-promoting political extremists, but the causal mechanisms translating extremism in the hostland into increased conflict in the homeland identified by each diverge slightly. While the 'greed' argument considers diaspora financial contributions to rebels to be the crucial mechanism, the 'new wars' argument views diaspora political support and ideological influence in addition to financial support as important mechanisms fuelling 'new wars'.

Proponents of the 'greed' argument contend that economic incentives, rather than socio-economic or political injustice, are adequate to explain the outbreak, duration and intensity of civil war. Modelled as an industry, rebel groups are motivated by economic benefit and are dependent upon opportunity and an adequate supply of resources. Contributions from the diaspora are seen as a key resource to rebels in civil wars. After the cold war ended, in most of the cases the support to rebels provided by the superpowers waned (Lacina, 2006). In light of this reduction in state sponsorship, rebels increasingly seek the support of other external sources, a key example being diaspora finance. Empowered by economic development, with access to international banking and travel, diasporas are provided the means by which they support their extreme political views through financial contributions to insurgent groups unobstructed by homeland government oversight.

The motives of the diaspora for supporting rebellion are theorized to be hatred, romanticized views of the war, and the protection of an identity formed around grievances (Collier, 2000, p. 14; Collier and Hoeffler, 2004, p. 575). Their opportunity to support rebellion is their relative wealth and access to technology granted by asylum in industrialized states and globalization, which supplies the means to transfer money more easily between hostland and homeland. Living abroad, diasporas avoid the costs of war and thus evade the moderating experience of it. During periods of peace, 'rebellion-specific capital' in the homeland is thought to decrease as tensions ease, while hatreds harboured by the diaspora remain strong (Collier and Hoeffler, 2004, p. 575). Acknowledging the limits of their investigation,[2] Collier and Hoeffler (2004, p. 588) are confident in asserting a causal relationship between diaspora remittances and civil war onset, citing similar findings in case study research.

There are numerous examples of rebel groups receiving direct financial support from members of diaspora communities (cf. Adamson, 2005; Angoustures and Pascal, 1996). The Real Irish Republican Army and Irish Republican Army, the Kosovo Liberation Army and the Kurdish Workers Party (PKK) serve as prominent examples. Perhaps the most frequently cited case is that of the Tamil diaspora and its support of the Liberation Tigers of Tamil Eelam (LTTE) in Sri Lanka (cf. Byman et al. 2001; Gunaratna, 2003). Although the Tamil diaspora was first established during British colonization of South Asia, the majority of Tamils in the diaspora were displaced from Sri Lanka by the eruption of civil war in the late 1980s (Fair, 2005). Donations to the LTTE from abroad, both voluntary and those gained through extortion, originate largely from wealthy states with large ethnic Tamil communities, such as Australia, Canada, England and Scandinavian countries. According to recent estimates, diaspora donations constitute approximately 80 per cent of the LTTE's 82 million dollar annual revenue (Gunaratna, 2000). The LTTE maintains substantial assets within the diaspora, and invests in business ventures with Tamil entrepreneurs from which it gains substantial profits. The diaspora facilitates the financial infrastructure of the LTTE through the operation of its offices in over 40 countries, not to mention related non-governmental organizations that directly or indirectly finance the LTTE. While Colombo and like-minded governments view such activities with distress, they fall within the bounds of the law in states where the LTTE is viewed as a legitimate organization. However, the Sri Lankan Tamil diaspora has also been implicated in the illicit trafficking of weapons, people and narcotics in support of the insurgency in the homeland (Fair, 2005).

Proponents of the 'new wars' argument claim that the nature of warfare fundamentally changed around the end of the cold war. While 'old wars' were motivated by inclusive ideologies (e.g. nationalism, democracy and socialism), were fought between states, and were characterized by military restraint; 'new wars' are motivated by exclusive identities (e.g. religion, ethnicity and new exclusivist nationalisms), are fought within failing or failed states, and are characterized by unrestrained warfare (Kaldor, 2001). In the post-cold war conflicts, the belligerents – a myriad of non-state actors – aim not to resolve conflict, but rather to sustain it, to take advantage of economic opportunities afforded by looting, rent seeking, taxing or siphoning off humanitarian aid and remittances, and by illicit trade.

Diasporas form an important aspect of the new globalized war economy. In addition, they provide political support to insurgencies and propagate exclusive ideologies. Diasporas supply financial support through direct contributions and the facilitation of smuggling between conflict zones and global markets (Duffield, 2001). As lobbyists, propagandists, spokesmen and grassroots organizers, diasporas lend their political support to insurgencies in the homeland. Their unique position also allows them to go beyond playing a mere supporting role in the conflict. Through manipulation of media, propaganda and publications, diaspora communities seek to influence the identity of the global diaspora community, as seen, for example, in online forums such as www.tamilnation.org or www.somalinet.com, which extend their communicative reach to the global level.

With little accountability to their homeland kin (Anderson, 1992), diasporas are thought to selfishly propagate exclusive identities, such as ethnic nationalism, at the expense of inclusive identities, such as those associated with cosmopolitanism (Kaldor, 2001; 2003). By influencing the perceptions and identity formation of the 'nation' (Shain and Barth, 2003), diasporas embolden ethnic entrepreneurs in the homeland and constrain the political choices of otherwise more moderate leaders, increasing the likelihood of violence. For these reasons, proponents of the 'new wars' argument refer to diasporas as 'long-distance nationalists' (Anderson, 1992) or 'regressive globalizers' (Anheier *et al.* 2003).

There are numerous examples of diasporas acting politically to support ethnic kin in the homeland One prominent example is the Jewish diaspora and its activities through the pro-Israel lobby in Washington – The American Israel Public Affairs Committee (AIPAC) – which arguably has been successful in influencing the United States to pursue a pro-Israel stance even when the cost of doing so exceeds the benefits (Mearsheimer and Walt, 2006). The influence of the Iraqi diaspora has been implicated in the Bush administration's decision to invade Iraq in 2003 (Vertovec, 2005). During the cold war, the United States, the Soviet Union and their allies followed asylum policies which encouraged citizens from the opposing blocks to 'defect' (Gibney and Hansen, 2003). In many cases of insurgency, the core leadership, or elements of it, often spend time abroad, or are forced to lead the insurgency from the diaspora, as in the case of Yasser Arafat and the PLO staging its operations against Israel from Jordan in the 60s, Lebanon in the 70s, and Tunisia in the 80s. It is difficult to pinpoint through case studies the way in which the identity of homeland kin is shaped by the diaspora. Part of the reason for this is the difficulty of establishing the causal direction in the relationship. While some argue that the diaspora may be a strong influence, others argue that identities are simply reproduced in diaspora communities (Brown, 2004). However, one element of their identity that has arguably influenced the identity of the nation is their attachment to the homeland territory (Lyons, 2004). The mechanism through which this occurs is the success of their support for territorial sovereignty or independence in the homeland, driven by the enthusiasm for such an agenda among members of the diaspora. The case of Sikh diaspora support for territorial independence in the Punjab is illustrative (Fair, 2005). There is evidence that the view of the Punjab as the Sikh homeland originated in India in the early 1900s. Yet political mobilization for this objective did not occur until the 70s and 80s, during which the diaspora played an active and crucial role in fomenting the insurgency, providing critical financial and political support, making public speeches and campaigning for support. In fact, the term Khalistan itself originated in diaspora circles, first in London, and became prominent in the homeland after a much-publicized speech in the early 1980s by a prominent member of the diaspora. While events such as Operation Blue Star to flush out militants from the Sikh holy shrine in Amritsar and the anti-Sikh riots following the assassination of Indira Gandhi equally inflamed support for independence among those in the homeland and those living in the diaspora, the ability to campaign abroad and harness international media resources enables the diaspora to greatly influence the discourse in which homeland conflicts are understood.

### Diasporas as Moderates

Others dispute the claim that diaspora financial contributions, political activities and ideological influence contribute overwhelmingly to war efforts in the homeland. Within the quantitative literature on civil war, a consistent finding is that war is driven, among other things, by poverty and economic inequality (Sambanis, 2002). The size of diaspora remittances to poor countries is thought to be nearly double that of international aid (Sørensen, 2002). As part of a larger stream of financial transfers between diasporas and their homelands, remittances are thought to play an important role in preventing conflict (Martin, 2001; Van Hear, 2002; Van Hear et al. 2004); reducing the effects of wars (Fagen and Bump, 2006; Goodhand et al. 2000); and contributing to post conflict reconstruction (Cheran, 2003; Koser and Van Hear, 2003). According to Naim (2002), migration provides 'new opportunities for trade and foreign investment as well as a powerful font of entrepreneurial energy'. As a major source of investment and tourism in states where poverty and war otherwise discourage it, and as key donors to charity, diasporas are drivers of economic development in their homelands (Fagen and Bump, 2006; Mohamoud, 2005). In the midst of ongoing wars, these resources are largely channelled to populations directly affected by the violence (Van Hear, 2002). By protecting the livelihood of those who stay behind to defend their assets, remittances reduce the scope of forced migration (Fagen and Bump, 2006). And by supporting basic services such as healthcare and education, remittances sustain the structures that foster social capital and provide a basis for future economic development (Goodhand et al. 2000).

Through lobbying hostland governments and international organizations and aiding processes of transition, diasporas may play an important role in achieving political compromise and non-violent conflict resolution in their homelands. For example, the Greek lobby in the US House of Representatives has actively lobbied the American government to be proactive in its stance towards conflict resolution in Cyprus, and the German–Cypriot Forum has lobbied German and EU Parliaments to continue the momentum of recent conflict resolution efforts (Zunzer, 2004, pp. 30–2). In Britain, a group of parliamentarians have lobbied for greater engagement of the British government in conflict resolution between Greece and Turkey, a result attributed to their dependence upon Cypriot–British constituencies. Other forms of pressure may be applied to homeland governments and rebels in order to promote non-violent conflict resolution and democratic development. For example, diaspora organizations pressure warring parties in the homeland to refrain from violence and engage in non-violent modes of interaction by discovering and drawing attention to their human rights abuses (Zunzer, 2004, p. 25).

A prominent example is the influence that the Irish American diaspora community has had on efforts to achieve a settlement to the conflict in Northern Ireland, for example in the successfully lobbying and support of then president Bill Clinton and the achievement on 10 April 1998 of the Good Friday Agreement (Cochrane, 2007).

Furthermore, by promoting non-violent forms of conflict resolution in the homeland, diasporas may avert civil war altogether. Campaigning by the Philippine diaspora is credited with an important role in peacefully unseating the Marcos regime, which might otherwise have led the country to a civil war (Newland and Patrick, 2004, p. 27). Similarly, South African diaspora were to a large extent responsible for the success of the anti-apartheid movement. During peace processes, diasporas are able to provide crucial professional resources, such as representation and consultancy. For example, members of the diaspora either negotiated directly on behalf of the warring parties or were involved as advisors during talks between Afghan factions in 2001, the Sri Lankan LTTE and the Government of Sri Lanka in 2002–3, and between Somali warlords in 2003–4 (Zunzer, 2004). Diaspora groups can help the international mediators to establish contact with the warring group leaders to facilitate the peace process. Their involvement may also provide much needed trust and assurance to both the warring parties and also to the mediators to engage in the peace process. Giving insights to the local issues, historical complexities and personal characteristics of the group leaders, diaspora can really provide invaluable help to the mediators to make right and appropriate moves before and during negotiations. During periods of transition, diaspora provide new ideas, values, skills and know-how important for the creation of institutions (for example during the drafting of the Eritrean constitution in 1993), and for the strengthening of civil society, the private sector and government infrastructure (for example by advising non-profit organizations, facilitating business networks between hostlands and homelands), and by consulting or even filling newly created government posts, as in the recently formed Afghan and Iraqi governments (Cheran, 2003; Mohamoud, 2005; Nassery, 2003; Zunzer, 2004).

By disseminating moderate perspectives, diasporas may influence their homeland kin towards supporting non-violent conflict resolution and democratic development. Diasporas usually enjoy a superior social status in their homelands. Due to their access to the freedom, wealth and knowledge needed to create and disseminate various forms of media, diasporas are particularly capable of influencing the identity and interests of their homeland kin (Levitt 1998; Shain and Barth 2003). Where migrants and refugees form diaspora communities in democratic states, the ideas and attitudes they develop during the process of integration into the hostland (e.g. preferences for political compromise, tolerance, human rights, gender equality etc.) may, through their dissemination via diaspora-controlled media, encourage more pro-peace attitudes among their homeland kin. Through their work as artists, intellectuals and journalists, many Bosnians living in Western Europe aim to spread a multicultural and inclusive view of politics in Bosnia-Herzegovina (Al-Ali *et al.* 2001b, p. 624). In the Sri Lankan diaspora, the growth of 'Tamil diasporic literature' includes a broad range of perspectives on topics such as 'peace and war', 'free expression', 'strengthening of civil society' and 'changing gender roles' (Cheran, 2003, p. 18), revealing the creation of an important social space in which the free exchange of ideas thrives, a process far less extensive in the homeland due to extensive government monitoring. Owing to lack of press freedom in Sri Lanka, these discussions offer an important avenue for increasing understanding, discovering and promoting new approaches to conflict resolution in the homeland. There are a number of Tamil organizations in North America and Europe who, albeit often anonymously, are critical of the approach of the LTTE (Zunzer, 2004, p. 25). Examples include the Tamil Eelam Development Organization (Canada), the Tamil Rehabilitation Organization (Europe, Canada and the USA), and the Tamil Information Centre (United Kingdom). By criticizing homeland governments and rebels for engaging in human rights abuses, diaspora civil society organizations decrease incentives for violence and increase incentives for engaging in dialogue and compromise.

## Conclusion

In light of ongoing globalization, environmental degradation, economic maldevelopment and violent conflict in many parts of the world, high levels of transnational migration flows will continue for the foreseeable future (Salehyan, 2005). Both home and host countries share a strong interest in understanding how diasporas may be encouraged to support peacebuilding efforts rather than foment ethnic nationalism and war. For homelands, moderating key diaspora communities and supporting their peacebuilding efforts may help to prevent the development of transnational insurgencies and terrorist networks that might otherwise prove difficult and costly to defeat. For hostlands, it is important to prevent, or avoid inadvertently fuelling, conflicts that lead to humanitarian crises, deteriorating relations with homelands, and greater externalized costs paid by the international community (e.g. accommodating refugee outflows and subsequent repatriation endeavours, demand for humanitarian aid and development assistance, and international terrorism).

Diasporas are diverse sets of communities which, though spread across state borders, possess a sense of shared identity. While some elements within them have supported war efforts, others have promoted peaceful conflict resolution. This leads us to a crucial element in the debate that has not been adequately explored: how do different diaspora communities become more extreme or more moderate? Their characteristics are probably not static, but rather change over time in response to particular circumstances. Diaspora communities not only respond to the changing character of the conflicts in their homelands, they also initiate and lead insurgencies or peacebuilding efforts. What are the most influential factors affecting diaspora identities, interests and capabilities?

These questions have yet to be adequately addressed in the emerging debate over the role of diasporas in conflict and peace processes. One reason for this has to do with the lack of theoretical development on both sides of the debate, although the impoverishment of ideas is more acute on the 'diasporas as moderates' side. Below we outline the theoretical components of the 'diasporas as extremists' argument, juxtaposing these with their logical theoretical counterpoints.

The political economy of civil war literature views diasporas as extreme by virtue of their being in the diaspora. The experience of life outside the homeland is thought to affect their capabilities as well as interests. However, understanding what influences their capabilities is its key preoccupation. In terms of the factors that shape diaspora interests, three main elements are identified: 1) grievances/hatred, 2) attachment to territory and 3) idealism. Diaspora grievances are born out of the conflict itself, particularly the experience of violence. Hatreds, formed during war and displacement, remain strong among those in the diaspora, whereas their kin in the homeland are tempered by the reality of war and, in peacetime, the experience of positive gains. The attachment of diaspora to the homeland territory is theorized to be shaped by their often-violent displacement from, and myth of return to, the homeland, which provides a central narrative and set of symbols around which to organize diaspora identity. Diasporas are thought to be idealistic due to their distance from the conflict, which renders their understanding of it simplistic, opening the door to idealism or romanticism. While those in the homeland are faced with the complexity of the conflict, members of the diaspora construct a more simplified and thus idealistic or romantic view of reality. While identity and interest are necessary, they are construed as basically constant, emerging from the experience of being in the diaspora, and thus deemed largely irrelevant in explaining patterns of their behaviour.

The key to explaining patterns of diaspora support for armed conflict in the homeland is believed to be the structure of their resources and opportunities, which together form the extent of their capabilities. This theorizes two main causes of diaspora extremism. By virtue of living abroad, they 1) avoid the experience of war (decreased costs), and 2) enjoy greater wealth and freedom (increased opportunities).

While this explanation follows a logical cost/benefit analysis approach, it lacks rigorous development and thus falls prey to oversimplification. It is far from clear that the experience of violence in the homeland can be considered a cost that makes support of violence less likely. Violent actions and reactions spiral during civil wars. While war is undoubtedly a costly endeavour and requires adequate resources, the experience of violence is threatening to survival, and given sufficient resources these threats will often be met with counter-threats. Although members of the diaspora arguably have more resources at their disposal, they have less of an immediate reason to participate in such cyclical violence. However, due to security dilemmas, when, for example, defensive preparations are interpreted as offensive intentions, those in the homeland will make plans for war and carry out preventive, pre-emptive and retributive attacks. They clearly have more of an immediate reason to do so in comparison to their kin abroad who escape the pressure of preoccupations with immediate security.

Furthermore, the situation in the diaspora is characterized by much more than simply increased opportunities. In many host societies, there exist strong incentives to eschew violent approaches to resolving political disputes in the homeland. For one, host state governments are often held responsible for the actions of their citizens and thus discourage them from undermining the governments of other states. An obvious example of this is the magnitude of attention states give to avoid being labelled supporters of terrorism in the current global context, and the proliferation of international agreements on approaches to counterterrorism. Even the diasporas themselves have strong reasons to avoid incurring new restrictions on sending money and investments to and from hostlands and conflict areas, which would adversely affect diasporas and their family in the homeland. Second, it is logical to assume that integration into liberal and democratic societies should to some extent encourage the adoption of new and more moderate views of the means through which political change should be pursued. Tolerance and dialogue are normative elements of many host societies, which arguably should have an effect on the diaspora community. Host countries and societies most likely play a defining role in turning diasporas into peace entrepreneurs as opposed to conflict instigators. More importantly, diasporas themselves would like to end conflict, because the post-conflict peacebuilding period provides enormous economic opportunities.

Similarly, the account of diaspora interests is also incomplete and thus problematic. First, a great deal more people than those directly displaced by violence form the diaspora. The current stock of migrants in the world totals approximately 174 million, of which the total number of refugees, approximately 8.4 million, makes up only a fraction. Thus large numbers of diasporas do not harbour grievances born out of the experience of violence. Furthermore, internal displacement is equally atrocious to displacement abroad, a fact that balances the equation of displacement-induced grievances between homeland and hostland. In fact, as mentioned above, grievances are likely to increase in the homeland during conflict due to the cyclical nature of the dynamics of violence. In peacetime, the kin in the homeland are plagued with great uncertainty and insecurity, which, as mentioned earlier in the case of Bosnia-Herzegovina, renders reconciliation between ethnic groups extremely difficult. While in the diaspora, as mentioned in the case of Sri Lanka, space is provided for interethnic dialogue to occur in a context of security guaranteed by the hostland. Regarding diaspora idealism and romanticism, such as their attachment to goals of sovereignty or independence, diasporas are arguably no longer isolated from what is happening in their homelands in the current era of increased global connectivity and communication. Through personal connections, travel and the use of information technology, the diaspora is very likely to achieve an intimate perspective of homeland conditions.

The argument for accounting for the causes of civil war by modelling the rebel movement as an industry requiring resources and opportunity is based upon the notion that grievances are so ubiquitous that they cannot explain changes over time in the outbreak, duration and intensity of civil war. Conceptually, considering the role of the diaspora in civil wars challenges this model in at least two ways. First, the diaspora may go beyond playing merely a supporting role to ethnic counterparts in the homeland, influencing the formation of preferences. And second, there is no reason to turn the assumptions made in the political economy of war literature about the constant nature of grievances onto the diaspora. They may require resources and opportunity to engage in conflict, however it is entirely possible, even more logical, to assume that their preferences will be shaped by emigration from their homeland and integration into hostland society. Theoretically, the identity of the diaspora cannot be assumed to be static, but rather should be seen as a perspective undergoing a process of change. The same could be said for their counterparts in the homeland. To move forward the debate over the role of diasporas in conflict and peace, the various elements influencing this process should be fleshed out, evaluated and comprehended along side a more rigorous examination of the resources and opportunities provided by the experience of life in the diaspora.

Chapter Eight

# UN PEACE OPERATIONS AS NORM ENTREPRENEURS: THE CHALLENGE OF ACHIEVING COMMUNICATIVE ACTION ON HUMAN RIGHTS

## Katarina Månsson

## Introduction

The far-reaching scope of peacekeeping mandates and the multitude of actors deployed in contemporary peace operations render the application of peace operations as human rights mechanism, much more difficult compared to traditional UN human rights mechanisms. An often overlooked but significant challenge for peace operations acting in such capacity is the establishment of mutual understanding and agreement on human rights between civilian and military peace actors, and the impact of such an agreement – or absence thereof – on the success of peace operations. This aspect involves issues as diverse as inter-agency cooperation, cultural differences between military and civilian actors and how international human rights law is accepted, embraced and 'operationalized' in such complex multicultural and politicized settings. Above all, it addresses the issue of how and under which conditions human rights standards and norms are best advocated by peace actors.[1]

The aim of this article is to examine how UN peace operations may enhance their potential of promoting human rights by analysing how peace actors communicate and reach agreement on human rights. The underlying presumption is that effective human rights promotion and protection is contingent on the existence of a common understanding of human rights among different components of a peace operation. Such examination will be undertaken by analysing data collected in the field in the light of discourse theories of human rights, drawing primarily on Jürgen Habermas' theory of communicative action. The analysis is premised on the suggestion that the institutional design of UN peace operations may either facilitate or undermine inter-agency communication on human rights. To explore this hypothesis, the operations deployed in Kosovo (United Nations Interim Administration Mission in Kosovo (UNMIK)/Kosovo Force (KFOR)) and in the Democratic Republic of the Congo (MONUC) are analysed, focussing on integration of human rights within the police and military components.

## UN Peace Operations as Norm Entrepreneurs

An examination of peacekeeping understood as a human rights tool contingent on communication and mutual understanding on human rights necessitates a novel theoretical approach to the study of peace operations. To date, most studies on peace operations have focused on the legal and political dimensions of such missions from a generic, system-wide perspective. International relations scholars have presented important insights to understand the human rights dimension of peace operations in liberal democratic peace theory as well as in critical theory (Paris 2004; Pugh 2004; Williams *et al.* 2004). Scholars of the former theoretical strand suggest that peace operations are instruments deployed to maintain stable peace across the globe by promoting liberal political and economic practices within states (Bellamy *et al.* 2004: *supra* note 2, p. 26). Critical theorists, on the other hand, claim that the liberal democratic agenda reflects a deliberate perpetuation of unequal distribution of power within the international system. Established by 'rich and powerful states and institutions', UN peace operations constitute 'arenas for acting out power relations' (Simmons and Martin, 2002, p. 194) and thus illustrate 'the disempowering effects of statist sovereignty and globalization' (Pugh 2004, p. 50).

In contrast to such theoretical focus on power politics and interests, social constructivists emphasize the potential role of institutions in advocating and shaping global norms. Institutions, they argue, reflect not only states' ambitions to maximize political gains but also commonly shared meanings and values which facilitate the maintenance of an international social order (Kratochwil 2000, p. 56). Based on the trust of institutions' ability to create and reflect intersubjective normative understandings, the theory of the 'norm life cycle' (Schmitz and Sikkink, 2002, p. 52; Finnemore and Sikkink, 1998) appears particularly useful when developing a new theory on UN peace operations as a human rights mechanism. In this interpretation, I argue that UN peace operations may be construed as instruments for human rights protection and promotion in that they may set in motion the constitutive three stages of a 'norm life cycle': norm emergence, norm cascade and norm internalization Briefly summarized here, peace operations may perform the role of norm entrepreneurs by introducing a new legal framework, that of international human rights law, which 'emerge in a highly contested normative space where they must compete with other norms and perceptions of interest' (Finnemore and Sikkink, 1998, p. 44). Norm emergence also requires 'organizational platforms' which, in this context, are represented by human rights components since they carry the main responsibility for coordination of human rights issues within peace operations (UN Secretary General 2005). Second, for a norm cascade – the process by which norm breakers become norm followers – to come into effect, a certain degree of 'institutionalization in the specific sets of international roles and organizations' is necessary (Finnemore and Sikkink, 1998). In the context of peace operations, human rights must thus first be institutionalized within the operation itself in order to effectively promote human rights in post-conflict settings. Following this logic, the higher the level of human rights institutionalization in peace operations, the better equipped they are to engender a process of domestic human rights *socialization* (Risse and Sikkink, 1999, p. 5; Risse, 2000).[2] Applied to this study, UN peace operations should stimulate and encourage such processes allowing for enduring *internalization* of human rights.[3]

This framework, however, examines peace operations primarily from a systemic (macro) perspective. In order to understand the dynamics of human rights considerations among peace actors and between peace actors and local actors at the field (micro) level, a theoretical framework which recognizes the importance of intercultural communication and interaction among peace actors is required. Agreeing with Selznick that 'in social inquiry, all description and explanation must respect the motives and contexts of human actors' (Selzinck, 2005, p. 61) insights from sociology and anthropology will provide additional useful perspectives to this analysis. At this micro level, UN peace operations furthermore represent a most interesting and unexplored field of study which will examine the encounter of global versus local cultures and the challenges involved in 'localizing' universal values such as human rights in such contexts (Rubinstein, 2005).

## Integration of Human Rights in UN Peace Operations through Communicative Action

Having established that institutionalization of human rights in UN peace operations is key to domestic human rights socialization, a closer examination on *the process of institutionalization* is vital. Habermas' theory of communicative action serves as the main theoretical tool to assess how integration of human rights within peace missions' military and police components may materialize. The main reason for relying upon Habermas is the assumption that integration presupposes a common understanding of human rights and a shared agreement on the importance of the human rights mandate for the overall success of a mission. Such agreement, it is suggested, may, in turn, depend on different degrees of institutionalization of human rights (reporting and monitoring structures, joint operations, training, etc.). An 'integrated mission', as recently defined by the UN Secretary General, is one in which

> [...] there is a *shared vision* among all UN actors as to the strategic objective of the UN presence at country level. [....] An Integrated Mission is one in which the structure is derived from *an in-depth understanding* of the specific country setting; of the evolving security, political, humanitarian, *human rights* and development imperatives in that particular country. (United Nations Integrated Mission Planning Process 2006, p. 3)

The core elements of a theory of communicative action are language and intersubjective understanding. Actors engage in communicative action when the 'actions of the agents involved are coordinated not through egocentric calculations of success but *through acts of reaching [mutual] understanding*' (Habermas, 1984, p. 286). Communicative action, or an ideal speech act, occurs when speaking and acting subjects engage in the process of reaching mutual understanding (*verständigung*) and are free, in this process of reaching agreement (*einigung*), to criticize the validity claims pursued. Habermas draws upon this idea of communicative action when elaborating a discourse theory of law and democracy according to which the legitimacy of the law leans not exclusively on individual rights and popular sovereignty but on *communicative mediation*: just those action norms are valid to which all possible affected persons could consent as participants in rational discourses (Erman, 2005, p. 56). Communicative action as discursive interaction in which interests and identities are constantly subject to change by the 'power of the better argument' is based, according to Thomas Risse, on primarily three preconditions. First, the ability of arguing actors to emphasize or to see things through the eyes of the interlocutor. Second, the need for actors to share a 'common lifeworld'. Finally, the need for actors to recognize each other as equals and to have equal access to the discourse (Risse, 2000, *supra* note 11, pp. 10–11).

The antonym of communicative action is *instrumental* or *strategic* action which occurs when actors are oriented towards success by exerting influence *upon* others. Both communicative and strategic actions constitute the main elements of social action and are directly linked to the concepts of the lifeworld and the system respectively. Communicative action is the guiding principle of the *lifeworld* (the background knowledge that we as social being always carry with us, the totality of socio-cultural facts), while strategic action is the guiding principle of the *system* (representing various integrated apparatuses such as the market and political organizations constituting modern society) (Risse, 2000, p. 6). Habermas recognizes that the complexity of human interaction and communication precludes a strict categorization of language use as either strategic or communicative action. Therefore, communicative action can be either 'weak' (actors merely recognize and *understand* the other's perspective, but without necessarily agreeing on the normative rightness of the action) or 'strong' (actors not only understand but *agree* with the other about a common position on the action which is understood as normatively valid from an inter-subjective perspective) (Risse, 2000, p. 41–3). Importantly, communicative action provides for the reproduction of the lifeworld since rational argumentation aimed at intersubjective understanding involves parallel processes of both individualization and socialization:

> Under the functional aspect of *mutual understanding*, communicative action serves to transmit and renew cultural knowledge; under the aspect of *coordinating action*, it serves social integration and the establishment of solidarity; finally, under the aspect of *socialization*, communicative action serves the formation of personal identities (Habermas 1987, p. 137).

Understanding human rights integration as integration in the intersubjective sense thus implies that civilian and military actors act in a spirit of mutual understanding of and agreement on human rights in order to effectively protect and promote human rights. If peace actors succeed in engaging in communicative action on human rights it entails, therefore, that they have resolved raised validity claims of human rights in an open discourse and that human rights activities therefore may be considered legitimate. According to the norm life cycle model, norms must be considered legitimate if they are to be socialized and eventually internalized in a society, and is closely linked to Thomas Franck's theory of compliance and legitimacy (Carlsnaes *et al.* 2002: *supra* note 7, p. 541). Habermas holds that communicative action takes place primarily in the lifeworld which has been 'colonized' by the system and is thus influenced by both spheres. In the context of peace operations, a plethora of various 'lifeworlds' exist (represented by the diversity of cultural and professional backgrounds of civil and military staff from different member states) and the 'system' may be conceived as represented by the financial and political interests of UN member states (primarily Security Council members). Applying the theory of communicative action, the three preconditions as outlined above must be satisfied if effective human rights integration in peace operations shall materialize: (i) the existence of *mutual empathy* among peace actors, which implies knowledge of and respect for each others' professions; (ii) the creation of *common lifeworld* between civilian and military actors and

(iii) *equality of actors*, primarily equality of the human rights component with the military and police, and equal access of the different components to the human rights discourse.

The theoretical framework, as presented here, suggests that various lifeworlds and systems are in constant competition within UN missions – a dynamics which may influence the degree of communicative action on human rights. For instance, a strong 'system' and the existence of very divergent lifeworlds of peace actors would result in 'weak' communicative action on human rights or predominantly strategic action on human rights among peace actors. This interplay may depend, however, I suggest, on the level of institutionalization of human rights within peace operations. Lifeworlds may be positively reproduced and strategic action minimized if the institutional framework is such that it provides for the inclusion of human rights considerations in reporting, monitoring, training and recruitment policies of the different mission compo-nents. The negative impact of disparate lifeworlds, i.e. cultural and normative perceptions and backgrounds, may then be outweighed by a functioning institutionalization of human rights (Erman, 2005, *supra* note 17, p. 173). Furthermore, the significant role played by personalities in leadership positions, if negative, may have less impact if clearly outlined mechanisms for inter-agency coordination and communication are outlined from the UN Secretariat, and the Department of Peacekeeping Operations (DPKO) in particular. Effective institutionalization may also allow for a 'reproduction of the system' (thus not only reproduction of the lifeworlds, as suggested by Habermas) in that political interests and actions are sensitized to and supportive of human rights protection and promotion. This may indeed be at the core of successful human rights integration. As expressed by a senior human rights expert: 'You work within an environment whereby you need to be politically useful, militarily useful and you want the Special Representative of the Secretary-General (SRSG) to agree with your work and you need to be relevant'. [4]

## Communicative Action, Cross-Cultural Perspectives and Action Rules of Language

Since key to this analysis on integration and institutionalization of human rights is the creation of a common understanding on human rights, Eva Erman's identification of the necessary conditions of language together with Abdullahi An-Na'im's and Richard Falk's deliberations on cross-cultural dialogues on human rights are helpful to further refine the foundations of a theory of communicative action on human rights in the context of peace operations. Erman sets out to amend Habermas' theory of communicative action by reducing its ethnocentric underpinnings (validity claims[5]) and by reinforcing its intersubjective contents (language), to render it universally applicable when applied to a human rights context. By emphasizing the power of action (language) and institutions (UN human rights bodies), Erman develops a discourse theory of human rights which is particularly relevant in this context since it links communicative action to institutions rather than to law (Erman, 2005, *supra* note 17, p. 206).[6] Drawing support for its normative claims from a universal pragmatics based on an epistemology of language rather than on any natural rights or cultural relativist approach, Erman's discourse theory may constitute a more universally justifiable tool when analysing human rights in the multicultural environments that UN peace operations represent. Habermas' preconditions for communicative action are thus complemented by Erman's necessary conditions of language, expressed as twelve action rules. These action rules are subdivided under five subheadings (Erman, 2005, *supra* note 17, pp. 81–112)[7] which may be modified and crystallized as follows to fit the purpose of this study:

- Since actors' understanding of human rights is intricate to their respective lifeworld, peace actors must be open to a *mouldable conceptualization of the lifeworld* to make it possible for different participants to act communicatively on human rights;
- Since all possibilities of action is limited by our environment and social norms, peace actors *must treat each other as subjects not objects*;
- Since we cannot recognize difference unless we also recognize similarity, peace actors need *to conceive of each others as mutually equal* in order to understand how different actors contribute in different ways to the common goal of human rights and peace in the host state of a mission.

These necessary conditions of language are based on a similar thought of line as the cross-cultural quest for human rights advocated for by An-Na'im. Because cultures are not static but constantly in a state of flux, a cross-cultural legitimacy of universal human rights recommends that 'processes of intercultural relations [...] be more deliberately and effectively utilized to overcome cultural antagonism to human rights norms that are problematic in a given context' (Na'im, 1992, p. 5). This emphasis on transcultural dialogues on human rights is also reflected in Falk's contention that for human rights to be effective at a local level, the imposition of the universal must be by way of an opening in the culture itself, and never by external imposition (Falk, 1992, *supra* note 29, p. 49). According to Falk, 'without mediating international human rights through the web of cultural circumstances, it will be impossible for human rights norms and practices to take hold in non-western societies' (Falk, 1992, *supra* note 29, p. 45).

This reasoning reverberates in Habermas: it is the *arguing* process in itself whereby actors are open to being convinced by the better argument of the other which is key to sustainable and positive change. 'Interests and identities are no longer fixed, but subject to interrogation and challenges and, thus, to change. The goal of discursive action is to achieve argumentative consensus with the other, not to push one's own view of the world or moral values.' (Risse, 2000, *supra* note 11, p. 10).

## From Theory to Practice: The Cases of Kosovo and the DRC

Following the methodological approach of qualitative comparative analysis, a dual approach is taken here to allow for a within-case as well as cross-case analysis of the two peace operations under scrutiny. Such an approach is appropriate in view of the vast differences of MONUC and UNMIK/KFOR in terms of mandate and context while the fact that both are multidimensional operations under Chapter VII of the UN Charter with shared features in common, allows for a cross-case analysis.[8] In view of the present delimitation, the application of data collected in Kosovo and the DRC[9] to the theoretical discussion presented here will focus on three phases which jointly provide the basis for preliminary recommendations to the UN or other international organizations:

- The impact of the missions' overall *structures* (regionalized vs UN-led) on the level of general human rights integration;
- The level of substantive integration of human rights within military and police in view of various institutional/structural measures *within a mission* (focus on MONUC);
- How *communicative action* on human rights between human rights actors, international military and police, can be enhanced, thus allowing for improved human rights integration (focus on MONUC Military and Human Rights Divisions respectively);
- Recommendations for future field deployments.

## Human Rights Integration in Regionalized v UN-led Peace Operations

No peace operation has seen such far-reaching delegation of responsibilities to regional organizations as that in Kosovo. Implementation of the mandate of the UN transitional administration, UNMIK, is divided under the overall authority of the SRSG, between the UN (Pillar I: Police and Justice and Pillar II: Civil Administration), the OSCE (Pillar III: Institution-building) and the EU (Pillar IV: Reconstruction and Economic Development).[10] The international security presence, KFOR, established as a separate entity out-side the remit of UNMIK, is led and commanded by NATO (UN Doc. S.C. Res. 1244, 1999, Para 18; Annex 2, Para. 4). Two aspects are of particular importance. First, the OSCE was given responsibility for institution-building, *including* that of human rights protection and promotion. The human rights mandate was thus bestowed upon a regional organization, operating under the overall authority of the Deputy SRSG of Pillar III and SRSG (OSCE Permanent Council decision PC.DEC/305 1999). Second, KFOR, mandated to establish a safe and secure environment in Kosovo, has operated in parallel to UNMIK outside the purview of the civilian authority de facto in charge of the territory (UN Doc. SC Res 1244 1999, Para 6). UNMIK Police forms part of Pillar I (Police and Justice) alongside UNMIK's Department of Justice with a three-fold mandate to (i) provide interim law enforcement, (ii) develop and deploy a Kosovo Police Service (KPS) and (iii) transfer police authority to KPS (Pillar, 2004, p. 6).

MONUC, on the other hand, is representative of a more traditionally structured UN peace operation where both the civilian and military components operate under the civilian command and control of the SRSG. MONUC's present institutional design, following the new model of 'integrated missions' (UN Guidelines on Integrated Missions Planning Process 2006),[11] allows for a SRSG with overall responsibility over (i) MONUC Force Commander, (ii) DSRSG/RC/HC (Resident Coordinator and Humanitarian Coordinator, including responsibility for humanitarian affairs and coordination of UN specialized agencies), (iii) DSRSG (including responsibility for the Human Rights Division, UN Police, and Rule of Law Division) and (iv) Director of Administration (DOA).[12] At a quick glance, thus, MONUC Human Rights Division not only operates under the same Deputy SRSG as MONUC Police but also under the same civilian umbrella as MONUC Military Division. In Kosovo, on the contrary, not only is the Human Rights Division one of several components of the OSCE mission in Kosovo (OMIK), but also operates within a separate pillar system distinct from that of UNMIK Police. Furthermore, OMIK is, like UNMIK, completely separated from KFOR. From a structural point of view thus, the operation in the DRC appears to provide a more advantageous model with respect to human rights integration than Kosovo.

Preliminary findings from field research in Kosovo and the DRC seem to uphold this hypothesis. All but one of the OSCE human rights officers interviewed believed that the institutional structure of UNMIK and KFOR impacted negatively on UNMIK's overall mandate to protect and promote human rights. This may be contrasted with the cautiously positive perception by MONUC human rights officers with respect to overall human rights integration in MONUC: it was generally felt that integration worked better in MONUC compared to other operations and, importantly, acknowledgement was made that the military and police had recently begun to show serious interest in human rights issues. With respect to the status, respect and independence of MONUC Human Rights Division vis-à-vis other mission components; there was a unison positive attitude.[13] In Kosovo, while unanimous at the high priority given to human rights within OMIK and its independence to operate as such, the majority of its human rights staff was dissatisfied with how human rights were generally taken into consideration by other units and departments of UNMIK. Recurring complaints concerned a lack of understanding of human rights among individual UNMIK officials, that lip service was being paid to human rights, and that the pillar system in general was not conducive to integration. Some believed that few UNMIK employees understood the mandate and activities of the OSCE and that the structure had prompted a system whereby anything labelled 'human rights' was automatically relegated to the OSCE. This perception of human rights as a subject matter confined to the 'jurisdiction' of the OSCE was indirectly upheld by one UNMIK official:

> We have improved coordination to some degree, with human rights not as well as we would have liked. It is easy to say "the OSCE is responsible for human rights". This is completely unfortunate.[…] Human rights have not been fused as well as it should have been within the mission. It also seems to me that institutions have tended to keep comparative advantages for themselves which has not been good for the mission as a whole.

The Inter-Pillar Working Group on Human Rights (IPWGHR), established as the main forum to 'ensure that human rights concerns are an integral part in the formulation of UNMIK's policies and legislation' (Review of the work of the IPWGHR 2006, p. 1), was subject to two general criticisms. First, that human rights experts[14] were given far too little time to comment in substance upon draft UNMIK legislation and, second, that its outcome was recommendatory in nature and seldom implemented in practice. While the IPWGHR and the Human Rights Oversight Committee were welcomed bodies, the question remained: Did they really operationalize human rights mainstreaming or were they not more of a cosmetic measure? It must be recalled, however, that UNMIK operates under extreme political pressure from the Security Council and Member States and under severe time pressure from UN Secretariat in

New York; thus strict time frames are rather due to institutional and political realities more than anything else. The IPWGHR was created in 2002 as a 'replacement' for the Special Adviser on Human Rights to the SRSG, a position which was discontinued in early 2000 after having operated for little more than six months. In response to the question why that position was discontinued, a senior OMIK official acknowledged that 'we have to do some digging on that issue'.[15] One OSCE human rights officer was of the opinion that the discontinuation was 'symptomatic' of the 'very, very poor' integration of human rights within UNMIK.

KFOR's separate status, particularly considering that it is exempt from any review mechanism,[16] was described as 'indefensible' by one human rights officer. Interaction between the OSCE and KFOR has been limited the past few years,[17] particularly after the ad hoc Task Force on Minorities[18] and OSCE's monitoring of KFOR were discontinued in the early 2000s. While human rights training has been provided to all military observers arriving in MONUC until December 2005, no systematic human rights training by OSCE has been provided to KFOR. Apart from its autonomous standing in relation to civilian structures, three recurring difficulties in interacting with KFOR were identified by OSCE human rights officers interviewed: first, the frequent rotation of troop contingents; second, the existence of multiple interlocutors and entities which may be attributed to the allegiance by troop contingents to national command rather than unified command under the Commander of KFOR (COMKFOR) and finally, *who* to engage with and *how* to engage with, that is, interaction '[e]ven in terms of simple communications perspective'.[19] A more direct statement to this dilemma was that many KFOR troops [here US marines] were 'trained to kill, but not to build peace, neither to keep peace [...] It is difficult even to talk to the officers'.[20]

An analysis of human rights integration at a *general* level in terms of overarching institutional design thus does not speak in favour of the model presented in UNMIK/KFOR. A 'public sphere' within the international peace mission where issues of human rights can be freely debated will have difficulty to gain ground in this institutional framework. While the socio-political backgrounds of UNMIK, OSCE and KFOR personnel (mostly of Western origin) are more similar than those of MONUC peacekeepers and police (predominantly from developing countries) and MONUC human rights officers (predominantly of Western origin),[21] the structural design of UNMIK and KFOR (representing the 'system') appears to outweigh any potential fertile ground for common action that the peace actors' similar lifeworlds could provide. Apart from attending a few common meetings, the lack of a structural, institutional framework that could allow for a natural flow of information and joint actions makes communicative action between military and human rights actors in Kosovo difficult. In this respect, several interviewees regretted the lack of systemic information gathering and reporting structures, both within UNMIK and between UNMIK and KFOR. In fact, there seems to be little interaction at all between OSCE and KFOR.[22] In addition, if the de facto military-politico purpose of the massive presence of KFOR is to train new NATO members[23] rather than proactively assist UNMIK in implementing its mandate to promote human rights in Kosovo, strategic interests may dominate and mutual understanding in communication with OSCE representatives and other civilian actors be undermined.

Both MONUC and UNMIK, as any UN peace operation, are political instruments per definition, but political interests may appear even more tangible in UNMIK due to the very sensitive context in which UNMIK operates. Several interviewees believed human rights were theoretically integrated in the mission but not in practice. UNMIK's structures, reflective of the strong politicization of the operation, appear not conducive to communicative action also *within* the civilian structures per se. A senior official of OMIK Human Rights and Rule of Law Department described this lack of dialogue as follows: 'The failing of UNMIK is that there are so many organizations that do not speak or plan in consultation with others. They operate in vacuum with directives from Brussels, from Vienna, Geneva etc. [...] This is the big failing of Kosovo'.[24]

### Communicative Action on Human Rights in View of the Degree of Institutionalization of Human Rights in Peace Operations: The Case of MONUC

Considering that MONUC's Human Rights Division is small in comparison to the mission's Military and Police Divisions,[25] it is remarkable that it appears to have succeeded in establishing itself as one of the most respected units of MONUC. Three key factors seem to have played a key role in this regard: first, the Division managed, from the outset, to gain political support from both MONUC political leadership and the Congolese Transitional Government; second, its independence, impartiality and extensive presence in the field has made the Division one of MONUC's most important sources of information; third, investigations conducted by the Division's Special Investigation Unit have been particularly successful in prosecuting individual perpetrators of gross human rights violations, which appear to have constituted an important, independent tool with which MONUC has been able to put political pressure on the Congolese authorities. Both MONUC Military Division and MONUC Police considered information provided by Human Rights Division to be very important. For the military, such information could prompt MONUC forces to take action against *Forces Armées de la République*

*Démocratique du Congo* (FARDC) forces in cases of harassment or mistreatment, warn civilian populations and, even, if necessary, modify deployment plans. For MONUC Police, interaction with human rights officers, while not necessarily without friction, was nevertheless perceived as fundamental due to them, inter alia, reminding the *Police Nationale du Congo* (PNC) of the legal benchmarks for democratic policing and due to the authority of the Division to intervene with the national police authorities on human rights issues.

Almost opposite to the situation in Kosovo, where cooperation between OSCE human rights officers appears to be closer with UNMIK Police than with KFOR in recent years, relations between the Human Rights Division and MONUC Military Division appear more advanced and mutually conducive than those with MONUC Police.[26] Reason for this may be the establishment of a more clear division of labour between MONUC Human Rights Division and MONUC Military Division. Both Divisions appear to be in the process of identifying and benefitting from each others' comparative advantages, because of, or as a result of, the establishment of institutional mechanisms for cooperation and information sharing. Similar structures, it appears, have, as of yet, not been put in place between the Human Rights Division and MONUC Police. Here, lessons could have been drawn from the experience of the Human Rights Expert Programme of the OSCE with UNMIK Police and KPS, which consists of OSCE human rights monitors and advisers deployed in regional police stations throughout Kosovo. This programme was warmly commended by a senior official in UNMIK Police and Justice Pillar since it epitomized how human rights officers with 'practical experience and knowledge how the police operate'[27] managed to get concrete results – contrary to the 'uselessness' of receiving an OSCE report long after events.

While this points at the significance of institutional structures to facilitate communicative action and thus substantive integration of human rights, some outstanding dilemmas on communication and perception of the other remain, both within MONUC Military, Police and Human Rights Division. These will be discussed below, focusing on integration of human rights in the fields of (i) training, (ii) information-sharing and reporting and (iii) joint operations. This will subsequently be measured against the three prerequisites identified above for communicative action: empathy and knowledge, common lifeworlds and equality of actors.

## Integration of Human Rights in MONUC Military Division

Some pioneering work appears to be underway in MONUC as far as integration of human rights within a peace operation's military division is concerned. This concerns primarily the work and role of MONUC's military observers, generally perceived as the 'eyes and ears' of the mission. Unprecedented in the context of UN peace operations, it is planned that certain MONUC Military observers be designated as human rights focal points for interaction with human rights officers in the field. Furthermore, a merged human rights report has been issued on a monthly basis by the Military and Human Rights Divisions since January 2006.

### Training

One of the weaker areas of interaction between MONUC Military and Human Rights Divisions appears to be that of training; acknowledged by representatives from both Divisions. While neither senior military nor civilian personnel are briefed on human rights or any other substantive work of MONUC, all incoming military observers have had a one hour's human rights briefing upon arrival as part of a general induction course. As of December 2005, the briefing was discontinued as part of a general reduction of the course.[28] Human rights training for military contingents, it was contended, is only carried out on an ad hoc basis at their deployment sites by the nearest human rights office and not at MONUC HQ.[29]

In military jargon, human rights training was referred to by one MONUC staff as fitting into the NENI (Non-Examinable and Non-Interesting course), a category of MONUC briefings. The relevance of the briefing for the military observers was partly confirmed, partly refuted by observers deployed in eastern Congo. One claimed it was very useful to be knowledgeable of the Human Rights Division's activities and stressed the need for the briefing to be upheld. Another observer was of the opinion that it had no relevance to his work; the briefing, he claimed, had only outlined the mandate and the activities, organization and reporting of the Division, nothing of which was considered to be of relevance to his own work. A senior MONUC Military officer stressed the need for any human rights training addressed to the military to be more dynamic, with more visualization and without moral teaching. A general assessment, in this regard, could be that the lifeworlds of military and the human rights staff are too disparate for a fifty minutes briefing to have any impact on the military's understanding of human rights. If training is to have any bearing, military staff stressed, it should be done in the field directly upon deployment, focus on very practical measures such as patrolling, area control, monitoring – not on abstract norms – and, if possible, be carried out jointly with the military. Needless to say, pre-deployment training would enhance the process of internalizing human rights knowledge within the military. This was confirmed by one military legal adviser working in MONUC: 'It is a waste of time doing it [training] in the mission, you have to approach the troop contributing countries and ask them to integrate it at home in the training courses'.

Rather than providing training, the most meaningful way of imparting human rights awareness and knowledge within the military was considered to be by way of working together directly in the field. As expressed by one human rights officer: 'I don't believe in training at all. This human rights induction course is so useless. [...] I think that the best way to get the message through is to be with them in the field. Then, from a practical point of view, they will see what needs to be done'. Working together is considered to be mutually beneficial to both sections – the military and the human rights officers. The human rights work needs to be visualized to the military and the human rights officers need to understand better the conditions in which the military works. A military observer in Beni described meaningful integration in following terms: 'Don't let [the human rights officers] sit in an office with the other civilians, but let them live directly with us. They can stay with us. It is here that they are needed. Sometimes we get the impression that they are "too important" to live in the field'.[30] Often overlooked in theory and practice, it highlights the need not only for military staff to learn about human right but vice versa. 'Human rights officers have legal training but they need [to know the] practicalities too'.[31] Both the lack of common lifeworlds and a sense of inequality by both divisions vis-à-vis the other render direct communication though joint activities in the field, rather than training, fundamental to reaching mutual understanding on human rights.

### *Information-Sharing and Reporting*

Information-sharing and reporting has, until recently, been more reactive than proactive, but military information appears, in general, to have been instrumental to the work of the Human Rights Division, particularly as far as human rights investigations are concerned. In general, MONUC Military observers play a key role with respect to the increased emphasis on human rights in information-sharing and reporting.[32] In the field, military observers may inform the nearest human rights officer (or child protection officer) if help has been requested and would subsequently report on the incident up the chain of the command to MONUC Force Headquarters. Also, military observers perform an indispensable role in areas where the Human Rights Division has no field presence. 'They are very good to go and check [out an incident] when we are not there, and then sending back messages that they think we should come'.[33] MONUC Force also informs the Human Rights Division on possible effects that a MONUC operation in a certain area may have on internally displaced persons and other vulnerable populations.[34]

In terms of reporting, the Military Division contends that it has reported on human rights as a separate heading since the outset of the mission.[35] More systematic reporting on human rights, based primarily on reports by military observers regarding complaints on FARDC, was initiated in February 2005 and culminated in a huge report on FARDC in January 2006 (covering all 2005). This initiative by MONUC Force Commander was welcomed by the Human Rights Division. '[I]n principle, this is a good initiative [...] because it shows that the military feels that human rights is also their task. So I think it [has] an excellent effect'.[36] This has developed into a system of joint human rights reports by MONUC Military and Human Rights Divisions, whereby the Military's reports are merged with the Human Rights Division's monthly reports, and subsequently submitted to the Congolese civil and military authorities on a monthly basis.

An issue of some contention, however, appeared to be the fact that the merged reports are handed over to the leadership of FARDC not by the Human Rights Division but by MONUC Force Commander. The explanation given by the Human Rights Division was: 'You do not know how to talk to them'. In this respect, it was felt that little improvement had been seen with respect to human rights integration. Similarly, it was also regretted that the leadership of MONUC Police maintains monopoly on communication on human rights issues with the leadership of the Congolese National Police. This perception may be based on a feeling among the military and police that human rights officers approach and communicate with the military establishment in a manner considered inappropriate. In this regard, one senior military officer stressed that the expectations of human rights officers must be pitched down to a pragmatic level, i.e. mindful of the socio-economic realities of sub-Saharan countries.[37] It is likely that the existing information-sharing and reporting system will improve considerably once the new 'incident form' reporting system is put in place. Drafted by the Human Rights Division and developed jointly with the MONUC Force HQ, such incident forms aim at educating all reporting sources, both military observers and troops, how to report on a human rights incident.

### Joint Operations

At least four areas can be identified where MONUC Military and Human Rights Division engage in joint operations *in situ* to protect and promote human rights in the DRC: human rights mobile teams, special investigations, interaction between military observers and human rights officers, and the protection of victim and witnesses.

The first MONUC human rights mobile team was established in 2005 to monitor the human rights situation in Masisi and Rutshuru territories in

North Kivu. During two and a half month, the team worked closely with the military which, among other things, provided mobile team escort upon request. This was a way in which the Human Rights Division '[…] could explain to our South African contingents and Indian contingents that this is what MONUC can do when it comes to human rights issues'.[38] The concept proved successful in terms of early warning, effectiveness of investigation, outreach to the civilian population and follow up of cases with previous judicial and military authorities.[39]

The second, and related, area is the role of the military in the conduct of special human rights investigations. For the purpose of investigating gross human rights violations, the Human Rights Division has since late 2002 established multidisciplinary teams composed by human rights and civilian experts, civilian police and military observers, initially in coordination with OHCHR DRC-field office personnel (Secretary General's Report on MONUC 2003, paras 8, 35). It was acknowledged that coordination aspects between the military (reporting on cases) and the civilian and human rights (follow-up and prosecution) had not always been ideal. Improvement in terms of cooperation between human rights officers and military observers, however, may be expected after a new system of designated military observers coordinators as focal points for interaction with the nearest human rights office or human rights mobile team will be put in place. According to an agreement between MONUC Force Headquarters and Human Rights Division, such focal points should be trained by the nearest human rights office over the basics of UN methodology for human rights investigation and should report daily to MONUC HQ.

Finally, military observers play an important role in locating and identifying vulnerable populations in need, upon which MONUC human rights officers would be informed and/or individuals in need would be physically brought by the observers to the human rights office.

## Analysis: How to Improve Integration of Human Rights through Communicative Action

While the process of institutionalizing human rights within MONUC Military Division is recent and ongoing, the fact that the initiative to embark upon this process partly came from the military itself is crucial. It indicates a willingness of the military to open their set of culture to that of Human rights, resonating Falk's philosophy as outlined above. In this sense, human rights training which is too legalistic, not designed to 'encounter' the military language, mentality or modes of operation may well be interpreted as an imposture to teach the military a moral lesson (Blocq, 2005, p. 210). In a hierarchic culture such as that of the military, any move from civilian actors to 'impose' a certain course of action is likely to meet resistance. When institutionalization of human rights in reporting and information-sharing occurs on the military's own initiative, human rights may more likely be perceived as legitimate by the military and a process of arguing and debating their validity on an equal footing may then begin.

While institutionalization of information-sharing and reporting may certainly facilitate communicative action on human rights, the foregoing discussion points at the importance of direct interaction if human rights officers and military are to reach mutual understanding of human rights field work. If adopted simultaneously, institutionalization *and* possibilities for direct interaction, the preconditions for communicative action may be fulfilled by (a) mutual empathy and knowledge; (b) common lifeworlds; (c) equality of actors and equal access to the discourse. How to enhance and improve human rights integration within the military, and police, may thus be assessed through an analysis against these three benchmarks.

(a) *Empathy and knowledge*: Given that military and human rights officers operate according to very disparate lifeworlds, direct interaction in the field appears fundamental prerequisite for both the actors as they will be 'able to see things through the eyes of the other'. Communication in terms of action, whereby human rights protection work is visualized, appears to be the 'language', which will be best understood by the military. While basic *knowledge* on the existence, mandate and activities of the Human Rights Division is crucial and should be transmitted through either briefings or other information-sharing processes, proper knowledge in terms of understanding and *empathy* for the other's work seem to be conditioned on face to face interaction.

According to Sajó, human rights claims are always credible if reinforced by empathy; such claims are 'good candidates for universal acceptance' (Sajó, 2006, *supra* note 13, p. 22). Working together in the field to achieve a common goal of protecting basic human rights (right to life, personal liberty and security, public liberties) will indirectly increase knowledge of and empathy for each other, and, importantly, create trust. Through institutionalization, MONUC Military will be knowledgeable of a basic principle of human rights reporting and monitoring – non-disclosure of sources. Through direct interaction, be it repatriation of internally displaced persons, provision of protection to a human rights witness, or successful prosecution of war criminals, the results-oriented military may in concrete action witness his or her personal contribution to human rights protection and thus experience work satisfaction. This way, understanding and empathy for the mandate and viewpoints of a human rights officer may be enhanced within the military. Human rights officers, on the other hand, may improve their comprehension of the challenging tasks of the military in upholding security and protecting civilians when directly deployed with them in the field.

Similarly, if senior MONUC military or police officers have no or little knowledge of the limited but important institution-building activities of the Human Rights Division, stereotypic views of human rights officers as denouncing without constructively recommending agents will be upheld. This may be detrimenta rights institution-building activities undertaken by the Human Rights Division, such as training for local police, are made known mission-wide. Likewise, empathy on the part of human rights offl to the establishment of a shared, positive approach vis-à-vis domestic law enforcement agencies. It is imperative, in this sense, that senior mission leadership provide proper information asanmestic law enforcement agencies. It is imperative, in this sense, that senior mission leadership provide proper information as llegial relationships. Some MONUC police officers underlined the importance that their human rights colleagues better understand that the establishment of trust between local and international police is a prerequisite if MONUC Police's advice and recommendations shall have effect. In this respect, human rights interventions, unless carefully coordinated with international police, could at times be perceived as disruptive to the effort of establishing such relationship of trust.

(b) *A common lifeworld*: The inherent challenge between the ordinary peacemakers and the human rights officers in building mutual understanding is that the lifeworlds of the two are diametrically opposite. The lifeworld of the former is, in *grosso modo*, created against military doctrine and training where the aim is to identify and eliminate the enemy,[40] not to protect vulnerable populations or disperse violent demonstrations and other public disorders. The lifeworld of the human rights officer, on the other hand, is often formed against the background of NGO activism or other advocacy work, where denouncing violations (often committed by the police and military) and demanding accountability for such breaches, is a key feature of their work. It is thus more challenging for the military peacekeeper (or police, who is not educated to train or advice other national police) to adapt his/her lifeworld to the setting of a peace operation than it is for a human rights officer to reproduce his/her lifeworld to the same aim. As a result, the military has to change not only *environment* but also *tasks*.

Acknowledging such disequilibria may be a first precondition if reproduction of the lifeworld of respective actors is to materialize, because only then are actors open to a mouldable conceptualization of their lifeworld. Once both actors are open to revisit their own values and perceptions, a reproduction of the lifeworld can be made either through direct interaction, 'coaching', or institutionalization, or ideally, both. Reproduction of the military's lifeworld in order to comprehend human rights work is more likely to materialize if the military is given the opportunity to actively contribute or assist in human rights field work, for example, by escorting human rights mobile teams or providing shelter to persecuted human rights witnesses. However, also by reporting, the lifeworld of the military may be able to give verbal expression to a human rights situation. Institutionalization of human rights can thus activate both processes of individualization and socialization entailed in the reproduction of the lifeworld. A military observer designated as human rights focal point will not only renew his individual knowledge and understanding of human rights; by coordinating action, he will also serve as a social integration between the Military Division and the Human Rights Division.

Human rights officers, on the other hand, may facilitate and enhance this reproduction of the military lifeworld by adapting their use of language and attitude. The methodology of human rights field work has been highlighted by a senior OHCHR staff member as 'extremely important, absolutely important', underlining that 'one of the [OHCHR's] biggest challenge is identifying and recruiting enough qualified human rights specialists to do this job. And the reality of the situation is that they are not out there. You can't find them, you have to *create* them'. If human rights officers assume a broader understanding of how human rights relate to the larger social and political context, their own lifeworld can also reproduce the same. This may be why some human rights officers have expressed the need 'for people [in peace operations] who are able to bring human rights to the political side [...] because if we just criticize we will not make any change or get anywhere'.[41] In Kosovo, while the quality of human rights colleagues was undisputed, it was stressed that '[i]f anything, perhaps we would need more non-lawyers. Legal justifications are important, but the sociological perspectives are important [too]'.[42]

(c) *Equality of actors*: The challenging security context and rough living conditions in which MONUC troops operate appears to have created a sense of inequality within the military.[43] Novel initiatives such as that of mobile human rights teams in MONUC which provides for real interaction under the same conditions are important to enhance equality among peacekeeping actors. According to Erman, the action rules of language and human rights imply, among other things, '[...] an ethics of reciprocity and recognition, where equality is founded on mutuality rather than symmetry' (Erman, 2005, *supra* note 17, p. 221). This necessary condition of language, *mutuality*, implies that we cannot recognize difference unless we also recognize similarity. This is one area where Erman redefines Habermas' notion of intersubjectivity, based on symmetry, to one based on mutuality since it more properly captures the internal relationship between similarity and difference in relation to interaction. When working together, human rights officers and military will understand their similarities despite their differences since their actions will be directed to a common goal and aim. It will also reinforce MONUC's potential in implementing its mandate. When asked what advice to give the Human Rights Division in order to synchronize better its work with the military, one MONUC Commander stated: '[I]f the Human Rights Division, a few uniformed people, we'll all go in the same name, singing the same song, it will be more effective, everyone will expect more from MONUC, everyone will know it is MONUC, no matter the agency, [and] the message will go deeper'.[44]

At the same time, a feeling of inequality appears to prevail also within the Human Rights Division. For instance, the Division appears, on occasions, to be denied direct access to and interaction with the leadership of the Congolese Police and Military (exemplified in the joint monthly human rights report to FARDC along with the fact that interaction with the PNC leadership is dealt with by MONUC Police senior leadership). In addition, a recurrent and significant dilemma: human rights components often have no operational budget for their activities (why they are, for example, dependent on military facilities for shelter purposes). Indeed, at UN Headquarters, as well as in the field, the lack of assessed contributions for human rights activities was highlighted as an outstanding obstacle to effective integration of human rights in UN peace operations.

## Implementation through Communication: Recommendations for Future Operations

Drawing on preliminary findings from field research and interviews with human rights officers, police and military personnel in Kosovo and the DRC as well as with UN staff at UN Headquarters, analysed through a new theoretical framework on peacekeeping, I have argued that communication skills among peace actors are an underestimated factor in analyses on integration of human rights in peace operations. I suggest that institutionalized mechanisms in forms of information-sharing, joint reporting and field activities may bridge, or at least reduce, communication barriers which are inherent in the diverging lifeworlds of human rights officers, police and military. Such initiatives are also likely to reduce feelings of inequality, boost mutual respect for the other, and enhance the aim of each mission to implement its mandate in a coherent and professional fashion.

If UN peace operations deliver contradictory messages with respect to protection and promotion of international human rights standards to local authorities and communities, they may run the risk of undercutting instead of enhancing the process of human rights socialization in a post-conflict society. Each peace actor should realize that his/her individual behaviour and actions affects, positively or negatively, the credibility and legitimacy of a UN mission.

Jean-Marie Guéhenno, Under-Secretary General for Peacekeeping Operations, recently stated: 'I have seen by visiting many missions that the credibility of peacekeepers whether of military commanders or civilian staff, is a key to the success of an operation. If you have a good concept but the people are not right, you will fail' (Press conference by Jean-Marie Guéhenno, 2006, p. 4). This echoes a comment from a MONUC police officer, which this author holds as a truism of any UN peace operations: 'Integration of a concept is integration of people'.

Empirically focused research ultimately aims at providing practice-oriented suggestions to relevant institutions and policymaking bodies. It is thus found appropriate to conclude with some specific recommendations, targeting both the field and Headquarters' levels, which may enhance processes of human rights communication and socialization and, as a consequence thereof, positively reinforce the larger and long-term aim of sustainable peacebuilding. Following the article's focus on human rights officers, police and military troops, the recommendations are subdivided into these three categories.

### Human Rights Field Deployments

*Focus on priorities and thematic issues from the start.*
*Include lawyers as well as non-lawyers in 'human rights teams'.*
*Enhance human rights officers' cooperation and communication skills with respect to interacting with military and police.*
*Engage with and respect local civil society actors from the outset of deployment.*
*Appoint senior leadership with management skills and vision.*
*Train human rights experts on the military and police profession and cultures.*

### Police Deployments

*Deploy police officers with specific monitoring and training skills.*
*Establish a pool of police officers with specific knowledge in international human rights law.*
*Establish a clear policy of cooperation and coordination between human rights experts and civilian police and effectively communicate that to the local police authorities.*
*Deploy police teams with mixed cultural backgrounds.*
*Police officers should be well versed in the local law.*

### Military Deployments

*Prioritize deployment of military observers and enhance their reporting and monitoring skills.*

*Engage in joint operations with human rights experts.*

*Provide proper and practice-oriented pre-deployment training in international human rights law.*

*Establish human rights focal points within military (observer) deployments.*

*Train military in how to be peace-builders and on 'how to be bored'.*

*Consistent and coherent rules of engagement, translated in clear language understandable to all nationalities represented in the peace mission.*

## Chapter Nine

# TO PRACTICE WHAT THEY PREACH: INTERNATIONAL TRANSITIONAL ADMINISTRATIONS AND THE PARADOX OF NORM PROMOTION

## Annika Björkdahl

### Introduction

Since mid-1990s the United Nations and other multilateral organizations have through the establishment of international transitional administrations assumed responsibility for governance of war-torn territories. United Nations Interim Administration Mission in Kosovo (UNMIK) is one of the bold experiments in internationally supported post-conflict state reconstruction, democratization and peacebuilding. International transitional administrations, such as UNMIK can be regarded as unparalleled opportunities to exert a normative influence and mould the state in reconstruction into a peaceful, liberal democracy. When the United Nations itself assumes a governing role, there is a temptation to demand the highest standards of democracy, human and minority rights, the rule of law etc. However, UNMIK was established through democratically deficient international processes and it is obviously not a representative democracy and should therefore not be held to the standards of a liberal democratic state. Yet, the mission is mandated to promote democracy and build democratic institutions of governance in Kosovo. How can liberal democratic norms be diffused in war-torn societies? What affects the ability to adopt norms of liberal democracy in societies that lack democratic culture? Through what means and channels is the UN promoting liberal democratic norms in Kosovo? To what extent are the Kosovars adopting these norms?

Taking the social constructivist assumption about norms and practices as mutually constitutive, this chapter sets out to explore the discrepancy between UNMIK's norm advocacy and practice of democracy. It attempts to analyse the effects of this inconsistency between rhetoric and practice on the ability of

UNMIK to exert a normative influence and diffuse liberal democratic norms in Kosovo. The analysis presented here illustrates that the democratic deficit of UNMIK, in terms of its lack of accountability and legitimacy, raises concerns about power abuse and this may well undermine its overall promotion of liberal democratic norms. Clearly, the mission is not leading by setting an example, and it fails to provide a model of good governance according to liberal democratic norms for the Kosovars to mimic. This failure to respect and comply with the norms of liberal democracy has eroded the authority of UNMIK as a norm advocate, weakened the norms and closed a channel for norm-promotion. The obvious gap between what the UN preaches and what it practices also challenges the conventional assumption that norm advocates respect and comply with the international norms they champion and attempt to diffuse norm followers. Furthermore, the authoritarian style of governance has undermined UNMIK's efforts to build sustainable democratic institutions and practices in Kosovo, to calm down tension in the relationship between UNMIK and the Kosovars, and it has potentially contributed to distort the Kosovars' vision of democracy.

This chapter provides an analysis of one aspect of the internationally led democratization process in Kosovo namely the democratic elections. A focus on democratic elections assists us in analysing both the rhetorical norm advocacy and the practices of the UN's democracy promotion. Democratic elections can be interpreted as a way to demonstrate how the promoted liberal democratic norms are translated into fundamental democratic practices. In addition, such analytical focus makes it possible to depict the pedagogical value of repeated elections for the social learning process central to adoption and socialization of liberal democratic values. Chesterman (2004, p. 205) argues elections are 'viewed as the preferred mechanism of handing over power from the undemocratic, yet internationally legitimate transitional administration to a democratic and (ideally) locally legitimate government'. Yet, the elections held in Kosovo were used less to elect legitimate representatives of the population than they were to engage the Kosovars in non-violent political activity (Chesterman 2004, pp. 205–6). Despite organizing and holding elections to the Provisional Institutions of Self-Government (PISG), UNMIK retained real powers, for example the power to resolve the Assembly. Slowly, and according to many Kosovars too slowly, authority and power are now transferred to local institutions, and local politicians are brought to power through democratic election processes.

## Promoting Democracy – On the Mutual Constitution of Norms and Practices

Different theoretical approaches allow us to pose different questions. The questions I am investigating concerns the relationship between norms and practice and how this relationship may affect the promotion of norms and I find social constructivism particularly pertinent in capturing this relationship and in providing us with some potential answers. Although a body of literature concerning norm promotion takes such a point of departure, the value added by this analysis presented here is the focus on the mutual constitution of norms and practices, i.e. how the norm advocacy may be strengthened or undermined by consistent or inconsistent practices. The UN and its democracy promotion in Kosovo well illustrate this dilemma. Although the UN norm advocacy concerning democracy is convincing, UN's practices have not always been up to standard. In this chapter, I focus on the two strategies of democracy promotion, namely norm advocacy and practices and the relationship between them.

## On Norm Advocacy

Norm advocacy is about the power of values, norms and ideas, such as democracy, and it has been particularly important in value-laden debates over human rights, the environment, gender equality and minority rights (cf. Keck and Sikkink, 1998, p. 9; Risse *et al.* 1999; Prügel, 1999). Such advocacy is about conscious efforts to promote norms by attempting to persuade and convince a potential norm-taker to adopt and comply with the advocated norms. In general, norm advocacy is based on norm diffusion through persuasion, teaching and normative suasion (cf. Checkel, 2005, pp. 801–26). The norm advocate has at its disposal a number of resources, such as diplomatic, rhetorical and pedagogical skills, moral authority and legitimacy, ideational as well as material carrots and sticks. Conducive conditions for norm advocacy can be provided by, for example, an institutional setting that permits consistent and intense contact with the potential norm-taker. Furthermore, if the norm advocate is perceived as trustworthy, legitimate and knowledgeable, and of high moral standing the norms he/she promotes are more likely to be persuasive (Björkdahl, 2002). Hence, promoting democracy is about spreading these norms, for example, to states in transition, to weak and undemocratic states, and to societies emerging from violent conflict (cf. Paris, 2004).

## On Practice

The second strategy of democracy promotion is practice. Norms are frequently defined as an outcome of common practices and as intersubjective understandings of appropriate behaviour. Norms also have 'constitutive effects'. Democratic norms, for example, will regulate and prescribe the appropriate mode of governance of a particular state as well as define the identity of a liberal democratic state (Katzenstein, 1996, p. 5). Yet, we should keep in mind that 'practices do not simply echo norms', practices make norms real. Practices in accordance with liberal democratic norms may, therefore, strengthen both the norms of liberal democracy and facilitate their promotion, since norms and practices are mutually constitutive – 'norms have power in, and because of, what people do' (Keck and Sikkink, 1998, p. 35). In that sense, democratic practices of the actor promoting liberal democratic norms are of great importance. Norm advocates can in this way lead by example, and provide a model to imitate. Then, as this article argues norm advocacy could be facilitated by activities that demonstrate the applicability and feasibility of the norm in practice and such practices could thereby actually be a mechanism for norm promotion (Björkdahl, 2006). The demonstrative effect of practicing what you preach may be a compelling and powerful way of promoting norms.

## The UN and Democracy Promotion

Since the early 1990's, the United Nations has increasingly been involved in teaching the values and norms pertaining to liberal democracy to its member states. According to Roland Rich (2004, p. 65), the UN Security Council has adopted 26 resolutions concerning mission mandates containing democratization or state-building aspects, the vast majority in the post-cold war era. In that sense, the UN has a broad experience in promoting democracy around the world. When the UN has undertaken these extensive peace- and state-building tasks and assumed governance of war-torn societies the functioning, legitimacy and accountability of these international governance structures are of immense importance in achieving the goal of establishing a self-sustainable liberal democracy.

## Ambiguous Normative Support

Even though the UN has adopted democracy promotion as an important objective there is not a word about 'democracy' in the UN Charter and democracy promotion is not one of the stated purposes of the UN (Farer, 2004, p. 32–4). Democracy is not even a prerequisite for UN-membership and many members are not multi-party democracies, and even fewer could be seen as liberal democracies. Nor is the UN a democratic organization (Falk, 1998). Yet, there is a strong foundation for the UN to advocate democracy as the linkage between democracy and peace is well established among both academics and policymakers, and so is the linkage between democracy and human rights (cf. Rich and Newman et al. 2004). The General Assembly's adoption of resolution 46/137 of 1991 on 'enhancing the effectiveness of the principle of periodic and genuine elections' illustrates the emerging consensus within the UN on norms pertaining to democratic governance (A/RES/46/137). The Secretary General, Boutros Boutros-Ghali developed *An Agenda for Democratization* presented in 1996 to construct a normative context supporting norms pertaining to liberal democracy. In addition, the Human Rights Commission's resolution 2000/47 is an important value added to the UN's ambition to strengthen democracy.[1] These landmark documents underscore the UN's support for democratic norms, democratic forms of governance and democratic elections. Yet, it is a thin conceptualization that the UN is diffusing mainly constrained to an understanding of democracy as free and fair elections (cf. Newman and Rich *et al.* 2004). Through organizing, monitoring and evaluating elections around the world, the UN has assisted in transitions to democracy. Most commonly, the UN has provided election assistance, and an Electoral Assistance Division has been set up within the Department of Political Affairs (DPA) to provide transitional countries with expertise and technical advise (Ludwig, 2004, p. 173). Holding elections has also frequently been the UN's exit strategy from its engagement in peace, state and democracy-building missions (Paris, 2004; Caplan, 2005, p. 213–29).

## UNMIK – Preaching Democracy

Since the Kosovo war of 1999, the international community has been deeply involved in the peace-and- democracy-building efforts in Kosovo. To some extent this can be seen as an attempt to project into Kosovo the Western community model for liberal democratic states, consisting of shared norms pertaining to democratic principles, good governance, rule of law, respect for human and minority rights and peaceful conflict resolution (cf. Paris, 2004).

## Resolution 1244 – A Mandate to Support the Development of Democracy in Kosovo

By virtue of UN Security Council Resolution 1244, passed on 10 June 1999, the Security Council authorized the Secretary General to establish an international civil presence know as UNMIK with the mandate 'to provide an interim administration for Kosovo under which the people of Kosovo can enjoy substantial autonomy within the Federal Republic of Yugoslavia and to provide transitional administration while establishing and overseeing the development of provisional democratic self-governing institutions to ensure conditions for a peaceful and normal life for all inhabitants of Kosovo' (SC/RES/1244). Resolution 1244 demonstrates that 'democratization has found a place in UN rhetoric and mandates' and that also non-democratic governments accept mandates with formulations stressing democracy and free and fair elections (Rich, 2004, p. 83). Hence, a mandate, like UNMIKs can therefore be seen as the beginning of the long process of democratization. Using its mandate, the UN has deeply permeated Kosovar society, and unlike many resolutions 1244 has had '[...] quite an impact on the situation on the ground' (Muharremi *et al.* 2003).

The Security Council Resolution 1244 was the result of diplomatic efforts and political compromise before and after the NATO air campaign (24 March to 10 June 1999) (Reka, 2003, p. 44). Attached to Resolution 1244 were annexes drawn from negotiations conducted outside the UN, in the G8 setting and within NATO (Hysa, 2004). According to Rich (2004, p. 79), 'the United Nations was constantly playing catch up, first in the process leading to the Rambouillet Accords and then after the humanitarian intervention by NATO-forces'. Through UNMIK, the international community assumed sovereignty and governed the territory with the reluctant consent of the Kosovo–Albanians, the Serb minority and Belgrade. The political process of drafting resolution 1244, however, failed to create a clear and practical mandate. Instead the mandate contains ambiguous and inconsistent obligations and an unclear end point. UNMIK's mandate stressed that it should organize and oversee the development of provisional institutions for democratic and autonomous self-government pending a political settlement, including holding elections. Furthermore, it should also transfer, as these institutions are established, its administrative responsibilities while overseeing and supporting the consolidation of Kosovo's local provisional institutions. No specific end date was set for completing the transition from UNMIK to the Provisional Self-Government and the final status of Kosovo was not decided. The Security Council thread careful on the issue of Serbian sovereignty, and in resolution 1244, the Council preserved the sovereignty of the Federal Republic of Yugoslavia over Kosovo (Hysa, 2004, p. 288). UNMIK assured that the Yugoslav laws should continue to be applied in Kosovo as long as they did not conflict with internationally recognized norms and values, such as human rights, minority rights, and the fulfilment of the mandate given to UNMIK or any regulation issued by UNMIK and the SRSG. The ambiguity of the resolution led to conflicting interpretations, but it was also used by UNMIK in its norm promotion to spur the Kosovars to adapt and implement the standards set by the international community.

## Translating International Norms of Liberal Democracy into Standards for Kosovo

In December 2003, at a meeting in the Pristina City Hall with representatives of the PISG, representatives of KFOR, the liaison offices of the international communities, members of the Kosovo civil society and numerous senior UN officials, the *Standards for Kosovo* document was inaugurated (UNMIK/PR/1079). SRSG Harri Holkeri and Prime Minister Bajram Rexhepi launched this landmark document translating some of the international norm advocacy into local standards and eventually if successfully implemented also would translate into local practices. This document outlined international standards of appropriate behaviour, i.e. eight benchmarks for achieving a functioning multi-ethnic democratic Kosovo. First, functional democratic institutions were to be established, such as a professional media, and a working civil society with minorities in civil service. Second, rule of law was stressed, including development of a police force, and court system able to control extremists and organized crime as well as international recognition of the Kosovo Police Service as reliable partner and a strong customs service. Third, freedom of movement of minorities without police or army escort within the territory was believed to be crucial in creating a multi-ethnic Kosovo. Fourth, so was the ability to create conditions for safe return of refugees, particularly to urban locations and a special budget targeted for refugee return as well as provide appropriate information regarding returning refugees. Fifth, in order to strengthen the weak economy and facilitate economic recovery, efforts to improve the collection and registration of taxes and encourage privatization as well as create legislation for safe investment were needed. Sixth, set up institutions that will safeguard private property and establish conditions and protections for reacquiring private property was also needed. Seventh, the Kosovo–Albanians were to set up a direct contact with Belgrade and restart business relationships. Eight, a multi-ethnic civilian emergency agency and police force was to be established, i.e. the Kosova Protection Corps (SC/7985).

The outlined standards were used in the norm advocacy of the SRSGs and various other UNMIK officials to measure progress leading to rewards or retributions, and it was clear that the benchmarks were to be met before talks about the final status of Kosovo would be conducted. Hence, the process has been about standards before status and it has forced the Kosovo–Albanians to undertake a number of reforms in order to meet the standards as for example incorporate minority rights (Ingimundarson, 2003, pp. 19–35). The reward for meeting these internationally set standards can be independence and sovereign statehood.

## Advocating Norms of Liberal Democracy

The SRSGs and UNMIK officials have been very forceful in their argumentation about the need for a multi-ethnic, democratic Kosovo. In speeches to the public, in meetings with the political elite and in statements, the SRSGs have pointed out the importance of free and fair elections in the process of democratization. Yet, when faced with realities in Kosovo, they have scaled back on their rhetoric of reconciliation and norm advocacy particularly concerning tolerance and multiculturalism and instead emphasize coexistence.

Prior to the first Kosovo-wide municipal election of 28 October 2000, the first appointed SRSG Dr Kouchner emphasized the importance of a peaceful election in an outreach campaign around the Kosovo countryside. In a speech at a town hall meeting in Obelic, Dr Kouchner promoted democracy by stating: 'building a democratic Kosovo without fear and discrimination must be the main objective, in order to show the world that they [the Kosovars] are ready for self-governance' (UNMIK/PR/333). He also offered a pact promising that UNMIK will assist the Kosovars to develop self-governance if local elections were conducted freely, openly and without violence (UNMIK/PR/351). The role of UNMIK as a teacher of liberal democratic norms is clear. Self-government as well as the opportunity to improve Kosovo's international image was used as carrots for conducting elections in a proper democratic way. Through holding and participating in democratic elections the international community's intentions were that the voters would be socialized into adopting the underlying liberal democratic norms.

On 17 November 2001, the people of Kosovo voted in Kosovo-wide, multi-party elections for the first time. The Kosovo Transitional Council (KTC) was to be replaced by new self-government institutions and an Assembly. United Nations Secretary General, Kofi Annan, welcomed the conduct of the elections and congratulated the people of Kosovo '[…] on the commitment to democratic norms through peaceful adherence to the electoral rules shown throughout the campaign and on Election Day' (UNMIK/PR/666). The Secretary General's statement can be interpreted as part of the overall norm advocacy and as using normative suasion. It was also an acknowledgement of the initiation of the process of socialization into accepting norms pertaining to democracy. As the transfer of power gradually progressed during 2002 the third SRSG, Michael Steiner, very forcefully spoke about democratic principles, about responsibility of authority and the accountability of the PISG. 'This is about recognizing the need for modern administration in line with European standards, in line with what Kosovo really needs' (UNMIK/PR/863). UNMIK's chief executive also stated that 'the better you handle the authority you already have, the more authority will come' (UNMIK/PR/732). The 26 October 2002 election was judged a success, and in compliance with international standards for free and fair elections, and the SRSG argued that, '[…] this election in particular shows the people of Kosovo want a democratic society' (UNMIK/PR/863). Hence, the SRSG constantly reminded the Kosovo political elite that transfer of additional powers to local institutions would meet progress toward democracy.

The March riots of 2004 disrupted the progress towards democracy, and the riots were condemned by SRSG Holkeri who stated that '[...] yesterday Kosovo saw the worst possible violence since UNMIK and KFOR came here five years ago' and that protests and violence were 'the worst possible message Kosovo could send to the international community [...] these acts are destroying the image of Kosovo and sending the worst message about its people and its future' (UNMIK/PR/1142). The international image of Kosovo is important for many reasons, but particularly for development aid, investments and the potential for support for an independent Kosovo. Hence, the rhetoric of Holkeri implies certain covert threats although not clearly expressed, but few would mistake the message. Due to the riots, the UN norm advocacy was more forceful prior to the election of 2004. The UN Secretary General Kofi Annan used his diplomatic skills and the legitimacy of his office to urge 'members of the Kosovo Serb community to participate in the election and in this way to ensure that their interests and concerns are represented and promoted within Kosovo's provisional institutions' (UNMIK/PR/1251). The 2004 election resulted in a change of power (UNMIK/PR/1270). The peaceful change of government based on a willingness to accept defeat in democratic elections can be interpreted as a sign of political maturity and as the process of socialization into the liberal democratic norms has moved forward.

## Preaching Democracy

It was in its capacity as embodiment of a presumably superior–normative context that UNMIK could become engaged in teaching the 'correct' norms of liberal democracy to Kosovo. UNMIK and the SRSGs took on the role of educator in the learning process, key to transforming Kosovo into a liberal democratic entity. The moral authority of the Secretary General and the legitimacy of his office combined with forceful persuasion of the SRSG attempted to convince the Kosovars to change their normative convictions in favour of multi-ethnic democracy. The authority and rhetorical skill of the SRSG were of importance in this type of norm advocacy. As were the timing. Most of the norm advocacy activities peaked prior to elections and it was directed not only to the political elite but also to the public encouraging everyone to participate and to ensure a non-violent election environment. UNMIK's acceptance of the role as teacher was reflected in the organiza- tion's institution-building efforts. To some extent it is a mutual learning process where norms are shaped and reshaped in the interaction, in order to facilitate norm adoption and localization. Although, true norm socialization is more likely to be achieved if norm adoption does not rely on promises of rewards and benefits, such incentives clearly played a role in the norm advocacy of the SRSGs. Shaming and arms-twisting are not likely to provide authentic norm socialization, yet it was used to ensure multi-ethnic diversion in various political bodies. Neta Crawford (1993, p. 52) observes that, '[…] norms established through coercion […] lack legitimacy'. Rewards such as increased power and authority or coercive approaches, such as threats of resolving the Assembly combined with norm advocacy do not promote authentic socialization in a constructivist understanding, because in the absence of rewards or forced compliance the actor would not adhere to the norm. Such approaches lead only to rhetorical acknowledgement of the norms, i.e. paying 'lip service' to liberal democracy and to rational or strategic compliance because it is expected of them and because it will be rewarded. This is not adoption based on change of normative convictions in favour of democracy. Furthermore, democracy promotion may be undermined in case of breakdown of trust and erosion of legitimacy due to tensions between the norms promoted and the practices of UNMIK.

## UNMIK – Failing to Practice Democracy

Practice as a channel for norm promotion provides norm advocates with an opportunity to act out on principles, i.e. comply with the norms the advocates are promoting. This path for norm promotion is obviously only open to norm advocates if they also practice what they preach. This chapter is concerned with providing a better understanding of norm complying practices as a means of norm promotion. Here, the rhetoric behind democracy promotion is translated to practice, in order to make the norms of liberal democracy more persuasive and convincing. One particularly useful way of diffusing norms is to lead by example. In this respect, UNMIK could provide a model of good, democratic governance rather than an autocratic system of governance that lacks accountability, transparency of decision-making and fails to consult the local population and thereby looses parts of its legitimacy. The benefits of cooperating closely in the process of transferring powers and authority from internationals to locals and of creating teams with both international and local staff within the transitional administration are that the interaction provides ample opportunities for norm advocacy and teaching. UNMIK could through its practices demonstrate the feasibility and applicability of the norms pertaining to liberal democracy and good governance in the Kosovo context, and thereby further advance democratization, foster democratic practices and promote democratic norms.

## The Institutional Structure of UNMIK

UNMIK is not providing a model of good, liberal democratic governance. It consists of a pillared structure with each of the principal agencies or organizations operating under the authority of the Special Representative of the Secretary General, the head of UNMIK and also the Transitional Administrator (TA) and the highest international civilian official in Kosovo. The international civil administration as originally designed was composed of four main components: the UN was responsible for civil administration, UNHCR for humanitarian issues, OSCE for institution-building, and the EU was responsible for economic reconstruction (Caplan, 2002, p. 25). The thought behind the design was that each organization should assume responsibility in areas where they had the capabilities and expertise. According to the Ombudsperson Institution in Kosovo 2002, 'UNMIK is not structured according to democratic principles, does not function in accordance with the rule of law, and does not respect important human rights norms. The people of Kosovo are therefore deprived of protection of their basic rights and freedoms three years after the end of the conflict by the vary entity set up to guarantee them' (Second Annual Report of the Kosovo Ombudperson 2001–2). Although conditions have improved as power has been transferred to local authorities, UNMIK was not intended to and will never be a democratic organization even if consultation mechanisms were better developed.

## Establishing a Supreme Authority

Upon arrival in Kosovo, it was important for UNMIK to establish its authority both within Kosovo, but also in relations with the Federal Republic of Yugoslavia. UNMIK is unprecedented as it has more extensive authority than any previous UN mission. In performing the duties vested in UNMIK, the SRSG issued legislative acts in the form of regulations. In its first regulation, UNMIK Regulation No. 1999/1, signed by Special Representative of the Secretary General (SRSG) Dr Bernard Kouchner, the mission asserted plenary powers: 'All legislative and executive authority with respect to Kosovo, including the administration of the judiciary, is vested in UNMIK and is exercised by the Special Representative of the Secretary General'. Furthermore, the SRSG was empowered to appoint and remove any person to or from positions within the civilian administration, including judges and may use these powers vested in him at his discretion (Chesterman, 2004, p. 86). Using these extraordinary powers, Kouchner for example, secured the demobilization of the Kosovo Liberation Army (KLA) and dismantled the parallel and provisional structure of self-government established by the Rugova's Democratic

League of Kosovo (LDK) and KLA (IICK 2000, p. 104). Between June 1999 and December 2005 UNMIK passed 289 regulations and 86 administrative directions covering all areas of law, such as criminal law, civil/commercial law and public/administrative law (www.unmikonline.org/regulations/index_reg_2001.htm). This legislative activity has had an enormous impact on the legal system of Kosovo (Muharremi *et al.* 2003).

The ambivalence of resolution 1244, made it absolutely important to establish the authority over the territory of Kosovo in relations to the Federal Republic of Yugoslavia (FRY). One very clear illustration of this is UNMIK's response to the attempt by FRY to conduct an election on the 24 September 2000 that included Kosovo. SRSG Bernard Kouchner issued the following statement:

> Under UNSCR 1244, UNMIK bears the sole responsibility for interim administration in Kosovo. There is only one electoral process organized by UNMIK/OSCE in Kosovo, and that will be the Municipal Elections for Kosovo scheduled to take place on 28 October. In fact, the attempt to stage the 24 September elections within Kosovo – without any formal discussion with UNMIK, disregarding the most elementary democratic rules, without adopted electoral lists, without international supervision, and in which a leading candidate has been indicted by the ICTY – amounts to nothing more than a farce, a crude attempt to disrupt the properly organised election process of 28 October. Therefore, UNMIK will not participate in, support, organise, or in any other way condone or legitimise the so-called election organised by Belgrade. (UNMIK/PR/339)

In this statement, Kouchner managed to both stress the authority of UNMIK and demonstrate how a properly organized election was conducted to strengthen the understanding of the principles of liberal democracy.

## Establishing Local Political Institutions

The international community perceived Kosovo as *tabula rasa*. Previous structures of governance were disregarded by UNMIK in the democratization and institution-building efforts (cf. Chopra, 2002). Instead, UNMIK attempted to import an abstract model of civil society largely divorced from recent Kosovar history, particularly its nearly four decades of building appropriate institutions for an independent state (Independent International Commission on Kosovo (IICK 2000, p. 104). The Government of the Republic of Kosova – the parallel government headed by President Ibrahim Rugova of the LDK – which claimed legitimacy on the basis of unofficial elections held in early 1990s, was not taken into account when structuring the new institutions. Strong KLA-structures also faced UNMIK upon arrival, and the first six months UNMIK authorities competed with local parallel structures for influence (IICK, 2000, p. 115). UNMIK also abandoned the 1974 Kosovo constitution and drew up a new constitutional framework. A joint working group comprising UNMIK representatives, lawyers from headquarters in New York and Kosovo–Albanians and representatives of the Serb minority (although they only participated the first and final day of the two-month process) drafted a new Constitutional Framework from scratch, disregarding the 1974 Constitution of Kosovo under the Yugoslav Federation. Instead of assisting the Kosovars to adapt and advance their old constitution, UNMIK assured itself special prerogatives and powers that could be more than advisory if the situation warranted and many Kosovars considered the new constitutional framework regressive (ICG Report No. 120, 2001). The Kosovars suggested that a Constitutional Court should be established to act as a check on the Special Representative of the Secretary General, who was not subject to international or national checks and balances. This suggestion was disregarded. The constitutional framework established four primary Provisional Institutions of Self-Government (PISG): the Assembly (with seats set aside for the different minorities), the President, Government and Judicial System (The Constitutional Framework of 2001). This set-up was intended to provide a framework for sharing responsibilities for provisional administrations with representatives of a broad cross-section of Kosovar society (Caplan, 2002). However, the Constitutional Framework clearly states that, the prerogatives of the SRSG under the Security Resolution 1244 are not diminished by the new set-up, leaving the Assembly with very limited authority. No one according to Chesterman (2004b, p. 91) 'was under the illusion that these bodies wielded any actual power'. It also consented to the establishment of 20 departments, each of which was controlled by two heads, an international and a local. This dual structure provided a number of opportunities for interaction, for mutual learning and exchange of ideas and solutions. Yet, there has been obvious dissatisfaction with the interim power-sharing arrangements as the creation of these consultative mechanisms limited the influence and power that the local politicians could exercise (Caplan, 200, p. 42). Still, parallel structures in, for example, Mitrovica continued to defy UNMIK and the Provisional Government (PISG) (ICG Report No. 170, 2006). Furthermore, the Constitutional Framework also stipulated the electoral system. In devising the system UNMIK (through OSCE) strongly favoured a simple system of a universal and secret franchise directly electing government representatives (Chesterman, 2004, p. 219). As their own suggestions and ideas on the election system were disregarded, the Kosovo–Albanians adopted the system favoured by UNMIK and OSCE so as not to delay the elections. The election system made it difficult for any single party to dominate the Assembly and power-sharing is the most likely outcome of elections. The electoral system also included a provision for closed candidate list (meaning that the ranking of the candidates on the lists cannot be changed by the voters) and quota for women (ICG Report No. 120, 2001).

One important reason for disregarding previous structures and the old constitution was that the UN representatives insisted that Kosovo must have a multi-ethnic character, and that Kosovo's autonomy (independence) was linked to its ability to develop into a multi-ethnic democracy (ICG Report No. 170, 2006). The PISG was, however, to guarantee multi-ethnicity by holding PISG and the Albanian majority to a tabulated programme of democratic norms and standards. So, in a sense the constitution provided a temporary foundation to establish democratic practices, such as elections. However, there was a debate concerning whether holding elections was to take place prior to the establishment of the democratic institutions, whether the local institutions were able to shoulder parts of the responsibility in this process, and whether political violence would be triggered by the elections (Hysa, 2004, p. 296).

## Organizing Elections and Promoting Democratic Practices

On 28 October 2000 the first elections were held only at the municipal level. This occurred 16 months after the establishment of UNMIK, to give time for moderate political forces to mobilize support and gain ground, and for voters to shift attention away from the issue of independence and sovereignty where the international community and the local community clearly had conflicting views (Caplan, 2002). The turnout was high and about 79 per cent cast their ballot in the first election under UNMIK administration.[2] Ibrahim Rugova's Democratic League of Kosovo (LDK) swept aside Hashim Thaci's Democratic Party of Kosovo (PDK). The October municipal elections were qualified as 'the best in the region' (Hysa, 2004, p. 296). Despite the elections, the international munici-pal administrators had exclusive rights to veto all decisions, and the SRSG had the final word in decision-making. This procedure did not 'sit comfortably with the need to develop democracy in Kosovo', according to Hysa (2004, p. 297).

The elections for a new Kosovo Assembly of 17 November 2001 represented a landmark in the international efforts to build democratic institutions. Yet, all of the major parties in the 2001 election complained about the electoral system's provision of a closed list and argued that '[…] it was an infringement of their democratic latitude', and that 'Kosovo democracy was to follow standards concerning gender quota that no Western democracy practiced'. Yet,  all of the major parties in the 2001 election complained about the electoral system's provision of a closed list and argued that 'it was an infringement of their democratic latitude', and that 'Kosovo democracy was to follow standards concerning gender quota that no Western democracy practiced' (ICG Report No. 120, 2001). However, the November 2001 elections for the new Kosovo Assembly could not qualify for the international standard as 'free and fair' due to the security situation of the non-Kosovo–Albanian minorities. Rather, the international community judged the election to fulfil the lower standard of 'legitimate and credible' (ICG Report No. 120, 2001). Furthermore, the election was followed by a three-month stalemate, which ended with a grand coalition government. Ibrahim Rugova became President, and PDK nominee Bajram Rexhepi Prime Minister. The grand coalition model saw PDK–LDK tensions soften, but also a directionless, corrupt and incompetent government (*Ibid*.).

Key powers were retained by UNMIK. The April 2001 Constitutional Framework defined which powers the provisional institutions of self-government (PISG) could wield. UNMIK officials showed a lack of faith in the ability of Kosovo leaders to manage Kosovo's internal politics. After the municipal elections of 2000 and the national Assembly elections of 2001, international officials continued in practice to be the real authorities at local and national level (ICG Report No. 120, 2001). The SRSG still maintained significant areas of competences, such as the right to dissolve the Assembly if the provisional institutions are '[…] deemed to act in a manner which is not in conformity with UNSCR 1244, or in the exercise of the SRSG's responsibilities under that resolution' (Constitutional Framework art. 8.1.). Limited authority of elected representatives and frequent elections explain the low turn out of only 711.205 voters (54) in the 26 October 2002 elections, which was Kosovo's second municipal election and third overall election in as many years (UNMIK/PR/863). The limited authority of the Kosovo Assembly is illustrated by how SRSG Steiner overturned an elections law adopted by the Assembly in 2003, clarifying that all matters related to holding elections in Kosovo were within the sole competence of UNMIK in accordance with paragraph 11 (c) of the United Nations Security Council resolution 1244 (UNMIK/PR/951). Constant interference by the SRSG and UNMIK in the Assembly's affairs and to invalidate and revoke its decisions undermined the authority and the legitimacy of the Assembly in the eyes of the people entitled to vote.

Elections were still a reserved responsibility of the UN interim administration in Kosovo, but UNMIK established local election institutions, the Central Election Commission (CEC) and its Secretariat (CECS) to build local capacity to run elections. The elections of 2004 were the first to be organized and run by the people of Kosovo themselves. These elections could be regarded as a significant step in the consolidation of Kosovo's representative and democratic provisional institutions of self-government and a demonstration of Kosovo's progress on the path of normalization and stability (UNMIK/PR/1251). The turnout rate was 54 per cent.[3] However, the Serbian government orchestrated a Serb boycott of the election, and the boycott marred otherwise peaceful and well conducted parliamentary elections. A new narrow governing coalition forged between Rugova's LDK and Ramush Haradinaj's Alliance for the Future of Kosovo (AAK) party, with Haradinaj appointed prime minister took power in January 2005 (ICG Report No. 163, 2005).[4]

## Teaching Democracy

Democratic practices of elections have had an educational role and this has contributed to establish democracy through local self-government institutions. The pedagogical value of elections should not be underestimated. Through technical assistance and effective civic and voter-education programmes, both prior to and following elections the UN may teach electoral practices and expand democratic participation. The ongoing, systematic interaction between UNMIK officials and the Kosovo leadership facilitated the democratic education and provided the Kosovo leadership with assurance of their progress towards democracy. The swift presidential election of February 2006 and the smooth succession from the late President Rugova to Fatmir Sejdiu, demonstrated political maturity, which appears to have strengthened the political fabric of Kosovo (UNMIK/PR/1487). The SRSG congratulated the Kosovo Assembly and all political parties to the 2006 elections, for '[...] once again upholding democratic values in challenging circumstances. Every such occasion, and there have been so many in the past year, contributes to building a strong democratic tradition that will hold Kosovo in good stead in its journey to Europe' (UNMIK/PR/1509). This is interesting as this advocacy highlighted the progression and the learning process and that democratic values take root slowly. It was obviously also connected to a future for Kosovo in Europe, if Kosovo adheres to the liberal democratic norms shared by the Western European states. Yet, democracy in Kosovo is still in the hands of the international community as the SRSG Jessen-Petersen, postponed the 2006 municipal elections for a period not exceeding twelve months to allow for the status talks to be conducted uninterrupted (UNMIK/PR/1567).

## The Effects of the Discrepancy Between UNMIKs Norm Advocacy and Norm Compliance

Norm promotion is clearly not only about rhetorical moral appeals invoking norms of liberal democracy. It is also about complying with the norms

UNMIK promotes. The more the SRSG and other officials of UNMIK 'talk the talk' of liberal democracy, the more they entangle themselves in a moral discourse, which they cannot escape. This implicitly creates expectations that the practice of UNMIK would be consistent with the promoted norms, i.e. that UNMIK would act in a democratic manner. Yet, UNMIK fails to provide a democratic model of governance, to establish channels and mechanism for local influence in the decision-making processes, and the power of UNMIK to overturn local decisions are not conducive for UNMIKs norm advocacy and for establishing a self-sustainable democracy in Kosovo. The way the authority of UNMIK and the SRSG undermines any attempt at local democratic practices and local leadership accountability is counter productive to establishing democratic values and practices.

## Undermined UNMIKs Norm Advocacy

The democratic deficit of UNMIK affects its norm advocacy, which is perceived as less convincing, trustworthy and legitimate. The legitimacy of UNMIK is derived from the legal authority of Security Council Resolution 1244, and the UN Charter. These sources of legitimacy are all international and not from the people of Kosovo. Attempts to set up various institutions for consultations with the local population, such as the KTC, the JIAS and the JIAC were less successful. The PISG set up partly for consultation purposes lost some of their attraction, as their real authority was very limited. The sweeping powers of the SRSG have, for example, efficiently undermined the authority of local institutions and limited the accountability of local political leaders. Hence, the municipal and national elections loose their political significance. The decreasing voter turnout may be an indication that the voters are realizing this. The Ombudsperson is the only mechanism available for the Kosovars to raise complaints or challenge UNMIK's decisions and actions. Chesterman (2004b, p. 102) concludes that UNMIK is '[...] exercising power in a manner that contradicts principles intended to bind future local regimes – such as democratic principles, the rule of law, separation of powers, respect for human rights – may actually harm the prospect of good governance in the long run. And, he criticizes UNMIK for its 'failure to embrace the norms it bears primary responsibility for espousing'. Some Kosovars, as a consequence perhaps, did not regard UNMIK as a legitimate teacher of norms, and some of them, particularly nationalist Kosovo–Serbs, associated the presence with Western neo-imperialism, and American and EU-conspiracy to break up rump-Yugoslavia by granting Kosovo sovereign rights or extensive autonomy.

## Adopting Norms of Liberal Democracy in Kosovo

The prevailing vision of a democracy in Kosovo is flawed, as it is based on a fundamental misconception of the proper relationship between state and civil society, and an obvious lack of respect for minority rights. According to the International Crisis Group's analysis 'the Kosovo-Albanian concept of government is defensive, inspired by Yugoslavian communism, centralized and with limited understanding for the need for decentralization' (ICG Report No. 170, 2006). Kosovo–Albanians have constructed their national identity in the struggle against Serbia and their conceptualization of Kosovo is not as a multi-ethnic state. Other minorities such as Bosniaks, Goranis, Roma, Ashkali and Egyptians are too vulnerable not to side with the Kosovo–Albanians, forcing the Serbian community to rely on Serbia. The March 2004 riots shattered the international confidence that the Kosovo–Albanians were committed to a multi-ethnic Kosovo. The Security Council and UNMIK responded with demands for decentralization of powers to the Kosovo–Serb communities. This in turn was a clear signal of the international communities loss of confidence in the PISG central institutions. The SRSGs have repeatedly stated that Kosovo's self-determination (or sovereignty) is conditioned by concrete measures to accommodate the Serb and other minorities, including decentralization in a multi-ethnic, democratic Kosovo (Interview in Pristina with SIDA official 2004).

## Democratic Practices in Kosovo

Some doubt whether UNMIK has supported the creation of sufficiently independent political institutions to maintain a functional state and democratic practices once UNMIK winds down. An inability to delegate and a lack of devolution of authority to local structures has rendered all levels of government dependent on international structures. As a consequence, this has created a growing dependency on UNMIK. Caplan (2002, pp. 51–2) also argues that '[…] early devolution also helps to prevent the administrative equivalent of aid dependency, in which the local population becomes accustomed to international representatives making decisions for them, including some of the harder decisions that they can choose to ignore'. UNMIK's decisions concerning a closed-list election system have facilitated hardened party hierarchies, weakened internal party democracy and have limited the accountability of politicians to voters. Such election system, it has been argued, 'has limited the democratic space and further marginalized already weak groups such as women and youth' (ICG No. 170, 2006). In UNMIK's final year international staff is gradually being replaced with locals and the main political parties are struggling for control of the institutions.

## UNMIK– Kosovo Relations

Even though the NATO attack against Serbian forces in 1999 and the continuing KFOR military presence remain widely popular, Kosovo–Albanians long ago became impatient with UNMIK as transitional administrator (Interview in Pristina with local NGO representative 2004). Some Kosovo–Albanians perceive that the Serbian regime has been followed by a new kind of 'occupation' that wears a 'humanitarian mask' (Cintron *et al.* 2003/2004). Underlying this opposition to a 'new kind of occupation' is the main concern about the viability of democratic processes when installed in top-down fashion. One local civil servant summarized the years of growing resentment: 'Still we collectively sit and wait. First there were the Yugoslav Communists and then the Serbian occupation, and now this international administration is imposing upon us another form of waiting. It feels as if we have been in an institutional vacuum forever' (quoted from Cintron *et al.* 2003/2004). The speaker of the Kosovar parliament, Nexhat Daci, in late April 2003 expressed to the BBC in a statement: 'If we ask UNMIK, they will never go; they stay here because of nice restaurants, large salaries, and beautiful women' (cited in Cintron *et al.* 2003/2004). In Pristina and other cities, the youth movement 'Vetevendosje!' (Self-determination) argued that Kosovo should reject UNMIK and KFOR by popular demonstrations. Through provocative actions, such as spray graffiti on buildings and UNMIK cars, throw eggs at UNMIK headquarters, flatten UNMIK car tires and call for hackers to attack the KFOR website, this and other youth organizations have gained publicity and attention (ICG No. 170, 2006). Some of the graffiti in Prishtina – *UNMIK Jasht* (UNMIK Out) – has been expressing the same sentiment for years (Cintron *et al.* 2003/2004). In different parts of the countryside, new liberation armies announced themselves in 2005. Although very weak and composed of fringe figures and criminals, the slow moving processes towards independence gave these liberation armies publicity (ICG No. 170, 2006).

## Conclusion

Liberal democratic norms may be successfully diffused to war-torn societies although norm advocacy in Kosovo occurred against a background of vicious state persecution, ethnic conflict, secessionist pressures and international military intervention. This is by no means an ideal situation for promoting values and norms pertaining to liberal democracy and fostering democratic practices. UNMIK had modest success in contributing to fostering democratic values and practices through establishing local democratic institutions. However, the ability for these democratic institutions to survive UNMIK's departure is questionable and the quality of democracy – in terms of accountability, transparency in political decision-making, participation and inclusion of minorities in determining the future of Kosovo – is also questionable. Although most benchmarks are still unmet, the downsizing of UNMIK has already begun. Staff members in both UNMIK and the Provisional Self-Government expect that status will be decided in 2007. For most Kosovo–Albanians the transition cannot occur fast enough. On the 17 November 2005, the Kosovo–Albanian political parties unified and unanimously adopted a 'Resolution on Reconfirmation of Political Will of the Kosovo People for Kosovo as an Independent and Sovereign State', reaffirmed their commitment to the independence referendum of 1991. The Kosovars focus on the future status of Kosovo has, however, been a major impediment for the transfer of meaningful power to local institutions.

What affects the ability to adopt norms of liberal democracy in societies that lack democratic culture? The discrepancy between the UNMIK's rhetoric in support of democracy and its lack of democratic practices may, however, affect its standing as a trustworthy and credible norm advocate. These inconsistencies may ultimately result in a process of superficial norm adoption that is based on strategic calculation, paying lip service to the norms but as incentives and pressure are removed the superficial commitment to these norms will disappear as convictions, preferences etc. are constant and have not changed, i.e. a true socialization processes has not happened and hence no sustained compliance with the norms. The norms are not internally validated and still perceived as something externally imposed. To practice what UNMIK preaches is therefore a way to close the gap between the rhetoric and practice, and may demonstrate that the UN is serious about the norms of democracy.

The UN's work in Kosovo also highlights the complexities involved when the international community tries to impose its universal norms and ambitious plans on local efforts and hopes. The mixed results suggest a need for caution especially when – as in Afghanistan and Iraq – conditions are considerably less favourable than they are in Kosovo.

# Chapter Ten

# RE-EXAMINING THE ROOTS OF WAR IN WEST AFRICA IN A GLOBALIZING WORLD

## Cyril I Obi

## Introduction

According to the Uppsala Conflict Data Programme (2005) about one-third of all armed conflicts in the post-cold war world era have taken place in African countries (Cited in Harbom and Forsberg, 2005). On a global ratio, Africa in 2004, accounted for 10 out of 30 armed conflicts. Most of these conflicts have been intrastate in nature, but in several cases, as in West Africa and the Great Lakes region, they 'crossed border' and mutated into cross-border or the so-called 'networked' wars. A lot of these wars have their roots in historically constructed social contradictions and inequities that have alienated large sections of the citizenry, the foreclosure of peaceful change by authoritarianism and repression, and an altered global context following the end of the cold war. Increased transborder flows of people, goods and arms, and decades of misrule and socio-economic crises also contributed to the outbreak of these wars. In most cases, the trigger for the descent into violent conflict lay in the combination of political and economic policies that deepened social contradictions, and resulted in the massive erosion of the state's welfare role(s) and capacities in the face of globally-led reforms.

After the cold war, West Africa was ravaged by bloody and highly destructive conflicts (Obi, 2005, pp. 4–5). Of note are the decade-long civil wars in Liberia from 1989 to1996 and from 1999 to 2003 and in Sierra Leone from 1991 to 2002 that also became regionalized before they were ended through international intervention, first by Economic Community of West African States Monitoring Group (ECOMOG), the UN and then with some support from the UK, US and the international community. There was also civil war in Guinea-Bissau, followed by the outbreak of war in 2002 in Cote d'Ivoire hitherto considered a bastion of peace and prosperity in the region. Although the rather uneasy ceasefire and peace process brokered by France, ECOMOG and African Union (AU), and backed by the UN, between rebel forces largely in control of the north and government forces in the south is in place, the situation in Cote d'Ivoire is far from settled. In Nigeria's volatile oil-rich Niger Delta, there has been an escalation of violence by insurgent ethnic minority (Ijaw) youth militia groups involving high-profile kidnapping of expatriate oil workers, and attacks on oil multinationals' installations and Nigeria's military forces intent on crushing any resistance to oil production (Human Rights Watch, 2005a, Okonta, 2006).

Thus, as global interdependence and competitiveness continue to intensify, it is possible to discern a twin-faceted trend towards the securitization of development, and a new emphasis on the developmental spin-offs from conflict prevention and resolution, peace building and security. Largely framed within the notions of the liberal peace (Paris, 2002, pp. 637–9) and the Global War on Terror, this trend more than ever before underscores the link between the roots of war and the dominant liberal peace paradigm. It is, therefore, important to revisit the root causes of war, first as a way of evaluating the basis upon which some of the basic assumptions of the dominant paradigm of peacebuilding in West Africa rests, and second to analyze the ways in which the structures and processes of globalization are involved in the 'production' and 'reproduction' of 'civil' war in West Africa.

Although there is a sense in which West Africa had been 'globalized' over the past four hundred years, the closing decades of the twentieth century witnessed the emergence of the most recent phase of globalization, which coincided with the end of the cold war with far reaching consequences for the region. Part of the fallouts from this period included the initial decline in the strategic value of the states and withdrawal of support to erstwhile cold war allies and dictators in the region, the intensification of popular protests and demands for democracy in the face of economic crises, socially harsh economic reform programmes and conditionalities imposed on the region by the Bretton Woods Institutions, creditor agencies and global powers. In all cases, the states resorted to increased repression to contain the popular protests against the socially harsh neo-liberal economic reforms.

The undermining of the welfare gains of independence by economic reforms and the gradual erosion of the state's welfare policies in a period of crises fed into mass alienation and anomie, leading to violent resistance by marginalized segments of society and the implosion of some states. The implosion of these states among others provided the context for local as well as transborder and transglobal forces actors to unleash and reproduce violence against such societies. While it is often easier to focus on the immediate triggers of the West African wars, it is more rewarding to critically examine the root causes, which were deeply embedded in the complex and historically constructed contradictions in the region, and were further sharpened by processes and forces directly connected to the most recent phase of globalization. At the core of the concerns of this chapter lies the quest to re-examine the roots of these wars, rather than accept the hasty conclusion that they are the latest throw ups of the predatory states, retribution from the 'resource curse' or the opportunities that the 'production' of violence provide to men (and women) with guns.

## Globalization

While some have focussed on the economic dimension of globalization, others have concentrated on its ideological, technological, historical, geographical and cultural aspects. However, there is an emerging consensus that it is hinged on transforming social relations on the basis of an integrative, transformatory and transcendental process on a global scale (Amin, 2003; Mittleman and Chin, 2005; Bello, 2002; Held, McGrew, Goldblatt and Perraton, 1999). Petras and Veltmeyer (2001, p. 11), note that it '[...] refers to the widening and deepening of the international flows of trade, capital, technology and information within a single integrated global market'. They also note that globalization is '[...] an epoch-defining set of changes that is radically transforming social and economic relations and institutions in the 21st century'.

One of the critical elements of the most recent phase of globalization has been increased power and influence of the transnational political, regulatory and economic institutions: multinational corporations, international financial institutions, World Bank, International Monetary Fund and the World Trade Organization. Other aspects include the intensified struggles for the world's finite resources and the global market. At another level, it refers to the rapid increase in transborder flows of people, capital and goods, including arms, raw materials and minerals. Taking advantage of the ways in which processes of globalization has empowered non-state transborder actors – including transglobal informal and criminal networks, while simultaneously undermining certain aspects of state capacity, it is rather easy to glean some of its linkages with the eruption of violence in certain parts of the world.

The fact that the wars in West Africa burst forth after the end of the cold war is significant. While the roots of the wars lay in internal contradictions, these were not completely independent of global influences, processes and actors.

## The Causes of War in Post-Cold War Africa

There has been a considerable amount of literature on the causes of war in post cold war Africa. Some analysts, strategists and policy think tanks have continued to devote resources and energies towards explaining and demonstrating how 'looting', 'corruption', 'failed states', 'warlordism' and the 'resource curse or 'environmental scarcities' in Africa breed violent conflict, perpetrate crises and threaten global peace and security. In some cases, such analyses are hinged upon typologies, pathologies and descriptive name-calling (accusing someone without proper evidence), which tend to distort the roots of violent conflict, but more fundamentally, turn a blind eye to the role of transglobal actors whose interventionist and economic roles, deepen local contradictions and contribute to the outbreak and reproduction of violent conflict in Africa. African states or 'rebels' are often blamed for the 'habit of conflict', a point that runs through sensational global media reports on war, political crises, famine, disease, corruption and poverty on the continent.

This tendency is also evident in mainstream 'new' political economy of war analysis, and the policy documents of multilateral and development agencies. It is a perspective that concentrates more on the failings of Africa, and the need for the international community to intervene to put a stop to the endless misery, corruption, the so-called 'new barbarism', poverty and violent conflict. The emphasis is on showing how the struggles over (scarce) resources and patrimonial networks of corruption by African 'statist' elites or warlords conspire to undermine and subvert the state and economy, provoke and sustain violent conflict. It is also keen on showing how Africa has failed to evolve or imbibe 'modern(ist) rationalities' or overcome 'backward cultural habits', leading to the subversion and collapse of its institutions, violence, and generating security threats to the rest of the world (Bayart, Ellis and Hibou, 1998; Chabal and Dialoz, 1999). There is a rational choice underpinning to some of the dominant perspectives that present the struggles over economic resources by corrupt elites, states or rebels as the primary motive for violent conflict. Such assumptions also filter through to the policy outputs of international agencies, and where these assumptions are based on faulty or wrong premises, the policy outputs (that they impose on post-conflict societies in the name of peacebuilding) are wrong-headed, and end up further complicating or worsening the problem of conflict, rather than resolving it.

It is therefore important to raise certain questions about this representation of the roots of conflict on the continent. Apart from addressing some of the risks attendant to some of the limitations of the explanations for violent conflict, it would form a basis for directing more attention to the processes of globalization (and transglobal actors) in the deepening crises and conflicts on the continent. Thirdly, by making the case for re-examining the roots of conflict in West Africa, it would establish a balanced and firmer footing and an alternative basis for examining conflicts and peacebuilding in West Africa.

## War Economies

The new political economy of war as postulated by Collier and his group within the World Bank, and which generated some controversy and spirited debates in the 1990's, is hinged on the position that '[…] economic considerations often shape the calculations and behaviour of parties to a conflict, giving rise to a particular war economy' (Berdal and Malone, 2000, p. 2; Ballentine and Sherman, 2003). It imposes the logic of economic rationality on civil wars. Posing the issue in terms of the greed versus grievance binary logic, the war economy perspective initially dismissed grievance as a cause of war, by demonstrating how greed was the main motive for war.

Economic predation is thus located at the core of conflict with the entrepreneurs of violence targeting 'lootable resources'. Orogun (2004) argues with reference to the wars in Angola, Democratic Republic of Congo (DRC), Liberia and Sierra Leone, that '[…] protracted internal and interstate armed conflicts have been triggered, sustained and funded by the economic imperative of capturing and monopolizing territorial control over the lucrative diamond producing areas'. In another article Smillie, Gberie and Hazleton (2000) argue that '[…] diamonds have been the cause of widespread death, destruction and misery in the small West African country of Sierra Leone', lending much credence to the view, as they put it, that 'the point of the war may not actually have been to win it, but to engage in profitable crime under the cover of warfare'. Keen (2000, p. 22) also notes that conflicts create war economies, in which winning is not the issue, but the creation of the conditions where plundering can be done without any accountability or questioning.

The most sophisticated articulation of the war economy perspective comes out in the observation by Collier (2000, p. 91) that '[…] economic agenda appear to be central to understanding why civil wars start'. He further argued that grievance was often used to mask economic motives in order to gain support, legitimacy locally and within the international community. Collier and Hoeffler (2001), in their attempt to predict the risk of the outbreak of war using a data set of conflicts from 1960 to 1999, and 'logit regressions' seek to draw the connection between greed and conflict. Conflict is also linked to the nature of the economy. Economies which export relatively more primary commodity are likely to fuel conflict. Primary commodities do not require 'complex and delicate networks of information and transactions such as manufacturing', and are not capital intensive, tend to breed conflict Also those who control the territory within which extraction is done can impose tax on or collect rents from the trade. Such rents, 'predatory' taxes and profits are used in buying arms and paying fighters thereby perpetuating war, and making it a means of livelihood.

In response to the criticism of his early war economies postulations, Collier diluted his highly statistical and economic determinants of war, by shifting the emphasis to the 'conflict trap'(Collier, 2003). He then linked conflict to 'opportunity for organised violence' (Berdal, 2005, p. 689) and not to 'the motives of rebel actors'. Some of such opportunities are believed to lie in the proportion of young men in the population, and their levels of education. More men with lower levels of education are more likely to be involved in violence for greed or private gain. Other opportunities lie in the nature of natural resource endowments of a particular country. But in the final analysis, while the war economy perspective has basically rejected 'greed over grievance' as the main cause of conflict, a lot of premium is still placed on opportunities for, and the feasibility of rebellion in resource-rich contexts (Collier, 2005; Berdal, 2005, p. 689), as a cause of violent conflicts.

As Berdal has noted (2005, pp. 688–9), Collier and others' explanations of the 'principal cause and driver of civil wars, has had a marked impact on international policy-making towards civil wars, especially within the United Nations'. Part of the attraction is purportedly related to the desire of the policy community for 'quick fixes' and technical solutions that economic and quantitative analyses appear to provide. At a more fundamental level, it provides justification for certain kinds of international intervention, targeted at the economic motives and opportunities for conflict and more fundamentally tied to state reform in ways that promote market-led development. While for the most part, the transnational component/actors are hardly sanctioned, the real causes of the conflict are not identified and attended to, thereby raising the risk of a future regression.

Yet when we examine the roots of conflicts in Sierra Leone, Liberia and Nigeria's Niger Delta, it is possible to establish several trends. First, the wars in Sierra Leone and Liberia were the result of a complex combination of political, economic and historical factors, as well as the deep-seated crises that engulfed both countries (Abdullah and Rashid, 2004; Ukeje, 2003). Secondly, the crisis coincided with the fall in global prices of the countries traditional exports and the rise in the costs of imports, particularly petrol. Thirdly, the descent to civil war coincided with the implosion of the state and the rupturing of the social contract between the state and its citizens and increased external pressures for economic reforms policies, which undermined the capacities of the states to offer social protection and deliver on welfare to its citizens.

As a result, the states resorted increasingly to repression to keep protests against unemployment, devaluation, increased user fees and inflation in check, further eroding their legitimacy, and opening the door to civil war as their claim to authority was violently challenged. In the case of Cote d'Ivoire, the collapse of the cash crop economy following the fall in global coffee and cocoa prices led to drastic cuts in state welfare spending, the adoption of drastic IMF austerity measures including the devaluation of the national currency – the CFA Franc, by one hundred per cent and the appointment of an IMF technocrat Allasane Ouatarra as Prime Minister. The protests provoked by the growing unemployment and the attendant social crises were compounded by the death of the country's President and patriarch, Houphouet Boigny in 1993. After his death, a power tussle ensued between Allasane and Konan Bedie, the president of the National Assembly. In the course of the struggle, the notion of citizenship became part of the conflict. The use of 'Ivorite' 'as the criteria for participation in the distribution of scarce resources (jobs, property power) within the country' and 'national preference' (Akindes, 2004, p. 26), was used to exclude Allasane from all subsequent elections (allegedly one of his parents was Burkinabe), but more fundamentally stripped all suspected immigrants (including indigenes of communities in northern Cote d'Ivoire) of their citizenship. Even those who were born in the country by parents or grandparents that had migrated from neighbouring countries were basically stripped of their citizenship rights. The atmosphere of mistrust, and fear driven largely by the manipulation and deployment of identity politics and exclusion eventually contributed to the outbreak of civil war in 2002 and the de facto division of the country into two, separated by French and a multi-national UN peacekeeping force: north controlled by rebels and the south controlled by the government.

The implication of the foregoing is that the roots of the civil wars in West Africa are more complex and lie in a combination of factors. It also echoes the point well made by Berdal (2005, p. 689) that the greed of rebels alone cannot explain the cause of civil wars. Beyond this, it makes the case for a more nuanced reading of the 'multi-causal' roots of war, based on a case-by-case approach, rather than broad generalizations that are not well anchored historically and empirically.

## Shadows of Violent Conflict? State Predation, Failure and Collapse

Another significant perspective is represented in the works of Reno (1996; 2000; 2003), de Soysa (2001) and Ikelegbe (2006) among others. War is presented, not just as the opposite of peace, but as the emergence of an alternative political economy of violence hinged upon 'shadow states and economies' (Reno, 2000; 2003). Reno constructs economic predation around the shadow state that exemplifies the 'nexus between corruption and politics', in which public office holders create a parallel state built on personal ties, patronage and illicit deals that profit their patrimonial networks.

The shadow state is built upon personal ties that exploit (subvert) state institutions for private gain. It is based on a 'kleptocracy' in which leaders and public officers pilfer state resources and undermine public institutions, while the real state collapses. In this connection, a collapsing shadow state breaks up into several factions that pursue conflicting personal economic interests, hence the descent into warlordism and civil war. Reno illustrates the connections between the shadow state and violent conflict in Africa, by drawing on cases in Sierra Leone, Liberia, Nigeria, Rwanda, Zimbabwe, Uganda and the DRC (Reno, 2000, p. 58). He paints a rather sobering picture of the ways in which state officials, armies and rebel movements across the continent are engaged in 'free style looting', and concludes that 'the economic interests of belligerents may be an obstacle to the termination of conflict' (Reno, 2000, p. 64).

While Reno goes to a great length to explain why African states are 'failing', he brings back 'grievance' into the debate about the roots of conflict. However, this time grievance is linked to injustice and insecurity, which sometimes drives the 'aggrieved' into predatory organizations. To break this circle of grievance, it is suggested that the roots of 'popular experiences of personalist rule and state collapse be addressed' (Reno, 2003, p. 47).

While Reno places most of the emphasis on how patrimonial political networks, corruption and state collapse, breed feelings of injustice, violence and predatory behaviour, he primarily presents corruption and the struggle for resources as the main source(s) of conflict. This kind of reading of the roots of conflict seems to lock Africa into an inescapable logic of violence. By hemming state collapse in Africa into a fixed frame of corruption, it cannot provide a basis for explaining contexts where corruption has not led to conflict and risks promoting a stereotype and static representation of African states and politics. Rather than locating 'state collapse' exclusively in 'corruption', it would have been more analytically rewarding to locate the weakening or 'implosion' of some African states in several complex factors, including the collapse of the 'post-colonial mode of accumulation' that was, in part, linked to the pressures from globalization, and 'the anti-state market reform agenda promoted by the IMF, World Bank and other donors' (Olukoshi, 2005, p. 185).

By neglecting a particular aspect of globalization that adversely affected some African states and over-emphasising the role of corruption, Reno glosses the ways in which globalization contributes to the post-cold war intrastate violent conflicts in Africa. In the same manner, his perspective may not be able to provide explanations to cases like Somalia, where in spite of 'state collapse' since 1990's, 'sub state polities' has emerged to provide some of the 'core functions of government' (Menkhaus, 2004, p. 11). This perspective promoted by Reno, also feeds into the 'good governance' agenda that emphasizes managerial policies hinged on transparency and accountability of African governments, even if, in practice, such policies hardly ever guarantee welfare interests of popular domestic constituencies.

## Resource Curse/Environmental Scarcities

The resource curse thesis is hinged upon the resource wealth- violent conflict nexus. It attempts to explain, why in spite of being relatively well endowed with resources, African countries remain poor and conflict-ridden. Ross (2003) presents a concise description of the resource curse based on findings 'that natural resources play a key role in triggering, prolonging, and financing conflicts'. In an earlier article, he had observed that 'many of the poorest and most troubled states in the developing world have, paradoxically, high levels of natural resource wealth. There is a growing body of evidence that resource wealth may harm a country's prospects for development' (Ross, 2001, p. 328; Soysa, 2001, p. 17). In looking at the resource dependency-conflict linkage as it relates to oil and democracy Ross (2001, pp. 325–61), argues that oil does greater damage to democracy in poor countries (such as provoking conflict) than in rich ones.

This perspective combines three objectives: explaining how economic predation of resources fuel violent conflict, why resource-rich states fail to transform into prosperous industrialized economies and how natural resource wealth can contribute to (the lack) of development and democracy. It shows how resource abundance tends to nurture misgovernance and the absence of the rule of law, and blocks economic development, subverting the state and feeding conflict. In a sense, conflict is seen as being one of the consequences of the absence of growth in paradoxically resource-rich, but impoverished contexts. Beyond this lie the attempts to demonstrate how institutional weakness or poor governance could translate into the inability to effectively manage resource wealth and contribute to the lack of development, stability or even conflict (Boschini and Patterson, 2003).

Boschini and Petterson also argue that resource-rich countries are only 'cursed' if they have 'low quality institutions' and what they refer to as the 'appropriability' or profitability of the resource based on institutional capacities and national control. They further contrast resource-rich but poor economies like Angola, Sierra Leone and DRC, with an oil-rich and developed Norway, explaining that the latter was able to transform its resource wealth on the basis of its institutional capacities. On this basis they doubt the veracity of perspectives that draw a simplistic linkage between resource wealth and the lack of economic development.

The 'resource curse' thesis is of limited analytical value. In a rapidly globalizing world, it has been argued that the international scramble for, and exploitation of Africa's resources has been intensified (Bond, 2006), leading to unprecedented poverty, de-industrialization and social crises, which deepen the conditions for civil strife. The nature of the resource: economic and strategic, the power relations that its control and production spawns, and the ways such relations feed into issues of access, ownership, distribution, democracy and social justice are fundamental in understanding the conflict nexus. It only partly explains why a resource-rich Norway is not embroiled in 'resource wars'; while a resource-rich Nigeria is confronted by insurgent Ijaw militia in the Niger Delta. Violent conflict is not just produced by internal contradictions or factors, but more often is not embedded in globally refracted contradictions arising from the intensified exploitation of Africa's resources and the predations of transnational elite – local, national and global. A lot of literature has emerged showing how the contradictions of intensified globalized oil exploitation in Africa had fed into the deepening of social contradictions and violence in the Niger Delta region, for example Obi, 2001, 2004, 2006; Fleshman, 2001; Okonta and Douglas, 2001. Indeed it is not possible to fully grasp the roots of the escalating conflict in Nigeria's Niger Delta outside the 'unique qualities of oil itself' (Watts, 2004, p. 76), and the role of the state, local elite, oil multinationals and youth militia in the volatile politics spawned by oil. In the same manner, the Angolan and Sudanese civil wars were in part prolonged because of the role of oil multinationals in profiting from the vast oil riches of those countries, and the contestations between the states and the warring factions/rebels movements to control access to these strategic energy resources that are highly valued and much sought after in the global market.

## Environmental Scarcities

This approach is essentially hinged on the view that population growth beyond a particular threshold places pressures/stresses on renewable natural resources/the environment leading to the relative scarcities of resources (Homer-Dixon, 1994; Myers, 1993). Environmental scarcities are also noticeable where resources are being rapidly depleted as a result of degradation or unsustainable forms of exploitation and production. Such scarcities are most associated with the developing countries, where they trigger conflicts over shrinking renewable resources. At the heart of this perspective to violent conflict is the population size-natural resource linkage. Kaplan (1994), a decade ago, constructed a frightening picture of a coming anarchy in a 'Hobbesian' West Africa, as the result of an imminent demographic-environmental catastrophe. Thus, in a neo-Malthusian fashion it assumes that population growth beyond the rate of replenishment of renewable resources (leading to scarcity) triggers off violent conflict in developing countries. The primary concern is therefore with environmental security, which among others seeks to prevent threats emanating from the environment – environmental conflicts or resource wars, from threatening global security (Obi, 2000, p. 47).

The resource curse and scarcities approach are indeed related and tend to proffer explanations for 'resource conflicts'. They are writ large in the explanations for Africa's civil wars that are often presented as resource conflicts. Yet, rather than providing explanations on how these scarcities are 'produced', they are often presented as natural, often linked to natural resources that occur as if placed in particular regions/countries by some 'invisible hand'. However, in some cases, the paradox of resource-rich areas such as the Niger Delta being one of the poorest and underdeveloped regions in Nigeria does show that scarcity may indeed be the result of distributive inequities that could be the result of historical injustices and political marginalization.

Thus, it would be more accurate to analyse how the 'politics' that revolve around the exploitation of natural resources by forces of transnational capital deepen social contradictions and conflict in Africa. As in politics, given the dominant mode of production that is tied to land, resource conflicts do not arise from the mere occurrence/location of these resources, but rather from the power relations surrounding their ownership and control, and the distribution of the benefits: accumulation versus dispossession, leading to a cycle of exploitation, resistance and repression. Therefore, what appears on the surface in most of Africa as 'resource conflicts' are linked to demands for redistribution, citizenship and social justice – in fundamental terms, to self-determination and democratic struggles. This much can be gleaned from the ongoing low intensity conflicts in Nigeria's oil-rich Niger Delta where insurgent Ijaw ethnic militia are locked in a confrontation with state security forces and oil multinationals in a struggle over the control of oil (Okonta, 2006; ICG, 2006).

Thus, there is a need for an alternative debate or analysis that should inform the understanding of wars and armed conflicts in Africa. A starting point will be to move more in the direction of a holistic analysis that draws upon the interrelated nature of social phenomena, rather than mono-causal explanations, or stereotypes of political behaviour in Africa. Emphasis should be placed on the substance and dynamics of 'irreconcilable differences between actors', or the connections between violent conflict and 'structural inequality or injustice' (Richmond, 2003, p. 292). Apart from this, some focus should be placed on the differences in the 'cocktail of causes' that vary from one country to the other. Economic factors alone do not explain conflict. They could be useful in explaining why wars could be prolonged or how global networks and hegemonic forces can also benefit from wars in West Africa. It is also necessary to include a critical appraisal of the role of external or global hegemonic factors, policies or triggers, in the eruption and prolongation of civil wars in Africa.

## Conclusion

The foregoing shows that the dominant perspectives are inadequate for fully understanding the complex roots and dynamics of conflict in West Africa. A re-examination of the causes of wars in West Africa reveals their origins in historically rooted contradictions that are further complicated by socio-economic factors and the politics of exclusion, as well as changes linked to the end of the cold war. As Hutchful and Aning (2004, p. 199), rightly observe, the roots of the conflicts in Africa 'are intertwined with the issues of political and economic marginalisation, as well as social exclusion, identity and citizenship'. Thus the core issues in the understanding of wars in West Africa relate to issues of inequality, injustice, social and power struggles at the local, national, (sub) regional and global levels. Mainstream conflict analysis on West Africa appears to privilege struggles over resources, state failure and warlordism', over the quest for justice, democracy, power, and the role of various fractions of international community and transnational networks in creating 'scarcities', and deepening internal contradictions that directly influence the outbreak and duration of war.

A related point that flows from the foregoing is the impact of globalization, and the increased role of regional and global actors in the conflicts in West Africa. Such international actors either in the form of diamond and gold traders, suppliers of ammunitions, mercenaries, private security companies, mining companies and oil multinationals appear to indirectly benefit more from conflict, as violence also provides them with a cover for lack of transparency, and opportunities for profit, even as they provide the resources for the combatants and states in the region. What is important to note is that violent conflict in West Africa is often the product or result of the collusion between internal and international players or factors. It is the outcome of a rather pernicious relationship that feeds on and off the interests of local, hegemonic and extractive external interests, in spite of indications that the end of the cold war has also meant a decline of the proxy status of some of the states in the region. While it is possible to note the diminishing presence of France in its former colonies, a trend emphasized by the devaluation of the CFA Franc in 1994, and which can be gleaned from more recent acts of hostility against France and its citizens in Cote d'Ivoire, France, Belgium, the UK and increasingly the US are deeply involved in conflicts and conflict resolution in Africa. But it is important to understand US renewed involvement more in terms of its strategic, security and energy interests particularly in the wake of the 9/11 terrorist attacks, the Global war on Terror, and the 'new' scramble for West Africa's oil resources as an alternative to total dependence on a volatile Middle East.

The notion of the new political economy of war cannot be understood outside the centrality of politics to violent conflict. At the regional level, conflicts in the region in a rapidly globalizing world have had the tendency to cross borders, as in the case of the Mano River states and Cote d'Ivoire, not primarily for economic reasons, but because of several reasons: historical, the movement of refugees and fighters across the borders, the unresolved crisis of citizenship in some West African states, and the security and other calculations of the leaders of neighbouring states in the region.

Although it could be argued that Taylor intervened in Sierra Leone to lay his hands on diamonds, it should be noted that his intervention was partly directed towards assisting his ally Foday Sankoh to seize power, after Tejjan Kabah, Sierra Leone's elected President had shown what was seen as hostility towards Taylor, by providing troops and logistics for ECOMOG, which the latter saw as a Nigerian-led West African force standing between him and power in Liberia. In the same manner, the conflict in Cote d'Ivoire is tied to the question of citizenship, which became an issue following economic crisis and structural adjustment, the post-Houphouet Boigny era in which the notion of Ivorite was used to exclude some Ivoriens from power and access to resources (Akindes, 2004; Ahonji, 2003; Chaleard, 2003; ICG 2004; Coulibaly, 2003). Houphouet too, had earlier provided support to Charles Taylor's National Patriotic Front of Liberia (NPFL), during the Liberian war, in an effort to avenge the murder of Liberia's President, and son-in-law, William Tolbert by Samuel Doe in the 1980 coup that brought him to power.

From the foregoing, the key issues revolve around the causes and dynamics of violent conflict in West Africa, and the roles played by domestic, regional and international actors in perpetrating, or resolving conflicts. Special attention needs to be placed on the role of ECOWAS and ECOMOG in conflict resolution in the region. It is also important to explain the nature of the narratives of violence in the region and the role of alienated youth (and children) as perpetrators as well as the victims of violence (Human Rights Watch 2005b; Utas, 2003). For it is by understanding these issues that intervention directed at promoting peace, reconciliation and reconstruction can become more sustainable. In the final analysis Hutchful and Aning (2004, p. 217) correctly note that '[...] conflicts in West Africa tend to have multiple causes, but the most important single cause is poor governance over a sustained period coupled with the frustrated aspirations for political change, often occurring in a context of profound state debilitation'. The latter observation on 'state debilitation' partly ties into the earlier observations on how the processes of economic globalization eroded and undermined state capacities in the socio-economic spheres through the imposition of market-led reforms in the 1970s to the early 1990s.

In relation to methodology, there should be deeper studies hinged on each specific conflict, and on comparative studies of conflicts within West Africa. For this reason apart from informed fieldwork in which international and local actors (and victims) in conflict are interviewed, there is a need to focus more on the fundamental causes of conflict by examining how political closures, exclusion, the social dimensions of economic crises, reform and the crises of state legitimacy fuel war. Then, it is also important to understand the international context of the political economy of conflicts in West Africa in a holistic and integrated sense. For therein lies the kernel of the nexus between international interventionism, the deepening of socio-economic crisis, the politics of exclusion, and the descent into violent conflict.

Finally, where violent conflict ends, the door to peace (and development) may or may not open. But the roots of peace themselves are embedded in a critical understanding of the roots of conflict, the character of the actors and the weapons of war. It takes two to tango, and conflict does involve local and international forces. But the locale is both the site of violent conflict and accounts largely for the more obvious factors and fighters. Thus, at one level, peace in West Africa can only be properly located in the context of a new social contract that provides equal access to power, and makes the rulers accountable to the people. Also the states and political elites must begin to respond more to the demands of the people to economic and social justice, while economic reform programmes and educational policies should be sensitive to the quality of life of the people, and their right to a dignified and meaningful existence. Social development, justice and peacebuilding programmes that attend to the need of the youth and children as demobilized combatants and victims of conflict should occupy a central place in the rebuilding of war-torn societies.

For post-war reconstruction and reconciliation to progress, there should be carefully designed projects hinged on locally-owned (rather than hegemonic externally imposed solutions) initiatives that balance impunity against justice, and brightens the hopes for an equitable and better future as the guarantee against a return to the horrors of a painful past. Rather than, the penchant of the international community to impose the 'liberal peace' model, or what Paris (2002), aptly calls a *mission civilisatrice* (2002, p. 637), there should be a return to the developmental, democratic and socially responsive state that would address the need for equitable access to power and resources, as necessary ingredients for development in West Africa. It is also critical that the current inequities in a rapidly globalizing world, where the gap between the rich and poor, within and between counties is widening, and the powerful countries promote neo-liberal reforms that disempower people of poor(er) countries be redressed, in ways that provide access to resources, markets and technologies so important to build firmer roots for peace in Africa.

In the final analysis, West Africa's development after devastating wars ultimately lies in the hands of Africans and their states, but it is equally important that those external hegemonic forces that exploit the continent and impose solutions and models of development that further their own interests, but contribute to Africa's underdevelopment, should respect the humanity and rights of African people to own and direct their collective democratic and developmental aspirations towards their own liberation, dignity, welfare and human security.

# Chapter Eleven

# THE AFRICAN UNION (AU) AND ITS COMMITMENT TO NON-INDIFFERENCE: CAN THE AU BE AN ACTOR FOR THE PROMOTION OF HUMAN SECURITY?

## Linnea Bergholm

The development of a new AU peace and security architecture attracts much interest today from academic and policy communities alike. Various organizations, not least the UN, are zealously debating the nature of such institutional structures and what best role external actors can play to support and bolster them. Many interesting changes are underway with regards to African security sector reform, combating terrorism and small arms proliferation as well as early warning frameworks. I will focus specifically on one aspect – peacekeeping and peacebuilding capabilities, where there has been a prominent change in emphasis from the Organization of African Unity (OAU) to the AU. Before the end of the cold war the OAU had started putting human beings more and more at the centre of their management of peace and security issues. I provide a broad account of how the OAU was severely constrained in doing so. The AU, since its succession to the OAU in 2002, has continued this transformation in concerns and priorities. As well as elucidating and explaining some background factors to why the AU has started couching its conflict resolution mechanisms in human security language, I analyse to what extent the AU can be an actor for the promotion of human rights and human security. This increasing importance can be seen in many ways but I will focus specifically on the cases of the African Union peace missions in Darfur, Sudan and in Burundi. The African Mission in Sudan (AMIS) has been seen as a test case for the African solution to African problems agenda. It has also put many of the AU's new institutions and Charter provisions to test.

In particular, it shows how the term 'civilian protection' has been given a prominent place in the planning of peace operations of the organization. Indeed, I show how the AU has already been, in a limited but very important sense, an actor that has promoted human security through tasks related to its civilian protection mandate.

## The OAU Birth and Charter

The OAU was established in 1963 at the Summit for African Heads of State and Government (AHSG) in Addis Ababa, around the time when most African states had just received their hard-won independence. The OAU Charter reflected the time in which it was conceived; a new era for equal and sovereign states in Africa. It was state-centric, emphasizing the respect for territorial integrity, non-interference and peaceful settlements of disputes.

The Charter Article III stated that the following Principles were to be adhered to:

- The sovereign equality of all Member States.
- Non-interference in the internal affairs of States.
- Respect for the sovereignty and territorial integrity of each State and for its inalienable right to independent existence.
- Peaceful settlement of disputes by negotiation, mediation, conciliation or arbitration.
- Unreserved condemnation, in all its forms, of political assassination as well as of subversive activities on the part of neighbouring States or any other States.

The OAU may be thought of as a 'Cold war Animal' in that the security context of the cold war helps elucidate why the OAU operated according to the sacrosanct principle of non-intervention. Africa was at that time rated as a central region to the stability of the spheres of interest of the superpowers. African states were encouraged to adopt the political ideologies of one or the other of the superpowers in efforts to expand their spheres of influence into Africa. The character of African regimes was not considered an important issue, indeed; brutalities committed by authoritative regimes were often ignored by major powers that often provided arms to them in exchange for military loyalty (Vogt, 1999; Ayoob, 1995, p. 95–6).

The OAU lacked a vision to work for human rights for all Africans. In fact, the OAU never pretended to be, first and foremost, an organization working for individual human rights. Nevertheless, Walraven elucidates how the massive rise in armaments, increasing super-power rivalry and the worsening economic crisis that the continent suffered since the mid-1970s and onwards led to a progressive deterioration in security. The OAU's blatant silence in the face of internal conflicts, indifference towards ethnic strife and the disregard of persecution and human rights violations belatedly led to serious criticism both from internal and external actors (Walraven, 1999, pp. 311–4). The early 1990s saw a general intensification of domestic and interstate conflicts with civil wars in Liberia, Sudan, Ethiopia, Rwanda and Mozambique. Once the cold war ended, authoritarian regimes and repressive governments that had operated under the protection of one or the other of the superpowers or former colonial powers were challenged as this protection was now gone. Many governments were confronted with internal and external pressure for democratization and they found themselves economically marginalized (Walraven, 1999, p. 298). As the OAU's member states enthusiasm for its conflict management methods declined, new reforms and considerations with regards to management of intrastate conflicts and human rights were considered as a response (Murray, 2004, p. 25). The OAU slowly started the arduous process towards prioritising human rights.

## The OAU and Human Rights

The Charter committed the organization to the establishment and maintenance of international peace and security, in particular founded upon the UN Charter and the Universal Declaration of Human Rights (UDHR), and complemented by African legal human rights instruments. The Charter, therefore, does make a reference to human rights in its preamble, where it records the adherence of the member states to the UN Charter and the UDHR. As Naldi points out however, these are not binding legal norms; the preamble simply reaffirms the existing rules and states the objectives to be achieved (1990, p. 3).

The most important sign that the OAU slowly became more sensitive to human rights considerations was the signing of the African Charter of Human and People's Rights (ACHPR) in 1981, coming into force five years later. Known as the Banjul Charter, this was a regional legal human rights instrument, representing African values and an African notion of human and people's rights (Naldi, 1999, p. 156). It gave the OAU Assembly the responsibility of composing an African Commission on Human and People's Rights. The Protocol to the Charter envisaged the establishment of an African Court on Human and People's Rights by 1998. The Banjul Charter had a critical role to play in the establishment of a new humanitarian order in Africa (Ouguergouz, 2003, p. 797). Yet, while the OAU did begin to recognize that human rights conditions in one state were a matter of concern for other states, this was not accompanied with an effective enforcement mechanism within the Charter.

Another important sign was the 1999 'Grand Bay Declaration and Plan of Action on Human Rights in Africa' which acknowledged that 'observance of human rights is a key tool for promoting collective security, durable peace and sustainable development as enunciated in the Cairo Agenda for Action on relaunching Africa's socio-economic transformation'. This was the first example of an African Ministerial conference on human rights (Ouguergouz, 2003, pp. 793–4; CONF/HRA/DECL (1) issued 16 April 1999, 7th preambular paragraph).

## The OAU and Responses to Humanitarian Crises Within Member States

External intervention and outside interference was seen as clearly jeopardizing the African influence in world politics and it was, therefore, the main source of fear among African regimes (Walraven, 1999, p. 269). The OAU was labelled a 'trade union for dictators', and was negatively viewed as a top-down organization that concerned itself very little with domestic conflicts, civil wars or the lives of ordinary Africans.

While superpower and western interference were both loathed and needed by African regimes, attempts were made to limit their own inter-ference in each other's affairs. The norm of *uti possidetis*[1] adopted by the OAU Assembly ensured that the colonial boundaries remained intact. While this contributed to interstate stability, it has often been argued that it was very detrimental to the individual security for the majority of African citizens (Andemicael, 1976, p. 57). Additionally, the OAU's record shows that a policy of non-intervention was applied to the extreme point of African nation states oppressing their people with impunity and doing little or nothing to prevent massive human rights violations in their neighbouring countries (Walraven, 1999; Murithi, 2005).

Despite playing an active and imaginative role in conflict management the OAU still had an unimpressive record in terms of practical outcomes. The OAU used informal conflict resolution procedures of an ad hoc nature. These included mediation, conciliation, diplomacy, ad hoc committees, good offices committees and 'presidential mediation' (Sesay, Ojo and Fasehun, 1984, p. 36). Without an institution given the authority to mandate peacekeeping operations, and without the political will to create one, the OAU was severely hampered in its attempts at anything resembling peacekeeping activities.

One exception was the only deployed OAU peacekeeping force in Chad in the 1980s, and it was not a very successful one. The civil conflict in Chad provided the OAU with its first opportunity to involve itself in peacekeeping operations. By the late 1970s the conflict saw the involvement of France, Libya, Nigeria, the US and the UK among other states (Mays, 2002, p. 17). The OAU Assembly deployed a peacekeeping force destined for Chad in 1981, amid considerable difficulties with regards to the funding modalities and the unwillingness by OAU members to provide soldiers for purposes within other member states. The Chad mission had an unclear mandate, suggesting both Chapter VI and Chapter VII functions to ensure the defence and security of the country while awaiting the integration of government forces. The OAU mission for Chad was a traditional peacekeeping mission in the sense that a ceasefire document was established, and it was invited by the government prior to the deployment. It was not officially concerned with the humanitarian situation, but with restoring the territorial integrity and law and order of the Chadian legitimate government. The organization's limited financial, logistical and military capacities for peacekeeping and peace enforcement severely hampered the Chad mission, which was withdrawn in 1982. The disappointment with the Chad operation made African regional hegemons seek alternatives to trying to mobilize the OAU into military-related cooperation thereafter. For example, Nigeria began using the framework of the Economic Community of West African States (ECOWAS) and South Africa opted to call upon the Southern African Development Community (SADC) (Mays, 2002, p. 157). One outcome of this first African attempt at peacekeeping on a large scale was that the OAU felt unable or unwilling to seriously contemplate peacekeeping operations under the OAU banner for more than ten years.

During the 1990s many African sub-regional organizations became aware of a sense of duty, partly out of humanitarian concerns, to contribute to regional stability and peace. ECOWAS, for example, has deployed peacekeeping missions in Liberia (1991), Sierra Leone (1993), Guinea-Bissau (1998) and most recently in Cote d'Ivoire (2003). ECOWAS has pioneered new ground for an African regional organization in the realms of peacekeeping and became a model for those who propagated a similar role for the OAU (Ero, 2000). Among others, Erskine argues that ECOWAS decided to intervene in Liberia partly because of the humanitarian need, and ECOMOG was indeed involved in humanitarian tasks of protecting, preserving and sustaining human lives (2000, pp. 81, 178–9). Adebajo describes how there was a sense of urgency among African policymakers and scholars in the search for mechanisms to solve Africa's conflicts (2002), much because of the manifest reluctance by the international community to deploy troops in Africa after the devastating experiences in Somalia and Rwanda.

In 1990 the OAU was given a formal prerogative to concern itself with internal conflict when the Assembly adopted a 'Declaration on the Political and Socio-Economic Situation in Africa and the Fundamental Changes Taking Place in the World'. This Declaration reflected the OAU's commitment to begin working towards the speedy resolution of conflicts, including those deemed as solely domestic, on the continent.

The Mechanism for Conflict Prevention, Management and Resolution (MCPMR), endorsed formally in 1993, was the response to the desire of establishing a permanent and more effective and interventionist conflict resolution mechanism. The 1993 Mechanism did not give the organization a blanket right of intervention in internal conflicts; an intervention had to be decided on by the central organ of the new mechanism, this decision in turn needed the consent of the disputants. However, Walraven argues that it did have the right to intervene in the exceptional cases marked by severe human suffering as well as collapse of the state (1999, p. 320). The mechanism was very active in terms of diplomacy, mediation and fact finding missions. The International Panel of Eminent Personalities investigating the causes and atrocities committed in the Rwandan genocide was an important example of the OAU's widening range of post-conflict peacebuilding activities and increasing concerns for the humanitarian situation in war zones. In 1993, at the news of an alleged attempt at a coup in Burundi, the Mechanism discussed the humanitarian need for rapid measures. The OAU intervened with a limited monitoring commission, the OAU Military Observer Mission to Burundi (OMIB). What was remarkable was that the Rwanda and Burundi cases show that humanitarian concern could be a sufficient ground for the activation of the MCPMR. The Mechanism did in some way continue to prepare the ground for future possibilities of African peacekeeping forces. Nonetheless, it largely continued operating in accordance with the OAU principles, especially in respect of the sovereignty and territorial integrity of Member States, non-interference in the internal affairs of states and the inviolability of borders.

## Birth of African Union and the Charter

The AU has set out to adopt a policy of 'non-indifference'. Ambassador Saïd Djinnit, the African Union's Commissioner of Peace and Security, said in Addis Ababa, 28 June 2004: 'No more, never again. Africans cannot [...] watch the tragedies developing in the continent and say it is the UN's responsibility or somebody else's responsibility. We have moved from the concept of non-interference to non-indifference. We cannot as Africans remain indifferent to the tragedy of our people'.

Creating the AU was an attempt to depart from the old organization and to create a Union with an explicit objective to be a security organization.

This may be seen in the Article 3 of the Constitutive Act, which spells out that the AU's objectives, among others, are to:

(a) Defend the sovereignty, territorial integrity and independence of its Member States.
(b) Encourage international cooperation, taking due account of the Charter of the United Nations and the Universal Declaration of Human Rights.
(c) Promote peace, security, and stability on the continent.
(d) Promote and protect human and peoples' rights in accordance with the African Charter on Human and Peoples' Rights and other relevant human rights instrument.

The Article 4 commits the AU to the principles of

(a) Sovereign equality and interdependence among Member States of the Union.
(b) Respect of borders existing on achievement of independence.
(c) Participation of the African peoples in the activities of the Union.
(d) Establishment of a common defence policy for the African Continent.
(e) Peaceful resolution of conflicts among Member States of the Union through such appropriate means as may be decided upon by the Assembly.
(f) Prohibition of the use of force or threat to use force among Member States of the Union.
(g) Non-interference by any Member State in the internal affairs of another.
(h) The right of the Union to intervene in a Member State pursuant to a decision of the Assembly in respect of grave circumstances, namely war crimes, genocide and crimes against humanity.
(i) Peaceful co-existence of Member States and their right to live in peace and security.
(j) The right of Member States to request intervention from the Union in order to restore peace and security.
(k) Promotion of self-reliance within the framework of the Union.
(l) Promotion of gender equality.
(m) Respect for democratic principles, human rights, the rule of law and good governance.

The most significant difference between the Charters of the AU and the OAU can be seen in the Article 4 (h) and (j) above. Principle 4 (h) marks a different stance with regard to the issue of military interventions in member states domestic affairs, due to humanitarian concerns. The Charter is still 'pro-sovereignty', but it has placed important limitations on the right for sovereigns to act in whatever way they wish. In contrast to the OAU, the AU does not require the consent of a state to intervene in its internal affairs in situations where populations are at grave risk (Powell, 2005, p. 12). Abass and Baderin among others have observed the potential problematique presented by the Constitutive Act, in that it contains provisions preserving the non-intervention principle 4(g) and also provisions enabling humanitarian interventions 4 (h) (2002, p. 14).[2] It may be argued that the AU Charter provision does not restrain the Union from interfering in internal affairs of a member state; it only restrains its members from doing so unilaterally.[3] The AU therefore has an institutional *right* to intervene in its members' conflicts, not a privilege or a duty.

Something that remains to be seen is what importance the amendment to Article 4 (h) – passed by the AHSG – will have within seven months of the launch of the organization. This was a contradictory move, showing that the interventionist stance of the AU is by no means consolidated or unproblematic. Baimu and Sturman argue that this clause, aiming to uphold state or regime security, is inconsistent with the other grounds for intervention, which aim to protect African people from grave violations of human rights when their governments are unable or unwilling to do so (2003).

## The AU and Human Rights

A case can be made that there is, since the 1990s, a noteworthy increase in political will for the promotion and protection of human security and human rights by African leaders. If the AU is to match its current statements with action, there must be a consolidated and coherent institutional approach to the benchmarks made regarding human rights. Murray contends that the AU has developed a vision for the continent and that this is a crucial time to ensure that the opportunity for human rights is not lost, preferably through enforcement mechanisms and an elaboration of standards and their implementation (2004, pp. 267–70).

The Constitutive Act does not explicitly discuss human rights issues but it attaches great importance to their protection and promotion, since acts such as genocide and crimes against humanity can effectively trigger intervention. This suggests that the AU recognizes the idea that security on the African continent is inextricably linked to the observance of human rights of their people. The Common African and Defence and Security Policy (CADSP) that was adopted at the AHSG Extraordinary Session held in Sirte, Libya, towards the end of February 2004 interestingly makes such links and aims to redefine the vision of security. It thereby alludes to the common security of all of Africa and how an emphasis on human security, not just traditional state-centric security, is needed. It declares that a multi-dimensional vision of security for all Africans embraces such issues like human rights. Although an effective human rights protection system in Africa is linked and essential to the effectiveness of the security organization in Africa, the AU human rights regime still remains undeveloped and ineffective (Abass and Baderin, 2002, p. 28).

The Constitutive Act grants respect for human rights, the rule of law and good governance (Ouguergouz, 2003, p. 794) as seen in the Objectives of the Union where Article 3 states that the Union shall '[…] promote democratic principles and institutions, popular participation and good governance' and shall 'promote and protect human and peoples' rights in accordance with the African Charter on Human and Peoples' Rights and other relevant human rights instruments'. It can also be seen in the Principles, Article 4 states that the Union shall function in accordance with, inter alia, the principles of respect for democratic principles, human rights, the rule of law and good governance; promotion of social justice to ensure balanced economic development; respect for the sanctity of human life, condemnation and rejection of impunity and political assassination, acts of terrorism and subversive activities; condemnation and rejection of unconstitutional changes of governments.

Another important step is that the African Court on Human and Peoples Rights had its Protocol ratified on 25 January 2004 and is envisaged to merge with the African Court of Justice in the future. This Court will become the main judicial organ of the AU and rule on human rights abuses under the ACHPR and under general international human rights law.[4] The challenges facing the Court are primarily political. As an illustration of this, the AU decided to suspend a report critical of Zimbabwe's human rights record (Murithi, 2005, p. 105). Compiled by the AU Commission of Human and People's Rights, the report is thought to contain political sensitivities. Funding and logistical support remain two other challenges.

## The AU and Responses to Humanitarian Crises Within Member States

The development of its peace operations capabilities play a central role because they reflect most notably how different the political climate of the AU is from the OAU. Since its inception, the AU has taken important steps to become the lead agent of peacekeeping on the continent. Two important examples have already been set in Burundi and Sudan where the AU has demonstrated its tenacity when it comes to assembling capabilities for full-fledged peace operations. This is a development that has received much enthusiasm from international, particularly Western, actors and donors. Commentators often argue that the AU is significantly different from the OAU in that it is more 'interventionist' and more sensitive to human rights considerations (Murithi, 2005; Powell, 2005). What is particularly striking is that since the early 1990s, with regards to peace operations in Africa, military measures in domestic conflict are increasingly considered by the OAU/AU due to humanitarian concerns.

The most significant organ when it comes to peacekeeping capabilities is the AU Peace and Security Council (PSC), established in 2003. Africa has for the first time established a higher authority, above state level, that is mandated to authorize and legitimize AU interventions in internal conflicts. Article 7, item (e), of the PSC Protocol reaffirms the AU's right to intervene as already stated in the Constitutive Act Article 4(h). It states that the PSC can recommend to the Assembly of Heads of State (AHS) '[...] intervention, on behalf of the Union, in a Member State in respect of grave circumstances, namely war crimes, genocide and crimes against humanity, as defined in relevant international conventions and instruments'. The PSC is composed of an African Standby Force (ASF), a continental army of multidisciplinary military and civilian contingents prepared for rapid deployment. By 2010 it is envisaged that this force will provide the AU with a combined standby capacity of 15,000 to 20,000 troops, incorporating five sub-regional standby arrangements, each of brigade size (3,000–4,000 troops). The PSC is additionally composed of a Panel of the Wise (POW), which advises the council on issues relating to the maintenance and promotion of peace, a continental Early Warning System, which facilitates anticipation and prevention of conflicts, and a Military Staff Committee (MSC). It is underpinned by two pillars, the Protocol and the Common Africa Security and Defence Policy (CSDP).[5] Although the ideas of enhanced common African defence and military cooperation hark back to the early days of the OAU, these were never translated into concrete policies accompanied with the political will to implement them.

So far, the AU has mandated and fielded two missions in Burundi and Sudan. The two cases are pivotal because each reflects how human beings are more centrally placed in the African Peace and Security agenda today. Both, however, had the consent of the host government and had followed the signing of peace or ceasefire agreements.

## The African Union Mission in Burundi (AMIB)

On 3 February 2003, Pierre Buyoya, President of Burundi, declared his willingness to see African peacekeepers in the country to help end the civil war. A Ceasefire Accord signed on 3 December 2003 established that an AU Force would monitor its implementation. For the then Chairperson of the AU, Thabo Mbeki, and for other African leaders, the deployment of AMIB was among other things an opportunity to demonstrate the AU's departure from the OAU and to assume a lead role in delivering on a peace and security agenda in Africa (Powell, 2005, p. 35). The OAU had been engaged in efforts to resolve the conflict in Burundi since 1993 but it was first during the last phase of the transition to establish the AU that this peacekeeping mission was a tangible option. Around 3,000 troops from mainly South Africa, Ethiopia and Mozambique were deployed in April 2003 to monitor the peace process, the implementation of the signed Ceasefire Accord and to provide security.

AMIB engaged in violent conflict prevention and peacebuilding activities during a very complex phase of the whole effort; despite the Ceasefire Accord the AU troops found that there was no peace to keep on the ground. Yet, in February 2004 a UN evaluation team concluded that the conditions were appropriate to establish a UN peacekeeping operation in the country (Murithi, 2005, p. 93). Thus, despite several shortcomings and insurmountable challenges, AMIB succeeded in bringing some peace to almost all provinces and created conditions where the UN felt that it could take over and intervene with its peacekeeping forces. AMIB forces became UN mandated United Nations Operation in Burundi (ONUB, Opération des Nations Unies au Burundi in French) forces and were boosted with around 2,000 additional troops.

The mission was not given an explicit mandate to protect civilians, but Powell notes that after some time on the ground, senior AMIB officials drafted rules of engagement (ROEs) to allow their troops to use force to protect civilians in imminent danger of serious injury or death. According to these ROEs, and with prior authorization from military and civilian officers, force could be used to protect civilians in cases of genocide and mass killings. This, for Powell, signifies 'new thinking on the specific challenges of protecting vulnerable populations in the context of an African-led peacekeeping mission' (Powell, 2005, pp. 3, 35). It can be argued that despite PSC being partially operational in 2003, AMIB left an important footprint with the positive outcomes in procuring human security of the population of Burundi. Even if AMIB cannot be said to have performed the civilian protection functions successfully, this does not negate its accomplishments and successes.[6]

## The African Union Mission in Sudan (AMIS)

On 8 April 2004 the Government of Sudan (GoS) and the two main rebel groups, the Sudan Liberation Movement/Army (SLM/A) and the Justice and Equality Movement (JEM), signed the AU and Chad mediated Humanitarian Ceasefire Agreement (HCFA). This step forward in the peace process meant that the AU established and deployed a ceasefire verification mission and an Armed Protection Force, comprising about 300 troops from Rwanda and Nigeria, to the Western Sudanese region of Darfur (Murithi, 2005, p. 88).

The small force could however do little beyond having a preventive effect; subsequent violations of the ceasefire agreement continued to plague the mediation efforts. The scale and brutality of this complex crisis in Darfur caused many observers to call for international intervention in accordance with humanitarian principles and for civilian protection. On the one hand, the GoS would not allow any other organization than the AU to deploy armed peacekeepers in Darfur. On the other hand, the AU, still busy putting in place and operationalizing its new structures, was eager to 'do something' in the face of the appalling human rights conditions in Darfur. The AU has all along shown remarkable willingness to assume a protective role (Powell, 2005, p. 60). The humanitarian situation and the deliberate targeting of civilians in the fighting was a great concern, as shown in resolutions and protocols.[7] Despite this, AMIS was not provided with an explicit protection mandate. Instead the mandate is complex, and incorporates a seeming inconsistency. AMIS is to 'Protect civilians whom it encounters under imminent threat and in the immediate vicinity, within resources and capability' but at the same time the mandate continues 'it being understood that the protection of the civilian population is the responsibility of the GoS'.[8]

AMIS became, with time, a more significant peace mission, thanks to troop build-ups during 2004 and 2005 it was transformed from a contingent primarily of unarmed military observers to a contingent of around 7,000 personnel; armed force protectors, unarmed civilian police and support teams. It was hoped that AMIS would then stand a better chance to achieve the civilian protection mandate. However, the protection mandate itself was unclear in the sense that it did not give AMIS the mandate to enforce the cease-fire, i.e. it was not accompanied with a Chapter VII mandate. AMIS has instead attempted to deter violations through monitoring. The civilian protection man-date has been interpreted in a number of different ways. National contingents within the mission have attached varying weight to this mandate and its corresponding mission tasks. The ROE's have not been sufficiently disseminated and explained to the contingents, leaving some soldiers and commanders uncertain on how to use force and how to react to threats. Still, AMIS has made and continues to make some contribution to the stabilization of the security and humanitarian situation in Darfur.

AMIS has throughout been under-equipped and under-resourced and suffers operational, logistical and capability shortfalls. It still encounters problems with command and control, and logistical support. AMIS' deployment was delayed at least partly due to insufficient planning capacity at the AU HQ in Addis Ababa. It is also hampered by lack of sufficient troops on the ground, most of which have not received their salaries for several months. In these circumstances, it is a matter of hope that AMIS has brought relief to internally displaced persons and that it stabilized the security situation in Darfur for some time. Although it is difficult to estimate the number, AMIS has saved countless lives. It has helped accumulate evidence through monitoring of human rights abuses, and has provoked the outside world's continued attention and condemnation. AMIS has incorporated, for the first time in AU's history, a CivPol section to the mission. Furthermore, and not insignificantly, AMIS has helped further our knowledge of the conflict through escorting and protecting numerous research teams, diplomatic and humanitarian missions in their wishes to document, interview and understand the atrocities that are underway in Darfur. Arguably, these are small but necessary accomplishments in the direction of a civilian protection capability.

## Conclusion

The beginning of the twenty-first century has witnessed a renewed resolve by African leaders to address conflicts in the region, including internal ones. What is more, there has been engagement in complex intrastate conflicts with references to the need to end large-scale humanitarian suffering. The designers of the AU have shown a will to create an organization and a Constitutive Act that will have the teeth and interventionist powers that the OAU always lacked. As a result, commentators often argue that the AU is significantly different from the OAU in that it is more interventionist and more sensitive to human rights considerations. High hopes are invested in that the AU will become an agent to intervene when necessary in the affairs of its member states to stop war crimes and genocide.

However, the challenge remains to assemble the necessary capabilities for the implementation and enforcement potential of these provisions. It is still early days to assess if the AU is in the process of creating a much more interventionist model for peacekeeping operations, despite the fact that concrete proposals, such as the Article 4(h) Charter provision, have seen the light. The litmus test of what seems to be a significant transformation, most scholars concede, rests in translating these statements and policies into measures that have impact on the ground, for the security of African civilians (Francis, 2006).

Therefore, the civilian protection activities that the AU has carried out thus far, in Burundi and Darfur, are important steps in the direction of creating a more human centred conflict management framework. The relative stabilization of conflict, the saving of lives and the lessons learned from these cases are laudable and are likely to contribute to a capacity building process that is well worth studying.

# Chapter Twelve

# HAMAS BETWEEN SHARIA RULE AND DEMO-ISLAM[1]

## Michael Schulz

[D]emocracy is inside Islam, there is no conflict between Islam and the democracy. (Interview with Hamas leader, 14 October 1997)

We do not wish to throw them into the sea... If Israel declares that it will give the Palestinian people a state and give them back all their rights, then we are ready to recognize them. (From an interview with Ismail Hanyeh, Prime Minister of the PA, 26 February 2006. http://www.washingtonpost.com)

This chapter examines the vexed issue of the place for Arab Islamic movements, such as Palestinian Hamas – The Islamic Resistance Movement – within democracy and democratic peace. Some analysts would claim that Arab Islamic movements have no place within democracy, due to Islam's inherent incompatibility with democracy (see Sörensen, 1993; Huntington, 1993; Tibi, 1998; Kramer, 2001; Spencer, 2005). Spencer asserts that in Islamic law, all non-Muslims are considered inferior to Muslims. Another claim often aired is that Islam constitutes a threat to the basic values of the West, including its democratic mode of governance. Others contradict these claims, highlighting democratic, grassroots level structures that Islamic organizations have built throughout history (Esposito and Voll, 1996; Midlarsky, 1998). Furthermore, the democratic popular political culture of the (mostly) religious Arab masses, in contrast with the undemocratic political structures of their governing regimes, forms the setting within which Islamists must act. (Goddard, 2002; Tessler, 2002; Inglehart, 2004)

Hamas's election victory in January 2006, handing it control of the Palestinian parliament, is the first time that an Arab Islamist party has ascended to power democratically in the Arab world. Studies in this area to date have considered

Islamist movements or parties *outside the government* (Norton, 1995; Persson and Özdalga, 1997), or have considered situations *outside the Arab world*, such as Iran (Ansari, 2000) or Turkey (Özdalga, 1998; Liel, 2003). Otherwise they may relate to *failed* attempts to seize power in the Arab world (for example, Algeria). Few studies have connected analyses concerned with political behaviour of Islamist parties/movements, with a political-cultural analysis (see Tessler, 2002).

This study aims to explore the proclivity for Hamas to develop a democratic or a theocratic influence over the Palestinian Authority (PA). Will it act as other Islamic *Sharia* ruled regimes have done, and seek to suppress or abolish the secular and democratic aspects of the PA? The perception that Islam is incompatible with democracy is not always borne out in reality. The forms of social infrastructure and networking established by Islamist organizations might indeed act as catalysts for more participatory politics. Islamic institution-building and networking in the form of schools, mosques, health clinics, kindergartens, charities, sports clubs, choirs, computer centres and the like are forms of mobilization from below, although there are instrumentalist reasons behind this that has gradually demonstrated the capacity to provide social welfare to the poorest (Mashal and Sela, 2000; Hroub, 2000).

This emerging capacity for public service cannot be seen to minimize Hamas's militant activities. However, as Bloom has shown, Hamas's use of suicide attacks against Israeli civilians is highly influenced by pragmatism: 'The social and public meaning of their activity is no less important than its religious legitimacy' (Bloom, 2005, p. 32). Hence, the critical issue explored in this study is in what way militants and moderates within Hamas will adapt to the new political reality now that it holds power within the PA.

With the establishment of the Arafat-led PA in 1994, initial public hopes for democratization were soon replaced by a more traditional political culture of scepticism, and of distrust of authority, policies and institutions (Schulz, 2006; Ghanem, 2001; Lindholm Schulz, 1999; Robertson, 1997). Existing non-democratic structures within the Palestine Liberation Organization (PLO) and the newly established PA regime further strengthened this mistrust. Opposition towards the PA, and in particular towards the Fatah party (the largest faction within the PLO), saw Hamas emerge as the major opponent to Fatah. Furthermore, the Palestinian public judged the PA in relation to its performance in the peace process, in the context of the Palestinians' ongoing conflict with Israel (Schulz, 2006; Lindholm Schulz, 2003; Shikaki, 2005, 1996). Hamas gained public support during the *al-Aqsa intifada* for its operations inside Israel, and was seen as the main catalyst for Israel's unilateral withdrawal from the Gaza Strip in 2005 (Shikaki, Jerusalem Media Communication Centre (JMCC), 2005). Hence, we would expect to find empirical evidence for a continuation of the Palestinian public's distrust of its political leaders, directed now against Hamas, if the new PA does not remain firmly committed to both democratic principles and its hard line against Israel. Hamas is simultaneously under political pressure internationally, in its new position of political responsibility. This pressure comes primarily from the USA and the EU, who consider Hamas a terrorist organization. They demand that Hamas recognize Israel and its right to exist, and that it end all violent means against Israel.

This study was guided by the following research questions:

- In what way is democracy defined in the Hamas movement and how is Hamas's perception of Islam linked to democracy?
- What are the expectations among Palestinians concerning the evolution of Hamas in relation to democracy and the peace process?
- What expectations do Palestinians have about the peace process and Hamas, and how will Hamas adapt to these public demands?

## Methods

The analysis proceeded from a study within two distinct levels: first, concerning popular attitudes and second, concerning leadership attitudes and strategies. The political culture of the Palestinian public and the Hamas leadership were considered to provide key indicators to the prospects for a democratic Hamas. Public expectations were compared with the manifested strategies of Hamas. Interviews with the Hamas leadership had been conducted in 1994 (Lindholm Schulz, 1999) and in 1997 (Schulz and Lindholm Schulz, 1998). The present study aims to follow up these interviews during 2008, thereby revealing actual and potential shifts in perceptions and strategies of the Hamas leadership.

The present study incorporates the findings of three previous surveys of Palestinian public opinion. The survey data stem from a joint research project between the Department of Peace and Development Research at Göteborg University (Sweden) and the Department of Sociology at Birzeit University (West Bank) on *Democracy and State Building in Palestine*, which was initiated in 1996. The three surveys were conducted in November 1997, July 2001, and April/May 2006. A random sample of 1,308 Palestinians was selected for the 1997 survey, 1,492 for the 2001 survey and 1,500 for the 2006 survey. Each survey contained between 150 and 200 questions. The target population were individuals, 18 years of age or older and were residents of the West Bank, the Gaza Strip or the city of Jerusalem (under Israeli control). The samples were constructed with the help of the Palestinian Central Bureau of Statistics (PCBS). Although some of the questions were amended, removed, or newly added between periods, several of the study's central foci have been measured throughout.

The accumulated data collected within this study revealed strong empirical evidence of a democratic Palestinian political culture. More than two-thirds of Palestinians are committed to democratic attitudes and behaviour. The surveys also revealed a stable democratic political culture over time, with no major shifts in attitudes and behaviours between the three periods.

There was strong support among Palestinians for continued armed struggle against Israel, but also simultaneously support for continued negotiations with Israel. In the context of this evident tension within an overtly democratic political culture, the study explored how stable is this democratic tendency under Hamas's stewardship of the PA. A further key issue concerning Palestinian public opinion is the extent to which Palestinians see a political solution in the conflict with Israel. The 2006 survey enabled comparison with the period during which Fatah dominated the PA. Hence, in this chapter, data collected since 1997 is used. The following aspects have been considered:

- *Popular* attitudes have been measured through a survey based on a question-naire concerning preferred systems of governance, definitions of democracy, commitment to democracy within Hamas and the PLO, commitment to democracy within the PA, assurance of human rights and freedoms in the new political environment, media and democracy, Islam and democracy, and democracy and the peace process.
- *Leadership* attitudes and strategies have been analysed through qualitative, semi-structured interviews with representatives of Hamas and the PA, and Hamas members of the Palestinian Legislative Council (PLC), about preferred systems of governance, the roles of the PA and the Palestinian Council in enhancing democracy, and potential impediments to democracy.

## The Political Culture of the Hamas Leadership

Approximately 50 leaders and representatives, drawn from all factions in the previous PLC, ministers from the previous Executive Authority and represen-tatives from parties that were outside the PLC[2] before Hamas's 2006 election victory, were interviewed in semi-structured surveys in 1994–5[3] and 1997.[4] Each was asked questions concerning the current political situation in the self-rule areas and the role that democracy is or should be playing there. Issues such as multi-party systems, basic law, human rights, freedom of opinion, character of a future Palestinian state, and the role of religion were discussed. The attitudes and perceptions of competing factions towards the Palestinian leadership were explored.

The role of the factions – for decades the cornerstone of Palestinian politics and activism – was critical in this study of PA institution-building and politics.

Here, some of the existing data presented results at variance with the present study. Some studies, such as a 1996–7 study conducted by the Centre for Palestine Research and Studies (CPRS), claimed that the role of all factions was declining. The survey results of the present study showed, in contrast, a growing polarization between Fatah and Hamas. The 2001 and 2006 surveys indicated that this polarization was widening over time. Significantly, the 2006 survey was launched a few months after Hamas's surprise election victory. A declining role of factions may prove counterproductive to democracy if pluralism – a cornerstone of democracy, and an element that has, historically, been relatively healthy within the PLO – also declines. The existence of several ideological streams within the PLO has facilitated robust political debate within that organization (Hassasian, 1993; Abu, Amr 1994). In addition, the existence of political parties is seen generally to be a crucial factor in democratization processes (see, for example, Rueschemeyer *et al.* 1992). If the trend towards polarization indicated in this study implies political debate and robust dialogue, this may in fact foster an emerging democracy. The success of an emerging democracy may depend upon common understandings among the elite groups about the codes of conduct for the democratization process.

## From Opposition to Power

Although there are two Islamic movements – the Hamas[5] and the Islamic Jihad – Hamas was the only real opposition force in Palestinian society before its January 2006 election victory. Hamas had become the second largest political group in the West Bank and Gaza, second only to Fatah. Opposition Islamist movements are grappled with the issues of submitting to mainstream political processes and participating in elections, and with the consequences of doing so, if, in fact, they were permitted to enter the mainstream. Algeria and Jordan provide examples of marginalized groups entering the mainstream fray in semi-democratic political systems. However, Hamas's 2006 election victory – one which international observers endorsed as free and fair – appears to be a unique case in the Arab world.

Hamas's public support rose and fell according to successive successes and failures in the peace process, and according to the timing of Hamas-sponsored suicide attacks on Israeli society. For instance, support for Hamas declined dramatically in relation to the devastating bomb attacks of February/March 1996, when several suicide bombings occurred over an eight-day period, killing approximately 60 Israelis. In September/October 1996, Hamas's support was down to 8 per cent, the lowest recorded by the CPRS (CPRS, Public Opinion Poll, No. 24, 26 September – 17 October 1996). The 1996 attacks also highlighted fractures within Hamas; between the traditional leadership and younger activists, between inside and outside leadership groups, and between the political and military wings. Through the mixture of repression and coercion that had characterized President Yasser Arafat's regime at the helm of the PA (see Robinson, 1997) some parts of Hamas's political wing were co-opted into the mainstream political process. Several politically moderate Hamas leaders were convinced, in contrast to the politically staunch military wing of the organization, to take more moderate positions, and to renounce military operations in particular. Almost one and a half years later, two similar attacks were executed in Jerusalem; one in the Mahane Yehuda Market in July 1997, and, in September of that year, in the pedestrian street Ben Yehuda. At that time Hamas was still wracked by internal conflict and burdened by hostile public opinion. The suicide bombings, against the Israeli military as well as civilian targets, failed to impress the Palestinian populace, evidenced by the 9 per cent indicative support of Hamas (CPRS No. 29, 18–20 September 1997). Not until the end of 1997 did public support for Hamas begin to climb again. In December 1997 it stood at 11.6 per cent (CPRS, No. 31, 22–30 December 1997). This increase is most likely explained by the release of Hamas's spiritual leader, Sheikh Ahmed Yassin, imprisoned since 1989, and whose release was precipitated by a failed assassination attempt on Khaled Masha'al by Israeli security forces, when the Hamas leader was in Jordan. Jordan's King Hussein was infuriated over the Israeli violation and his strong representations led to Yassin's immediate release. His return was widely celebrated in the West Bank and Gaza. However, it was problematic for PA leader Yasser Arafat for two reasons. First, Yassin was released without Arafat's involvement, but instead with Israel, Jordan and Hamas as the key players, relegating Arafat to a mere bit part. Second, the symbolic power of the release of an imprisoned spiritual leader eroded some of Arafat's radiance as the incarnation of Palestine. The 1997 survey revealed that Hamas would have garnered the support of almost 20 per cent of the population if an election had been held in November 1997.

The relationship between the PA and Hamas during the period from 1994 until the outbreak of the *al-Aqsa intifada* in September 2000 was highly ambiguous. Hamas struggled with its identity; on the one hand that of a military resistance movement with a strategy of excessive violence and the use of terror tactics, and on the other, an aspiring cooperative political partner to the PA. The elite within Hamas and Islamic Jihad still see themselves as representatives of an alternative to the existing 'secular' regime.[6] Empirical support from the present study suggests that parallel democratic and Islamic versions of the political system have been developing, and will continue to develop.

Some Hamas leaders expressly differentiate between Islam and democracy:

> First of all, we have our private self-control, consultations or *shura*, which is totally different from what is called democracy. Democracy in the sense of [the] Europe[an] concept has no actual justice. (Interview with Hamas leader, 15 October 1997.)

This interpretation of Western democracy sees it as underlining the 'tyranny of the majority' that enforces its will over the large minority. In Islam this would not occur, according to Islamic leaders. Nevertheless, one leader stresses the importance of following a democratic process:

> [I]t's up to the people to choose the way of life they prefer. If they prefer a religious life, it should be accepted [by] everyone; Sharia to be the rule of our life. If they will accept that – I think they should – ... Sharia should be applied. If they will not, then we will wait until the change of our community. This is our way, in [our] struggle for applying the Sharia, in a democratic way. (Interview with Hamas leader, 12 October 1997)

In other words, such Islamic leaders believe that the democratic system should be used in order to first achieve power and then to create a theocratic state. Meanwhile the PA was seen as a temporary representative of self-rule. Islamists were highly critical of the performance of the PA:

> They [the PA] are responsible [for] all the corruption and the absence of democracy. So they are responsible for all the misery of the Palestinians. [T]hey have to change their attitude, but according to my mind it is impossible for them, because they actually practise corruption, practise this absence of democracy among the PLO system [for] more than 35 years. (Interview with Hamas leader, 15 October 1997)

Hamas leaders expressed the reluctance of Hamas to see itself as an opposition party to the allegedly undemocratic ruling PA:

> We are not the opposition. We have different groups, we are from the PLO, [and] we are committed to our religion. [W]e are not a member of the Council to say that we are the opponent, maybe we are. [W]e represent the majority of the people, so we can't say that we are the opponents, without real elections, we can't say that we are the majority and you are the minority or the reverse. (Interview with Hamas leader, 15 October 1997)

The interviews found, in general, that the Islamist opposition was critical of the PA and the peace process at large; however it indicated a willingness to join future elections in order to test its political strength. Hamas was not prepared or ready to participate the January 1996 elections. However, Hamas participated in municipality elections in 2005, winning some districts, and in the national election in January 2006, where, of course, it achieved its unexpected victory. However, on several occasions prior to these plebiscites taking place, Arafat delayed or postponed them, giving Hamas the opportunity to criticize the PA as undemocratic. Only after Arafat's death, in 2004, was it possible to hold new elections.

> Yes, yes, we are ready to take part in municipality elections, but the question is, do you think that Mr Arafat is going to permit or run elections for [the] municipality? He is afraid [of] Hamas winning, so he postponed it, postponed it forever. (Interview with Hamas leader, 15 October 1997)

Evidence supporting the assertion that Hamas has shifted positions – from a radical militant movement to a political pragmatic one – can be found in three major documents that Hamas uses as its political and electoral platform. These documents contrast with the commonly quoted Hamas Charter of 1988. Hroub has analysed these documents, and has argued:

> Hamas continues to be characterized with reference to its 1988 charter, drawn up less than a year after the movement was established in direct response to the outbreak of the first intifada and when its raison d'âitre was armed resistance to the occupation. Yet when the election and post-election documents are compared to the charter, it becomes clear that what is being promoted is a profoundly different organization. (Hroub, 2006, p. 6)

The following is the most commonly quoted passage from the 1988 Charter:

> For our struggle against the Jews is extremely wide-ranging and grave, so much so that it will need all the loyal efforts we can wield, to be followed by further steps and reinforced by successive battalions from the multifarious Arab and Islamic world, until the enemies are defeated and Allah's victory prevails. (Passage from the Introduction to the Hamas Charter, 1988, www.palestinecenter.org/cpap/documents/charter.html)

This passage is widely seen as an evidence of the militant and violent strategy that Hamas has pursued against Israel. Less attention has been paid to the documents that were used by the Change and Reform list that Hamas constructed for the January 2006 Palestinian election. Although, the documents can be dismissed as, and may indeed prove, mere lip service, they nonetheless indicate a clear democratic strategy, including political promises to the public, capable of judgment by Palestinians via the ballot. The documents indicate a shift within Hamas towards a more politically mature actor, which has developed concrete suggestions for reform and change in various spheres of society. They spell out the political reforms that are needed within the PA, and suggest how corruption should be handled, how the judiciary and legislative policies should be developed, and how public freedoms and citizen rights should be protected. Education, social and media policies are also mentioned in these documents. The suggestions for change are formulated in a language that 'overall is secular and bureaucratic' (Hroub, 2006, p. 14). The remnants of religious language in the document are primarily used by opponents of Hamas as proof that its real intention remains that of the Islamization of Palestinian society. However, documents from 2005's National Unity Government Programme, which declare Hamas's preference for a unity government with the other Palestinian factions (National Unity Government Programme), support the perception of Hamas as a democratic coalition partner. The idea behind the National Unity Government Programme was to muster a joint force behind the aim of liberating Palestinian society from Israeli occupation. Its critics, in contrast, claim that Hamas in fact never believed in an election victory, and that this declaration was made as a tactical move, rather than representing a real change in its positions.

However, evidence suggests Hamas's increasing awareness of the need to adjust its position in relation to Fatah, and to respond to pressure from the international community to recognize Israel. In Article 9 of the National Unity Government Programme Hamas confirms that

The government will deal with the signed agreements [between the PLO/PA and Israel] with high responsibility and in accordance without compromising its immutable prerogatives. (From Hroub, 2006, p. 17)

Furthermore, Hamas states in Article 10 that

The government will deal with the international resolutions [on the Palestine issue] with national responsibility and in accordance with protecting the immutable rights of our people. (*Ibid*.)

For Israel in particular, but also for the international community and for Fatah, this was not enough. However, when compared with the Charter of 1988, the contents of the National Unity Government Programme suggest that Hamas has made a major shift. Others claim that traces of this position were already evident in 1989 (see, Lindholm Schulz, 1999). Still, Article 10 can be given numerous interpretations. One view is that Hamas will respect the basis of the Oslo agreements, but only if Palestinian rights are fulfilled. These rights could include the establishment of an Islamic Palestinian state in the whole of Palestine, thereby implying the destruction of Israel. However, it could also be seen as an indirect acceptance of a two-state solution, although this is not explicit. Another major rift that developed between Fatah and Hamas after the 2006 election concerned the movements' respective positions towards the PLO. Hamas has, since 1996, demanded to be accepted as a PLO member. By 2005, when Hamas and Islamic Jihad were discussing with Fatah the possibility of joining the PLO, Hamas had also begun to discuss reforming the PLO. Article 23 of the National Unity Government Programme states the need for 'Developing administrative and financial reforms, strengthening the role of oversight and accountability, establishing a *diwan al-mazalem* (court of complaints and injustices), activating the laws against illegal profiteering, corruption, and the squandering of public funds' (*Ibid., p.* 18).

In Article 7, Hamas underlines the need to rebuild institutions on 'democratic, professional and nationalist foundations rather than on the basis of *unilateralism* (a surrogate reference to one-man or one-party rule) and factional affiliation' (*Ibid*, emphasis is the author's). Hamas's intention to reform the PLO, as well as the PA, has further fuelled the tension and power struggle between Fatah and Hamas. Hamas has not been willing to accept the PLO as the sole representative of the Palestinian people unless Hamas is permitted entry into that organization. In contrast with the international community's, and the Arab League's, positions (seeing the PLO as the sole Palestinian representative), Hamas sees itself as a popular representative, but is at the same time intent on entering the PLO. If this occurred, Hamas would indirectly take a step closer to recognizing Israel's right to exist. Hamas has evolved from a movement that was heavily influenced, in its formation, by the first intifada, to become a more established political actor, standing on a more detailed political platform and reform programme, and adapting to the reality of the political system in which it must operate. It is not accurate to characterize this evolution as an internal struggle between so-called moderates and militants. Rather, it is the culmination of a continuous, robust debate that has revolved around Palestinian public opinion, as well as around contextual changes in relations with Israel and the Arafat-and Fatah-led PA. In particular, Hamas's relations with Israel have been discussed within the movement over a long period. On several occasions less hostile options have been on the organization's agenda. Lindholm Schulz identified a potential future dialogue between Hamas and Israel through a 1994 interview with a Hamas leader:

> I believe that there must be, and it is not impossible or strange to have, such a dialogue between the Islamist movement and the Israeli government [...] I believe that there must be an equal dialogue, no-one is high, no-one is down, and equal dialogue on political or social or any other matter between the Israeli government and the Islamic movement. (From Lindholm Schulz, 1996, p. 242)

Of course, Hamas's readiness for dialogue is also dependent upon the degree to which public opinion will pressurize it to eschew violent policies towards Israel.

## Public Opinion and Hamas

All polls that have been conducted since the start of the peace process evidence a large majority of the Palestinian population as supporting a democratic system, of a similar, although not identical, style to the Western representative system. According to the Hanf & Sabella study, conducted in the period during the first Palestinian elections in January 1996, 36 per cent of the population *favoured* some kind of consociational democracy, whereas 43 per cent favoured a representative, competitive democracy. 76 per cent would have *accepted* consociational democracy and 71 per cent would have accepted competitive democracy, although not necessarily favouring it above other alternatives (Hanf & Sabella, 1996, 121 ff.). A majority of those sympathetic to the Islamist movements favoured consociational or majority rule (59 per cent). The secularists (Popular Front for the Liberation of Palestine (PFLP), Democratic Front for Liberation of Palestine (DFLP), Palestinians People's Party (PPP) and the Palestine Democratic Union (Fida) demonstrated the most democratic tendencies, with 86 per cent favouring one of the two 'democratic' options in the sample. Fatah supporters fell in between these extremes – 78 per cent favoured one of the two democratic options, while 22 per cent opted for less democratic alternatives (*Ibid.*, p. 123). There was also strong support for an accountable government, independent courts and a free press (*Ibid.*, p. 125). Those that supported the Islamists also generally favoured a separation of powers (*Ibid.*, p. 126).

One of the crucial issues that were identified as foci of this study's 1997 survey was to determine the extent to which Palestinians are committed to democracy. One of the most frequently asked research questions in Palestinian opinion polls designed to measure public commitment to democracy has been,

'Do you support a government whose policies you believe in (such as economic and foreign policy) but that is not democratic?'. The 1997 survey of this study showed that 75.5 per cent of Palestinian respondents did not support such a government.[7] When the question was directed towards whether the PA, in 1997, was democratic, 25.4 per cent of respondents disagreed with that statement.

In 2001, in the context of the continuing *al-Aqsa intifada*, ongoing then for one year, the Palestinian public's dissatisfaction with the Arafat-led PA and its undemocratic performance had increased to 45.2 per cent. Despite the fact that Palestinians were in the midst of a violent struggle with Israel, Arafat failed to create a sense of national unity that could obscure the flaws and misbehaviours of the PA.

However, by 2006, after Hamas had taken control of the PA, only 12.9 per cent of Palestinians surveyed considered the PA undemocratic. This indicates the Palestinian public's high expectations about the future democratic performance of Hamas. Hence, Palestinians not only prefer a democratic government, but also appear to perceive the current Authority as democratic. Although Palestinians perceive the PA as democratic, it is reasonable to surmise that the public's perceptions will be critical if the present Hamas government departs from a democratic course.

When Palestinians were asked an open question about the preferred character of a Palestinian future state, the answers clearly indicate a preference for an Islamic state. In 1997, 54.7 per cent of respondents selected this alternative, while only 39.5 per cent chose a democratic state. When respondents were asked about the best solution to the Palestinian Israeli conflict, the Islamic option was most frequently chosen.

When an open question was asked on this same issue, 34.9 per cent answered that an Islamic state in all of Palestine would be the best solution. The option of an independent state in the West Bank and Gaza was chosen by 28.4 per cent of respondents. Support for the Islamic state option in 2001 was 43.6 per cent, but it had risen to 52.5 per cent in 2006. This open question does

*Table 1.* **The PA is a Democratic Authority**

|  | 1997 Valid per cent | 2001[8] Valid per cent | 2006 Valid per cent |
|---|---|---|---|
| Don't agree | 25.4 | 45.2 | 12.9 |
| Agree to some extent | 36.1 | 28.5 | 21.8 |
| Agree | 31.4 | 23.2 | 42.4 |
| Agree strongly | 7.0 | 3.1 | 23.0 |
| Total | 100.0 (1,251) | 100.0 (1,489) | 100.0 (1,469) |

*Table 2.* **The Preferred Solution to the Overall Palestinian–Israeli Conflict**

| What is according to you the preferred final solution to the Palestinian–Israeli–conflict? | 1997 | 2001 | 2006 |
|---|---|---|---|
| Islamic state in the whole of Palestine | 34.9 | 43.6 | 52.5 |
| Arab state in the whole of Palestine | 13.9 | 12.2 | 12.9 |
| Secular and democratic state in the whole of Palestine | 6.4 | 1.8 | 3.6 |
| Bi-national state in the whole of Palestine | 2.1 | 3.8 | 3.0 |
| Palestinian independent state according to UN 1947 partition plan | 7.9 | 6.2 | 11.6 |
| Independent state in the West Bank and Gaza | 28.4 | 22.9 | 14.6 |
| Palestinian entity in West Bank and Gaza in confederation with Jordan | 1.5 | 0.5 | 1.0 |
| Other | 4.9 | 8.9 | 0.8 |
| Total | 100.0 | 100.0 | 100.0 |
| | (1,278) | (1,487) | (1,481) |

not reveal more nuanced respondent-preferences. The answers reveal preferences for an independent state, but not more specific criteria for an alternative state structure. However the combination of these two questions suggests that Palestinians might see Islam and democracy as intimately related.

The issue remains in what respects do Islamic values overlap with democratic principles in Hamas's ideology, and how this is implemented in political practice. To assess this requires an investigation of how the population relates to the performance of the PA and the official national discourse about Palestinian national identity. It is one thing to say that a population is satisfied or dissatisfied with its authorities, but quite another to say that it perceives them as democratic (although both opinions may indeed co-exist).

Table 3, (Next page), indicates that Palestinians are very optimistic concerning Hamas's capacity to improve democracy and human rights issues and to act within the PA in an honest and efficient way. At the same time, Palestinians expect that the chances of peace with Israel and improved relations with the EU and the USA will worsen dramatically. The Hamas-led PA's relations with the Arab countries are expected to improve. However, despite the negative expectations about the future relations with Israel, the USA and the EU, it does not follow that Palestinians think that the Hamas government should be more conciliatory towards the West.

On the contrary, when asked if Hamas should abandon its armed struggle in its resistance to Israeli occupation, 77.2 per cent rejected this option. Furthermore, when asked if Hamas should recognize Israel and, in return, that

*Table 3.* **Palestinians' Hopes and the New Hamas-led PA's Performance**

| | State of democracy and HR | Honesty and efficiency of PA administration | Relations of PA with USA | Relations of PA with EU | Relations of PA with Arab countries | Chances of peace with Israel |
|---|---|---|---|---|---|---|
| | Valid per cent | Valid per cent | Valid per cent | Valid per cent | Valid per cent | Valid per cent |
| Will worsen | 16.9 | 12.8 | 64.3 | 51.7 | 29.6 | 66.6 |
| Remain the same as now | 25.9 | 15.7 | 17.0 | 23.1 | 29.6 | 17.6 |
| Will improve | 57.2 | 71.5 | 18.7 | 25.2 | 40.9 | 15.9 |
| Total | 100.0 | 100.0 | 100.0 | 100.0 | 100.0 | 100.0 |
| | (1,481) | (1,474) | (1,480) | (1,481) | (1,480) | (1,479) |

**Table 4. Do you Support that Hamas Abandon Violence (or Armed Struggle) in Its Resistance to Israeli Occupation?**

|  | Valid per cent |
|---|---|
| Do not support | 77.2 |
| Support to some extent | 12.1 |
| Support | 8.6 |
| Strongly support | 2.1 |
| Total | 100.0 |
|  | (1,470) |

Israel recognize Hamas as a national liberation movement, 67.3 per cent were against such a political compromise. This option would in fact almost exactly mirror the agreement that the PLO and Israel made in 1993 in signing the Oslo Accords. Despite the worsening of relations with the West, it can be expected that Palestinians will continue to see liberation from Israeli occupation as a central issue of justice. Palestinians will, of course, be highly reticent to compromise over issues in the conflict that they perceive as fundamental national rights.

**Table 5. Do you Support that Hamas Recognize Israel and, in Return, Israel Recognizes Hamas as a National Liberation Movement?**

|  | Valid per cent |
|---|---|
| Do not support | 67.3 |
| Support to some extent | 13.6 |
| Support | 16.2 |
| Strongly support | 2.9 |
| Total | 100.0 |
|  | (1,471) |

Furthermore, in 2006, this study asked questions related to factors or issues that were decisive for the way Palestinians voted in the national elections. Table 6 shows that the political factions' proposed solutions to the Palestinian problem was the core issue deciding how Palestinians voted. The issues linked to non-corrupt performance, religious programme, the candidates themselves, economic programme and health, education and social issues were less important to voters.

Clearly Palestinians expect Hamas to act in accordance with democratic principles. Interestingly, Hamas did, during the early part of 2006, signal an ambiguous position regarding Israel. On the one hand, a hard-line position towards Israel and its right to exist appears to be evident. On the other, some

***Table 6.*** **Which of the Following Considerations Affected Your Choice on the List Most?**

|  | Valid per cent |
|---|---|
| Position regarding the solution of Palestinian problem | 38.6 |
| Formation of honest and efficient administration | 16.8 |
| Religious programme | 14.8 |
| Economic programme | 8.8 |
| Education, health and social issues programme | 5.3 |
| The list candidates | 12.1 |
| Other | 3.5 |
| Total | 100.0 |
|  | (1,042) |

of the official statements made by the Hamas leadership apparently suggest that the leadership is searching for a way to indirectly recognize Israel. Thereby, Hamas is trying to avoid being seen as weak by the Palestinian public, if it were to directly recognize Israel under international pressure. Ismail Abu Shanab, a moderate Hamas spokesman, stated in 2002 that Hamas could agree with the Saudi plan that was accepted by the Arab League members, which called for Israel to return to its pre-1967 borders in return for 'normal relations' with Arab nations, and that Hamas would then 'cease all military activities' (www.sfgate.com/cgi-bin/article.cgi?f = /c/a/2002/04/28/MN222422.DTL).

In March 2006, Haniyeh said Hamas would establish 'peace in stages' if Israel would withdraw to its boundaries before the 1967 war. But he immediately distanced himself from those remarks by saying Hamas was interested in a long-term truce with Israel, but did not seek peace with it. (www.foxnews.com. Hamas Leader Hanyeh: 'We Could Make Peace With Israel One Day' 17 March 2006)

Currently, with fresh memories of the mid-2006 clashes between the Palestinians and Israel, and with the negative impact from the Israel–Hezbollah war, the chances for dialogue appear dim. However, the numerous moderate statements made against Israel since the election victory in 2006 evoke the signals that the PLO gave before shifting its position towards Israel prior to the Oslo process. Significantly, Hamas has declared a willingness to build Palestinian society, and the PA itself, on a democratic basis. Whether Hamas achieves such a democratic sea change will hinge, not only on Hamas's own resolve, but also on the latitude it receives for that project from the Palestinian population themselves, and from Fatah, Israel and the rest of the international community.

## Conclusions

Hamas is a movement that has come to terms with the political realties of the Oslo process, the Oslo Accords that prepared the ground for the establishment of the PA. From being an opponent of the Oslo process and a critic of the PA and its handling of Palestinian democracy, it has finally emerged as a participant in, and finally a leader of, the Palestinian political system. Its readiness to engage in these realities has also led to the development of a more pragmatic strategy within Hamas. Hence, Hamas is now demonstrating that it is listening to Palestinian public opinion, and that it has dramatically shifted some of its positions, particularly those concerning relations with Israel.

Palestinians have high expectations that Hamas will democratize Palestinian society more effectively then the previous Fatah-led PA. Furthermore, in light of the present stalemate in the peace process, Palestinians expect Hamas to be more assertive in its position towards Israel.

Paradoxically, while it appears that Hamas has come closer to recognizing Israel, and is even closer to formally accepting, at least temporarily, a two-state solution, the Palestinian public opinion has become more radicalized, and less amenable to compromise and to accept a two-state solution, as compared with the earlier days of the peace process. In this sense, we can observe Palestinian public opinion and Hamas's set of positions following opposite trajectories. The fleeting convergence of these trajectories in January 2006 is the most likely explanation for Hamas's election victory. However, if the Palestinian public continues towards a radical position it will be crucial to see how Hamas will respond to the public mood. It is possible that Hamas may return to not only using violent means against Israel, but also to less moderate positions concerning democratic issues. Whether Hamas follows its more moderate recent political programmes, or returns to its militant 1988 Charter, remains to be seen.

The central theme of this study was to explore whether Islamic parties could develop a 'Demo-Islam' character, and eschew more fundamentalist elements. The concept of Demo-Islam implies that Islamic parties could exhibit similarities with European Christian Democratic parties (Liel, 2003). Hence, such a symbiosis between Islam and democracy – Demo-Islam – could develop in Palestine, in a similar way Islamic Justice and Development Party emerged in Turkey. This study indicates that Arab Islamist parties, such as Hamas, have the potential to follow this Demo-Islamic path. How Hamas executes its leadership of the PA over the next two to three years may prove crucial in determining whether this potential is realized or not.

# Chapter Thirteen

# ENVIRONMENTAL SCARCITY AND INTRASTATE CONFLICTS: THE CASE OF NEPAL[1]

## Fiona J Y Rotberg

### Introduction

Nepal is poised on the verge of a historic and precarious precipice. Nepal, having suffered from a more than decade long armed conflict with devastating impacts on the social and political foundations of the country, is on the verge of peace. Although in size, Nepal is only 855 km from east to west and 193 km from north to south, and populated by 24.2 million people, it is situated between India and China, having potentially large geopolitical and strategic impacts on world politics. Members of the Maoist insurgents are poised to become part of the mainstream political structure. Yet, if they were to be dissatisfied with the peace process and stage a coup for example, strong reactions would come from both of its neighbours.[2] The way in which Nepal chooses to solve its conflict and address the primary and secondary causes of it, certainly has implications for leaders and international security policy experts with interests in countries with similar preconditions; they can potentially learn from the Nepali case, and avoid thousands of unneeded lost lives.

At the writing of this chapter, peace talks between the Maoist talk team and the Seven Party Alliance (SPA) were underway. Although the appointment in August 2006 of Mr Ian Martin, Personal Representative of the United Nations Secretary General in Nepal for Support to the Peace Process (a choice hailed by all parties to the conflict) the inability of the parties to advance on topics such as the role of the monarchy and the management of arms and armies, has led to untenable peace and a future with potential further violence. As these historic negotiations take place and the world community waits to see how and whether Nepal will become a democratic nation, it is important for scholars, civil society leaders and others to assess the causes of the Nepali conflict, including environmental scarcity issues.

When roots to intrastate conflicts are traced, it is often the case that there are many interlinked factors. Nepal is no exception. There are important linkages between the historical, economic, cultural, political, social, developmental and environmental structures and norms of the country. This chapter addresses environmental scarcity in the context of population issues, unequal access to resources, agricultural poverty, land holdings and state legitimacy.

## Environmental Scarcity

> Acute inequalities, absolute poverty, lack of access to resources and the failure of political structures to address these issues, have made Nepali society extremely vulnerable to conflict and mass movements like the Maoists [...]. (Upreti, 2004, p. 281)

As Bishnu Upreti states in the above quote, the connection between environmental scarcity and failing political structures can make a society vulnerable to internal conflict. Environmental scarcity incorporates several sources of scarcity into one term; natural resource scarcity; population growth (which leads to a reduction in per capita availability of a resource); and unequal resource distribution (such as unequal land holdings, with more in the hands of elites, for example).

The increase in environmental scarcity is linked both to the decline of the state's capacity to secure basic public goods and an increase in civil violence (the Maoist insurgency) and as a result, in the Nepali case, leaving its state in disarray and incapable to provide for its people. Because environmental scarcity causes economic deprivation, that in turn causes institutional disruption and civil strife; and a potential eventual breakdown of the state.

This is not to suggest that environmental scarcity and related issues are the sole cause of the recent conflict in Nepal, but rather that they can not be ignored. It is argued here that natural resource scarcity, connected to unequal access to natural resources, is one of the central political causes of the Maoist insurgency. A May 2006 study, commissioned by United States Agency for International Development (USAID), similarly concluded that 'resentment over discriminatory natural resource access is one of the underlying political causes' of the conflict in Nepal (USAID, 2006). Indeed, the increase in environmental stress throughout the Nepali country side, in combination with an increasing population, contributed to a situation of 'acute insecurity and instability' (Matthew and Upreti, 2006, p. 1).

Much of Nepal's land is severely constrained by rugged terrain, and thus the lives of many Nepalese people inhabiting the hilly and often remote areas depend on the surrounding ecosystems and the natural resources therein (Bhurtel and Ali, 2006, p. 8). However, these ecosystems tend to be fragile. Flooding and land scarcity has led people to depend on fragile areas. For example, the Midland region is severely deforested and there is a shortage of wood, fuel wood and fodder to carry out daily life. Floods, landslides and soil erosion are ever present. In many of the hill districts, there is shortage of food supply and the carrying capacity of the land has been destroyed (Sharma, 1998, p. 6).

Forests have typically been a source of livelihood for many Nepalese, through the provision of food, medicine, wood and animal feed. In the Terai region, tropical hardwoods have had commercial value, but there are few resources left, due to illegal harvesting. Reportedly, Maoists have demanded a 'tax' (ranging from 2 per cent to 50 per cent) on each harvested product by individuals and logging contractors with government harvesting permits (USAID 2006, p. vi). (Ironically, Nepal's success in community forestry initiatives has been hailed throughout the world. While an impressive 13,300 forest user groups have been identified, with 1.1 million hectares of forest land under management, the poor are not benefiting.) According to a USAID study, research indicates that '[…] socially dominant and relatively wealthier villagers capture most of the benefits from community forests, while poorer […] members bear a disproportionate share of the management costs' (USAID 2006, p. vii).

A similar situation can be evidenced with water resources; large landowners own the land, while poor farmers who do not own irrigated land, farm the land of the large landowners. Rivers flow out of the Himalayas, supplying large quantities of water to Nepal. Historically, Nepal has had several government institutions and procedures that work to manage irrigation and water distribution.[3] Many of the rural households have limited supply of water: women and girls must often walk long distances each day to fetch water. Further, people from the *Dalit* caste are prohibited by religious belief to take water from the same source as others within the community (USAID 2006, p. 8).

In 1911, the population in Nepal was 5.6 million, while in 2003, it had increased to 24.1 million (Central Bureau of Statistics 2002, p. 3). The population growth rate in Nepal was at 2.25 per cent in 2001, and total fertility rate stood at 4.1. According to the World Bank, approximately 50 per cent of the population in Nepal tries to make ends meet on one US dollar a day.

## Unequal Access and Distribution of Resources

It is argued here that another factor that promoted the conflict in Nepal was economic motives of the elite and the exploitation of natural resources by powerful groups. Because the rich and elite class has traditionally had a loud and successful voice in policy making in Nepal, they have been able to maintain dominance and keep the peasants at the low end of the class and caste system. And as a result, Maoists strategically and conveniently found peasants, as a group, a useful set of ears to fertilize their promises of better economic, social, cultural and political policies to benefit all Nepalese. 'Initially, the insurgents chose the Mid-western hills [...] to begin their war because the location is remote [...] and an oppressed ethnic population was an easy recruitment option for the Maoists [...]' (Bhurtel and Ali, 2006, p. 7).

Unequal resource distribution can be viewed as a factor that led to the Maoist insurgency and subsequent violence. In a recent academic workshop facilitated by the author, parties to the Nepali conflict agreed that unequal distribution was indeed a historical and current factor that needed to be solved in order to avoid similar unrest festering in the country side. The Nepali population can roughly be said to live in three main areas – the Mountain region (7.3 per cent of total population living here); Hill region (44.3 per cent); and Terai region (48.4 per cent), according to the 2001 Census.

Nepal is a 'resource-thin country' (Matthew and Upreti, 2006, p. 4) making it difficult for the population to depend on its resources for a living. While 90 per cent of the population relies on subsistence agriculture, only 20 per cent of the land is arable (Rizal and Yokota, 2006, p. 262) and many of the peasants do not have secure land titles. In fact, close to 69 per cent of land holdings are less than one hectare, making it nearly impossible to make a living.

Indeed, the Nepal Human Development Report 2004 indicates that the lower 47 per cent of households only own 15 per cent of the total arable land, while the top 5 per cent own approximately 37 per cent. Clearly, the distribution of land favours the elites; land distribution is one of the issues that the Maoist leaders say, exemplifies inadequate and unfair government policy. Table 1 depicts the unequal land distribution in Nepal.

The correlation between inequitable land holdings and Maoist violence can be linked directly. This correlation of unequal distribution of land and political violence can also be traced to similar insurgencies in Nicaragua, Peru, Chile and El Salvador (Packenham, 1992; Paige, 1975). For Nepal, Rizal and Yokota conclude that

> The development regions, ecological belts and cluster districts, where the number of holdings and average holding size are low, the Maoist influence, consolidation and violence seems maximum [...] Concentration of land in the hands of few elite classes and severe exploitation of the peasantry through the excessive expropriation of labour and land revenue

has been the principal policy adopted by the rulers through much of the nations' history. (Rizal and Yokota, 2006, p. 278)

Historically, the *Panchayat* system was introduced in Nepal in 1962, when the King ruled democratically with the support of councils, or *panchayats*. It, however, did little other than keep the feudal structure in place, and thereby furthering disparities among the different Nepali regions. In fact, the semi-feudal economic structure, combined with livelihoods based on subsistence agriculture, essentially ensured that rural areas would be unable to develop. Meanwhile, the political elites continued neglecting the realities of the rural level, thus 'providing the poor with no tangible redress of their frustration' (Rizal and Yokota, 2006, p. 276).

Table 2 depicts the linkage between poverty and farm size in the three regions of Nepal; the concentration of poverty is higher in landholdings below 0.5.hectares as compared to those up to 1.0 hectares (UNDP, 2006, p. 233).

Social inequalities can be traced to historical factors that include cultural, religious, caste structures and feudal rule. The resentment among the groups and the bottom rungs of Nepalese society festered and grew for centuries. 'Social inequality is comprehensive, including disparity of access to livelihood resources, government services, and economic opportunity' (USAID 2006, p. v).

How does environmental scarcity, linked with poverty and social inequality, lead to civil strife? It has been argued that the Maoist rebellion was simply a political movement, resulting from poverty among the rural population (Bhurtel and Ali, 2006, p. 2). An online conference organized by the Programme on Humanitarian Policy and Conflict Research at Harvard University, for example, identified only political, legal, social, economic and ethnic factors as the main causes of the conflict. Environmental causes were not included.

*Table 1.* **Land Distribution by Farm Size in Nepal, 2001–2**

| Size of holdings (*in* Hectare) | Holdings | | Total area | |
|---|---|---|---|---|
| | Number | % | Hectares | % |
| No land | 32,109 | 1.2 | 1,571 | 0.1 |
| Holding with land | 2,703,941 | 99.9 | 259,400 | 98.8 |
| Below 1 Ha | 1,877,702 | 68.8 | 791,883 | 30.5 |
| 1–2 Ha | 529,467 | 19.4 | 716,533 | 27.6 |
| 2–3 Ha | 168,449 | 6.2 | 400,227 | 15.4 |
| 3–5 Ha | 88,165 | 3.2 | 328,089 | 12.6 |
| 5 Ha and above | 40,158 | 1.5 | 360,669 | 13.9 |

Source: Rizal and Yokota, 2006, p. 276.

***Table 2.*** **Poverty Incidence by Farm Size**

| Poverty incidence | (%) |
|---|---|
| Mountains | |
| Below 0.5 hectare | 77.8 |
| Between 0.5 – 1.0 hectare | 67.3 |
| Above 1.0 hectare | 39.7 |
| Hills | |
| Below 0.5 hectare | 70.3 |
| Between 0.5 – 1.0 hectare | 64.3 |
| Above 1.0 hectare | 51.0 |
| Terai | |
| Below 0.5 hectare | 39.7 |
| Between 0.5 – 1.0 hectare | 32.3 |
| Above 1.0 hectare | 23.6 |

Source: United Nations Development Programme (UNDP) 2004.
Nepal Human Development Report 2004. Empowerment
and Poverty Reduction. Kathmandu, UNDP, 2006.

However, the scarcity of natural resources and the unequal distribution of resources can be linked to the Maoist insurgency in, at least, five important ways: 1) *Underlying cause:* resentment over discriminatory natural resource access is one of the underlying political causes that attracted early Maoist recruits; 2) *Funding Source:* Maoist military operations are funded partially by taxes on natural resources; 3) *Refuge:* Forests provide bases of operation and refuge for Maoists which leads to restricted access by rural farmers; 4) *Altered Dynamic of Natural Resource Use and Conflict by User Groups*: the insurgency has made proper management of forest and water resources near impossible, given that there is fear, distrust and insecurity on the part of users. Government rules have essentially been dismantled by Maoists and conflicts among the users have become chronic; 5) *Forest Management and Biodiversity Conservation Disruption:* the government has been unable to enforce management laws, leading to forest degradation and poaching (USAID 2006, p. viii).

This chapter will now turn to the discussion of how the legitimacy of the state and its capacity to provide for its people, such as ensuring equitable land distribution and access to natural resources, is linked to the above discussion and to the Maoist insurgency.

## Linkages between Resource Scarcity and State Capacity

The lack of the Nepalese Monarch's legitimacy and its inability to cope with both the insurgency and the environmental pressures led the way to total state disarray. Thus, Nepal's lack of state capacity, as a function of legitimacy, internal coherence and responsiveness (Homer-Dixon, 2001) certainly resulted in civil violence. To what extent does the state's capacity to cope with environmental pressures and the regimes legitimacy determine *its* capacity to provide legitimate goods to its people? State capacity incorporates the distinct concepts of state effectiveness (in terms of order and organizational capacity) and state legitimacy (in terms of authority) (Goldstone, 2000, p. 52). State capacity is viewed by the Project on Environmental Scarcities, State Capacity, and Civil Violence as '[...] a function of variables such as the state's fiscal resources, political autonomy, legitimacy, internal coherence, and responsiveness' (Homer-Dixon, 2001, p. 1). The findings from this study that are applicable to the Nepal case are as follows:

• Environmental scarcities do increase financial and political demands on the state;
• Resource scarcities affect the state via their effects on elites;
• Predatory behaviour of elites can evoke defensive reactions among weaker groups that directly depend on the resources in question; and
• The impact of resource scarcity affects the states overall productivity, leading to decline in tax revenues of local and national governments.

Environmental scarcities, as in Nepal, can indeed

> [...] affect a number of the variables measuring state capacity. It can directly constrain a state's fiscal resources, and by encouraging predatory behavior by elites, it can reduce state autonomy. Rivalry among political elites reduces coherence, and competition among groups over resources weakens civil society. (Homer-Dixon, 2001, p. 1)

The combination of competition over natural resources and rivalry among different members of the Nepalese society curtailed the state's ability to respond and supply to the need of basic social goods in terms of clear and fair property rights, and an effective and fair judicial system.

In the spring of 2006, the world held its breath and watched the Nepalese people demonstrate in the streets. Would Nepal pull itself from where it had sunk? Would Nepal become a failed state? Or would Nepal march towards historic compromise. The initial answer is that Nepal, after the dust settled, pulled itself back from failure, remarkably so. The final analysis cannot be rendered, however, as peace negotiations and agreement details are presently underway. It remains to be seen whether the Maoists and the Seven Party Alliance can manage to find an acceptable solution that leaves everyone confident and trusting, and resources more equally distributed.

Without the involvement of the peasant population in all areas of society, including agricultural policies, land policies, and the development of rules and laws, peace will remain fragile rather than solid and sustainable.

As the *Economist* magazine reported in the 10 October 2006 issue, presently the Nepali '[…] state is hardly functioning […]. This has been a boon for the Maoists […]. Until the government can re-establish itself, the Maoists will continue to grow stronger'. Meanwhile the leader of the Maoists is 'arguably the country's most popular politician now' (*Economist*, 2006, p. 64). This indicates that the demands of the Maoists have resonated with the majority of the population of Nepal. Roots of the insurgency can be traced, in part, to environmental disparities, including lack of access to land and natural resources. It is no surprise that the insurgency gathered momentum among the peasant population and majority of the willing recruits are from the countryside. Whichever path Nepal takes, a lesson can be learned within the scholarly and policy communities alike, that environmental scarcity issues should not be ignored when analysing direct and indirect causes to complex national conflicts.

# Chapter Fourteen

# NARCOTICS: THE NEW SECURITY THREAT FOR CHINA[1]

## Niklas Swanström

China is today facing a war against drugs, a war that has been threatening the very fabric of the state. The drug threat emanates from multiple sources ranging from states in its periphery, regional criminal networks to domestic actors, such as local triads, which account for the bulk of the production and sale of narcotics in China. As China gradually opens up, the drug problem is becoming increasingly serious and threatens China's progress, especially in the field of health, economy and public security. This development is driven by the rapid economic development and the creation of a strong consumer base in China for narcotics. As seen in Central Asia, Afghanistan and some Southeast Asian states, economies seriously affected by the narcotics trade usually have a worsened health situation with the increase in HIV/AIDS, Hepatitis C and other drug related diseases (Swanström and Cornell, 2006, pp. 10–28). There have also been cases of 'narcotisation' of states leading to political instability (Cornell, 2006, pp. 37–8; Swanström, 2007). They are usually associated with decreased competitiveness of the national economies as drug related industries offer steady incomes in states with high unemployment and where few opportunities exists for a secure income, at the legitimate market. One of the most problematic effects in such states has been weakening of the state apparatus by the criminal networks that deal with drugs. Such networks thrive in weak states where they exercise control over the political elite or simply become a part of the elite. The question remains what the current effects are for China and how long-term implications can be prevented.

During the Maoist time there were very little drugs in China. This situation has changed since then as impressive Chinese economic development has created a strong consumer base and China is today seen as a lucrative market by criminal networks dealing with narcotics. In response, the Chinese government has taken a strong stand against the production and sale of narcotics (Ting Chang, 2004).[2] China now is the largest seizure state of heroin (10,836 kg), the ninth largest of opium (890 kg), the seventh largest of ecstasy (300 kg) and the second largest of amphetamines (2,746 kg), (United Nations Office on Drugs and Crime (UNODC) 2006, pp. 71, 72, 136, 140). While these seizures indicate the importance and resources that China puts into combating the illegal narcotics trade, it also reflects the magnitude of the problem facing the government today. The number of addicts *registered* at the public security organs increased dramatically to more than a million registered users in 2003. While the statistics indicate a drop in the number to 771,579 registered addicts in 2004, it is clear that China still has a long way to go in its attempt to combat the drug abuse problem (White Papers of Chinese Government, 2003 p. 146; Ting, 2004, p. 20; UNODC 2006, p. 50). Heroin is used by 88 per cent of the addicts according to UN reports of 2006. According to Chinese statistics, 79.2 per cent of the registered addicts are under 35 years old and sexually active, which has a direct impact on the HIV/AIDS problem since 72.4 per cent of the 17,316 registered carriers of HIV/AIDS were intravenous users in 1999.

## Why has China Emerged as a Centre for Narcotics?

China has emerged as one of the major users of narcotics in the last few years due to a number of factors. First, the economic development that brought wealth and prosperity to its citizens created a market for the international narcotics trade. Just between 2000 and 2005, the Chinese GDP per capita has grown from US $ 3,980 to 6,292. Such a boost in purchasing power has enabled the average Chinese citizens with financial means to acquire more illegal stimulus (*Economist*, 2006). Expenditure on narcotics has decreased significantly in relation to the economic development and what used to cost a significant part of the income is today only a fraction of the income for the middle class. Economic development has been particularly high in the urban coastal areas where some of the greatest *increase* in narcotics abuse has been documented. It is also in the more affluent regions where we see the new designer drugs.

The second factor is the increased liberalization of the economic system, which has brought greater freedom to China and has opened borders with its neighbours in Southeast Asia, Central Asia, Afghanistan and North Korea (Democratic Peoples Republic of Korea). China has increased the legitimate trade with its neighbours significantly; the Sino-Burmese (Myanmar) trade is more than US $ 600 million/year, China and Central Asia trade has increased between 15 and 120 per cent per country from 2001 to 2003. China's total trade volume with Kazakhstan has, for example, expanded from a modest US $ 635.5 million in 1998 to US $ 1.3 billion in 2001, and to almost US $ 4.5 billion in 2004 and US $ 6.2 billion in 2005 (Ministry of Commerce of the People's Republic of China, 2005; 2004–5 Xinhua's China Economic Information Service, 7 February 2006). *Increased* legitimate trade has opened up the economies but this has also led to increasing amounts of narcotics being smuggled. There is today no possibility for the Chinese government, or for that matter, any government dependent on trade, to control inbound and outbound shipments. It seems that most of the narcotics trafficking is done through remote areas bordering Myanmar, Central Asia and North Korea where the figures of interception is far lower.

Three of the most important narcotics producers in the world, who are particularly active in the heroine trade, are Afghanistan, Myanmar and North Korea. All three share borders with China thereby making the mainland Chinese market relatively easy to penetrate. Myanmar's border is in a flux and geographically easy to penetrate with well established criminal organizations handling the trade. Afghanistan benefits from the established transit trade in Central Asia and the world's largest production of narcotics; North Korea is involved in a complicated political and economic relation with China and benefits from the Russian connections, and Russia benefits as a transit country. This has made China an important nexus in the narcotics trade, both as a consumer and as a transit route. The major influx of narcotics is still believed to be from the Golden Triangle, which is the world's second largest producer of heroin and opium with 7.8 per cent of the world production, and in particular, from Burma that exports about 80 per cent of its inland production through southern China (Yunnan) to its final destinations in China, the US and other places. Afghanistan's control of the opium production (88.7 per cent of world production) has made Burma less important and as a result, smuggling has increasingly shifted to the western part of China, namely Xinjiang. This is made possible by the changed political situation in Afghanistan and the lack of a strong central government. There has been a diversification of the production and refinement patterns in Afghanistan that has increasingly put the focus on Northern Afghanistan and Central Asia as a transit route. This positions China as a strong future market for Afghan heroin.

Furthermore, in recent years, United Nations has identified China as one of the main producing countries of illegal drugs, especially metham-phetamine, Amphetamine-Type Stimulants (ATS) and to some extent cannabis, (UNODC 2004, pp. 155, 161, 163, 260). On the positive side, there seems to be little opium production in China and there is limited number of heroin refineries as most heroin is refined in Burma, Afghanistan or North Korea. The domestic production of illegal drugs in China has created new problems with a large number of small but productive labs for methamphetamine and ATS production. This is reinforced by an improved industrial structure that can handle illegal production of narcotics with high quality output. This is especially true as China has emerged as a centre for chemical industries and is one of the leading producers of precursors in the world. In an effort to handle the problem Chinese government introduced its first administrative law on precursor chemicals (US Department of State, 2006). It is far reaching with real measures to handle manufacturing, perchance, distribution and export of precursor chemicals. This trade has made domestic production possible, and it has also made China an exporter of precursors to the narcotics industry in Asia, Russia and Europe.

## China as a Consumer

Chinese consumption is modest compared to the domestic levels of abuse in the late 1800s and early but the levels of consumption has increased significantly during the last ten years. The increase from 520 thousand *registered* addicts in 1995 to 770 thousand in 2005 is an indication of the growing problem that China is facing, (White Papers of Chinese Government, 2003, p. 146; UNODC, 2006, p. 50). These figures, however, only reflect the tip of the iceberg, as most addicts are not registered because stigmatization and punishment of narcotics addiction are severe in China. In private interviews conducted by the author with United Nations, NGOs, drug enforcement and intelligence staff both within and outside China, most estimate the actual figure to be higher than five million addicts and in some conservative assessments up to 15 million. In surveys of teenage drug abuse in China in 2003–4, 7.6 per cent of the teenagers surveyed in Shanghai replied that their peers frequently used narcotics and in Hong Kong, 20.6 per cent claimed that their friends or classmates used narcotics on a frequent basis (Washington Times, 2004).[3] In all major Chinese cities – under the influence of growing rave culture – ecstasy, amphetamine type stimulants and other design narcotics have been the preferred illegal substance of choice for the teens. This is a new form of abuse that is not reflected in the official figures.

Despite increased consumption of amphetamine type stimulants and designer narcotics, heroin is still the drug of choice and is consumed by 71.5 per cent of the addicts in China according to official Chinese sources for 2003; the United Nations's own estimates for 2006 puts the figure at 88 per cent, (White Papers of Chinese Government, 2003, p. 146; UNODC 2006, p. 50). Cannabis, ATS and methamphetamine usage have increased dramatically in China since 1997, partly due to the introduction of ecstasy then and

**Chart 1.** Number of addicts in PRC.

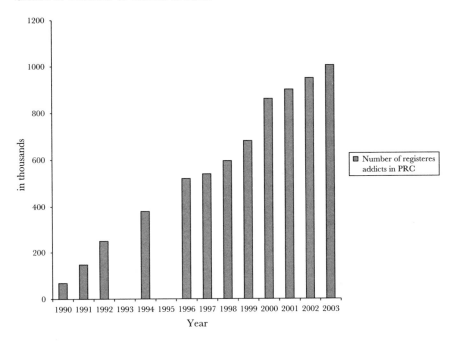

Source: UNODC 2004, p. 88.

the growing demand of cannabis in Xinjiang, (UNODC 2004, pp. 45–6). Moreover, an increasing amount of ATS and methamphetamine are locally produced and, therefore, all the more difficult for the Chinese authorities to intercept.

The prevalence of narcotics is growing rapidly. This is apparent both from the number of seizures the Chinese government has conduced and from the relative decline in prices of narcotics. Chinese law enforcement agencies seized 5,477 kg of heroin in 1997, 13,200 kg in 2001 and 9,290 kg in 2002, and as of August 2006 they have seized 9,228 kg (UNODC, 2004, pp. 255–331). The retail price for heroin varies between US $ 13 to 185 per gram with the highest prices in the coastal areas and the lowest prices in the entry points close to Burma, Central Asia, and to a certain extent, North Korea. Chinese drug enforcement officers have claimed that prices are declining in relation to median income which has made it possible for a larger population to abuse narcotics. The combination of decreasing costs and increasing prevalence of narcotics have led to the mushrooming of the number of addicts in the last few years.

The problem for China is not only the increase of narcotics addicts but also the age of the users, which is dangerously young. 79.2 per cent of the addicts are under 35 years old according to the official statistics based on registered users. These official figures do not take into consideration the escalating problem of ecstasy and the club culture that is developing in China. China View, a news agency in China, claims that the majority of the drug users are youngsters in the 20s and people under 18 are the main users of ecstasy (head-swaying pills) quoting to officials in Shanghai (China View, 2004; Ministry of Public Security, 2006). This is a pattern that has been acknowledged by a variety of NGO's and Chinese medical institutions. The trend is that abusers as well as HIV/AIDS victims are getting younger (Yan, 2006; French, 2006).

The dwindling age among abusers is problematic as they are sexually active. This has a direct impact on the HIV/AIDS problem since 72.4 per cent of the 17,316 registered new carriers of HIV/AIDS were intravenous users in 1999, and then in 2001 68.7 per cent of 28,000 were infected (White Papers of Chinese Government, 2003, p. 146; Ting, 2004, p. 20). In 2005, 44 per cent of the approximately 70,000 new HIV/AIDS infections were spread through needle sharing (Yan, 2006).

This rise in reporting of both HIV/AIDS cases and the number of intravenous users is staggering. In 2004, 9,787 HIV positive persons in Xinjiang alone were infected through needle sharing (Bates and Song, 2006, p. 39). Of the approximately 20 million that lives in Xinjiang there is an official estimate of 60,000 HIV/AIDS infections (French 2006).

The intravenous problem is not only combined with HIV/AIDS but also with Hepatitis C that is lethal in many cases. The spread of sexually transmitted diseases is accelerated by approximately 80 per cent of female addicts in China, who turn to prostitution to finance their dependence (Chang, 2004, p. 23). In 2006, China raised HIV prevention funding to US $ 185 million; an impressive increase from US $ 98.7 million in 2005 (Medical News Today, 2007). Other important steps are the Methadone Maintenance Therapy programmes that have been initiated in 58 clinics in 10 provinces with funding to reach more than 100,000 people (Malinowska-Sempruch and Bartlett, 2006, pp. 25–30).

Addiction, crime and prostitution are especially problematic among the so-called floating population that includes a significantly large number of narcotics abusers. This group (approximately 90–160 million people) is known to be involved in high levels of addiction as well as in the frequent visits to prostitutes (Thompson, 2004). The new patterns of very mobile abusers have spread the abuse of heroin all over China and risks spreading HIV/AIDS as well as intravenous habits to areas that so far has remained unaffected. The uneven economic development of China has created a large number of groups that end up outside the social security net and these groups are more exposed to narcotics than the more affluent groups, and often fail to register in the official numbers.

## China and Its Neighbours

The main gateway for narco trafficking into China has been, and still is, Burma and the Golden Triangle in Southeast Asia. According to various official sources between 65–90 per cent of narcotics is imported from the Golden Triangle. On a positive note however, the trend is that imports from Burma is decreasing. What is really worrying is the rapid increase in heroin trafficking from Afghanistan into China through its western provinces.[4] In the last two years, estimated import figures have risen from modest numbers under 5 per cent to official figures between 10–25 per cent. In interviews with security and police personnel, the increase is perceived to be even more significant, with some privately estimating that possibly 20–35 per cent is coming from Afghanistan. The increased market share for Afghan heroin (and to a lesser degree opium) has increased significantly with each passing year due to the economic development in China and the proximity to heroin producing states which has made heroin more widely accessible at low prices. The political chaos in Afghanistan and the relatively open borders and transit routes has made the Afghan heroin very competitive in the Chinese markets. The rapid decline of Burma as a production site has created a degree of turmoil in the transit trade of heroin. Just in 2006 alone, the land cultivation dropped by 29 per cent in Burma while in Afghanistan we witness an increase with a significant margin (UNODC, 2006a). The relative shift from Burmese to Afghani heroin is partly due to the Chinese and Burmese counter offenses against trafficking from Burma, as well as the relatively cheap heroin from Afghanistan which produced 88.7 per cent of the world's opium in 2005. Transaction costs in crossing the Sino-Burmese border has increased as the Chinese anti-narcotics forces have stepped up their struggle against the heroin trade in Burma. Russia is also a possible route of entry for some drugs from Afghanistan but more significantly from North Korea. Moreover, the Russian border has also functioned as a departure point for Chinese drugs and illegal precursors. However, the Chinese and Russian authorities have increasingly been trying to tighten border control and on the 26 June 2002 an agreement was signed between the Chinese province of Heilongjiang and the Russian Border area of Bihai to monitor the border area (The Ministry of Public Security, 2002). The success has been debatable as the region is heavily infested with illegal narcotics; some of it is believed to be of Russian origin; with the remaining coming from North Korea, not to mention Chinese designer narcotics and precursor trade.[5]

Cooperation between China and many of its neighbours have been important factors in the relatively successful attempt to curb the narcotics problem. An example of such regional cooperation has been joint investigation initiatives among Chinese, Lao, Thai and Burmese authorities that resulted, for example, in the seizure of 426 kg of heroin in Burma and the arrest of Chinese nationals for drug smuggling (Bullock, 2006). The Chinese anti-narcotics forces have attempted to intercept the transit route from Burma (primarily the Shan state) and Laos into Yunnan and Guangxi in China which remains parts of a major transit route to the costal provinces of Guangdong and Fujian. This effort has opened up alternative routes through the three major port areas in China, namely Qingdao, Shanghai and Tianjin. Similarly, the transit areas in the Northwest, such as the Wakhan corridor, Kulma Pass, Torughart, Khorgos to name a few are all increasingly used to transport heroin to China and precursors to Afghanistan.

International cooperation among governments has increased, this especially is true in regard to the US. Recently, offices have been established in both China and the US and an increased level of exchanges has been conducted. However, much of this cooperation still suffers from the same problem like all international cooperation efforts in fighting the narcotics industry. Many governments are reluctant to submit too much information and police forces are discouraged from cooperating too closely. There are also suspicions that some of the other states police, customs and officials are more involved in the trade and therefore it is unwise to work too closely. Different legal traditions and operative schemes also make closer cooperation difficult to implement.

China seized 10,836 kg of heroin in 2004 according to the UN and 890 kg of raw and prepared opium during the same time (UNODC, 2006, pp. 275, 287), which shows that the trade is primarily in heroin rather than the bulky and less profitable opium. As of August 2006, the Chinese authorities seized 9,228 kg of heroin (The Ministry of Public Security, 2006). Chinese police have reported that they seized over 160 tons of precursor chemicals and prevented a further 3,514 tons from leaving the country in 2004 (US Department of State, 2006). In the first eight months of 2006, China seized 117 tons of precursors and prevented a further 576 tons from leaving the country (The Ministry of Public Security, 2006). The pattern behind the seizures of precursors shows that the trade is quickly moving towards Afghanistan, as it produces the vast majority of the opium in the world and is an emerging producer of heroin. Estimates from the intelligence community in the US claims that the majority of Chinese precursors will be exported to Afghanistan in two–three years due to the relative decline of Burma as a producer.

The prior importance of southern China as a transit route was through its geographical advantages (4,060 kilometre inaccessible border region) and large uninhabited areas. The transit trade from Afghanistan through Pakistan and Central Asia benefits similarly from inaccessable road communication and a huge geographical area that is virtually impossible to monitor. The fastest growing consumer markets in China are the Northwest provinces, especially Xinjiang and the major cities on the east coast. However, the problem still remains severe in the provinces closer to Burma due to the relatively long history as an access point.[6] As of 2003, China has experienced an increase of narcotics abusers – representing an 11 per cent increase since 2001 – the majority being heroin users despite fastest growth in the number of ATS and methamphetamine (such as bingdu and ecstasy) users. According to Chinese official figures, the increase in Xinjiang and the north-western provinces might be double that figure of narcotic abusers (11 per cent).[7] There are estimates that put the figure as high as 180,000 narcotics abusers in Xinjiang alone as of 2005 (Bates and Song, 2006, p. 38). This increased demand for narcotics, in itself, will boost the role of Afghanistan as a drug export centre to China's north-western region.

## Central Asia and Afghanistan

China receives much of its narcotics import from the Central Asian states (as a transit line from Afghanistan). This import of heroin is rapidly increasing in relative and absolute terms when seen in comparison to the import from the Golden Triangle. Despite the fact that Central Asia is not a main producer of heroin, it has been important for the smuggling of precursors to Afghanistan and possibly to Europe, even if the European market for Chinese precursors is a minor one at this point in time. The importance of Central Asia as a transit route, and possibly export market, for Afghan heroin to China and vice versa for the precursor trade has increased dramatically, especially through Khorgos and Torughart. According to Chinese military sources, Central Asia as a transit route has witnessed an impressive surge in volume as part of the Chinese transit network. The reason for this is that China has attempted to close the Sino-Afghan border which has increased the relevance of both Central Asia and Pakistan as a transit route. This said, the possibility to use the Sino-Afghan border is limited by geographical conditions. The border is only 76 km long and the Wakhir pass, which is the only accessible route, is closed almost six months of the year due to weather conditions. The Central Asian states that would be most vulnerable in such a network are Kyrgyzstan and Tajikistan since both provide easy access into China and Afghanistan due to corruption at the national level and involvement of elite in the narcotics trade. Kyrgyzstan and Tajikistan, moreover, has ethnic links that stretches over the borders to China. This has simplified the transit trade immensely and has made it very difficult for the Han-Chinese police to infiltrate the criminal networks.

Pakistan is not a major transit route to China due to the relatively expensive transit route via Pakistan. Chinese border troops and local officials and their Central Asian and Afghani counterparts are more involved in the drug trade and therefore it is easier to corrupt and traffic narcotics. This might change in the near future as Afghanistan, Iran and Pakistan, often referred to as the Golden Crescent, are taking over more and more of the production of heroin and the criminal networks will move their attention towards Afghanistan and its neighbours. Many Chinese officials have reported uneasiness with the Pakistani border recently, as it could open up a new transit route of heroin to China and precursors to Afghanistan.

## North Korea

North Korea is another front in the war against narcotics. This is not only devastating on a socio-economic level, but politically sensitive too. Many Chinese officials have either denied any North Korean involvement in the narcotics trade or claimed that this is a political problem and is out of their reach.[8] The reality is that much of the narcotics in Northeast Asia (including Russia) today originate from North Korea and even states as far away as Australia have severe problems with narcotics originating from the country (Wortzel, 2003; Radio Free Asia, 2004). It is impossible with the limited information to estimate the magnitude of the trade. It is, however, evident that increasing number of seizures of North Korean heroin has been made. It is normally assumed in the West that the North Korean government is involved in the drug trade and there have been persistent accusations from the US, Japan, Australia, for a long time, that the North Korean government is directly involved in narcotics production. However, there is no direct evidence of the North Korean government's involvement since the 1970s when several North Korean embassies were caught selling narcotics, reportedly to sustain their diplomatic activity (Asher, 2005). The lack of appropriate measures from the North Korean government and the failure to provide valid information of the North Korean involvement in the narcotics trade is troubling.

The United Nations World Drug Report has not referred to North Korea as a major producer or transit country. This is due to the lack of information about the narcotics situation in North Korea. However, there have been unofficial references to North Korea as an emerging problem especially from Japan and Australia. The increasing seizures of large amounts of heroin smuggled by North Koreans to Australia, Japan and other important consumer states do indicate a disturbing development of major export of heroin through North Korean criminal networks (Perl, 2003; Savacool, 2005, pp. 497–520). In contrast to the earlier relatively minor exports size, this indicates a more aggressive trend and an increasingly important role of North Korean heroin on the world market.

Part of the evidence of North Korean involvement can be seen in the large quantities of heroin available in border areas close to North Korea, such as Dalian (Port Arthur), Jilin and Shenyang (Xinhua, 2004; Squires, 2003). This situation may be partly due to the transit trade from Afghanistan to the eastern part of Russia, but the high concentration of narcotics is more likely to indicate the existence of direct trade from North Korea. There have been several seizures of heroin from North Korea reported in Japan and Australia but very few reported by China (BBC 2004; Kim Young II, 2004). Several Chinese police sources have privately made it very clear, to this author, that North Korea is an emerging actor in the drug trade. Some even estimate the North Korean trade to be the third largest supplier of heroin into China after Burma and Afghanistan.[9] While there is neither official information nor public debate about this issue; reports from hospitals and civil society in China do appear to second such an opinion.[10]

## China as a Producer

China has traditionally been an importer of narcotics, especially from Burma. This has changed in the last few years and China has emerged as a producer and exporter of crystal methamphetamine (ice, shabu, bingdu), Methylene-dioxymethamphetamine (MDMA) (ecstasy) and chemical precursors such as pseudoephedrine and ephedrine that are primarily destined for heroin and cocaine production (UNODC, 2006; White Papers of the Chinese Government 2003). China is today one of the major producers of precursor's chemicals in the world, and it produces, for example, more than 100,000 metric tones of acetic anhydride each year (UNODC, 2006). This is a new trade which is hidden in the legal production and export. The Chinese government has taken this problem seriously and have taken several initiatives to curb the illegal export of precursors (The Ministry of Public Security, 2006).[11] China as a producer in the area of narcotics is a new phenomena and even though China is still a net importer of heroin it has become a net exporter of chemical based drugs and precursors according to reliable governmental sources in China. Opium is locally produced in Yunnan, Ningxia, north-western areas and Inner Mongolia in very small quantities and is not transformed into heroin but is consumed locally by the minority population of these remote areas in traditional ways.

The production of narcotics in China (primarily crystal methamphetamine and phenylpropylaminea) is, to a large degree, consumed domestically though there are indications that exports are on the rise. It is primarily ice, MDMA and other chemical narcotics that are consumed in the major cities, cannabis in the north-western provinces and the small amount of opium produced in China is locally used. The sale of Chinese crystal methamphetamine and phenylpropylamine is today primarily a domestic affair, but trade is increasing with the US, Russia, Central Asia and other states in the Pacific region.[12] It seems that Chinese narcotics are spreading in the same tracks as Burmese heroin that is smuggled through China. This makes the US and Japan the main importers, though the Central Asian states and Russia seem to have a liking for Chinese narcotics too.

Most important is, however, not the export of narcotics but the export of chemical precursors to the Golden Triangle mentioned earlier. Recently the export of precursors has, to a higher degree, gone to Afghanistan, Europe and possibly to Central Asia rather than to the traditional market in Burma.[13] The central position of China in producing legal precursors has inevitably created a black market of precursors directed towards the narcotics trade. The precursor trade is mainly with the producing states in Asia, then especially with Burma and Afghanistan, and also with Europe.[14] Specifically in the heroin trade, China has begun to export precursors to Burma and Afghanistan and has in return imported the final product of heroin. This put Central Asia as a very likely transit region and the booming of the precursor trade will create new routes to bring in heroin to China.

## State Infiltration and Actors

The main producers and traffickers from Afghanistan to China are known to be the members of the Northern Alliance.[15] What is more difficult to ascertain are who are smuggling on the Chinese side? Most of the traffickers are believed to be the Chinese Triads such as the 14K, but also ethnic Chinese groups living outside China that are loosely connected to the Triads. The trafficking from the Golden Triangle is conducted by effective cooperation between these Triads and militants, most importantly 14K, and the United Wa State Army (UWSA) and the Myanmar National Democratic Alliance Army (MNDAA–Kokang Chinese). These organizations are virtually unrestricted in their respective regions and free to engage in the narcotics trade as long as the national unity is preserved and have been so since early twenty-first century.

The assumption from the Chinese side is that Muslim terrorist and separatist groups in Xinjiang are involved in the smuggling of drugs to China and precursors from China as well as in the criminal organizations in the South. Chinese President Hu Jintao has, for example, claimed that there is a close relationship between international drug trade and separatism, extremism and terrorism in China.[16] In interviews and official documents, there is, however, few who can provide names and evidences on direct involvement in the drug trade by these groups, even if different East Turkestan liberation movements have been frequently cited. The lack of clarity among the Chinese attempts to link these movements to the narcotics trade indicates that they are not involved to the degree that the Chinese government would like us to believe. It is more likely that this is a question of traditional organized crime cooperating with separatist and terrorist groups to a certain degree but is in no way exclusive to these groups.

The connection between Chinese Muslim militants and their 'brethren' in the Central Asian states and Afghanistan should however not be dismissed. A large number of militants have received training in Afghanistan under the Taliban and created strong networks that could be used to traffic drugs and precursors. In interviews by the author with Uyghur activists in Beijing, they claimed that the 'cause' is increasingly dependent on narcotics trade and organized crime in general and that ethical and ideological ties with Afghanistan are helping this trade. It is, however, unlikely that these organizations are responsible for all the trafficking. There have also been suspicions of involvement by some corrupt Chinese border police, local politicians and military in the trade and this has been privately confirmed by some military sources. The ethnic component is, as previously mentioned, important but is largely limited to criminal organizations that overlaps in China, Tajikistan and Kyrgyzstan.

The internationalization of the trade has shown itself in the Chinese trade, Chinese criminal gangs not only cooperate with Burmese traffickers but increasingly with Colombian criminal networks and they have begun to penetrate weak states and poorly defended borders, where the Northeast Asian provinces in China and the Central Asia region seem to be legitimate targets. There are some intelligence reports that claim that there is a well developed relationship between criminal organizations in China and militants and warlords in Afghanistan and Central Asia. The extent of the proposed relationship is unclear, but it would explain the increased trade with China's western provinces.

Narcotics related corruption is rarely reported in media and the government claims that there are relatively few such cases. Most cases of reported narcotics related corruption in China involve low-level officials in the border provinces neighbouring Afghanistan, Burma, Taiwan and Hong Kong. So far there has been no official evidence that senior officials are co-opted or corrupted by narcotics money. The size of the narcotics trade that is prevalent in China today and the smuggling of precursors are evidence that there has to be some involvement of corrupt officials in the border areas as this illegal smuggling is simply too large to be conducted without official assistance. Taking Afghanistan as an example, it would not be too difficult to close that border section off and to stop large parts of the smuggling of heroin and precursors. The current level indicates some complicity from police, military or customs officials. The same is true of Burma, even if that border section is far more difficult than the Afghani border to seal off and defend.[17] The Central Asian states have borders that are relatively easy to penetrate in part because of the direct involvement of senior government officials in the smuggling trade.

Money laundering and other criminality related to the narcotics trade seem to be more related to traditional organized crime and till today no senior PRC official has been connected to narcotics money, even if there are high level corruption and several senior officials are found guilty of embezzlement, power abuse and fraud. China's economic development and internationalization has made it a likely laundering state, as its financial regulations are still relatively weak. There have been some Chinese attempts to prevent an infiltration of the Chinese banking system. This is a much needed attempt and could play out well if it increases the transaction costs and decreases the profit for the criminal organizations. The criminal organizations would target economic institutions with weak regulations and enforcement, as well as those with a relatively prosperous economy. If any significant improvement in this field would follow it would force the narco-industry to rethink China as a major laundering site and focus on weaker states and economic institutions.

In some interviews with senior officials, there have however been indications that the narcotics trade has corrupted more senior officials than earlier been known. There have been some charges that it is now more difficult to act against the narcotics trade due to some individuals' direct involvement in the trade. These allegations are however rare and it seems that most senior officials are in no way involved in the narcotics trade.

As noted, there is very little evidence that Chinese separatist groups are involved on the Chinese side. It is, however, more likely that Islamic Movement of Uzbekistan and other groups are involved in trafficking into China. There have been some indications from military officials that they 'share' problems with Tajikistan and Uzbekistan with regards to narcotics trafficking and terrorism. Militants of different sorts have been involved in the trade in China, some supportive of the separatist struggle in Xinjiang and Tibet; but most are related to 'international terrorism'. Like Chinese President Hu Jinto, several military officials have made the connection directly between terrorism and narcotics trade. Police officials and narcotics officers have been more reluctant to make that connection, and state that while it exists it is minor in relation to at the trade at large. This said, it seems evident that most of the traders in China are economic players and not political.

The trade towards Burma has directly involved separatists such as the Shan state and the MNDAA that has fought a long and bloody war against the

Burmese government. Moreover, it is apparent that North Korea has increased its heroin trade to China, through Russian criminal networks and directly through the North Korean minority in China and through Chinese officials. Interviews with North Korean and Chinese officials have indicated that this is an increasing problem affecting their relations, especially since it is in all likelihood supported by the North Korean government, at least tacitly.

In short, there is little reliable evidence that separatists, extremists and terrorists are controlling the trade and even though they are involved in some manner, their participation seems to be limited to minor operations. There seems to be more evidence that the trade is driven by purely economic incentives as a traditional criminal organization, this said, it is not impossible that political groups have made significant inroads in the trade.

## Winning the Opium War?

Despite some concerted efforts, the war against narcotics have met with limited success as witnessed in terms of increased addicts and increased tonnage of smuggled heroin, opium, precursors as well as the domestic production. It can however be regarded as a success in terms of the engagement from the Chinese government and the relatively low level corruption of the state, which narcotics trade normally bring in China. Without the measures China has put up, the drug problem in China would have been much worse. It should also be noted that China is far below the international average of abuse (5 per cent of the total population). Even if the level of narcotics abuse reaches 10 million, it would still be less than 1 per cent of China's total population which currently stands at 1.3 billion. Give and take a few million, China's drug situation remains well below the international average. However, it must be recognized that the situation is rapidly getting worse and China is in many ways the fastest growing market for narcotics, especially with the booming economy and easy access.

China is facing a double-edged sword with increased international engagement and the increased wealth of its people. The open door policy has made it much easier for criminals to penetrate the Chinese market and to transfer the funds necessary for conducting trade and investment to launder the illegal assets, as well as increase the legal trade with the outside world and foreign investments. The legal trade has also increased the buying power of the Chinese population and this has stimulated the illegal narcotics market. As the legal Chinese market further grows, the potential profit for the narcotics traders is also set to increase exponentially. Similarly, the growing openness of the Chinese economy has made it easier for smugglers to penetrate China's borders, and for the laundering of criminal assets in and out of China. As in many parts of the world, banks in China are used in laundering the criminal profits, much of which can be controlled but unfortunately some of which will be difficult to prevent. Open economies and increased economic interaction have brought increased costs to each state, some of which are directly related to the organized crime and the narcotics trade. The Chinese government has to continue with its open-door policy while putting safeguards to filter out the illegal narcotics trade. This is a situation that is difficult to resolve without major compromises that are, possibly, too politically sensitive to make.

China's problem is that there are currently good transit lines to and from China with rapidly improving infrastructure, but relatively weak border controls. It will be impossible to control all possible border crossings due to the enormous geographical area China encompasses and the relatively few police and border officials that could work on these issues. Much of the war against the narcotics trade will have to be a coordinated effort by increasing transaction costs for smugglers such as tighter control of the borders but more importantly, by assisting production states in their struggle against the narcotics industry, much of which was done in Burma by the Chinese police in training and operational support. To make this possible, there will be a need for greater cooperation between China and its international drug enforcement counterparts.

Criminals neither respect state sovereignty nor national boundaries. For the criminal organizations, borders and different policing systems are their best means to penetrate different states. This is because different legal policies and limited international cooperation make border control difficult and borders relatively easy to penetrate. Cooperation is there but there needs to be more integration among production, transit and consumer states. It is also evident that China's narcotics problem will continue as long as the weaker states in China immediate proximity can not resolve their own narco problems. To step up the fight against the narco industry China, and many other states, will need to equip the producing and transit states with tools to fight the illegal narcotics industry. This was done relatively successfully by China with Burma, but much remain to be done to effectively control the problem.

The Chinese government claims that the war against narcotics will be won, but in reality it is impossible to win the war due to the demand and the fact that the criminals are always one-step ahead of us. If the heroin trade is controlled, designer drugs will take over, and if Afghanistan manages to control its production the heroin trade will move to another state. Thus, the focus has to be on decreasing and controlling the demand and transit of narcotics in an effort to increase transaction costs and prevent a criminalization of the society. Profit is the primary interest behind the narcotics trade and to deal with this business the efforts has to be directed towards decreasing profit and increasing risk for traders.

# REFERENCES

## Chapter Two: The Problem of Peace: Understanding the 'Liberal Peace'

1 I take responsibility for all errors in this essay as is the custom. Thanks go Roland Bleikor, Neil Cooper, Costas Constantinou, Jason Franks, AJR Groom, Ian Hall, Vivienne Jabri, Anthony Lang, Farid Mirabagheri, Mike Pugh, Nick Rengger, Chandra Sriram, RJB Walker, Alison Watson and Peter Wallensteen. I would like to thank the many people, local and international, private or official, from East Timor, DRC, to the Balkans, who were willing to talk to me during the course of my fieldwork. I am also grateful to the Leverhulme Trust, the Carnegie Trust, and the Russell Trust for providing funding for various parts of the fieldwork. Oliver P Richmond, 2006, 'The Problem of Peace: Understanding the Liberal Peace', *Conflict Security and Development*, Vol. 6, No. 3, published by Taylor & Francis. Reprinted with permission of the publisher.

2 'Peace to the undefeated' or the victor's peace. Inscribed on the Tomb of the Unknown Solider in St Mary's Cathedral, Sydney, Australia.

3 This cliché has often been quoted to me during interviews with officials during fieldwork.

4 This was the conclusion offered by many of my interviewees, official and non-official during fieldwork in the Balkans in January 2005.

## Chapter Three: Pre-emptive Self-Defence New Legal Principle or Political Action?

1 The text of the Charter of The United Nations can be found on the web site of the United Nations (http://www.un.org/aboutun/charter/index.html).

2 This section is adapted from Amer, 1994, pp. 22–30. It is based on an overview of the following studies: Acevedo, 1984; Asrat, 1991; Bowett, 1955–6; Brownlie, 1962; Brownlie, 1963; Franck, 1970; Henkin, 1968; Kelsen, 1948; Reisman, 1984a; Reisman, 1984b; Waldock, 1952; Wright, 1957. For other studies see Gordon, 1985, pp. 271–8; Mrazek, 1989, pp. 83–91; Müllerson & Scheffer, 1995, pp. 100–3; Schachter, 1984, pp. 1624–8.

3 References to the discussions about Article 51 can be found in: Asrat, 1991, pp. 38–40 and 199–200; Bowett, 1955–6, p. 131; Brownlie, 1962: pp. 223–33.

4 In this context the listed weaknesses are only seen from the perspective of the provisions of the Charter of the United Nations, and they do not take into consideration

whether customary international law or General Assembly Resolutions address these weaknesses.

5  References to the discussions about Article 51 can be found in: Asrat, 1991, pp. 38–40 and 199–200; Bowett, 1955–6, p. 131; Brownlie, 1962: pp. 223–33.

6  In line with principle used in relations to Article 2(4), in this context the listed weaknesses are only seen from the perspective of the provisions of the Charter of the United Nations.

7  For a detailed analysis related to the claims made by the intervening states in the interventions in Grenada and Panama respectively, and the conceptual issues raised in the legal debates relating to the two cases see see Amer (1997, pp. 24–60).

8  In her study Sapiro states that the USA based its legal argumentation 'more on U.N. Security council resolutions that on the Charter's right of self-defense' (Sapiro, 2005, p. 359). The self-defence arguments she refers to were made in statements by the President of the USA and the Department of State's Legal Adviser (Sapiro, 2005, p. 359). Sapiro has not made use of the letter to the Security Council referred in this study.

9  After the military intervention had been launched against Afghanistan the Security Council adopted three resolutions in 2001. First, on 14 November Resolution 1378 was adopted (S/RES/1378 (2001)), Second, on 6 December Resolution 1383 was adopted (S/RES/1383 (2001)). Third, on 21 December Resolution 1386 was adopted (S/RES/1386 (2001)). In this context it should be noted that Resolution 1378 included the following Preamble Paragraph: '*Supporting* international efforts to root out terrorism, in keeping with the Charter of the United Nations, and *reaffirming* also its resolutions 1368 (2001) of 12 September 2001 and 1373 (2001) of 28 September 2001' (S/RES/1378 (2001)). Also Resolution 1386 included the same paragraph but 'reaffirming' was not in italic (S/RES/1386 (2001)).

## Chapter Four:  Beyond Criminal Justice: Promoting the Rule of Law in Post-Conflict Societies

1  The Council of Europe has the rule of law as one criterion for membership and the European Court on Human Rights has through its case law repeatedly confirmed the centrality of the rule of law to the European Convention on Human Rights. Similarly, the EU in the Treaty of the European Union, as amended by the Treaty of Amsterdam, stipulates that rule of law, liberty, democracy and human rights and fundamental freedoms as the foundation of the EU.

2  Consisting of the UN, World Bank, ECOWAS, AU, EU, USA, Ghana and Nigeria.

## Chapter Five:  Peace by Pact: Data on the Implementation of Peace Agreements

1  The research presented in this chapter is a follow-up project to the volume *From War to Democracy*, (eds.) Anna Jarstad and Timothy Sisk, Cambridge: Cambridge University Press (forthcoming). The research is funded by the Swedish Research Council.

2  The IMPACT dataset builds on the Terms of Peace Agreements Dataset (TOPAD) v 1.1. by Nilsson, Desirée, Isak Svensson and Ralph Sundberg, 2006, Department of Peace and Conflict Research. IMPACT adds unique data on the implementation of pacts.

3  In addition, economic power sharing, as stipulated in the Sudan 2005 peace accord can serve to distribute revenues from natural resources such as oil. See Hoddie and Hartzell on other examples of economic power sharing (2005).

4 Literature on credible commitment and costly signalling includes, for instance, Fearon (1995) and Reiter (2003).

5 Walter defines a settlement as successful if two criteria are met: violence needs to stop for at least five years and implementation of 'one part of the political agreement (either the installation of the transitional government or the formation of a new national government) and at least partial demobilization' (Walter, 2002, p. 54).

6 The available COW datasets only extend up until 1997. Available at http://www.correlates ofwar.org. Definitions and coding are elaborated upon in Small and Singer (1982).

7 We differ here from Walter's (2002) study in that she only includes settlements where all, or the main, warring parties were signatories.

8 The two scholars also pay an equal amount of attention to 'economic power sharing'. We have not focused on such 'pacts' or 'power sharing', since we do not deem them to be theoretically or empirically comparable with the other categories of pacts, even though they might have relevance in certain types of conflicts.

9 The creation of a joint command also qualifies as a guaranteed integration.

10 Examples of 'local self-government' are autonomy, regional autonomy, municipal autonomy or other forms of territorial decentralization based on a shift in territorial control from the central government to lower levels of governance.

11 Such as the ones in Romania, Russia, Azerbaijan and Georgia in the early 1990s.

12 Not only full regional autonomy is included in the definition of a territorial pact, but also lower forms of autonomy such as municipal autonomy, or other types of self-government that do not necessarily include full fiscal or juridical independence from the centre.

13 Such data is available in TOPAD v.1.1 (Nilsson, Svensson *et al.* 2006).

14 Case selection differs though, with Lake and Rothchild studying the 1945–92 period. In the period when the two time frames overlap IMPACT has found only one territorial pact, which was not implemented. Coding criteria also do not overlap, with Lake and Rothchild basing their coding of decentralization on a number of different datasets, such as Polity II and III (Gurr, 1989; Jaggers and Gurr, 1995) and Database of Political Institutions (Beck *et al.* 1998).

## Chapter Six:  Refugee Repatriation as a Necessary Condition for Peace

1 Adelman (2002, p. 273).

2 In most instances, the terms return and repatriation are used synonymously. In Guatemala, they took on different connotations with return implying an active subject deciding to return home as opposed to the passive object being repatriated. In this essay, the two terms are used synonymously.

## Chapter Seven:  Catapulting Conflicts or Propelling Peace: Diasporas and Civil Wars

1 Multiple armed conflicts may be fought simultaneously in a given state. For example, in India alone there were five conflicts active in 2005, one for control over state power (Government vs CPI-M) and four over geographical territories (Assam, Kashmir, Nagaland and Manipur) (Harbom, 2006). 'New refugees' refers to the number of people newly displaced during 2005 (figures do not include internal displacement).

'Total refugees' refers to the global population of refugees by country of origin as of 31 December 2005 (UN 2006, Annex 4).

2  Collier and Hoeffler (2004) rely on the size of the diaspora population relative to that of the homeland as a proxy for financial transfers between diasporas and rebels in the homeland. While possible endogeneity between diaspora size and civil war is controlled for, the sample size is small (29 civil wars) and is restricted to diasporas in the United States.

## Chapter Eight:  UN Peace Operations as Norm Entrepreneurs: The Challenge of Achieving Communicative Action on Human Rights

1  The concept of 'peace actors' refers to all personnel part of UN peace operations, while focus here is on military peacekeepers, civilian police and human rights officers.

2  An active process of international socialization is the primary mechanism of maintaining domestic change according to Risse and Sikkink.

3  Internalization encompasses the processes of (i) instrumental adaptation and strategic bargaining; (ii) moral consciousness-raising, argumentation, dialogue and persuasion; and (iii) institutionalization and habitualization.

4  Interview, UN staff, Geneva, May 2006.

5  Habermas three main validity claims connected to speech acts oriented towards communicative action are as follows: (1) that the statement is true, (2) that the speech act is right with respect to the existing normative context, (3) that the manifest intention of the speaker is intended as it is expressed, and (4) the claim's intelligibility.

6  This approach is possible because 'the international system is less organized by legislative structures than nation-state or federalist systems and could, therefore, not stabilize communicative action by way of law in the same way'.

7  (1) Knowledge and person; (2) subject and object; (3) language reflexivity and inter-subjective understanding; (4) interaction and possibilities of action; (5) mutuality involving both similarity and difference.

8  Both UNMIK and MONUC constitute 'integrated missions' that generally are concerned with the three overarching aims of (i) restoring stability, law and order, (ii) protecting civilians, (iii) providing the foundations for long-term recovery, development and democratic governance (Eide *et al.* 2005). Also, according to the Rules of Engagement, MONUC troops 'can and do arrest and detain civilian and militia elements that are caught red-handed engaging in obvious criminal acts[…]. At times, persons may be arrested for contravening orders imposed under MONUC's Chapter VII authority, for instance, refusal to disarm in the town of Bunia' (Ricci, 2004, pp. 100–101).There are thus similarities with KFOR's interim law enforcement role at the early stage of UNMIK.

9  Field research was undertaken in Kosovo from 15 November to 22 December 2005 and in Kinshasa from 28 April to 8 May 2006. The majority of interviews were conducted with senior representatives of the respective missions' military, police and human rights components, but local human rights experts were also interviewed in order to gain a local perspective. To gain a perspective of integration of human rights in UN peace operations from a macro-level, interviews with staff of DPKO and OHCHR at UN Headquarters, New York, were conducted from 1 to 29 October 2006.

10 See http://www.unmikonline.org/intro.htm.

11 On file with author.

12 Since 2002, MONUC has two Deputy SRSGs. DSRSG/RC/HC is not only Deputy SRSG with responsibility for Child Protection, Elections, Humanitarian, Gender, Mine Action, Security and HIV/AIDS activities but also Resident Coordinator and Humanitarian Coordinator of UN Specialized Agencies in the DRC. The other DSRSG has responsibility for Human Rights, UN Police, Rule of Law, Political Affairs, DDRRR/DDR and Public Information.

13 The fact that the Human Rights Division was under the same DSRSG as the Division for Political Affairs has been stressed as a crucial. Interview, UN staff, Geneva, May 2005.

14 The primary human rights actors of the IPWGHR are those of OMIK Human Rights and Rule of Law Department and the Office of the High Commissioner for Human Rights, OHCHR.

15 Interview, OSCE official, OSCE Mission in Kosovo, Pristina, December 2005.

16 This is also the case with respect to the newly created Human Rights Advisory Panel. See UNMIK 2006/12 (Para 1.2).

17 During the first years of operation, however, when the security situation was more acute, cooperation between KFOR and the OSCE was extensive. See Månsson (2001).

18 William O'Neill, the former Special Adviser on Human Rights in UNMIK, recalls that the Task Force on Minorities '[…] is the most effective example of inter-agency cooperation and protection that I have ever seen in a peacekeeping operation'. See O'Neill (2006, p. 139).

19 Interview, staff, OSCE Human Rights Division, Pristina, December 2005.

20 Interview, staff, OSCE Human Rights Division, Pristina, December 2005.

21 At least at the level of MONUC Headquarters.

22 This was revealed, inter alia, through the answers provided by a questionnaire distributed to senior or mid-level representatives from KFOR's Liaison Monitoring Teams (LMT) in KFOR MNB (C). Sixteen responded in the negative to the question 'Do you have any cooperation/coordination with OSCE Human Rights Division in your Area of Responsibility (AOR)?' and only two responded in the positive.

23 This was claimed by several people met with in Kosovo. Interviews, UN staff, Pristina, December 2005 and OSCE staff, OSCE Human Rights and Rule of Law Department, Pristina, December 2005.

24 Interview, staff, OSCE Department of Human Rights and Rule of Law, Pristina, December 2005.

25 As of May 2006, the Human Rights Division encompassed 117 officers (incl 74 international staff). The ratio of Congolese inhabitants per HR Officer is almost 600,000 (compared to almost 30,000 Kosovans per OSCE Human Rights officer). MONUC Military is 17,480 while UNPOL's strength is 1,103 (as of 30 April 2006).

26 It should be stressed however, that this assessment is based on interviews with staff at MONUC Headquarters, why interaction in the field may vary greatly. Indeed, many respondents were of the view that in general, cooperation was much closer in the field than at Headquarters.

27 Interview, UN staff, Police and Justice, Pristina, December 2005.

28 Interview, MONUC staff, Kinshasa, May 2006. The induction course was reduced from 10 to 6 days in December 2005.

29 Interview, Ibid.

30  Military Observer, Rutshuru, North Kivu, phone interview, Kinshasa, May 2006.
31  Senior Military Officer, Ituri Brigade, MONUC, phone interview, May 2006.
32  The military observers interviewed by phone all indicated quite or very close interaction with MONUC human rights officers.
33  Interview, staff, MONUC Human Rights Division, Kinshasa, May 2006.
34  Interview, Senior Military Officer, Western Brigade, MONUC, May 2006.
35  Interview, UN staff, Force HQ MONUC, Kinshasa, May 2006.
36  Interview, UN staff, MONUC Human Rights Division, May 2006.
37  Interview, Senior Military Officer, MONUC East Brigade, Interview, Kinshasa, May 2006.
38  Interview, UN staff, MONUC Human Rights Division, Kinshasa, May 2006.
39  Due to its perceived effectiveness, a request to establish three new mobile teams in South Kivu, Katanga and Ituri was subsequently made. See MONUC (2006, p. 18).
40  This would, of course, vary hugely in terms of troop contributing country and current training policies and modalities, linked to the overall purpose of national armed forces.
41  Interview, UN staff, MONUC Human Rights Division, Kinshasa, May 2006.
42  Interview, Senior Human Rights Officer, OSCE Human Rights and Rule of Law Department, Human Rights Division, Pristina, 1 December 2005.
43  This was also confirmed in the survey referred to by one of the interviewed military observers (Report of the Secretary General A/61/255 2006, Para 28).
44  Interview, Senior Military Official, Western Brigade, Military Division, MONUC, 5 May 2006.


## Chapter Nine:  To Practice What They Preach: International Transitional Administrations and the Paradox of Norm Promotion

1  See also resolutions 1999/57, of 26 April 1999, 2000/116, 2002/46 of 23 April 2002.
2  According to the OSCE certified results (http://www.osce.org/documents/html/pdftohtml/20458_en.pdf.html = ).
3  http://www.osce.org/kosovo/13208.html.
4  Haradinaj resigned 8 March 2005 after long-anticipated indictment by ICTY; turned himself in and released on pre-trial bail June 2005.


## Chapter Eleven:  The African Union (AU) and Its Commitment to Non-Indifference: Can the AU be an Actor for the Promotion of Human Security?

1  International legal principle advocates conversion of old administrative boundaries into international boundaries when a political subdivision achieves independence, i.e. the stability of the territorial status quo.
2  4 (h) has added weight since it is a Principle, not an Objective (that expresses the aspirations of the AU). Abass & Baderin argue that the principles are the main part of the lawmaking process of the AU. The Article 4 might, therefore, become part of the legal corpus of the Union (Abass & Baderin, 2002, p. 14).

3  This is a large step away from the OAU Charter Article 3 which was similar to the UN Charter 2(7). One problematic issue is whether the decision to intervene by the AU could be seen to violate the provision of Article 2(4) of the UN Charter and the customary principle of 'non-intervention' under general international law. For Abass and Baderin, the AU does have a right to intervene as long as the intervention is consistent with the purposes of the UN (2002, p. 11).

4  The operationalization of the African Court on Human and Peoples' Rights begun when, at the Eighth Ordinary Session of the Executive Council, 22 January 2006, the first eleven Judges were elected http://www.iss.co.za/AF/RegOrg/unity_ to_union/pdfs/au/khartoum06/ecordidec.pdf.

5  The PSC is made up of 15 member countries, ten elected for a term of two years and five for a term of three years. All countries serving on the PSC have equal voting rights; there are no veto rights or permanent members. The PSC meets regularly and recommends action to the Assembly of the Union, the supreme organ of the AU is composed of Heads of State and Government.

6  Explanations for the challenges and shortfalls of AMIB are adequately given elsewhere, see for example, Agoagye, F, 'The African Mission in Burundi: Lessons learned from the first African Union peace keeping operation', African Centre for Constructive Resolution of Disputes (*ACCORD*), 2, 2004; Boshoff, H, 'The United Nations Mission in Burundi', *African Security Review*, 2004, *Vol.* 13, No. 3; Powell, K, 'Opportunities and Challenges for Delivering on the Responsibility to Protect: The African Union's Emerging Peace and Security Regime', The North-South Institute, 2005, Monograph No 119.

7  For example, AU Special Envoy for Sudan, Ambassador Baba Gana Kingibe, had met with Sudanese and Chadian government officials in March 2004 to discuss the role of the AU in the Darfur crisis. These discussions paid particular attention to the humanitarian consequences of the ongoing conflict.

8  African Union Peace and Security Council Communiqué, PSC/PR/Comm (XVII), p. 2; http://www.africaunion.org/News_Events/Communiqués/Communiqué% 20_Eng%2020%20oct%202004.pdf.

# Chapter Twelve:  Hamas between Sharia Rule and Demo-Islam

1  This study is based on previous studies and data collection conducted jointly with Professor Mahmoud Miari from Birzeit University and Professor Helena Lindholm Schulz from Padrigu at Göteborg University. However, the study is also linked to the first phase of a new research project planned to continue over three years. Special thanks goes to Stuart Roberts who copy edited the language of the manuscript.

2  The political factions treated as outsiders with respect to the previous PLC in this study are Islamic Jihad, the Democratic Front for the Liberation of Palestine and the Popular Front for the Liberation of Palestine.

3  Interviews conducted by Helena Lindholm Schulz, published in the study *Between Revolution and Statehood: The Reconstruction of Palestinian Nationalisms*, 1996, Göteborg: Padrigu Papers, Doctoral dissertation thesis.

4  Interviews conducted by Helena Lindholm Schulz and Michael Schulz.

5  On Hamas see Milton-Edwards, 1996; Abu-Amr, 1994; Legrain, 1990.

6  There is an entire separate debate about whether Islamist movements are capable of embracing democratic principles: see, for example, Esposito, 1996.

7  Among the Palestinian public in the West Bank 15.4 per cent 'somewhat supported', 8.5 per cent 'supported' and 0.6 per cent 'strongly supported' a non-democratic government. A similar question was asked of the Israeli public in a survey carried out in September–October 1995: 'What would you prefer if you have to choose between a democratic government whose policies you oppose in principle and a non-democratic government whose policies you definitely support?' The Israeli Jewish population supported democracy to a slightly lesser extent than their Palestinian neighbours; 72.8 per cent supported the democratic option. Among the Israeli Arabs, 90.2 per cent were committed to democracy in this context (see Schulz, 1996, p. 210).

8  In the 2001 survey 9.0 per cent answered 'Do not know'.

## Chapter Thirteen:  Environmental Scarcity and Intrastate Conflicts: The Case of Nepal

1  A version of this chapter was presented at the Environment: Survival and Sustainability Conference, and is available at www.neuconference.org.

2  For details on the decade long Maoist insurgency that has led to 13,000 deaths in Nepal, please refer to Michael Hutt (ed.), *Himalayan "People's War": Nepal's Maoist Rebellio,*. 2004, Bloomingto, Indiana University Press.

3  For example, Farmer Managed Irrigation Systems, Government Managed Irrigation Systems, and Irrigation Water Users Associations.

## Chapter Fourteen:  Narcotics: The New Security Threat for China

1  The author is grateful for the financial support from the Swedish Foreign Ministry, Swedish Emergency Management Agency and the Swedish National Drug Policy Coordinator so that this research could be accomplished. The views of the author do not reflect these organizations in any way.

2  White Papers of the Chinese Government, Narcotics Control in China, 2003. The Chinese data on the narcotics problem deserves a note, especially as it is very low in an international perspective. Even with the higher informal estimates the consumption will only reach 1 per cent of the total population in comparison with the international average of 5 per cent. First, the Chinese estimates are based on registered users which are much lower than the factual numbers, this is, of course, always the case in all states but as China has begun relatively late in seriously analysing the numbers we are only seeing the tip of the ice-berg. Second, the actual numbers of abusers in China are probably much lower than in other states (as a percentage of the total population) due to the low economic development and underdeveloped market for illegal narcotics. This is changing rapidly now with the economic development and increased trade. Third, earlier the figures were kept down for propaganda purposes. This is no longer the case but the anti-narcotics efforts have a long way to go before the estimates of the user population and the size of the narcotics trade are at a realistic level. Finally, the new designer drugs are not represented in the figures. The increased usage of speed, ecstasy, ice etc. is virtually unaccounted for.

3  The term used in the surveys was 'mild stimulant drugs'.

4  'The drugs that flow in through the Golden Triangle remains as China's main drug problem', http://www.longhoo.net/gb/longhoo/news2004/china/userobject1ai 247226.html; 'Drugs from the Golden Crescent is rapidly penetrating China, drug routes have been restricted but not stopped', 19 February 2004, http://www.jschina.com.cn/gb/jschina/news/node4438/userobject1ai408921.html.

5  Interesting to note is that most Chinese law enforcement and military staff refuses to give any details on the North Korean transit route and claims the problem to be of a political nature, neither supporting nor refuting the North Korean involvement.

6  'The anti narcotics bureau officials of the Chinese Ministry of Public Security talks about China's anti-drugs efforts', 14 July 2004 http://www.fmprc.gov.cn/chn/zxxx/t143074.htm.

7  The anti narcotics bureau officials of the Chinese Ministry of Public Security talks about China's anti-drugs efforts', 14 July 2004 http://www.fmprc.gov.cn/chn/zxxx/t143074.htm.

8  Interviews with Chinese officials 2004–6.

9  Interviews with drug enforcement personnel, security forces and police in China, 2004–6.

10  Interviews in China, 2004–6, with medical staff and civil society in northern China.

11  'Annual Report on Drug Control in China, 2006' Available at: http://news.xinhuanet.com/legal/2006–06/23/content_4738474.htm.

12  'The drugs that flow in through the Golden Triangle remains as China's main drug problem', http://www.longhoo.net/gb/longhoo/news2004/china/userobject1ai 247226.html; 'Re-enforcing pragmatic cooperation for collective peaceful development' Hu Jintao's speech at the SCO Tashkent Summit Tashkent, 17 June 2004, http://www.fmprc.gov.cn/chn/wjdt/zyjh/t140098.htm.

13  'China's Five-year drug control plan', http://www.china.org.cn/chinese/law/591563.htm; 'Our country is bilaterally and multilaterally engaged in the international anti-narcotics effort' http://www.people.com.cn/GB/shehui/212/8467/8471/2593207.html; 'The anti narcotics bureau officials of the Chinese Ministry of Public Security talks about China's anti-drugs efforts'. On 14 July 2004, the PRC Ministry of Foreign Affairs Press and Media Service invited China's National Narcotics Control Commission (NNCC), Vice Secretary General and Director of the Anti-Narcotics Bureau of the Ministry of Public Security, Yang Fengrui to give an account of China's drug situation, the anti-narcotics measures taken by the Chinese government, the success attained, as well as the steps ahead to be undertaken, etc. to Chinese and foreign journalists. The Director General of the Information Department of the PRC Ministry of Foreign Affairs, Liu Jianchao presided over the briefing. http://www.fmprc.gov.cn/chn/zxxx/t143074.htm.

14  'The drugs that flow in through the Golden Triangle remains as China's main drug problem' http://www.longhoo.net/gb/longhoo/news2004/china/userobject1ai247226.html.

15  The Northern alliance (also known as the United Islamic Front for the Salvation of Afghanistan (UIF), *Jabha-yi Muttahid-i Islami-yi Milli bara-yi Nijat-i Afghanistan* ) is the military grouping of primarily Tajik, Uzbek, Persian speaking and other non Pashto elements that successfully defeated first the Soviets and then the Taliban. It has since then been the primarily collaboration partner for the West in Afghanistan.

16  'Re-enforcing pragmatic cooperation for collective peaceful development', 17 June 2004; Hu Jintao's speech at the SCO Tashkent Summit, Tashkent, 17 June 2004, http://www.fmprc.gov.cn/chn/wjdt/zyjh/t140098.htm.

17 'Heroin from here flows to the rest of the world, drugs taint the Silk Road', http://www.chinadaily.com.cn/gb/doc/2004-02/18/content_307027.htm, 18 February 2004. 'Re-enforcing pragmatic cooperation for collective peaceful development', Hu Jintao's speech at the SCO Tashkent Summit Tashkent, 17 June 2004, http://www.fmprc.gov.cn/chn/wjdt/zyjh/t140098.htm.

# BIBLIOGRAPHY

Abdullah, I. 2004. "Bush Path to Destruction: The Origin and Character of the Revolutionary United Front (RUF/SL)", Abdullah, I (ed.), *Between Democracy and Terror: The Sierra Leone Civil War*, Dakar: CODESRIA Books.

Abdullah, I and Rashid, I. 2004. "Rebel Movements", Adebajo, Adekeye and Rashid, I (eds.), *West Africa's Security Challenges: Building Peace in a Troubled Region*, Boulder, London: Lynne Rienner.

Abu-Amr, Ziad. 1994. *Islamic Fundamentalism in the West Bank and Gaza: Muslim Brotherhood and Islamic Jihad*, Bloomington and Indianapolis: Indiana University Press.

Acevedo, Domingo E. 1984. "Collective Self-Defense and the Use of Regional and Subregional Authority as Justification for the Use of Force", *American Society of International Law*, Proceedings of the 78th Annual Meeting, 12–14 April, Washington, D.C., pp. 69–74.

Adamson, F. 2005. "Globalisation, Political Mobilisation and Networks of Violence", *Cambridge Review of International Affairs*, Vol. 18, No. 1.

Addison, T and Murshed, S. 2005. "Post-Conflict Reconstruction in Africa: Some Analytical Issues", Fosu, A and Collier, P (eds.), *Post-Conflict Economies in Africa*, Hampshire and New York: Palgrave Macmillan.

Adebajo, A (ed.), 1999. *Comprehending and Mastering African Conflicts: The Search for Sustainable Peace and Good Governance*, London: Zed Books.

Adebajo, A and Landsberg, Chris. 2000. "Back to the Future: UN Peacekeeping in Africa", *International Peacekeeping*, Vol. 7, No. 4.

———. 2002. *Liberia's Civil War: Nigeria, ECOMOG, and Regional Security in West Africa*, Boulder, Colorado and London: Lynne Rienner.

Adebajo, A and Rashid, I, op. cit.

Adelman, Howard. 2002. "Refugee Repatriation", Stedman, Stephen John, Rothchild, D and Cousens, Elizabeth M (eds.), *Ending Civil Wars: The Implementation of Peace Agreements*, Boulder, London: Lynne Rienner.

Ademola, Abass and Mashood, Baderin. 2002. "Towards Effective Collective Security and Human Rights Protection in Africa: An Assessment of the Constitutive Act of the New African Union", *Netherlands International Law Review*.

*African Union Peace and Security Council Communiqué, PSC/PR/Comm (XVII)*.

Agoagye, Festus. 2004. "The African Mission in Burundi: Lessons Learned from the First African Union Peacekeeping Operation", *ACCORD 2*, Special Edition. *Peacekeeping*.

Ahonji, M. 2003. "Houphouet against the Nation", *African Geopolitics*, No. 9, Winter.

Akindes, F. 2004. "The Roots of the Military-Political Crises in Cote d'Ivoire, Research Report 128", Sweden: Nordic Africa Institute.

Al-Ali, N, Black, R and Koser, K. 2001a. "The Limits to Transnationalism: Bosnian and Eritrean Refugees in Europe as Emerging Transnational Communities", *Ethnic and Racial Studies*, Vol. 24, No. 4, pp. 578–600.

——. 2001b. "Refugees and Transnationalism: The Experience of Bosnians and Eritreans in Europe", *Journal of Ethnic and Migration Studies*, Vol. 27, No. 4, pp. 615–34.

Ali, Taisier M and Matthews, Robert O. 2004. "Conclusion: The Long and Difficult Road to Peace", Ali, Taisier M and Matthews, Robert O (eds.), *Durable Peace: Challenges for Peacebuilding in Africa*, Toronto: University of Toronto Press.

Alusala, Nelson. 2004. "African Standby Force", *African Security Review*, Vol. 13, No. 2.

Amer, Ramses. 1994. *The United Nations and Foreign Military Interventions: A Comparative Study of the Application of the Charter*, Uppsala: Department of Peace and Conflict Research: Uppsala University, Second Edition, Report 33.

——. 1997. "The Intervention Debate – New or Old Concepts?", Wallensteen, Peter (ed.), *International Intervention: New Norms in the Post-Cold War Era?*, Uppsala: Department of Peace and Conflict Research: Uppsala University, Report 45, pp. 17–60.

Amin, S. 2003. *Capitalism in the Age of Globalisation*, Cape Town, London and New York: IPSR and Zed Books.

Andemicael, Berhanykun. 1976. *The OAU and the UN: Relations between the Organization of African Unity and the United Nations*, New York: United Nations Institute for Training and Research by Africana Pub. Co.

——. 1983. *Imagined Communities: Reflections on the Origin and Spread of Nationalism*, New York: Verso.

——. 1992. "The New World Disorder", *The New Left Review*, Vol. 193, pp. 3–13.

Andemicael, B and Davidson, Nicol. 1984. "The OAU: Primacy in Seeking African Solutions within the UN Charter", El-Ayouty, Yassin and Zartman, I W (eds.), *The OAU after Twenty Years*, New York: Praeger Press, pp. 101–19.

Angoustures, A and Pascal, V. 1996. "Diasporas et Financement des Conflits", Jean, F and Rufin, J C (eds.), *Économie des guerres civiles*, Paris: Hachette.

Anheier, H, Glasius, M and Kaldor, M. 2003. "Global Civil Society in an Era of Regressive Globalisation: The State of Global Civil Society in 2003", Anheier, H, Glasius, M and Kaldor, M (eds.), *Global Civil Society*, Oxford: Oxford University Press.

Annan, K. 2002. "Democracy as an International Issue", *Global Governance*, Vol. 8, No. 2, pp. 4–142.

An Na'im, A A (eds.), 1992. *Human Rights in Cross-Cultural Perspectives: A Quest for Consensus*, Philadelphia: University of Pennsylvania Press.

Ansari, Ali M. 2000. *Iran, Islam and Democracy: The Politics of Managing Change*, London: Chatham House.

Archibugi, Daniele, Held, David and Köhler, Martin (eds.), 1998. *Re-Imagining Political Community: Studies in Cosmopolitan Democracy*, Stanford, California (CA): Stanford University Press.

Asher, D. 2005. "The North Korean Criminal State, its Ties to Organized Crime, and the Possibility of WMD Proliferation", Policy Forum Online, 15 November.

Asrat, Belatchew. 1991. "Prohibition of Force Under the UN Charter: A Study of Art. 2 (4)", *Studies in International Law*, Vol. 10, Uppsala University, Swedish Institute of International Law, Uppsala: IUSTUS förlag.

Audéoud, Olivier. 1983. "L'intervention Américano-Caraïbe à la Grenade" [The American–Caribbean intervention in Grenada], *Annuaire Français de Droit International*, Vol. 29, pp. 217–28.

Augustine. 1991. *City of God*, pp. XIX, 13, 1, London: Penguin Classics.

Baimu, E and Sturman, K. 2003. "Amendment to the African Union's Right to Intervene: A Shift from Human Security to Regime Security?", *African Security Review*, Vol. 12, No. 2.

Ballentine, K. 2003. "Beyond Greed and Grievance: Reconsidering the Economic Dynamics of Armed Conflict", Ballentine, K and Sherman, J (eds.), *The Political Economy of Armed Conflict: Beyond Greed and Grievance*, Boulder, London: Lynne Rienner.

Ballentine, K and Nitzschke, H. 2003. "Beyond Greed and Grievance: Policy Lessons From Studies in the Political Economy of Armed Conflict", *IPA Policy Report*, New York: International Peace Academy.

Ballentine, K and Sherman, J. 2003. "Introduction", Ballentine, K and Sherman, J, op. cit.

Bannon, I and Collier, P (eds.), 2003. *Natural Resources and Violent Conflict: Options and Actions*, Washington, D.C.: The World Bank.

Baral, Lok Raj (ed.), 2006. *Nepal Quest for Participatory Democracy*, New Delhi: Adroit Publishers.

Bates, G and Song, G. 2006. "HIV/AIDS in Xinjiang: A Growing Regional Challenge", *The China and Eurasia Forum Quarterly*, Vol. 4, No. 3, pp. 38–9.

Bayart, J, Ellis, S and Hibou, B. 1998. *The Criminalisation of the State in Africa*, Oxford: James Currey.

Beau, Christophe. 2003. "National Legislation", *Forced Migration Review*, No. 17, pp. 16–18.

Beck, Robert J. 1993. "International Law and the Decision to Invade Grenada: A Ten-Year Retrospective", *Virginia Journal of International Law*, Vol. 13, No. 4, pp. 765–817.

Beck, T, Clarke, G, Groff A, Keefer, P and Walsh P. 2001. "New Tools and New Tests in Comparative Political Economy: The Database of Political Institutions", *Working Paper, No. 2283*, Washington, D.C.: The World Bank.

Bell, Christine. 2000. *Peace Agreements and Human Rights*, Oxford: Oxford University Press.

Bellamy, A and Williams P (eds.), 2004. *Peace Operations and Global Order*, London: Routledge.

———. 2005. "The Responsibility to Protect and the Crisis in Darfur", *Security Dialogue*, Vol. 36, No. 1.

Bello, W. 2002. *Deglobalisation*, London: Zed Books.

Berdal, M and Keen, D. 1997. "Violence and Economic Agendas in Civil Wars: Some Policy Implications", *Millennium: Journal of International Studies*, Vol. 26, No. 3.

Berdal, M and Malone, D (eds.), 2002. *Greed and Grievance: Economic Agendas in Civil Wars*, Boulder, Colorado: Lynne Rienner.

Bergling, P. 2006. *Rule of Law on the International Agenda: International Support to Legal and Judicial Reform in International Administration, Transition and Development Co-operation*, Antwerpen: Intersentia.

Berkowitz, D, Pistor, Katharina and Richard, Jean-Francois. 2003. "The Transplant Effect", *American Journal of Comparative Law*, Vol. 51, No. 1, pp. 163–204.

Berman, Eric, Sams, Katie. 2000. "Peacekeeping in Africa: Capabilities and Culpabilities", Geneva: UNIDIR and ISS.

Best, S and Kemedi, D. 2005. "Armed Groups and Conflict in Rivers and Plateau States, Nigeria", Florquin, N and Berman, E (eds.), *Armed and Aimless: Armed Groups, Guns and Human Security in the ECOWAS Region*, Geneva: Small Arms Survey.

Beyers, Jan. 2005. "Multiple Embeddedness and Socialization in Europe: The Case of Council Officials", *International Organization*, Vol. 59, No. 4, pp. 899–936.

Bhatia, Michael. 2003. "Repatriation under a Peace Process: Mandated Return in the Western Sahara", *International Journal of Refugee Law*, Vol. 15, No. 4, pp. 786–822.

Bhurtel, Jugal and Saleem, Ali. 2006. *The Green Roots of Red Rebellion: Environmental Degradation and the Rise of the Maoist Movement in Nepal.* Draft.

Björkdahl, Annika. 2002. *From Idea to Norm – Promoting Conflict Prevention*, Lund: Lund University Press.

———. 2006. "Promoting Norms through Peacekeeping: UNPREDEP and Conflict Prevention", *International Peacekeeping*, Vol. 13, No. 2, pp. 214–28.

Blankenburg, E. 1997. "Civil Litigation Rates as Indicators for Legal Culture", Nelken, D (ed.), *Comparing Legal Cultures*, Aldershot: Dartmouth.

Bleiker, R. 2000. *Popular Dissent, Human Agency, and Global Politics*, Cambridge: Cambridge University Press.

Blocq, D S. 2005. "The Fog of UN Peacekeeping: Ethical Issues Regarding the Use of Force to Protect Civilians in UN Operations", *Journal of Military Ethics*, Vol. 5, No. 3, November 2006, pp. 201–13.

Bloom, Mia. 2005. *Dying to Kill: The Allure of Suicide Terror*, New York: Columbia University Press.

Bond, P. 2006. *Looting Africa: The Economics of Exploitation*, London and Pietermaritzburg: Zed Books and University of KwaZulu-Natal Press.

Bonoan, Rafael. 2001. "When is International Protection No Longer Needed? The 'Ceased Circumstances' Provisions of the Cessation Clauses: Principles and UNHCR Practice, 1973–1999", *The Rosemary Rogers Working Paper Series, No. 8.*

Boschini, A and Patterson, J. 2003. "Resource Curse or Not: A Question of Appropriability", *SSE/EFI Working Paper Series in Economics and Finance, No. 534*, September.

Boshoff, H. 2004. "The United Nations Mission in Burundi", *African Security Review*, Vol. 13, No. 3.

Boshoff, H and Francis, D. 2003. "The AU Mission in Burundi: Technical and Operational Dimensions", *African Security Review*, Vol. 12, No. 3.

Boulden, Jane (ed.), 2003. *Dealing with Conflict in Africa: The United Nations and Regional Organizations*, New York: Palgrave Macmillan.

Boutros-Ghali, Boutros. 1992. *An Agenda for Peace: Preventive Diplomacy, Peacemaking and Peace-Keeping. A/47/277 – S/24/111*, New York: United Nations.

———. 1996. *An Agenda for Democratization*, New York: United Nations.

Bowett, D W. 1955–6. "Collective Self-Defence Under the Charter of the United Nations", *British Yearbook of International Law*, Vol. 32, pp. 130–61.

Braumoeller, Bear F and Goertz, Gary. 2002. "Watching Your Posterior: Comment on Seawright", *Political Analysis*, Vol. 10, No. 2, pp. 198–203.

Bring, Ove. 2006. "Efter den 11 September – en rätt till väpnat självförsvar mot internationell terrorism?" [After 11th September – A Right to Armed Self-Defence against International Terrorism?], Bring, Ove and Mahmoudi, Said, *Internationell våldsanvändning och folkrätt* [International Use of Force and International Law], Stockholm: Norstedts Juridik, pp. 77–88.

Brown, G S. 2004. "Coping with Long-Distance Nationalism: Inter-Ethnic Conflict in a Diaspora Context", PhD dissertation, University of Texas, Austin, USA.

Brownlie, Ian. 1962. "The Use of Force in Self-Defence", *British Yearbook of International Law*, Vol. 37, pp. 183–268.

———. 1963. *International Law and the Use of Force by States*, Oxford: Oxford University Press.

———. 2001. "International Law and the Use of Force by States Revisited", *The Australian Year Book of International Law*, Vol. 21, pp. 21–37.

Bullock, T. 2006. *China Taking "Great Strides" Against Narcotics Trafficking, State Department Annual Report cites rise in drug abuse, transit flow*, 1 March.

Bunce, Valerie. 2005. "Promoting Democracy in Divided Societies", Paper prepared for the American Political Science Association Task Force on 'Difference and Inequality in the Developing World' and presented at the University of Virginia, 22–3 April.

Byman, D L, Chalk, P, Hoffman, B, Rosenau, W and Brannan, D. 2001. *Trends in Outside Support for Insurgent Movements*, Santa Monica, California: RAND Cooperation.

Cambell, D. 1992. *Writing Security*, Minneapolis: University of Minnesota Press.

Caplan, R. 2002. *A New Trusteeship? The International Administration of War-Torn Territories (Adelphi Paper)*, Oxford: Oxford University Press for the IISS.

———. 2002. *A New Trusteeship? The International Administration of War-Torn Territories (AdelphiPaper 341)*, New York: Routledge.

Carlson, S. 2006. "Legal and Judicial Rule of Law Work in Multi-Dimensional Peacekeeping Operations: Lessons Learned Study", UN Peacekeeping Best Practice Section.

Carothers, T. 1998. "The Rule of Law Revival", *Foreign Affairs*, Vol. 72, No. 2.

———. 1999. *Aiding Democracy Abroad: The Learning Curve*, Washington, D.C.: Carnegie Endowment for International Peace.

———. 2001. "The Many Agendas of Rule of Law Reform in Latin America", Domingo, P and Sieder, S (eds.), *Rule of Law in Latin America*, London: Biddles Ltd.

———. 2006. "The Problem of Knowledge", Carothers, T (ed.), *Promoting the Rule of Law: In Search of Knowledge*, Washington, D.C.: Carnegie Endowment for International Peace.

Cater, C. 2003. "The Political Economy of Conflict and UN Intervention: Rethinking the Critical Cases of Africa", Ballentine, K and Sherman, J, op. cit.

Carter, W H. 1936. In foreword to Vollenhoven C Van, *The Law of Peace*, London: Macmillan.

Ceadel, M. 1987. *Thinking about Peace and War*, Oxford: Oxford University Press.

Chabal, P and Dialoz, J. 1999. *Africa Works: Disorder as a Political Instrument*, Oxford: James Currey.

Chaleard, J. 2003. "Cote d'Ivoire's Shattered Unity", *African Geopolitics*, No. 9, Winter.

Chandler, D. 2002. *From Kosovo to Kabul: Human Rights and International Intervention*, London: Pluto.

———. 2004. "The Responsibility to Protect: Imposing the 'Liberal Peace' ", Bellamy, A and Williams, P, op. cit.

Chandler, David P. 2000. "Will There Be a Trial for the Khmer Rouge?", *Annual Journal of the Carnegie Council on Ethics and International Affairs*, Vol. 14.

Channell, W. 2006. "Lessons Not Learned: Problems with Western Aid for Law Reform in Postcommunist Countries", Carothers, T, op. cit.

Checkel, Jeffrey. 2005. "International Institutions and Socialization in Europe: Introduction and Framework", *International Organization*, Vol. 59, No. 4, pp. 801–26.

Cheran, R. 2003. "Diaspora Circulation and Transnationalism as Agents for Change in the Post-Conflict Zones of Sri Lanka", A Policy Paper submitted to the Berghof Foundation for Conflict Management, Berlin, Germany.

Chesterman, Simon. 2004. *You, The People: The United Nations, Transitional Administration, and State-Building*, Oxford: Oxford University Press.

———. 2004b. "Building Democracy through Benevolent Autocracy: Consultation and Accountability in UN Transitional Administrations", Newman, Edward and Rich, Roland *et al*, *The UN Role in Promoting Democracy: Between Ideals and Reality*, Tokyo, New York, Paris: United Nations University Press, pp. 86–112.

Chimni, B S. 2003. "Post-Conflict Peace-Building and the Return of Refugees: Concepts, Practices, and Institutions", Newman, Edward and Selm, Joanne Van (eds.), *Refugees and Forced Displacement: International Security, Human Vulnerability, and the State*, Tokyo: United Nations University Press.

——. 2004. "From Resettlement to Involuntary Repatriation: Towards a Critical History of Durable Solutions to Refugee Problems", *Refugee Survey Quarterly*, Vol. 23, No. 3, pp. 55–73.

*China View.* 2004. "Drug Use of Youngsters on the Rise",17 June.

Chirayath, L *et al.* 2005. "Customary Law and Policy Reform: Engaging with the Plurality of Justice Systems", prepared as a background paper for the World Bank, *World Development Report 2006: Equity and Development.*

Chopra, Jarat. 2002. "Building State Failure in East Timor", *Development and Change*, Vol. 33, No. 5, pp. 979–1000.

Chopra, J and Hohe, T. 2004. "Participatory Intervention", *Global Governance*, Vol. 10, No. 3, pp. 289–305.

Cilliers, Jakkie and Mills, Greg (eds.), 1999. *From Peacekeeping to Complex Emergencies: Peace Support Missions in Africa*, Johannesburg and Pretoria: South African Institute of International Affairs and Institute for Security Studies.

Cintron, Ralph, Weine, Stevan and Agani, Ferid. 2003–4. "Exporting Democracy: The UN and the Rebuilding of Kosova", *Boston Review.*

Clapham, Christopher. 1999. "The UN and Peacekeeping in Africa", Mark, Malan (ed.), *Whither Peacekeeping in Africa?* Pretoria: Institute for Security Studies.

——. 2002. "Problems of Peace Enforcement: Lessons to be Drawn from Multinational Peacekeeping Operations in Africa", Williams, Zack, Frost, Tunde, Thomson, Diane, Alex (eds.), *Africa in Crisis: New Challenges and Possibilities*, London: Pluto Press, pp. 196–215.

Clark, I. 2001. *The Post-Cold War Order*, Oxford: Oxford University Press.

Clark, Kevin A. 2002. "The Reverend and the Ravens: Comment on Seawright", *Political Analysis*, Vol. 10, No. 2, pp. 194–7.

Clarke, W and Herbst, J. 1997. *Learning from Somalia: The Lessons of Armed Humanitarian Intervention*, Boulder: Westview Press.

Cleaver, Gerry and May, Roy. 1995. "Peace keeping: The African Dimension", *Review of African Political Economy*, Vol. 22, No. 66.

Clemens, Walter C Jr. 2002. "Complexity Theory as a Tool for Understanding and Coping with Ethnic Conflict and Development Issues in Post-Soviet Eurasia", *International Journal of Peace Studies*, Vol. 7, No. 2, pp. 1–15.

Cliffe, S and Rohland, C. 2002. "The East Timor Reconstruction Program: Success, Problems and Trade Offs", *World Bank CPR Working Papers, No. 2.*

Cochrane, Feargal. 2007. "The Power of the Diaspora: Lessons from Irish-America in Building Constituencies for Peace", *Journal of Peace Research* (forthcoming).

Collier, P. 2000. "Doing Well out of War: An Economic Perspective", Berdal, M and Malone, D, op. cit.

——. 2000. *Economic Causes of Civil Conflict and Their Implications for Policy*, Washington, D.C.: The World Bank.

——. 2003. *Breaking the Conflict Trap: Civil War and Development Policy*, Washington, D.C.: The World Bank.

Collier, P and Hoeffler, A. 1998. "On the Economic Causes of Civil War", *Oxford Economic Papers*, Vol. 50, No. 4, pp. 563–73.

——. 2001. "Greed and Grievance in Civil War", Washington, D.C.: The World Bank.

——. 2004. "Greed and Grievance in Civil Wars", *Oxford Economic Papers*, Vol. 56, No. 4, pp. 563–95.

*Common African Security Defence and Security Policy (CADSP)*. 2004. AHSG Extraordinary Session, Sirte, Libya, February.

Conca, Ken. 2006. "Peacebuilding and Environmental Challenges in War-Torn Societies", Seminar organized by the Swedish Network of Peace, Conflict and Development Research, 7 December, Uppsala.

Conference on 'Security and Co-operation in Europe (CSCE)'. 1990. Document of the Copenhagen Meeting of the Conference of the Human Dimension of the CSCE, 29 June.

*Constitutional Framework*. 2001. Constitutional Framework, signed on 15 May 2001, by SRSG Hans Hackkerup.

Cooper, R. 2003. *The Breaking of Nations*, London: Altantic Books.

Cornell, S E. 2006. "The Narcotics Threat in Greater Central Asia: From Crime-Terror Nexus to State Infiltration", *The China and Eurasia Forum Quarterly*, Vol. 4, No. 1, pp. 37–68.

Costello, Cathryn. 2005. "The Asylum Procedures Directive and the Proliferation of Safe Country Practices: Deterrence, Deflection and the Dismantling of International Protection?", *European Journal of Migration and Law*, Vol. 7, No. 1, pp. 35–69.

Cotterrell, R. 1997. "The Concept of Legal Culture", Nelken, D, op. cit.

Coulibaly, A. 2003. "Cote d'Ivoire's Seven Deadly Sins", *African Geopolitics*, No. 9, Winter.

Cousens, E M and Kumar, Chetan (eds.), 2001. *Peacebuilding as Politics: Cultivating Peace in Fragile Societies*, Boulder, Colorado: Lynne Rienner.

——. *Ibid.* "Introduction".

Cox, R W. 1981, "Social Forces, States and World Orders: Beyond International Relations Theory", *Millennium: Journal of International Studies*, Vol. 10, No. 2, pp. 126–55.

Crawford, Neta. 1993. "Decolonization as an International Norm: The Evolution of Practice, Arguments and Beliefs", Reed, Laura W and Kaysen, Carl (eds.), *Emerging Norms of Justified Intervention: A Collection of Essays*, Cambridge MA: American Arts and Society, pp. 37–61.

Crépeau, François and Nakache, Delphine. 2006. "Controlling Irregular Migration in Canada: Reconciling Security Concerns with Human Rights Protection", *IRPP Choices*, Vol. 12, No. 1.

Crocker, C A and Hampson, F O. 1996. "Making Peace Settlements Work", *Foreign Policy*, No. 104, Autumn, pp. 54–71.

Daci, Nexhat. 2003. Statement in a BBC Interview, April.

De Coning, C. 2004. "Refining the African Standby Force Concept", *Conflict Trends Magazine*, Vol. 2.

Deng, Francis M, Kimaro, Sadakiel, Lyons, Terrence, Rothchild, D, Zartman, W I. 1996. *Sovereignty as Responsibility: Conflict Management in Africa*, Washington, D.C.: The Brookings Institution Press.

Deng, Francis M, Zartman, W I. 2002. *A Strategic Vision for Africa: The Kampala Movement*, Washington, D.C.: Brookings Institution Press.

Der Derian, J. 2001. *Virtuous War*, Boulder, Colorado: Westview Press.

Dion, Douglas. 2003. "Evidence and Inference in the Comparative Case Study", Goertz, Gary and Starr, Harvey (eds.), *Necessary Conditions: Theory, Methodology, and Applications*, Lanham: Rowman & Littlefield.

Doswald-Beck, Louise. 1984. "The Legality of the United States Intervention in Grenada", *Netherlands International Law Review*, Vol. 31, No. 3, pp. 355–77.

Downs, G and Stedman, S J. 2002. "Evaluation Issues in Peace Implementation", Stedman, S J, Rothchild, D and Cousens, E M, op. cit.

Doyle, M. 1983. "Kant, Liberal Legacies, and Foreign Affairs", *Philosophy and Public Affairs*, Vol. 12, No. 3, pp. 205–35.

Duffield, M. 2001. *Global Governance and the New Wars: The Merging of Development and Security*, London: Zed Books.

Dwan, R and Bailey, L. 2006. "Liberia's Governance and Economic Management Assistance Programme (GEMAP): How it Came into Being, What it is and What we Might Learn from the Process", A Joint Review by the Department of Peacekeeping Operation's Best Practice Section and the World Bank's Fragile States Group.

Eastmond, Marita, and Öjendal, Joakim. 1999. "Revisiting a 'Repatriation Success': The Case of Cambodia", Black, Richard and Koser, Khalid (eds.), *The End of the Refugee Cycle? Refugee Repatriation & Reconstruction*, New York, Oxford: Berghahn Books.

Ehrenoeich–Brooks, R. 2003. "The New Imperialism: Violence, Norms and the 'Rule of Law' ", *Michigan Law Review*, Vol. 101.

Eide, E B, Kasperen, A T, Heppel, R K Von. 2005. *Report on Integrated Missions*, Independent Study for the Expanded UN ECHA Core Group.

El-Ayouty, Yassin and Zartman, I W, op. cit.

Eleventh United Nations Congress on Crime Prevention and Criminal Justice. 2005. "Making Standards Work: Fifty Years of Standard-Setting in Crime Prevention and Criminal Justice", UN Doc. A/CONF.203/8.

Ellis, S. 1999. *The Mask of Anarchy: The Destruction of Liberia and the Religious Dimension of an African War*, London: C Hurst.

Erman, E. 2005. *Human Rights and Democracy, Discourse Theory and Global Rights Institutions*, Hampshire: Ashgate.

Ero, Comfort. 1999. "The Future of ECOMOG in West Africa", Cilliers, J and Mills, G (eds.), 1999. *From Peacekeeping to Complex Emergencies: Peace Support Missions in Africa*, Johannesburg, Pretoria: South African Institute for International Affairs and Institute for Security Studies.

———. 2000. *ECOMOG: A Model for Africa?*, Pretoria: Institute for Security Studies.

Erskine, E A. 2000. *Peace Keeping Techniques for Africa's Conflict Management*, Ghana: Afram Publications Ltd.

Esposito, John and Voll, John. 1996. *Islam and Democracy*, Oxford: Oxford University Press.

Fagen, P W and Bump, M N. 2006. "Remittances in Conflict and Crises: How Remittances Sustain Livelihoods in War, Crises and Transitions to Peace", *International Peace Academy Policy Paper*, February.

Fair, C. 2005. "Diaspora Involvement in Insurgencies: Insights from the Khalistan and Tamil Eelam Movements", *Nationalism and Ethnic Politics*, Vol. 11, pp. 125–56.

Falk, Richard. 1992. "Cultural Foundations for the International Protection of Human Rights", An Na'im, A A (ed.), *Human Rights in Cross-Cultural Perspectives: A Quest for Consensus*, Philadelphia: University of Pennsylvania Press.

———. 1998. "The United Nations and Cosmopolitan Democracy: Bad Dream, Utopian Fantasy, Political Project", Archibugi, Daniele, Held, David and Köhler, Martin, op. cit. pp. 309–31.

Fallon, R. 1997. " 'The Rule of Law', as a Concept in Constitutional Discourse", *Columbia Law Review*, Vol. 97.

Farer, Tom J. 2004. "The Promotion of Democracy: International Law and Norms", Newman, Edward and Rich, Roland *et al. op. cit.*, pp. 32–61.

Faundez, J. 2001. "Legal Reform in Developing and Transition Countries: Making Haste Slowly", Puymbroeck, R (ed.), *Comprehensive Legal and Judicial Development*, Washington, D.C.: The World Bank.

Fearn, D. 2004. Personal Interview, Foreign and Commonwealth Office, London, 13 January.

Fearon, J D. 1995. "Rationalist Explanations for War", *International Organization*, Vol. 49, No. 3, pp. 379–414.

————. 2004. "Why Do Some Civil Wars Last So Much Longer Than Others?", *Journal of Peace Research*, Vol. 41, No. 3, pp. 275–301.

Finnemore, M and Sikkink, K. 1998. "International Norm Dynamics and Political Change", *International Organization*, Vol. 52, pp. 887–917.

Fleshman, M. 2001. "The International Community and Crisis in Nigeria's Oil Producing Communities: A Perspective on the US Role", *ACAS Bulletin*, Nos. 60–1, Fall.

Fletcher, G. 1996. *Basic Concepts of Legal Thought*, Oxford: Oxford University Press.

Foucault, M. 1991. "Governmentality", Burchell, G, Gordon, C and Miller, P (eds.), *The Foucault Effect: Studies in Governmentality*, Hemel Hempstead: Harvester Wheatsheaf.

Francis, David J. 2006. *Uniting Africa: Building Regional Peace and Security Systems*, Aldershot: Ashgate.

Franck, Joshua. 2006. "Kidnapped in Israel or Captured in Lebanon", *Global Research*, 25 July. (http://www.dailykos.com/storyonly/2006/7/25/92027/5840).

Franck, Thomas M. 1970. "Who Killed Article 2(4)? Or: Changing Norms Governing the Use of Force by States", *The American Journal of International Law*, Vol. 64, No. 4, pp. 809–37.

————. 2004. "Preemption, Prevention and Anticipatory Self-Defense: New Law Regarding Recourse to Force?", *Hastings International and Comparative Law Review*, Vol. 27, No. 3, pp. 425–35.

French, H. 2006. "China's Muslims Awake to Nexus of Needles and AIDS", *The New York Times*, 12 November.

Friedman, L. 1997. "The Concept of Legal Culture: A Reply", Nelken, D, op. cit.

Fukuyama, F. 2004. *State Building: Governance and World Order in the Twenty-first Century*, London: Profile.

Furley, Oliver, May, Roy (eds.), 1998. *Peacekeeping in Africa*, Aldershot: Ashgate.

————. (eds.), 2001. *African Interventionist States*, Aldershot: Ashgate.

Ganzglass, M. 1997. "The Restoration of the Somali Justice System", Clarke, W and Herbst, J (eds.), *Learning from Somalia: The Lessons of Armed Humanitarian Intervention*, Boulder: Westview Press.

Garth, G. 2003. "Building Strong and Independent Judiciaries through the New Law and Development: Behind the Paradox of Consensus Programs and Perpetually Disappointing Results", *DePaul Law Review*, Vol. 52.

General Assembly Resolution (A/46/137). 1991. "Enhancing the Effectiveness of the Principle of Periodic and Genuine Elections", Adopted in 17 December 1991.

Ghanem, As'ad. 2001. *The Palestinian Regime: A 'Partial Democracy'*, Brighton: Sussex Academic Press.

Gibney, M and Hansen, R. 2003. "Asylum Policy in the West: Past Trends, Future Possibilities", Helsinki: UNU/WIDER.

Giddens, A. 1991. *Modernity and Self-identity: Self and Society in the Late Modern Age*, Cambridge: Polity Press.

Gleditsch, N P, Wallensteen, P, Eriksson, M, Sollenberg, M and Strand, H. 2002. "Armed Conflict 1946–2001: A New Dataset", *Journal of Peace Research*, Vol. 39, No. 5, pp. 615–37.

Goddard, Hugh. 2002. "Islam and Democracy", *Political Studies Quarterly*, Vol. 73, No. 1, January–March.

Goertz, Gary and Starr, Harvey. 2003. "Introduction: Necessary Condition Logics, Research Design, and Theory", Goertz, Gary and Starr, Harvey (eds.), *Necessary Conditions: Theory, Methodology, and Applications*, Lanham: Rowman & Littlefield.

———.2003a. "Introduction: Necessary Condition Logics, Research Design, and Theory", Goertz, Gary and Starr, Harvey op.cit.

———.2003b. *Necessary Conditions: Theory, Methodology, and Applications*, Lanham: Rowman & Littlefield.

Goldstone, Jack, *et al.* 2000. *State Failure Task Force Report: Phase III Findings*, McLean: VA.

Golub, S. 2006. "A House without a Foundation", Carothers, T, op. cit.

Goodhand, J, Hulme, D and Lewer, N. 2000. "Social Capital and the Political Economy of Violence: A Case Study of Sri Lanka", *Disasters*, Vol. 24, No. 4, pp. 390–406.

Goodpaster, G. 2003. "Law Reform in Developing Countries", *Transatlantic Law & Contemporary Problems*, Vol. 13.

Gordon, Edward. 1985. "Article 2(4) in Historical Context", Special Feature – Restraints on the Unilateral Use of Force: A Colloquy, *The Yale Journal of International Law*, Vol. 10, No. 2, pp. 271–8.

Governance and Economic Management Assistance Programme (GEMAP), 9 September 2005, Monrovia.

Gray, C H. 1997. *Postmodern War: The New Politics of Conflict*, New York: Guilford Press

Grossman, H I, 1999, "Kleptocracy and Revolutions", *Oxford Economic Papers*, Vol. 51, pp. 267–83.

Gunaratna, R. 2000. "Bankrupting the Terror Business", *Jane's Intelligence Review*, Vol. 12, No. 8.

———. 2003. "Sri Lanka: Feeding the Tamil Tigers", Ballentine, K and Sherman, J, op. cit.

Gurr, T R. 1989. "Polity II Codebook", (http://www.bsos.umd.edu/cidcm/mar.)

———.1993. *Minorities at Risk: A Global View of Ethnopolitical Conflict*, Washington, D.C.: US Institute of Peace.

Gusmao, X. 2004. "Peacekeeping and Peacebuilding in Timor Leste", Seminar on 'The Role of the UN in Timor Leste', Dili, 26 November.

Habermas, J. 1984. *The Theory of Communicative Action, Reason and the Rationality of Society*, Cambridge: Polity Press.

———. 1987. *The Theory of Communicative Action, Reason and the Rationality of Society, Vol. II*, Boston: Beacon Press.

Hakimi, E *et al.* 2004. "Asymmetric Reforms in the Afghan Civil Service", *Independent Administrative Reform Commission, Report No SASPR–3*.

Haliday, F. 2001. "The Romance of Non-State Actors", Daphne, Josselin and Wallace, William (eds.), *Non-State Actors in World Politics*, London: Palgrave.

Hammergren, L. 2003. "International Assistance to Latin American Justice Programs", Jensen, E and Heller, T (eds.), *Beyond Common Knowledge: Empirical Approaches to the Rule of Law*, Stanford: Stanford University Press.

Hanf, T and Sabella, B. 1996. *A Date with Democracy: Palestinians on Society and Politics: An Empirical Survey*, Freiburg: Arnold-Bergerstraesser-Institute.

Harbom, L, Högbladh, S and Wallensteen, P. 2006. "Armed Conflict and Peace Agreements", *Journal of Peace Research*, Vol. 43, pp. 617–31.

Harbom, L and Wallensteen, P. 2006. "Patterns of Major Armed Conflicts, 1990–2005", Harbom, L (ed.), *States in Armed Conflict 2005*, Uppsala: Universitetstryckeriet.

Harbom, L and Forsberg, E. 2005. "Armed Conflict and Conflict Resolution Trends in Africa 1989–2004", Paper presented at Workshop: From Intrastate War to Durable Peace: Conflict and Conflict Resolution in Africa 1989–2004, Uppsala, 24–6 October.

Hardt, M and Negri, A. 2000. *Empire*, Cambridge, MA: Harvard University Press.

Hartzell, C. 1999. "Explaining the Stability of Negotiated Settlements to Intrastate Wars", *Journal of Conflict Resolution*. Vol. 43, 1 February, pp. 3–22.

Hartzell, C and Hoddie, M. 2003. "Institutionalizing Peace: Power Sharing and Post-Civil War Conflict Management", *American Journal of Political Science*, Vol. 47, No. 2, pp. 318–32.

Hassassian, Manuel. 1993. "The Democratization Process in the PLO: Ideology, Structure, and Strategy", Kaufman, Edy, Shukri, Abed B and Rothstein, Robert L (eds.), *Democracy, Peace and the Israeli–Palestinian Conflict*, Boulder: Lynn Reinner, pp. 257–85.

Hear, N Van. 2002. "Sustaining Societies under Strain: Remittances as a Form of Transnational Exchange in Sri Lanka and Ghana", Al-Ali, N and Koser, K (eds.), *New Approaches to Migration: Transnational Communities and the Transformation of Home*, London and New York: Routledge.

Hear, N Van, Pieke, N F and Vertovec, S. 2004. "The Contribution of UK-Based Diaspora to Development and Poverty Reduction", A Report by the ESRC Centre on Migration, Policy and Society (COMPAS): University of Oxford for the Department for International Development.

Held, D. 1995. *Democracy and the Global Order*, Cambridge: Polity Press.

Held, D, McGrew A, Goldblatt, D and Perraton, J. 1999. *Global Transformations: Politics, Economics and Culture*, Stanford: Stanford University Press.

Hempel, Carl G. 1945. "Studies in the Logic of Confirmation (I.)", *Mind*, Vol. 54, No. 213, pp. 1–26.

Henderson, Errol A. 2002. *Democracy and War: The End of an Illusion*, Boulder, Colorado: Lynne Rienner.

Hoare, Q, Nowel-Smith, G (eds.), 1972. *Selections from the Prison Notebooks of Antonio Gramsci*, London: Lawrence & Wishart.

Hoddie, M and Hartzell, C. 2003. "Civil War Settlements and the Implementation of Military Power-Sharing Arrangements", *Journal of Peace Research*, Vol. 40, No. 3, pp. 303–20.

——. 2005. "Power Sharing in Peace Settlements: Initiating the Transition from Civil War", Roeder, P G and Rothchild, D (eds.), *Sustainable Peace: Power and Democracy after Civil War*, Ithaca, London: Cornell University Press.

Holsti, K J. 1996. *The State, War and the State of War*, Cambridge Studies in International Relations, Cambridge: Cambridge University Press.

Homer-Dixon, Thomas. 1991. "On the Threshold: Environmental Changes as Causes of Acute Conflict", *International Security*, Vol. 16, No. 2, Fall, pp. 76–116.

——. 1994. "Environmental Scarcities and Violent Conflict: Evidence from Cases", *International Security*, Vol. 19, No. 1, Summer, pp. 5–40.

——. 2001. "Key Findings", Project on Environmental Scarcities, State Capacity and Civil Violence, University of Toronto.

Hooghe, Liesbeth. 2005. "Several Roads lead to International Norms, but Few via International Socialization: A Case Study of the European Commission", *International Organization*, Vol. 59, No. 4, pp. 861–98.

Howard, M. 2000. *The Invention of Peace and War*, London: Profile.

Khaled, Hroub. 2000. *Hamas: Political Thought and Practice*, Washington, D.C.: Institute for Palestine Studies.

———. 2006. "A 'New Hamas' through its New Documents", *Journal of Palestine Studies*, Vol. 35, No. 4, Summer.

Huang, R. 2005. "Securing the Rule of Law: Assessing International Strategies for Post-Conflict Criminal Justice", *International Peace Academy Policy Paper.*

Human Rights Commission Resolution 2000/47, "Promoting and Consolidating Democracy", adopted by The Commission on Human Rights, 25 April 2000.

Human Rights Watch. 2005. "Youth, Poverty and Blood: The Lethal Legacy of West Africa's Regional Warriors", *Human Rights Watch Report*, Vol. 17, No. 5(A), April.

———. 2005a. "Rivers of Blood, Guns, Oil and Power in Nigeria's River's State", *A Human Right Watch Briefing Paper*, New York: *Human Rights Watch*, February.

Human Security Centre. 2005. *Human Security Report: War and Peace in the 21st Century*, Oxford: Oxford University Press.

Huntington, Samuel. 1991. *The Third Wave: Democratization in the Late Twentieth Century*, Norman: University of Oklahoma Press.

———. 1993. *The Clash of Civilizations and the Remaking of World Order*, New York: Simon and Schuster.

Hutchful, E and Aning, K. 2004. "The Political Economy of Conflict", Adebajo, A and Rashid, I, op. cit.

Hutchinson, A and Monahan, P (eds.), 1987. *The Rule of Law: Ideal or Ideology*, Toronto: Carswell Legal Publications.

Hutt, Michael (ed.), 2004. *Himalayan 'People's War': Nepal's Maoist Rebellion*, London: C Hurst.

Hwang, B. 2003. "Curtailing North Korea's Illicit Activities", *Backgrounder*, No. 1679, Washington, D.C.: Heritage Foundation, August.

Hysa, Ylber. 2004. "Kosovo: A Permanent International Protectorat?", Newman, Edward and Rich, Roland *et al, op. cit.* pp. 282–301.

Ignatieff, Michael. 2000. *Empire Lite: Nation Building in Bosnia, Kosovo and Afghanistan*, London: Vintage.

Ikelegbe, A. 2006. "The Economy of Conflicts in the Oil Rich Niger Delta Region of Nigeria", *African and Asian Studies*, Vol. 5, No. 1.

Ikenberry, G J. 2001. *After Victory*, Princeton: Princeton University Press.

Independent International Commission on Kosovo (IICK). 2000. *The Kosovo Report*, Oxford: Oxford University Press.

Ingelhart, Ronald. 2004. *Islam, Gender, Culture and Democracy: Findings from the Values Surveys*, Ontario: De Sitter Publications.

Ingimunderson, Valur. 2003. "Pitting Democratic Standards against Sovereign Rights: The Nature of International Rule in Kosovo", *New Balkan Politics*, Vol. 8, pp. 10–36.

"International Commission on Intervention and State Sovereignty". 2001. *The Responsibility to Protect*, Ottawa: International Development Research Centre.

International Crisis Group. 2001. "Kosovo: Landmark Elections", *ICG Report*, No. 120, 21 November.

———. 2004. "COTE D'IVOIRE: No Peace in Sight", *ICG Africa Report*, No. 82.

———. 2005. "Kosovo after Haradinaj", *Europe Report*, No. 163, 26 May.

———. 2006. "Kosovo: The Challenge of Transition", *Europe Report*, No. 170, 17 February.

———. 2006. "Nigeria's Faltering Experiment", *Africa Report*, No. 119, 25 October.

Jabri, V. 1996. *Discourses on Violence*, Manchester: Manchester University Press.

Jaggers, K and Gurr, T R. 1995. "Polity III: Regime Change and Political Authority, 1800–1994", Second ICPSR Version.

Jensen, E. 2003. "The Rule of Law and Judicial Reform: The Political Economy of Diverse Institutional Patterns and Reformer's Responses", Jensen, E and Heller, op. cit.

Jensen, E and Heller, op. cit.

Juma, Monica and Mengistu, Aida. 2002. *The Infrastructure of Peace in Africa: Assessing the Peacebuilding Capacity of African Institutions*, New York: International Peace Academy, September.

Junne, Gerd and Verkoren, Willemijn (eds.), 2005. *Postconflict Development: Meeting New Challenges*, Boulder, Colorado: Lynne Reinner.

Kaldor, M. 2001. *New and Old Wars: Organised Violence in a Global Era*, Oxford: Polity and Cambridge: Blackwell.

Kaldor, M and Vashee, B (eds.), 1998. *New Wars*, London: Printer.

Kälin, Walter. 2003. "The Legal Dimension", *Forced Migration Review*, No. 17, pp. 15–16.

Kaplan, R. 1994. "The Coming Anarchy: How Scarcity, Crime, Overpopulation, Tribalism, and Disease are Rapidly Destroying the Social Fabric of our Planet", *Atlantic Monthly*, February.

Kassinger, T and Williams, D. 2005. "Commercial Law Reform Issues in the Reconstruction of Iraq", *Georgia Journal of International Law & Comparative Law*, Vol. 33.

Kaufmann, Chaim. 1996. "Possible and Impossible Solutions to Ethnic Civil Wars", *International Security*, Vol. 20, No. 4, pp. 136–75.

———. 1998. "When all else Fails: Ethnic Population Transfers and Partitions in the Twentieth Century", *International Security*, Vol. 23, No. 2, pp. 120–56.

Keck, Margareth and Sikkink, K. 1998. *Activists Beyond Borders: Advocacy Networks in International Politics*, Ithaca, New York, London: Cornell University Press.

Keen, D. 1998. "The Economic Functions of Violence in Civil Wars", *Adelphi Paper No. 320*, Oxford: IISS/Oxford University Press.

———. 2000. "Incentives and Disincentives for Violence", Berdal, M and Malone, D, op. cit.

———. 2003. "Greedy Elites, Dwindling Resources, Alienated Youths: The Anatomy of Protracted Violence in Sierra Leone", *Internationale Politik und Gesellschaft*, No. 2.

Keller, E J and Smith, L. 2005. "Obstacles to Implementing Territorial Decentralization", Roeder, P G and Rothchild, D, op. cit.

Kelsen, Hans. 1948. "Collective Security and Collective Self-Defence under the Charter of the United Nations", *The American Journal of International Law*, Vol. 42, No. 4, pp. 783–96.

Kim Young II. 2004. "North Korea and Narcotics Trafficking: A View from the Inside", *North Korea Review*, 27 February: The Jamestown Foundation.

Kindiki, K. 2003. "The Normative and Institutional Framework of the African Union Relating to the Protection of Human Rights and the Maintenance of International Peace and Security: A Critical Appraisal", *African Human Rights Law Journal*, Vol. 3, No. 1.

Kioko, B. 2003. "The Right of Intervention under the African Union's Constitutive Act: From Non-Interference to Non-Intervention, and Ewumbue-Monono, Churchill, Von Flüe, Carlo, Promotion of International Humanitarian Law through Cooperation between the ICRC and the AU", *International Review of the Red Cross*, Vol. 85, No. 852.

Knight, M and Özerdem, A. 2004. "Guns, Camps and Cash: Disarmament, Demobilization and Reinsertion of Former Combatants in Transitions from War to Peace", *Journal of Peace Research*, Vol. 41, No. 4, pp. 499–516.

Koser, K and Hear, N Van. 2003. "Asylum Migration and Implications for Countries of Origin", *UNU/WIDER Discussion Paper No. 2003/20*, Helsinki: UNU/WIDER.

Kosovo Ombudsperson. 2002. Second Annual Report of the 2001–2.

Kostic, Roland. 2007. "Ambivalent Peace: International Nation-building, Group Insecurity and Reconciliation in Bosnia-Herzegovina", PhD Dissertation, Department of Peace and Conflict Research, Uppsala University, Sweden (forthcoming).

Krain, Matthew and Myers, Marissa. 1997. "Democracy and Civil War: A Note on the Democratic Peace Proposition", *International Interactions*, Vol. 23, No. 1, pp. 109–18.

Kramer, Martin. 2001. *Ivory Towers on Sand. The Failure of Middle Eastern Studies in America*, Washington: The Washington Institute for Near East Policy.

Kratochwil, F. 2000. "How do Norms Matter?", in Byers, M (ed.), *The Role of Law in International Politics: Essays in International Relations and International Law*, Oxford: Oxford University Press.

Krygier, M. 2001. "Transitional Questions about the Rule of Law: Why, What, and How?", Paper delivered at the conference, *'East Central Europe: From Where to Where?'* Organized by East Central Europe/L'Europe du Centre Est. Eine wissenschaftliche Zeitschrift at Collegium Budapest, Institute for Advanced Study, Budapest, 15–17 February.

———. 2005. "Human Rights and a Humanist Social Science", Eisgruper, C L and Sajó, A (eds.), *Global Justice and the Bulwarks of Localism: Human Rights in Context*, Leiden, Boston: Martinus Nijhoff Publishers.

———. 2006. "Rule of Law: An Abusers Guide", Sajó, A (ed.), *Abuse: The Dark Side of Fundamental Rights*, Utrecht: Eleven International Publishing.

Kumar, Krishna (ed.), 1997. *Rebuilding Societies After Civil War: Critical Roles for International Assistance*, Boulder: Lynne Rienner.

Lacina, B. 2006. "Explaining the Severity of Civil Wars", *Journal of Conflict Resolution*, Vol. 50, No. 2, pp. 276–89.

Lacina, B, Gledistch, N P and Russett, B. 2006. "The Declining Risk of Death in Battle", *International Studies Quarterly*, Vol. 50, No. 1.

Lake, D A and Rothchild, D. 2005. "Territorial Decentralization and Civil War Settlements", Roeder, P G and Rothchild, D, op. cit.

Legrand, P. 2001. "What 'Legal Transplants'?", Nelken, D and Feest, J (eds.), *Adapting Legal Cultures*, Oxford: Hart Publishing.

Levitt, P. 1998. "Social Remittances: Migration Driven, Local-Level Forms of Cultural Diffusion", *International Migration Review*, Vol. 32, No. 4, pp. 926–48.

Liel, Alon. 2003. *Demo–Islam*, Jerusalem: Rubin Mass.

Lindholm, Schulz, Helena. 1996. *Between Revolution and Statehood*, Dissertation Thesis, Padrigu: Göteborg University.

———.1999. *The Reconstruction of Palestinian Nationalisms: Between Revolution and Statehood*, Manchester: Manchester University Press.

———. 2003b. "The 'Al-Aqsa Intifada' as a Result of Politics of Transition", *Arab Studies Quarterly*, Vol. 24, No. 4, Fall 2002, pp. 21–46.

(with Hammer, Juliane). 2003a. *The Palestinian Diaspora: Formation of Identities and Politics of Homeland*, London, New York: Routledge Taylor and Francis Group.

Linklater, A. 1998. *The Transformation of Political Community*, Columbia: University of South Carolina Press.

Lischer, Sarah Kenyon. 2005. *Dangerous Sanctuaries: Refugee Camps, Civil War, and the Dilemmas of Humanitarian Aid*, Ithaca, New York: Cornell University Press.

Loescher, Gil and Milner, James. 2005. "Protracted Refugee Situations: Domestic and International Security Implications", *Adelphi Paper No. 375*, Oxford: Oxford University Press.

Ludwig, Robin. 2004. "The UN's Electoral Assistance: Challenges, Accomplishments and Prospects", Newman, Edward and Rich, Roland *et al*, op. cit. pp. 169–87.

Lund, M S. 2003. "What Kind of Peace is Being Built: Taking Stock of Post-Conflict Peacebuilding and Charting Future Directions", Paper presented at the conference on 'The 10th Anniversary of Agenda for Peace', International Development Research Centre, Ottawa, Canada, January.

Lyons, T. 2004. "Engaging Diaspora Communities to Promote Conflict Resolution: Transforming Hawks into Doves", Mimeo, Fairfax: Institute for Conflict Analysis and Resolution, George Mason University.

Mack, Andrew. 2005. *The Human Security Report*, Oxford: Oxford University Press.

Mahmoudi, Said. 2006a. "USA:s attack mot Afghanistan", Bring, Ove and Mahmoudi, Said (eds.), *Internationell våldsanvändning och folkrätt* [International Use of Force and International law], Stockholm: Norstedts Juridik, pp. 137–41.

———. 2006b. "Self-Defence and International Terrorism", Bring, Ove and Mahmoudi, Said, op. cit, pp. 167–80.

Malinowska-Sempruch, K and Bartlett, N. 2006. "Who Needs Protecting?, Rethinking HIV, Drugs and Security in the China Context", *The China and Eurasia Forum Quarterly*, Vol. 4, No. 1, pp. 25–30. Mandelbaum, M. 2002. *The Ideas that Conquered the World*, New York: Public Affairs.

Mansfield, Edward D and Snyder, Jack. 2005. *Electing to Flight: Why Emerging Democracies Go to War*, Cambridge, MA: MIT Press.

Månsson, K. 2001. "Cooperation in Human Rights: Experience from the Peace Operation in Kosovo", *International Peacekeeping*, Vol. 8, Winter, pp. 111–36.

Markovits, I. 2004. "Exporting Law Reform – But Will it Travel?", *Cornell Internationall Law Journal*, Vol. 37.

Marshall, Monty G and Gurr, T R. 2005. *Peace and Conflict 2003: A Global Survey of Armed Conflicts, Self-Determination Movements, and Democracy*, College Park, MD: CICDM, University of Maryland at College Park.

Martin, S. 2001. "Remittance Flows and Impact", paper prepared for the regional conference on '*Remittances as a Development Tool*', organized by the Multilateral Investment Fund and the Inter-American Development Bank.

Matthew, Richard. 2005. "Sustainable Livelihoods, Environmental Security and Conflict Mitigation: Four Cases in South Asia", IUCN, *Working Paper Series*.

Matthew, Richard and Upreti, Bishnu Raj. 2006. *Environmental Stress and Demographic Change in Nepal: Underlying Conditions Contributing to a Decade of Insurgency: Special Report*, Unpublished Draft.

Mays, Terry M. 2002. *Africa's First Peacekeeping Operation: The OAU in Chad, 1981–82*, London: Praeger Publishers.

Mburu, C. 2001. "Challenges Facing Legal and Judicial Reform in Post-Conflict Environments: Case Study from Rwanda and Sierra Leone", World Bank conference on '*Empowerment, Security and Opportunity Through Law and Justice*', 8–12 July.

Mead, M. 1990 [1940]. "Warfare is Only an Invention – Not a Biological Necessity", Hunt, Douglas (ed.), *The Dolphin Reader*, Boston, MA: Houghton Mifflin, Second Edition.

Mearsheimer, J. 1998. "The False Promise of International Institutions", Brown, M E, Coates, O R, Lynn-Jones, S M and Millar, S E (eds.), *Theories of War and Peace*, Cambridge, MA: MIT Press.

Mearsheimer, J and Walt, S. 2006. "The Israel Lobby", *London Review of Books*, Vol. 28, No. 6.

Melander, E, Öberg, M and Hall, J. 2006. "The 'New Wars' Debate Revisited: An Empirical Evaluation of the Atrociousness of 'New Wars'", *Uppsala Peace Research Papers No. 9*, Uppsala: Department of Peace and Conflict Research, Uppsala University.

Menkhaus, K. 2004. "Vicious Circles and the Security-Development Nexus in Somalia", *Journal of Conflict, Security and Development*, Vol. 4, p. 2.

Mepham, D and Ramsbotham, A. 2007. *Darfur: The Responsibility to Protect*, London: Institute for Public Policy Research (ippr).

Messick, R. 1999. "Judicial Reform and Economic Development: A Survey of the Issues", *The World Bank Research Observer*, Vol. 14, No. 1.

Michal, Shaul and Sela, Avraham. 2000. *The Palestinian Hamas: Vision, Violence, and Coexistence*, New York: Columbia University Press.

Midlarsky, Manus I. 1998. "Democracy and Islam: Implications for Civilizational Conflict and the Democratic Peace", *International Studies Quarterly*, 1998, Vol. 42, pp. 458–511.

Ministry of Public Security of the People's Republic of China, Significant progress has been made in the "People's War Against Drugs", in the first eight months of 2006, 9 November 2006.

Mittleman, J and Chin, C. 2005. "Conceptualizing Resistance to Globalisation", Amoore, L (ed.), *The Global Resistance Reader*, London, New York: Routledge.

Mohammed, Ayoob. 1995. *The Third World Security Predicament. State Making, Regional Conflict, and the International System (Emerging Global Issues)*, Boulder, Colorado: Lynne Rienner.

Mohamoud, A A. 2003. "African Diaspora and Development of Africa", *Report prepared for the African Diaspora Summit in the Netherlands, Amsterdam*, 16 December.

———. 2005. "Mobilising African Diaspora for the Promotion of Peace in Africa", *Policy Report for the Netherlands Ministry of Foreign Affairs*, Sub Sahara Department, Amsterdam: SAHAN Research Bureau.

Mrazek, Josef. 1989. "Prohibition of the Use and Threat of Force: Self-Defence and Self-Help in International Law", *The Canadian Yearbook of International Law*, Vol. 27, pp. 81–111.

Mueller, John. 2004. *The Remnants of War*, Ithaca, New York: Cornell University Press.

Muharremi, Robert, Lulzim, Peci, Leon, Malzogu, Verena, Knaus, Teuta, Murati and Isa, Blum (eds.), 2003. *Administration and Governance in Kosovo: Lessons Learned and Lessons to be Learned*, Geneva: CASIN.

Müllerson, Rein and Scheffer, David J. 1995. "Legal Regulation of the Use of Force", Damrosch, Lori Fisler, Danilenko, Gennady M and Müllerson, Rein (eds.), *Beyond Confrontation: International Law for the Post-Cold War Era*, Boulder, San Francisco and Oxford: *American Society of International Law*: Westview Press, pp. 93–139.

Murithi, Tim. 2005. *The African Union: Pan-Africanism, Peacebuilding and Development*, Aldershot: Ashgate.

Murphy, Rachel. 2005. "UN Peacekeeping and the Use of Force – The Failure to Protect in Kosovo", *Baltic Yearbook of International Law*, Vol. 5.

———. 2004. *Human Rights in Africa: From the OAU to the African Union*, New York: Cambridge University Press.

Murshed, S. 2002. "Conflict, Civil War and Underdevelopment: An Introduction", *Journal of Peace Research*, Vol. 39, No. 4, July.

Myers, N. 1993. "Environmental Refugees in a Globally Warmed World", *BioScience*, Vol. 43, No. 11, December.

Nabudere, D. 2004. "Africa's First World War: Mineral Wealth, Conflicts and War in the Great Lakes Region", *AAPS Occasional Paper Series*, Vol. 8, No. 1, Pretoria.

Naím, Moisés. 2002. "The New Diaspora", *Foreign Policy*, July–August.

Naldi, Gino J. 1999. *The Organization of African Unity: An Analysis of its Role*, New York: Mansell Publishing Ltd., Second Edition.

Nanda, Ved P. 1990. "The Validity of United States Intervention in Panama under International Law", *American Journal of International Law*, Vol. 84, No. 2, pp. 494–503.

Naqvi, Yasmin. 2004. "Between a Rock and a Hard Place? A Legal Analysis of the Voluntary Repatriation of Guatemalan Refugees", *Refugee Survey Quarterly*, Vol. 23, No. 2, pp. 74–99.

Narayan, D *et al.* 2000. *Voices of the Poor: Crying Out for Change, Vol. 1*, Oxford: Oxford University Press.

Nassery, H G. 2003. "The Reverse Brain Drain: Afghan–American Diaspora in Post-Conflict Peacebuilding and Reconstruction". (http://www.aisk.org/reports/diaspora.pdf.)

National Planning Commission. 2003. *Tenth Five Year Plan*, Kathmandu: National Planning Commission. Nelken, D and Feest, J, op. cit.

Nelken, D (ed.), 1997. *Comparing Legal Cultures*, Aldershot: Dartmouth.

_____. 2001. "Towards a Sociology of Legal Adaptation", op. cit.

Newland, K and Patrick, E. 2004. *Beyond Remittances: The Role of Diaspora in Poverty Reduction in their Countries of Origin*, Washington, D.C.: Migration Policy Institute.

Newman, Edward and Rich, Roland *et al.* op. cit.

Nilsson, D, Svensson, I and Sundberg, R. 2006. *The Terms of Peace Agreements Dataset (TOPAD)*, Vol. 1.1, Uppsala University, Department of Peace and Conflict Research.

Noll, Gregor. 1999. "Rejected Asylum Seekers: The Problem of Return", *International Migration*, Vol. 37, No. 1, pp. 267–88.

Norton, Augustus Richard (ed.), 1995. *Civil Society in the Middle East*, Vol. 1 and 2, Leiden, New York, Köln: E J Brill.

O' Brien, Cruise, Conor. 1983. "Terrorism under Democratic Conditions: The Case of the IRA", Crenshaw, Martha (ed.), *Terrorism, Legitimacy, and Power: The Consequences of Political Violence*, Middletown, CT: Wesleyan University Press.

O'Donnell Guillermo and Schmitter, Philippe C. 1986. *Transitions from Authoritarian Rule: Tentative Conclusions about Uncertain Democracies*, Baltimore: Johns Hopkins University Press.

Obi, C. 2000. "Globalised Images of Environmental Security in Africa", *Review of Africa's Political Economy*, No. 83.

_____. 2001. "Global, State and Local Intersections: Power, Authority and Conflict in the Niger Delta Oil Communities", Callaghy, T, Kassimir, R and Latham, R (eds.), *Intervention and Transnationalism in Africa: Global-Local Networks of Power*, Cambridge: Cambridge University Press.

_____. 2004. "The Oil Paradox: Reflections on the Violent Dynamics of Petro-Politics and (Mis) Governance in Nigeria's Niger Delta", *Africa Institute Occasional Paper No. 73*, Pretoria.

_____. 2005. "Introduction", *African and Asian Studies*, Vol. 4, Nos. 1 and 2 (Special Issue on Conflict and Politics in Post-Cold War Africa).

_____. 2006. "Foreign Interests and Environmental Degradation", Rothchild, D and Keller, E (eds.), *Africa–US Relations: Strategic Encounters*, Boulder, Colorado: Lynne Rienner.

Odinkalu, C A. 2003. "Back to the Future: The Imperative of Prioritizing for the Protection of Human Rights in Africa", *Journal of African Law*, Vol. 47.

Öjendal, Joakim and Lilja, Mona. 2006. *Imagining Political Legitimacy in Cambodia*, Copenhagen: NIAS Press.

Okonta, I and Douglas, O. 2001. *Where the Vultures Feast: Shell, Human Rights and Oil*, San Francisco: Sierra Club.

Okonta, I. 2006. "Behind the Mask: Explaining the Emergence of the MEND Militia in Nigeria's Oil Bearing Niger Delta, Niger Delta Economies of Violence", *Working Paper No. 11*, Berkeley, Washington, D.C., Port Harcourt: University of California, United States Institute for Peace, and Our Niger Delta.

Olonisakin, F. 2004. "African Peacekeeping at the Crossroads: An Assessment of the Continent's Evolving Peace and Security Architecture", *External Study for the UN Peacekeeping Best Practices Unit*, September.

Olukoshi, A. 2005. "Changing Patterns of Politics in Africa", Boron, A and Lechini, G (eds.), *Politics and Social Movements in an Hegemonic World: Lessons from Africa, Asia and Latin America*, Buenos Aires: CLACSO Books.

Orjuela, Camilla. 2003. "Building Peace in Sri Lanka: A Role for Civil Society?", *Journal of Peace Research*, Vol. 40, No. 2.

Orogun, P. 2004. "'Blood Diamonds' and Africa's Armed Conflicts in the Post-Cold War Era", *World Affairs*, Vol. 166, No. 3, Winter, pp. 151–61.

Orth, John V. 1998. "Exporting the Rule of Law", *North Carolina Journal of International Law and Commercial Regulations, N C J INT'L L & COM. (REG)*. Vol. 24, pp. 71–6.

Østergaard-Nielsen, Eva. 2006. "Diasporas and Conflict Resolution: Part of the Problem or Part of the Solution?", *DIIS Brief*, March.

Ottoway, M and Carothers, T (eds.), 2000. *Funding Virtue: Civil Society Aid and Democracy Promotion*, Washington, D.C.: Carnegie Endowment for International Peace.

Ouguergouz, Fatsah, Robinson, Mary, Salim, S A and Bara-Rezag, Kamel. 2003. *The African Charter of Human and People's Rights: A Comprehensive Agenda for Human Dignity and Sustainable Democracy in Africa*, Netherlands: Kluwer Law International.

Özdalga, Elisabeth. 1998. *The Veiling Issue: Official Secularism and Popular Islam in Modern Turkey*, Richmond: Curzon.

Packenham, Robert A. 1992. *The Dependency Movements: Scholarship and Politics in Development Studies*, Cambridge, MA: Harvard University Press.

Paige, Jeffery M. 1975. *Agrarian Revolution*, New York: Free Press.

Paris, Roland. 2002. "International Peacebuilding and the 'Mission Civilisatrice'", *Review of International Studies*, Vol. 28, No. 4, pp. 637–56.

———. 2004. *At War's End: Building Peace after Civil War*, Cambridge: Cambridge University Press.

———. *Ibid.*

Peerenboom, R. 2005. "Human Rights and Rule of Law: What's the Relationship?", *Georgetown Journal of International Law*, Vol. 36.

Penn, W. 1993 [1693]. "An Essay towards the Present and Future Peace of Europe", *The Peace of Europe*, London: Everyman.

Perl, R. 2003. "Drug Trafficking and North Korea: Issues for U.S. Policy", *CRS Report for the Congress*, 5 December.

Pérouse de Montclos, M-A. 2005. "Diaspora, Remittances and Africa South of the Sahara: A Strategic Assessment", *Institute for Security Studies (ISS) Monograph Series No. 112*.

Persson, Sune and Özdalga, Elisabeth. 1997. "Civil Society and the Muslim World", *Transactions*, Vol. 7, Istanbul: Swedish Research Institute.

Petras, J and Veltmeyer, H. 2001. *Globalisation Unmasked*, Halifax, London: Fernwood Publishing and Zed Press.

Pevehouse, J. 2002. "Democracy from the Outside-In? International Organizations and Democratization", *International Organization*, Vol. 56, pp. 515–49.

Pillar, I. *Police and Justice*, Presentation Paper, June 2004. (http://www.unmikonline.org/justice/documents/PillarI_Report_June04.pdf.)

Pitts, M. 1999. "Sub-Regional Solutions for African Conflict: The ECOMOG Experiment", *Journal of Conflict Studies*, Vol. 19, No. 1.

Pogge, T. 2002. *World Poverty and Human Rights*, Cambridge: Polity Press.

Posen, B R. 1993. "The Security Dilemma and Ethnic Conflict", *Survival*, Vol. 35, No. 1, pp. 27–47.

Powell, Kristiana. 2005. "Opportunities and Challenges for Delivering on the Responsibility to Protect: The African Union's Emerging Peace and Security Regime", The North-South Institute, Ottawa, Canada, Monograph No. 119.

Prügel, Elizabeth. 1999. *The Global Construction of Gender: Home-based work in the Political Economy of the 20th century*, New York: Columbia University Press.

Przeworski, Adam. 1999. "Minimalist Conception of Democracy: A Defense", Shapiro, Ian and Cordon, Casiano Hacker (eds.), *Democracy's Value*, Cambridge, Cambridge University Press.

Pugh, M. 2004. "Peacekeeping and Critical Theory", Bellamy, A and Williams, P, op. cit. pp. 39–58.

———. 2004. "Peacekeeping and Critical Theory", *International Peacekeeping*, Vol. 11, pp. 39–58.

Puley, Greg. 2005. "Responsibility to Protect: East, West, and Southern African Perspectives", *Ploughshares Working Paper 05–5*.

Puymbroeck, R (ed.), *Comprehensive Legal and Judicial Development*, Washington, D.C.: The World Bank.

Quigley, John. 1990. "The Legality of the United States Invasion of Panama", *Yale Journal of International Law*, Vol. 15, No. 2, pp. 276–315.

Radio Free Asia, "Dozens of North Korean Diplomats Caught Smuggling Drugs", 15 December 2004.

Ragin, Charles C. 1987. *The Comparative Method: Moving Beyond Qualitative and Quantitative Strategies*, Berkeley: University of California Press.

———. 2000. *Fuzzy-Set Social Science*, Chicago: University of Chicago Press.

———. 2003. "Fuzzy-Set Analysis of Necessary Conditions", Goertz, Gary and Starr, Harvey, op. cit.

———. 2004. "Turning the Tables: How Case-Oriented Research Challenges Variable-Oriented Research", Brady, E Henry and Collier, David (eds.), *Rethinking Social Inquiry: Diverse Tools, Shared Standards*, Lanham, MD: Rowman & Littlefield Publishers, Inc.

Rashid, I. 2004. "Student Radicals, Lumpen Youth, and the Origins of the Revolutionary Groups in Sierra Leone, 1977–1996", Abdullah, I, op. cit.

Rasmussen, M V. 2003. *The West, Civil Society, and the Construction of Peace*, London: Palgrave.

Raystiala, K and Slaughter, A–M. 2002. "International Law, International Relations and Compliance", Carlsnaes, W, Risse, T and Simmons, B (eds.), *Handbook of International Relations*, London: SAGE Publications.

Raz, J. 1979. *The Authority of Law*, Oxford: Clarendon Press.

Reisman, Michael, W. 1984a. "Coercion and Self-Determination: Construing Charter Article 2(4)", *The American Journal of International Law*, Vol. 78, No. 3, pp. 642–5.

———. 1984b. "The Use of Force in Contemporary International Law", *American Society of International Law*, Proceedings of the 78th Annual Meeting, Washington, D.C., 12–14 April, pp. 74–87.

Reiter, D. 2003. "Exploring the Bargaining Model of War", *Perspectives on Politics*, Vol. 1, pp. 27–43.

Reka, Blerim. 2003. "UNMIK as an International Governance with Post-Conflict Societies", *New Balkan Politics*, Vol. 8, pp. 37–55.

Reno, W. 1996. "The Business of War in Liberia", *Current History*, May.

———. 2000. "Shadow States and the Political Economy of Civil Wars", Berdal, M and Malone, D, op. cit.

———. 2003. "Political Networks in a Failing State: The Roots and Future of Violent Conflict in Sierra Leone", *Internationale Politik und Gesellschaft*, No. 2.

*Report of the Secretary General's High Level Panel on Threats, Challenges, and Change*. 2004. New York: United Nations.

"Report of the Sierra Leone Truth and Reconciliation Commission".2004. *Witness to the Truth*, Vol. 2, Accra: GLP Press.

Ricci, R. 2004. "Human Rights Challenges in the DRC: A View from MONUC's Human Rights Section", Malan, M and Porto, J G (eds.), *Challenges of Peace Implementation: The UN Mission in the Democratic Republic of the Congo*, Pretoria: ISS.

Rich, Roland. 2004. "Crafting Security Council Mandates", Newman, Edward and Rich, Roland *et al*, op. cit., pp. 62–85.

———. 2003. "Realizing Hegemony? Symbolic Terrorism and the Roots of Conflict", *Studies in Conflict and Terrorism*, Vol. 26.

Richmond, O. 2002. *Maintaining Order, Making Peace*, London: Palgrave.

———. 2004. "UN Peace Operations and the Dilemmas of the Peacebuilding Consensus", *International Peacekeeping*, Vol. 10, No. 4, pp. 83–102.

———. 2005. *The Transformation of Peace*, London: Palgrave.

Rieff, D. 2002. *A Bed for the Night*, London: Vintage.

Risse, T. 2000. "Let's Argue! Communicative Action in World Politics", *International Organization*, Vol. 54, pp. 1–39.

Risse, T and Sikkink, K. 1999. "The Socialization of Human Rights Norms", Risse, T, Ropp, S C and Sikkink, K (eds.), *The Power of Human Rights: International Norms and Domestic Change*, Cambridge: Cambridge University Press.

Rizal, Dhurba and Yokota, Yozo. 2006. *Understanding Development, Conflict and Violence: The Cases of Bhutan, Nepal, North-East India and the Chittagong Hill Tracts of Bangladesh*, New Delhi: Adroit Publishers.

Roberts, Anthea Elizabeth. 2001. "Traditional and Modern Approaches to Customary International Law: A Reconciliation", *The American Journal of International Law*, Vol. 95, No. 4, pp. 757–91.

Robertson, A H and Merrills, J G. 1996. *Human Rights in the World*, Manchester: Manchester University Press.

Robinson, Glenn. 1997. *Building a Palestinian State: The Incomplete Revolution*, Bloomington and Indianapolis: Indiana University Press.

Roeder, Philip G. 2005. "Power-Dividing as an Alternative to Ethnic Power-Sharing", Roeder, P G and Rothchild, D, op. cit.

Rosenfeld, M. 2001. "The Rule of Law and the Legitimacy of Constitutional Democracy", *California Law Review*, Vol. 74.

Ross, M. 1999. "The Political Economy of the Resource Curse", *World Politics*, Vol. 51, January.

———. 2001. "Does Oil Hinder Democracy", *World Politics*, Vol. 53, April.

———. 2004a. "What Do We Know About Natural Resources and Civil War", *Journal of Peace Research*, Vol. 41, Issue 3, May.

_____. 2004b. "How Do Natural Resources Influence Civil War? Evidence from Thirteen Cases", *International Organizations*, Vol. 58, Winter.

_____. 2006. "Nepal: Environmental Scarcity and State Failure", *World Security Network*, 30 May.

Rotberg, Robert (ed.), 2003. *State Failure and State Weakness in a Time of Terror*, Washington, D.C.: Brookings Institution Press.

Rothchild, D. 2002. "Settlement Terms and Post-agreement Stability", Stedman, S J, Rothchild, D and Cousens, E M, op. cit.

_____. 2005. "Reassuring Weaker Parties after Civil Wars: The Benefits and Costs of Executive Power-Sharing Systems in Africa", *Ethnopolitics*, Vol. 4, No. 3. pp. 247–67.

Rothchild, D and Roeder, P G. 2005. "Dilemmas of State-Building in Divided Societies", Roeder, P G and Rothchild, D, op. cit.

Rubinstein, R. 2005. "Intervention and Culture: An Anthropological Approach to Peace Operations", *Security Dialogue*, Vol. 36, p. 534.

Rueschemeyer, Dietrich Stephens, Evelyne, Huber and Stephens, John D. 1992. *Capitalist Development and Democracy*, Cambridge: Polity Press.

Rumage, Sarah. 1993. "Panama and the Myth of Humanitarian Intervention in US Foreign Policy: Neither Legal Nor Moral, Neither Just Nor Right", *Arizona Journal of International and Comparative Law*, Vol. 10, No. 1, pp. 1–76.

Rummel, R J. 1985. "Libertarian Propositions on Violence Within and Between Nations: A Test Against Published Research Results", *The Journal of Conflict Resolution*, Vol. 29, pp. 419–55.

Rupnik, J. 2005, "Centre d'Etudes et de Recherches Internationales", *European Parliament, Committee on Foreign Affairs*, 25 January.

Sadako, Ogata. 1997. "Introduction: Refugee Repatriation and Peace-Building", *Refugee Survey Quarterly*, Vol. 16, No. 2, pp. vi–x.

Sajó, A (ed.), 2006. *Abuse: The Dark Side of Fundamental Rights*, Utrecht: Eleven International Publishing.

Salehyan, I. 2005. "Refugees, Climate Change, and Instability", Paper presented at the International Workshop on 'Human Security and Climate Change', Oslo.

Salim, S A. 1998. "The OAU Role in Conflict Management", Otunnu, O A and Doyle, M W (eds.), *Peacemaking and Peacekeeping for the New Century*, Lanham: Rowman & Littlefield, pp. 245–53.

Sambanis, N. 2000. "Partition as a Solution to Ethnic War: An Empirical Critique of the Theoretical Literature", *World Politics*, Vol. 52, No. 4, pp. 437–83.

_____. 2002. "A Review of Recent Advances and Future Directions in the Quantitative Literature on Civil War", *Defence and Peace Economics*, Vol. 13, No. 3, pp. 215–43.

Sapiro, Miriam. 2005. "Preempting Prevention: Lessons Learned", *New York Journal of International Law and Politics*, Vol. 37, No. 2, pp. 357–71.

Schachter, Oscar. 1984. "The Right of States to Use Armed Force", *Michigan Law Review*, Vol. 82, No. 5–6, pp. 1620–46.

Schmitt, C. 1996. *The Concept of the Political*, Chicago: University of Chicago Press.

Schmitz, H P and Sikkink, K. 2002. "International Human Rights", Carlsnaes, W, Risse, T and Simmons, B, op. cit.

Schulz, Michael. 1996. "Israel between Conflict and Accommodation: A Study of a Multi-Melting Pot Process", *Göteborg: Padrigu Thesis Series* (Dissertation Thesis).

———. (ed.), 2006 [2003]. "Democratization and Civil Society in the Middle East: Case Studies of Palestinian Self-Rule Areas and Iraqi Kurdistan, Stockholm and Göteborg", *Sida and Centre for Middle East Studies*, Sweden: Göteborg University.

Seawright, Jason. 2002a. "Testing for Necessary and/or Sufficient Causation: Which Cases are Relevant?", *Political Analysis*, Vol. 10, No. 2, pp. 178–93.

———. 2002b. "What Counts as Evidence? Reply", *Political Analysis*, Vol. 10, No. 2, pp. 204–7.

*Secretary General's Report on MONUC*, UN Doc. S/2003/211, 21 February 2003.

Sesay, Amadu and Ismail, W. 2003. "Introduction", Sesay, A (ed.), *Civil Wars, Child Soldiers and Post-Conflict Peace-Building in West Africa*, Ibadan: College Press.

Sesay, A, Olusola, Ojo, Orobola, Fasehun. 1984. *The OAU after Twenty Years*, Boulder, London: Westview.

Shain, Y. 2002. "The Role of Diaspora Communities in Conflict Perpetuation or Resolution", *SAIS Review of International Affairs*, Vol. 22, Baltimore: John Hopkins University Press.

Shain, Y and Barth, A B. 2003. "Diaspora and International Relations Theory", *International Organization*, Vol. 57, No. 3, pp. 449–79.

Simkhada, Shambhu Ram and Fabio, Oliva. 2006. *Causes of Internal Conflicts and Means to Resolve Them: Nepal a Case Study*, Geneva: PSIO.

Sharma, L P. 1998. "Geography", *CBS, A Compendium on Environmental Statistics of Nepal*, Kathmandu: CBS, pp. 20–7.

Shaw, M. 1999. "War and Globality: The Role and Character of War in the Global Transition" Jeong, H W (ed.), *The New Agenda for Peace Research*, Aldershot: Ashgate.

Shikaki, Khalil. 1996a. "The Peace Process, National Reconstruction, and the Transition to Democracy in Palestine", *Journal of Palestine Studies*, Vol. 25, No. 2, Winter, pp. 5–20.

———. 1996b. *Transition to Democracy in Palestine: The Peace Process, National Reconstruction and Elections*, Nablus: Centre for Palestine Research and Studies.

———. 2005. (www.pcpsr.org.)

Shklar, J. 1987. "Political Theory and the Rule of Law", Hutchinson, A, and Monahan, P, op. cit.

Simensen, Jarle. 1999. "Democracy and Globalization: Nineteen Eighty-Nine and the 'Third Wave'", *Journal of World History*, Vol. 10, No. 2, Fall, pp. 391–411.

Simmons, B and Martin, L. 2002. "International Organizations and Institutions", Carlsnaes, W, Risse, T and Simmons, B, op. cit.

Slomp, G. 1996. "Hobbes, Feminism, and Liberalism", *Political Studies Association*, Scotland, UK: University of Glasgow.

Small, M and Singer, D J. 1982. *Resort to Arms: International and Civil Wars 1816–1980*, Beverly Hills, CA: SAGE Publications.

Smilie, I, Gerie, L and Hazleton, R. 2000. "The Heart of the Matter: Sierra Leone, Diamonds and Human Security", *Partnership Africa*.

Smith, M G. 2003. *Peacekeeping in East Timor*, Boulder, Colorado: Lynne Rienner.

Smithson, Michael and Verkuilen, Jay. 2006. *Fuzzy Set Theory: Applications in the Social Sciences*, London: SAGE Publications.

Snow, D M. 1996. *Uncivil Wars: International Security and the New Internal Conflicts*, Boulder: Lynne Rienner.

Snyder, J. 2000. *From Voting to Violence*, London: W. W. Norton.

Sørensen, Georg. 1993. *Democracy and Democratization*, Boulder: Westview Press.

Sørensen, N, Hear, N Van and Engberg-Pedersen. 2002. "The Migration-Development Nexus Evidence and Policy Options: State-of-the-Art Overview", *International Migration*, Vol. 40, No. 5, Special Issue.

Sovacool, B K. 2005. "Constructing a Rogue State: American Post-Cold War Security Discourse and North Korean Drug Trafficking", *New Political Science*, Vol. 27, No. 4, pp. 497–520.

Soysa, D. 2001. "Paradise is a Bazaar? Greed, Creed, Grievance and Governance", *WIDER Discussion Paper No. 42.*

Spear, J. 2002. "Disarmament and Demobilization", Stedman, S J, Rothchild, D and Cousens, E M, op. cit.

Spears, I S. 2002. "Africa: The Limits of Power-Sharing", *Journal of Democracy*, Vol. 13, No. 3, pp. 123–36.

Spencer, Robert. 2005. *The Myth of Islamic Tolerance: How Islamic Tolerance Treats Non-Muslims*, Amherst, New York: Prometheus Books.

Squires, N. 2003. "North Koreas are linked to Heroin Haul in Australia", *South China Morning Post*, 28 May.

Stedman, S J. 2001. "International Implementation of Peace Agreements in Civil War", Crocker, C A, Hampson, F O and Aall, P (eds.), *Turbulent Peace: The Challenges of Managing International Conflict*, Washington, D.C.: United States Institute of Peace, pp. 737–52.

Stedman, S J, Rothchild, D and Cousens, E M, op.cit.

Stemmet, A. 2003. "From Rights to Responsibilities: The International Community's Responsibility to Protect Vulnerable Populations", *African Security Review*, Vol. 12, p. 4.

Strohmeyer, H. 2001. "Collapse and Reconstruction of a Judicial System: The United Nations Mission in Kosovo and East Timor", *American Journal of International Law*, Vol. 95, No. 1.

Stromseth, J *et al.* 2006. *Can Might Make Rights? Building the Rule of Law after Military Interventions*, Cambridge: Cambridge University Press.

Studdard, K and Hurwitz, A. 2005. "Rule of Law Programs in Peace Operations", *International Peace Academy Policy Paper.*

Summers, R. 1999. "The Principles of the Rule of Law", *Notre Dame Law Review*, Vol.74.

———. (ed.), 2005. *Education as Social Action: Knowledge, Identity and Power*, Houndmills and New York: Palgrave Macmillan and UNOISD.

Swain, Ashok. 1996. "Environmental Migration and Conflict Dynamics: Focus on Developing Regions", *Third World Quarterly*, Vol. 17, No. 5, December, pp. 959–73.

———. 2006. "Agenda 21", Robertson, Roland and Scholte, Jan Aart (eds.), *Encyclopedia of Globalization*, New York: Routledge.

Swanström, N. 2007. "Narcotics a Threat to Security? National and Transnational Implications", *Global Crime*, Vol. 8, No. 1.

Swanström, N and Cornell, S E. 2006. "The Eurasian Drug Trade: A Challenge to Regional Security", *Problems of Post-Communism*, Vol. 53, No. 4, pp. 10–28.

Tamanaha, B. 2004. *On the Rule of Law: History, Politics, Theory*, Cambridge: Cambridge University Press.

Tessler, Mark. 2002. "Islam and Democracy in the Middle East: The Impact of Religious Orientations on Attitudes toward Democracy in Four Arab Countries", *Journal of Comparative Politics*, Vol. 34, April, pp. 337–54.

Thapa, Deepak. 2004. *A Kingdom Under Siege: Nepal's Maoist Insurgency, 1996 to 2004*, London: Zed Books.

Thielemann, Eiko R. 2004. "Why Asylum Policy Harmonisation Undermines Refugee Burden-Sharing", *European Journal of Migration and Law*, Vol. 6, No. 1, pp. 47–65.

Thompson, D. 2004. "China Faces Challenges in Effort to Contain HIV/AIDS Crisis", Washington, D.C.: Population Reference Bureau.

Tibi, Bassam. 1998. *The Challenge of Fundamentalism [Electronic Resource]: Political Islam and the New World Disorder*, Berkeley, California: University of California Press.

Ting, C. 2004. *China Always Says "No" to Narcotics*, Beijing: Foreign Languages Press.

UCDP. 2006. "Uppsala Conflict Database: Definitions". (http://www.pcr.uu.se/database/definitions_all.htm.)

Ukeje, C. 2001. "Youth Violence and the Collapse of the Public Order in the Niger Delta of Nigeria", *Africa Development*, Vol. 26, Nos. 1 and 2.

———. 2003a. "State Disintegration and Civil War in Liberia", Sesay, A, op. cit.

———. 2003b. "Sierra Leone: The Long Descent into Civil War", Sesay, A, op. cit.

United Nations. 1992. "An Agenda for Peace Preventive Diplomacy, Peacemaking and Peace-keeping", Report of the Secretary General pursuant to the statement adopted by Summit Meeting of the Security Council on 31 January.

———. 1998. *Guiding Principles on Internal Displacement*, E/CN.4/1998/53/Add.2, Geneva: ECOSOC.

———. 2000. *Report of the Panel on United Nations Peace Operations*, A Far Reaching Report by an Independent Panel.

———. 2004. "World Economic and Social Survey 2004". *International Migration*, New York: United Nations.

———. 2004. *A More Secure World: Our Shared Responsibility-Executive Summary*. 2004: United Nations.

———. 2005. United Nations Secretary General's address to UNHCR Executive Committee, 6 October, Geneva: United Nations.

———. 2006. *2005 Global Refugee Trends: Statistical Overview of Populations of Refugees, Asylum-Seekers, Internally Displaced Persons, Stateless Persons, and Other Persons of Concern to UNHCR*, Geneva: UNHCR.

University of Minnesota Human Rights Library Charter of the Organization of African Unity, 479 UNTS. 39, entered into force 13 September 1963. Available online (http:// www1.umn.edu/humaNots/africa/OAU_Charter_1993.html.), accessed on 3 October 2007.

UN Department of Peacekeeping Operations. 2006. *Integrated Mission Planning Process (IMPP)*, Guidelines Endorsed by the Secretary General on 13 June.

United Nations Development Programme (UNDP). 2004. "Empowerment and Poverty Reduction", *Nepal Human Development Report 2004*, Kathmandu: UNDP.

———. 2006. *Economic Policies, Poverty and Human Development in Nepal: Reading in Human Development*, Kathmandu: UNDP.

UN Mission in Liberia. 2006. *Human Rights in Liberia's Rubber Plantations: Tapping into the Future*, Monorovia: UNMIL.

UN Secretary General Report (UNSG). 2004a. *Rule of Law and Transitional Justice in Conflict and Post-Conflict Societies*, UN Doc. S/2004/616.

———. 2006a. *First Report of the Secretary General on the United Nations Integrated Office in Sierra Leone*, UN Doc. S/2006/269.

———. 2006b. *Seventh Report of the Secretary General on the United Nations Operation in Burundi*, UN Doc. S/2006/429.

———. 2006c. *Report of the Secretary General on Timor-Leste Pursuant to Security Council Resolution 1690*, UN Doc. S/2006/628.

UNHCR Executive Committee. 2004. *Protracted Refugee Situations*. EC/54/SC/CRP.14: UNHCR.

———. 2006. *The State of the World's Refugees: Human Displacement in the New Millennium*, Oxford: Oxford University Press.

United Nations Office of Drugs and Crime. 2004. *2004 World Drug Report*, New York: United Nations.

———. 2006b. *2006 World Drug Report*, New York: United Nations.

———. 2006b. *Patterns and Trends of Amphetamine-Type Stimulants (ATS) and Other Drugs of Abuse in East Asia and the Pacific, 2005*, New York: United Nations, p. 50.

UNMOC. 2006. The Human Rights Situation in the Democratic Republic of the Congo (DRC) during the period of January to June 2006. (http://www.monuc.org/news.aspx?newsID_761&menuOpened_Activities.)

Upham, F. 2006. "Mythmaking in the Rule of Law Orthodoxy", Carothers, T, op. cit.

Upreti, Bishnu Raj. 2004. *The Price of Neglect: From Resource Conflict to Maoist Insurgency in the Himalayan Kingdom*, Kathmandu: Bhrikuti Academic Publications.

———. 2005. "Resource Governance, Resource Scarcity and Conflict in Nepal", A Discussion Paper.

———. 2006. "Nepal: A Tragedy of Triple Conflict", *South Asian Journal*, May.

USAID. 2006. *Conflict Over Natural Resources at the Community Level in Nepal: Including its Relationship to Armed Conflict*, Washington, D.C.: Prepared by ARD, Inc.

US Committee for Refugees. 2006. *World Refugee Survey 2006*, Washington, D.C.: USCR. Also 1989–2005.

US Department of State. 2006. "US Relations with the People's Republic of China", *International Narcotics Control Strategy Report – 2006*, Released by the Bureau for International Narcotics and Law Enforcement Affairs, March.

Utas, M. 2003. "Sweet Battlefields: Youth and the Liberian War", PhD Thesis, Uppsala: Dissertations in Cultural Anthropology and Ethnology (DICA), Department of Cultural Anthropology and Ethnology: Uppsala University.

Vogt, Margaret. 1999. *Co-operation between the United Nations and the OAU in the Management of African Conflicts*, Monograph, No 36, April 1999. Available online, accessed on 3 September 2007. (http://www.iss.co.za/Pubs/Monographs/No36/OAU.html.)

Waldock, C H M. 1952. "The Regulation of the Use of Force by Individual States in International Law", *Recueil des cours*, Vol. 81, No. 2: pp. 455–517.

Walker, R B J. 1992. *Inside/Outside: International Relations as Political Theory*, Cambridge: Cambridge University Press.

Wallensteen, Peter. 2002. *Understanding Conflict Resolution: War, Peace and the Global System*, London: SAGE Publications.

Walraven, K Van. 1999. *Dreams of Power: The Role of the Organization of African Unity in the Politics of Africa 1963–1993*, Aldershot: Ashgate.

Walter, B F. 1999. "Designing Transitions from Civil War: Demobilization, Democratization, and Commitments to Peace", *International Security*, Vol. 24, No. 1, pp. 127–55.

———. 2002. *Committing to Peace: The Successful Settlement of Civil Wars*, Princeton, Princeton University Press.

Watts, M. 2004. "Resource Curse? Governmentability, Oil and Power in the Niger Delta, Nigeria", *Geopolitics*, Vol. 9, No. 1.

Williams, A, Bellamy, P and Griffin, S. 2004. *Understanding Peacekeeping*, Cambridge, Oxford: Polity Press and Blackwell Publishing Ltd.

Wilmer, F. 2002. "The Social Reconstruction of Conflict and Reconciliation in the Former Yugoslavia", *Social Justice*, Vol. 24, No. 4.

Wilson, W. 1983. "Address to the Senate, 12 January 1917", Link, A S *et al* (eds.), *The Papers of Woodrow Wilson*, Vol. 40, Princeton: Princeton University Press.

World Bank. 2006. *Doing Business 2006*, Washington, D.C.: The World Bank.

Wortzel, L. 2003. "North Korea's Connection to International Trade in Drugs, Counterfeiting, and Arms", Washington, D.C.: The Heritage Foundation.

Wright, Q. 1957. "The Legality of Intervention under the United Nations Charter", *Proceedings of the American Society of International Law*, Vol. 51, pp. 79–90.

———. 1964. *The Study of War*, Chicago: University of Chicago Press.

Xhaferi, Arben. 2003. "The Paradox of Resolution 1244", *New Balkan Politics*, Vol. 8, pp. 71–5.

Yan, Z. 2006. "Methadone Therapy, Needle Exchanges Leading HIV Battle", *China View*, 23 October.

Zunzer, W. 2004. "Diaspora Communities and Civil Transformation", *Occasional Paper No. 26*, Germany: Berghof Research Centre for Constructive Conflict Management.